T0074938

Praise for *Machine Learning for High-Risk Applications*

Machine Learning for High-Risk Applications is a practical, opinionated, and timely book. Readers of all stripes will find rich insights into this fraught subject, whether you're a data scientist interested in better understanding your models, or a manager responsible for ensuring compliance with existing standards, or an executive trying to improve your organization's risk controls.

—Agus Sudjianto, PhD, EVP, Head of Corporate Model Risk,
Wells Fargo

Don't miss out on this must-read! Packed with a winning combination of cutting-edge theory and real-world expertise, this book is a game-changer for anyone grappling with the complexities of AI interpretability, explainability, and security. With expert guidance on managing bias and much more, it's the ultimate guide to mastering the buzzword bonanza of the AI world. Don't let the competition get ahead—get your hands on this indispensable resource today!

—Mateusz Dymczyk, Software Engineer,
Machine Learning, Meta

The book is a comprehensive and timely guide for anyone working on machine learning when the stakes are high. The authors have done an excellent job providing an overview of regulatory aspects, risk management, interpretability, and many other topics while providing practical advice and code examples. Highly recommended for anyone who prefers diligence over disaster when deploying machine learning models.

—Christoph Molnar, Author of Interpretable Machine Learning

Machine learning applications need to account for fairness, accountability, transparency, and ethics in every industry to be successful. *Machine Learning for High-Risk Applications* lays the foundation for such topics and gives valuable insights that can be utilized for various use cases. I highly recommend this book for any machine learning practitioners.

—*Navdeep Gill, Engineering Manager, H2O.ai*

Responsible AI—explained simply.

—*Hariom Tatsat, Coauthor of* Machine Learning & Data Science Blueprints for Finance

Machine Learning for High-Risk Applications is a highly needed book responding to the growing demand for in-depth analysis of predictive models. The book is very practical and gives explicit advice on how to look at different aspects, such as model debugging, bias, transparency, and explainability analysis. The authors share their huge experience in analyzing different classes of models, for both tabular and image data. I recommend this book to anyone wishing to work responsibly with complex models, not only in high-risk applications.

—*Przemysław Biecek, Professor at the Warsaw University of Technology*

A refreshingly thoughtful and practical guide to responsible use of machine learning. This book has the potential to prevent AI accidents and harms before they happen.

—*Harsh Singhal, Senior AI Solution Director, Financial Services, C3.ai*

This book stands out for its uniquely tactical approach to addressing system risks in ML. The authors emphasize the critical importance of addressing potential harms as necessary to the delivery of desired outcomes—noted as key to the very success of ML. Especially helpful is the focus on ensuring that the right roles are in the room when making decisions about ML. By taking a nuanced approach to derisking ML, this book offers readers a valuable resource for successfully deploying ML systems in a responsible and sustainable manner.

—*Liz Grennan, Associate Partner and Global Co-Lead for Digital Trust, McKinsey & Company*

This book is a comprehensive review of both social and technical approaches to high-risk AI applications and provides practitioners with useful techniques to bridge their day-to-day work with core concepts in Responsible AI.

—*Triveni Gandhi, PhD, Responsible AI Lead, Dataiku*

Unlocking the full potential of machine learning and AI goes beyond mere accuracy of models. This book delves into the critical yet often overlooked aspects of explainable, bias-free, and robust models. In addition, it offers invaluable insights into the cultural and organizational best practices for organizations to ensure the success of their AI initiatives. With technology advancing at an unprecedented pace and regulations struggling to keep up, this timely and comprehensive guide serves as an indispensable resource for practitioners.

—*Ben Steiner, Columbia University*

Machine learning models are very complex in nature and their development is fraught with pitfalls. Mistakes in this field can cost many's reputation and millions or even billions of dollars. This book contains must-have knowledge for any machine learning practitioner who wants to design, develop, and deploy robust machine learning models that avoid failing like so many other ML endeavors over the past years.

—*Szilard Pafka, PhD, Chief Scientist, Epoch*

Saying this book is timely is an understatement. People who do machine learning models need a text like this to help them consider all the possible biases and repercussions that arise from the models they create. The best part is that Patrick, James, and Parul do a wonderful job in making this book readable and digestible. This book is needed on any machine learning practitioner's bookshelf.

—*Aric LaBarr, PhD, Associate Professor of Analytics*

This is an extremely timely book. Practitioners of data science and AI need to seriously consider the real-world impact and consequences of models. The book motivates and helps them to do so. It not only provides solid technical information, but weaves a cohesive tapestry with legislation, security, governance, and ethical threads. Highly recommended as reference material.

—*Jorge Silva, PhD, Director of AI/Machine Learning Server, SAS*

With the ever-growing applications of AI affecting every facet of our lives, it is important to ensure that AI applications, especially the ones that are safety critical, are developed responsibly. Patrick Hall and team have done a fantastic job in articulating the key aspects and issues in developing safety-critical applications in this book in a pragmatic way. I highly recommend this book, especially if you are involved in building AI applications that are high stakes, critical, and need to be developed and tested systematically and responsibly!

—*Sri Krishnamurthy, QuantUniversity*

If you're looking for direction from a trusted advisor as you venture into the use of AI in your organization, this book is a great place to start. The authors write from a position of both knowledge and experience, providing just the right mix of baseline education in technology and common pitfalls, coverage of regulatory and societal issues, relevant and relatable case studies, and practical guidance throughout.

—*Brett Wujek, PhD, Head of AI Product Management, SAS*

Machine Learning for High-Risk Applications

Approaches to Responsible AI

Patrick Hall, James Curtis, and Parul Pandey
Foreword by Agus Sudjianto, PhD

Beijing · Boston · Farnham · Sebastopol · Tokyo 

Machine Learning for High-Risk Applications

by Patrick Hall, James Curtis, and Parul Pandey

Published by O'Reilly Media, Inc., 1005 Gravenstein Highway North, Sebastopol, CA 95472.

O'Reilly books may be purchased for educational, business, or sales promotional use. Online editions are also available for most titles (*http://oreilly.com*). For more information, contact our corporate/institutional sales department: 800-998-9938 or *corporate@oreilly.com*.

Acquisition Editors: Rebecca Novack and Nicole Butterfield	**Proofreader:** Kim Cofer
	Indexer: WordCo Indexing Services, Inc.
Development Editor: Michele Cronin	**Interior Designer:** David Futato
Production Editor: Gregory Hyman	**Cover Designer:** Karen Montgomery
Copyeditor: Liz Wheeler	**Illustrator:** Kate Dullea

April 2023:   First Edition

Revision History for the First Edition

2023-04-17:   First Release

See *http://oreilly.com/catalog/errata.csp?isbn=9781098102432* for release details.

978-1-098-10243-2

[LSI]

Table of Contents

Part II.   Putting AI Risk Management into Action

Part III.   Conclusion

Foreword

Renowned statistician George Box once famously stated, "All models are wrong, but some are useful." Acknowledgment of this fact forms the foundation of effective risk management. In a world where machine learning increasingly automates important decisions about our lives, the consequences of model failures can be catastrophic. It's critical to take deliberate steps to mitigate risk and avoid unintended harm.

Following the 2008 financial crisis, regulators and financial institutions recognized the importance of managing model risk in ensuring the safety of banks, refining the practice of model risk management (MRM). As AI and machine learning gain widespread adoption, MRM principles are being applied to manage their risk. The National Institute of Standards and Technology's AI Risk Management Framework serves as an example of this evolution. Proper governance and control of the entire process, from senior management oversight to policy and procedures, including organizational structure and incentives, are crucial to promoting a culture of model risk management.

In *Machine Learning for High-Risk Applications*, Hall, Curtis, and Pandey have presented a framework for applying machine learning to high-stakes decision making. They provide compelling evidence through documented cases of model failures and emerging regulations that highlight the importance of strong governance and culture. Unfortunately, these principles are still rarely implemented outside of regulated industries, such as banks. The book covers important topics ranging across model transparency, governance, security, bias management, and more.

Performance testing alone is not enough in machine learning, where very different models can have the same performance due to model multiplicity. Models must also be explainable, secure, and fair. This is the first book that emphasizes inherently interpretable models and their recent development and application, particularly in cases where models impact individuals, such as in consumer finance. In these scenarios, where explainability standards and regulations are particularly stringent, the explainable AI (XAI) post hoc explainability approach often faces significant challenges.

Developing reliable and safe machine learning systems also requires a rigorous evaluation of model weaknesses. This book presents two thorough examples alongside a methodology for model debugging, including identifying model flaws through error or residual slicing, evaluating model robustness under input corruption, assessing the reliability or uncertainty of model outputs, and testing model resilience under distribution shift through stress testing. These are crucial topics for developing and deploying machine learning in high-risk settings.

Machine learning models have the potential to disproportionately harm historically marginalized groups, and to deliver this harm rapidly and at scale through automation. Biased model decisions have detrimental impacts on protected groups, perpetuating social and economic disparities. In this book, the reader will learn how to approach the issue of model fairness through a sociotechnical lens. The authors also detail a thorough study of the effects of model debiasing techniques, and give practical advice on the application of these techniques within different regulated verticals.

Machine Learning for High-Risk Applications is a practical, opinionated, and timely book. Readers of all stripes will find rich insights into this fraught subject, whether you're a data scientist interested in better understanding your models, or a manager responsible for ensuring compliance with existing standards, or an executive trying to improve your organization's risk controls.

— Agus Sudjianto, PhD
EVP, Head of Corporate Model Risk, Wells Fargo

Preface

Today, machine learning (ML) is the most commercially viable subdiscipline of artificial intelligence (AI). ML systems are used to make high-risk decisions in employment, bail, parole, lending, security, and in many other high-impact applications throughout the world's economies and governments. In a corporate setting, ML systems are used in all parts of an organization—from consumer-facing products, to employee assessments, to back-office automation, and more. Indeed, the past decade has brought with it even wider adoption of ML technologies. But it has also proven that ML presents risks to its operators, consumers, and even the general public.

Like all technologies, ML can fail—whether by unintentional misuse or intentional abuse. As of 2023, there have been thousands of public reports of algorithmic discrimination, data privacy violations, training data security breaches, and other harmful incidents. Such risks must be mitigated before organizations, and the public, can realize the true benefits of this exciting technology. Addressing ML's risks requires action from practitioners. While nascent standards, to which this book aims to adhere, have begun to take shape, the practice of ML still lacks broadly accepted professional licensing or best practices. That means it's largely up to individual practitioners to hold themselves accountable for the good and bad outcomes of their technology when it's deployed into the world. *Machine Learning for High-Risk Applications* will arm practitioners with a solid understanding of model risk management processes and new ways to use common Python tools for training explainable models and debugging them for reliability, safety, bias management, security, and privacy issues.

We adapt a definition of AI from Stuart Russell and Peter Norvig's book, *Artificial Intelligence: A Modern Approach* (*https://oreil.ly/oosZs*): The designing and building of intelligent systems that receive signals from the environment and take actions that affect that environment (2020). For ML, we use the common definition attributed—perhaps apocryphally—to Arthur Samuel: [A] field of study that gives computers the ability to learn without being explicitly programmed (circa 1960).

Who Should Read This Book

This is a mostly technical book for early-to-middle career ML engineers and data scientists who want to learn about the responsible use of ML or ML risk management. The code examples are written in Python. That said, this book probably isn't for every data scientist and engineer out there coding in Python. This book is for you if you want to learn some model governance basics and update your workflow to accommodate basic risk controls. This book is for you if your work needs to comply with certain nondiscrimination, transparency, privacy, or security standards. (Although we can't guarantee compliance or provide legal advice!) This book is for you if you want to train explainable models, and learn to edit and debug them. Finally, this book is for you if you're concerned that your work in ML may be leading to unintended consequences relating to sociological biases, data privacy violations, security vulnerabilities, or other known problems caused by automated decision making writ large—and you want to do something about it.

Of course, this book may be of interest to others. If you're coming to ML from a field like physics, econometrics, or psychometrics, this book can help you learn how to blend newer ML techniques with established domain expertise and notions of validity or causality. This book may give regulators or policy professionals some insights into the current state of ML technologies that may be used in an effort to comply with laws, regulations, or standards. Technical risk executives or risk managers may find this book helpful in providing an updated overview of newer ML approaches suited for high-stakes applications. And expert data scientists or ML engineers may find this book educational too, but they may also find it challenges many established data science practices.

What Readers Will Learn

Readers of this book will be exposed to both traditional model risk management and how to blend it with computer security best practices like incident response, bug bounties, and red-teaming, to apply battle-tested risk controls to ML workflows and systems. This book will introduce a number of older and newer explainable models,

---

and explanation techniques that make ML systems even more transparent. Once we've set up a solid foundation of highly transparent models, we'll dig into testing models for safety and reliability. That's a lot easier when we can see how our model works! We'll go way beyond quality measurements in holdout data to explore how to apply well-known diagnostic techniques like residual analysis, sensitivity analysis, and benchmarking to new types of ML models. We'll then progress to structuring models for bias management, testing for bias, and remediating bias from an organizational and technical perspective. Finally, we'll discuss security for ML pipelines and APIs.

 The Draft European Union AI Act categorizes the following ML applications as high risk: biometric identification; management of critical infrastructure; education; employment; essential services, both public (e.g., public assistance) and private (e.g., credit lending); law enforcement; immigration and border control; criminal justice; and the democratic process. These are the types of ML use cases we have in mind when we refer to high-risk applications, and that's why we've chosen to focus the code examples in this book on computer vision and tree-based models for tabular data.

Readers should also be aware that in this first edition we focus on more established ML methods for estimation and decision making. We do not address unsupervised learning, search, recommendation systems, reinforcement learning, and generative AI in great depth. There are several reasons for this:

- These systems are not the most common commercial production systems, yet.

- Before moving on to more sophisticated unsupervised, recommendation, and reinforcement learning or generative approaches, it is imperative that we master the fundamentals. This first edition of the book focuses on the basics that will enable readers to take on more sophisticated projects later.

- Risk management for these systems is not as well understood as it is for the types of supervised models we concentrate on in this book. To be direct—as we often are in the remainder of the book—using models for which failure modes, mitigants, and controls are not well known can increase risk.

We do hope to return to these topics in the future and we acknowledge they are affecting billions of people today—positively and negatively. We also note that with a little creativity and elbow grease many of the techniques, risk mitigants, and risk management frameworks in this book can and should be applied to unsupervised models, search, recommendation, and generative AI.

Cutting-edge generative AI systems, like ChatGPT and GitHub Copilot, are an exciting way ML is impacting our lives. These systems appear to have addressed some of the bias issues that plagued earlier generations of similar systems. However, they still pose risks when working in high-stakes applications. If we're working with them and have concerns, we should consider the following simple guardrails:

Don't copy and paste from or into the user interface.
> Not using generated content directly and not pasting our own content directly into the interface can limit intellectual property and data privacy risks.

Check all generated content.
> These systems continue to generate wrong, offensive, or otherwise problematic content.

Avoid automation complacency.
> Generally, these systems are better suited to content generation than to decision support. We should be careful not to let them unintentionally make decisions for us.

Alignment with the NIST AI Risk Management Framework

In an attempt to follow our own advice, and to make the book even more practical for those working on high-risk applications, we will highlight where the proposed approaches in the book align to the nascent National Institute of Standards and Technology (NIST) AI Risk Management Framework (RMF). Application of external standards is a well-known risk management tactic, and NIST has an incredible track record for authoritative technical guidance. The AI RMF has many components, but two of the most central are the characteristics for trustworthiness in AI and the core RMF guidance. The characteristics for trustworthiness establish the basic principles of AI risk management, while the core RMF guidance provides advice for the implementation of risk controls. We will use vocabulary relating to NIST's characteristics for AI trustworthiness throughout the book: validity, reliability, safety, security, resiliency, transparency, accountability, explainability, interpretability, bias management, and enhanced privacy. At the beginning of each chapter in Part I, we'll also use a callout box to break down how and where the content aligns to specific aspects of the core NIST AI RMF map, measure, manage, and govern functions. We hope alignment to the NIST AI RMF improves the usability of the book, making it a more effective AI risk management tool.

NIST does not review, approve, condone, or otherwise address any content in this book, including any claims relating to the AI RMF. All AI RMF content is simply the authors' opinions and in no way reflects an official position of NIST or any official or unofficial relationship between NIST and the book or the authors.

Book Outline

The book is broken into three parts. Part I discusses issues from a practical application perspective, with dashes of theory where necessary. Part II contains long-form Python coding examples, addressing the topics in Part I from both structured and unstructured data perspectives. Part III imparts hard-won advice on how to succeed in real-world high-risk use cases.

Part I

Chapter 1 begins with a deep dive into pending regulations, discussions of product liability, and a thorough treatment of traditional-model risk management. Because many of these practices assume a somewhat staid and professional approach to modeling—a far cry from today's common "move fast and break things" ethos—we'll also discuss how to incorporate computer security best practices that assume failure into model governance.

Chapter 2 presents the burgeoning ecosystem of explainable models. We cover the generalized additive model (GAM) family in the most depth, but also discuss many other types of high-quality and high-transparency estimators. Chapter 2 also outlines many different post hoc explanation techniques, but with an eye toward rigor and known problems with this somewhat overhyped subfield of responsible ML techniques.

Chapter 3 tackles model validation, but in a way that actually tests models' assumptions and real-world reliability. We'll go over software testing basics as well as touch on highlights from the field of model debugging.

Chapter 4 overviews the *sociotechnical* aspects of fairness and bias in ML before transitioning to technical bias measurement and remediation approaches. Chapter 4 then treats bias testing in some detail, including tests for disparate impact and differential validity. Chapter 4 also addresses both established and conservative methods for bias remediation, and more cutting-edge dual-objective, adversarial, and pre-, in-, and postprocessing remediation techniques.

Chapter 5 closes Part I by laying out how to red-team ML systems, starting with the basics of computer security and moving into discussions of common ML attacks, adversarial ML, and robust ML.

Each chapter in Part I closes with a case discussion relating to topics like Zillow's iBuying meltdown, the A-level scandal in the UK, the fatal crash of a self-driving Uber, Twitter's inaugural bias bug bounty, and real-world ML evasion attacks. Each chapter will also outline alignment between content and the NIST AI RMF.

Part II

Part II expands on the ideas in Part I with a series of thorough code example chapters. Chapter 6 puts explainable boosting machines (EBMs), XGBoost, and explainable AI techniques through their paces in a basic consumer finance example.

Chapter 7 applies post hoc explanation techniques to a PyTorch image classifier.

In Chapter 8, we'll debug our consumer finance models for performance problems, and do the same for our image classifier in Chapter 9.

Chapter 10 contains detailed examples relating to bias testing and bias remediation, and Chapter 11 provides examples of ML attacks and countermeasures for tree-based models.

Part III

We end the book in Chapter 12 with more general advice for how to succeed in high-risk ML applications. It's not by moving fast and breaking things. For some low-risk use cases, it might be fine to apply a quick and dirty approach. But as ML becomes more regulated and is used in more high-risk applications, the consequences of breaking things are becoming more serious. Chapter 12 caps off the book with hard-won practical advice for applying ML in high-stakes scenarios.

Our hope with the first edition of this text is to provide a legitimate alternative to the opaque and compressed-time-frame workflows that are common in ML today. This book should provide a set of vocabulary, ideas, tools, and techniques that enable practitioners to be more deliberate in their very important work.

Example Datasets

We rely on two primary datasets in this book, to explain techniques or to demonstrate approaches and discuss their results. These are example datasets, not fit for training models in high-risk applications, but they are well known and easily accessible. Their shortcomings also allow to us to point out various data, modeling, and interpretation pitfalls. We will refer to these datasets many times in subsequent chapters, so be sure to get a feel for them before diving into the rest of the book.

Taiwan Credit Data

For the structured data chapters—Chapters 6, 8, 10, and 11—we used a slightly modified version of the Taiwan credit data available from the University of California Irvine Machine Learning Repository (*https://oreil.ly/xJ5u2*) or Kaggle (*https://oreil.ly/DmAWe*). The credit card default data contains demographic and payment information about credit card customers in Taiwan in the year 2005. In general, the goal with this dataset is to use past payment statuses (PAY_*), past payment amounts (PAY_AMT*), and bill amounts (BILL_AMT*) as inputs to predict whether a customer will meet their next payment (DELINQ_NEXT = 0). Currency amounts are reported in Taiwanese dollars. We've added simulated SEX and RACE markers to this dataset to illustrate bias testing and remediation approaches. We use the payment information as input features, and following best practices to manage bias in ML systems, we do not use the demographic information as model inputs. The complete data dictionary is available in Table P-1.

Table P-1. Data dictionary for the credit card default data

Name	Modeling role	Measurement level	Description
ID	ID	Int	Unique row identifier
LIMIT_BAL	Input	Float	Amount of previously awarded credit
SEX	Demographic information	Int	1 = male; 2 = female
RACE	Demographic information	Int	1 = Hispanic; 2 = Black; 3 = white;[a] 4 = Asian
EDUCATION	Demographic information	Int	1 = graduate school; 2 = university; 3 = high school; 4 = others
MARRIAGE	Demographic information	Int	1 = married; 2 = single; 3 = others
AGE	Demographic information	Int	Age in years
PAY_0, PAY_2–PAY_6	Input	Int	History of past payment; PAY_0 = the repayment status in September, 2005; PAY_2 = the repayment status in August, 2005; ...; PAY_6 = the repayment status in April, 2005. The measurement scale for the repayment status is: −1 = pay duly; 1 = payment delay for one month; 2 = payment delay for two months; ...; 8 = payment delay for eight months; 9 = payment delay for nine months and above
BILL_AMT1– BILL_AMT6	Input	Float	Amount of bill statement; BILL_AMT1 = amount of bill statement In September, 2005; BILL_AMT2 = amount of bill statement in August, 2005; ...; BILL_AMT6 = amount of bill statement in April, 2005

Name	Modeling role	Measurement level	Description
PAY_AMT1– PAY_AMT6	Input	Float	Amount of previous payment; PAY_AMT1 = amount paid in September, 2005; PAY_AMT2 = amount paid in August, 2005; …; PAY_AMT6 = amount paid in April, 2005
DELINQ_NEXT	Target	Int	Whether a customer's next payment is delinquent (late), 1 = late; 0 = on-time

[a] There is an ongoing debate as to whether "White" should be capitalized alongside "Black" when referring to racial demographic groups. Throughout this book, we have generally followed the lead of many authoritative voices (*https://oreil.ly/3iKFj*) in publishing and academia by capitalizing "Black," out of recognition of a shared history and cultural identity.

As readers will see in the following chapters, this dataset encodes some pathological flaws. It's too small to train usable high-capacity ML estimators and nearly all of the signal for DELINQ_NEXT is encoded in PAY_0. As the book progresses, we'll attempt to deal with these issues and uncover others.

Kaggle Chest X-Ray Data

For the deep learning chapters—Chapters 6 and 9—we will be using the Kaggle Chest X-Ray Images dataset (*https://oreil.ly/TsoGB*). This dataset is composed of roughly 5,800 images of two classes, pneumonia and normal. These labels were determined by human domain experts. The images are deidentified chest X-rays, taken during routine care visits to Guangzhou Women and Children's Medical Center in Guangzhou, China. See Figure P-1 for an example pneumonia image.

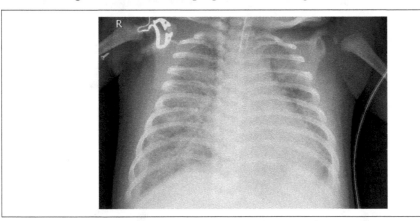

Figure P-1. An example pneumonia image from the Kaggle Chest X-ray dataset

The main issues we'll face with this dataset are small size—even for transfer learning tasks, misalignment between the images in the dataset, visual artifacts that can give rise to shortcut learning, and the need for domain expertise to validate modeling outcomes. As with the Taiwan credit data, we'll work through these issues and discover more in the later chapters of this book.

Conventions Used in This Book

The following typographical conventions are used in this book:

Italic
> Indicates new terms or important ideas.

`Constant width`
> Used for program listings, as well as within paragraphs to refer to program elements such as variable or function names, databases, data types, environment variables, statements, and keywords.

> This element signifies a general note or suggestion.

> This element indicates a warning or caution.

Online Figures

You can find larger, color versions of some figures at *https://oreil.ly/MLHA-figures*. Links to each figure also appear in their captions.

Using Code Examples

Supplemental material (code examples, exercises, etc.) is available for download at *https://oreil.ly/machine-learning-high-risk-apps-code*.

> Over time, code examples may change from those printed in the book.

If you have a technical question or a problem using the code examples, please send email to *bookquestions@oreilly.com*.

This book is here to help you get your job done. In general, if example code is offered with this book, you may use it in your programs and documentation. You do not need to contact us for permission unless you're reproducing a significant portion of the code. For example, writing a program that uses several chunks of code from this book does not require permission. Selling or distributing examples from O'Reilly books does require permission. Answering a question by citing this book and quoting example code does not require permission. Incorporating a significant amount of example code from this book into your product's documentation does require permission.

We appreciate, but generally do not require, attribution. An attribution usually includes the title, author, publisher, and ISBN. For example: "*Machine Learning for High-Risk Applications* by Patrick Hall, James Curtis, and Parul Pandey (O'Reilly). Copyright 2023 Patrick Hall, James Curtis, and Parul Pandey, 978-1-098-10243-2."

If you feel your use of code examples falls outside fair use or the permission given above, feel free to contact us at *permissions@oreilly.com*.

O'Reilly Online Learning

 For more than 40 years, *O'Reilly Media* has provided technology and business training, knowledge, and insight to help companies succeed.

Our unique network of experts and innovators share their knowledge and expertise through books, articles, and our online learning platform. O'Reilly's online learning platform gives you on-demand access to live training courses, in-depth learning paths, interactive coding environments, and a vast collection of text and video from O'Reilly and 200+ other publishers. For more information, visit *http://oreilly.com*.

How to Contact Us

Please address comments and questions concerning this book to the publisher:

O'Reilly Media, Inc.
1005 Gravenstein Highway North
Sebastopol, CA 95472
800-998-9938 (in the United States or Canada)
707-829-0515 (international or local)
707-829-0104 (fax)

We have a web page for this book, where we list errata, examples, and any additional information. You can access this page at *https://oreil.ly/machine-learning-high-risk-apps*.

Email *bookquestions@oreilly.com* to comment or ask technical questions about this book.

For news and information about our books and courses, visit *https://oreilly.com*.

Find us on LinkedIn: *https://linkedin.com/company/oreilly-media*

Follow us on Twitter: *https://twitter.com/oreillymedia*

Watch us on YouTube: *https://youtube.com/oreillymedia*

Acknowledgments

The authors thank our editors and production staff at O'Reilly, particularly Michele Cronin and Gregory Hyman; our copyeditor, Liz Wheeler; and our acquisitions editors, Rebecca Novack and Nicole Butterfield. Thanks also to our technical reviewers, Navdeep Gill, Collin Starkweather, Hariom Tatstat, and Laura Uzcátegui.

Patrick Hall

Thanks to Lisa and Dylan for love and support throughout the long drafting and editing process. Thanks also to my colleagues over the past decade at the Institute for Advanced Analytics, SAS Institute, the George Washington School of Business, H2O.ai, SolasAI, the AI Incident Database, NIST, and BNH.AI.

James Curtis

For my wife, Lindsey, whose unyielding love forms the bedrock of my life. My children, Isaac and Micah, did not help much with the writing of this book, but I appreciate them nonetheless. Finally, I must thank my former colleagues at SolasAI, especially Nick and Chris, for the many hours of insightful discussions.

Parul Pandey

I am incredibly grateful to have had the love and support of my husband, Manoj, and my son, Agrim, while writing this book. Both of them not only encouraged me to take up this mammoth task but also were deeply understanding when I would spend hours in my study working on the book.

## PART I

Theories and Practical Applications of AI Risk Management

## CHAPTER 1

Contemporary Machine Learning Risk Management

Building the best machine learning system starts with cultural competencies and business processes. This chapter presents numerous cultural and procedural approaches we can use to improve ML performance and safeguard our organizations' ML against real-world safety and performance problems. It also includes a case study that illustrates what happens when an ML system is used without proper human oversight. The primary goal of the approaches discussed in this chapter is to create better ML systems. This might mean improved in silico test data performance. But it really means building models that perform as expected once deployed in vivo, so we don't lose money, hurt people, or cause other harms.

 In vivo is Latin for "within the living." We'll sometimes use this term to mean something closer to "interacting with the living," as in how ML models perform in the real world when interacting with human users. *In silico* means "by means of computer modeling or computer simulation," and we'll use this term to describe the testing data scientists often perform in their development environments before deploying ML models.

The chapter begins with a discussion of the current legal and regulatory landscape for ML and some nascent best-practice guidance, to inform system developers of their fundamental obligations when it comes to safety and performance. We'll also introduce how the book aligns to the National Institute of Standards and Technology (NIST) AI Risk Management Framework (*https://oreil.ly/Or940*) (RMF) in this part of the chapter. Because those who do not study history are bound to repeat it, the chapter then highlights AI incidents, and discusses why understanding AI incidents is important for proper safety and performance in ML systems. Since many ML safety concerns require thinking beyond technical specifications, the chapter then blends model risk management (MRM), information technology (IT) security guidance, and practices from other fields to put forward numerous ideas for improving ML safety culture and processes within organizations. The chapter will close with a case study focusing on safety culture, legal ramifications, and AI incidents.

None of the risk management approaches discussed in this chapter are a silver bullet. If we want to manage risk successfully, we'll need to pick from the wide variety of available controls those that work best for our organization. Larger organizations will typically be able to do more risk management than smaller organizations. Readers at large organizations may be able to implement many controls across various departments, divisions, or internal functions. Readers at smaller organizations will have to choose their risk management tactics judiciously. In the end, a great deal of technology risk management comes down to human behavior. Whichever risk controls an organization implements, they'll need to be paired with strong governance and policies for the *people* that build and maintain ML systems.

A Snapshot of the Legal and Regulatory Landscape

It's a myth that ML is unregulated. ML systems can and do break the law. Forgetting or ignoring the legal context is one of the riskiest things an organization can do with respect to ML systems. That said, the legal and regulatory landscape for ML is complicated and changing quickly. This section aims to provide a snapshot of important laws and regulations for overview and awareness purposes. We'll start by highlighting the pending EU AI Act. We'll then discuss the many US federal laws and regulations that touch on ML, US state and municipal laws for data privacy and AI, and the basics of product liability, then end the section with a rundown of recent Federal Trade Commission (FTC) enforcement actions.

 The authors are not lawyers and nothing in this book is legal advice. The intersection of law and AI is an incredibly complex topic that data scientists and ML engineers are not equipped to handle alone. You may have legal concerns about ML systems that you work on. If so, seek real legal advice.

The Proposed EU AI Act

The EU has proposed sweeping regulations for AI that are expected to be passed in 2023. Known as the EU AI Act (*https://oreil.ly/x5dLT*) (AIA), they would prohibit certain uses of AI like distorting human behavior, social credit scoring, and real-time biometric surveillance. The AIA deems other uses to be high risk, including applications in criminal justice, biometric identification, employment screening, critical infrastructure management, law enforcement, essential services, immigration, and others—placing a high documentation, governance, and risk management burden on these. Other applications would be considered limited or low risk, with fewer compliance obligations for their makers and operators. Much like the EU General Data Protection Regulation (GDPR) has changed the way companies handle data in the US and around the world, EU AI regulations are designed to have an outsized impact on US and other international AI deployments. Whether we're working in the EU or not, we may need to start familiarizing ourselves with the AIA. One of the best ways is to read the Annexes (*https://oreil.ly/0k_TQ*), especially Annexes 1 and 3–8, that define terms and layout documentation and conformity requirements.

US Federal Laws and Regulations

Because we've been using algorithms in one form or another for decades in our government and economy, many US federal laws and regulations already touch on AI and ML. These regulations tend to focus on social discrimination by algorithms, but also treat transparency, privacy, and other topics. The Civil Rights Acts of 1964 and 1991, the Americans with Disabilities Act (ADA), the Equal Credit Opportunity Act (ECOA), the Fair Credit Reporting Act (FCRA), and the Fair Housing Act (FHA) are some of the federal laws that attempt to prevent discrimination by algorithms in areas like employment, credit lending, and housing. ECOA and FCRA, along with their more detailed implementation in Regulation B, attempt to increase transparency in ML-based credit lending and guarantee recourse rights for credit consumers. For a rejected credit application, lenders are expected to indicate the reasons for the rejection, i.e., an *adverse action*, and describe the features in the ML model that drove the decision. If the provided reasoning or data is wrong, consumers should be able to appeal the decision.

The practice of MRM, defined in part in the Federal Reserve's SR 11-7 guidance (*https://oreil.ly/xpr5P*), forms a part of regulatory examinations for large US banks, and sets up organizational, cultural, and technical processes for good and reliable performance of ML used in mission-critical financial applications. Much of this chapter is inspired by MRM guidance, as it's the most battle-tested ML risk management framework out there. Laws like the Health Insurance Portability and Accountability Act of 1996 (HIPAA) and the Family Educational Rights and Privacy Act (FERPA) set up serious data privacy expectations in healthcare and for students. Like the GDPR, HIPAA's and FERPA's interactions with ML are material, complex, and still debated. These are not even all the US laws that might affect our use of ML, but hopefully this brief listing provides an idea of what the US federal government has decided is important enough to regulate.

State and Municipal Laws

US states and cities have also taken up laws and regulations for AI and ML. New York City (NYC) Local Law 144, which mandates bias audits for automated employment decision tools, was initially expected to go into effect in January 2023. Under this law, every major employer in NYC will have to conduct bias testing of automated employment software and post the results on their website. Washington DC's proposed Stop Discrimination by Algorithms Act attempts to replicate federal expectations for nondiscrimination and transparency, but for a much broader set of applications, for companies that operate in DC or use the data of many DC citizens.

Numerous states passed their own data privacy laws as well. Unlike the older HIPAA and FERPA federal laws, these state data privacy laws are often intentionally designed to partially regulate the use of AI and ML. States like California, Colorado, Virginia, and others have passed data privacy laws that mention increased transparency, decreased bias, or both, for automated decision-making systems. Some states have put biometric data or social media in their regulatory crosshairs too. For example, Illinois' Biometric Information Privacy Act (BIPA) outlaws many uses of biometric data, and IL regulators have already started enforcement actions. The lack of a federal data privacy or AI law combined with this new crop of state and local laws makes the AI and ML compliance landscape very complicated. Our uses of ML may or may not be regulated, or may be regulated to varying degrees, based on the specific application, industry, and geography of the system.

Basic Product Liability

As makers of consumer products, data scientists and ML engineers have a fundamental obligation to create safe systems. To quote a recent Brookings Institute report, "Products Liability Law as a Way to Address AI Harms" (*https://oreil.ly/2K_R6*), "Manufacturers have an obligation to make products that will be safe when used in reasonably foreseeable ways. If an AI system is used in a foreseeable way and yet becomes a source of harm, a plaintiff could assert that the manufacturer was negligent in not recognizing the possibility of that outcome." Just like car or power tool manufacturers, makers of ML systems are subject to broad legal standards for negligence and safety. Product safety has been the subject of large amounts of legal and economic analysis, but this subsection will focus on one of the first and simplest standards for negligence: the Hand rule. Named after Judge Learned Hand, and coined in 1947, it provides a viable framework for ML product makers to think about negligence and due diligence. The Hand rule says that a product maker takes on a burden of care, and that the resources expended on that care should always be greater than the cost of a likely incident involving the product. Stated algebraically:

$$Burden \geq Risk = (Probability\ of\ loss)(Loss\ size)$$

In more plain terms, organizations are expected to apply care, i.e., time, resources, or money, to a level commensurate to the cost associated with a foreseeable risk. Otherwise liability can ensue. In Figure 1-1, Burden is the parabolically increasing line, and risk, or Probability multiplied by Loss, is the parabolically decreasing line. While these lines are not related to a specific measurement, their parabolic shape is meant to reflect the last-mile problem in removing all ML system risk, and shows that the application of additional care beyond a reasonable threshold leads to diminishing returns for decreasing risk as well.

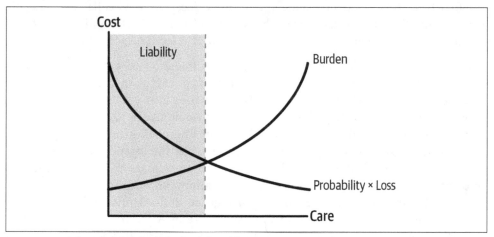

Figure 1-1. The Hand rule (adapted from "Economic Analysis of Alternative Standards of Liability in Accident Law": https://oreil.ly/9_u8H)

 A fairly standard definition for the *risk* of a technology incident is the estimated likelihood of the incident multiplied by its estimated cost. More broadly, the International Organization for Standardization (ISO) defines risk in the context of enterprise risk management as the "effect of uncertainty on objectives."

While it's probably too resource intensive to calculate the quantities in the Hand rule exactly, it is important to think about these concepts of negligence and liability when designing an ML system. For a given ML system, if the probability of an incident is high, if the monetary or other loss associated with a system incident is large, or if both quantities are large, organizations need to spend extra resources on ensuring safety for that system. Moreover, organizations should document to the best of their ability that due diligence exceeds the estimated failure probabilities multiplied by the estimated losses.

Federal Trade Commission Enforcement

How might we actually get in trouble? If you're working in a regulated industry, you probably know your regulators. But if we don't know if our work is regulated or who might be enforcing consequences if we cross a legal or regulatory red line, it's probably the US Federal Trade Commission we need to be most concerned with. The

FTC is broadly focused on unfair, deceptive, or predatory trade practices, and they have found reason to take down at least three prominent ML algorithms in three years. With their new enforcement tool, *algorithmic disgorgement*, the FTC has the ability to delete algorithms and data, and, typically, prohibit future revenue generation from an offending algorithm. Cambridge Analytica (*https://oreil.ly/cM3V8*) was the first firm to face this punishment, after their deceptive data collection practices surrounding the 2016 election. Everalbum (*https://oreil.ly/05SO5*) and WW (*https://oreil.ly/PMOq0*), known as Weight Watchers, have also faced disgorgement.

The FTC has been anything but quiet about its intention to enforce federal laws around AI and ML. FTC commissioners have penned lengthy treatises on algorithms and economic justice (*https://oreil.ly/v8Z4y*). They have also posted at least two blogs providing high-level guidance for companies who would like to avoid the unpleasantness of enforcement actions. These blogs highlight a number of concrete steps organizations should take. For example, in "Using Artificial Intelligence and Algorithms" (*https://oreil.ly/066Y-*), the FTC makes it clear that consumers should not be misled into interacting with an ML system posing as a human. Accountability is another prominent theme in "Using Artificial Intelligence and Algorithms," "Aiming for Truth, Fairness, and Equity in Your Company's Use of AI" (*https://oreil.ly/XMqKo*), and other related publications. In "Aiming for Truth, Fairness, and Equity in Your Company's Use of AI," the FTC states, "**Hold yourself accountable—or be ready for the FTC to do it for you**" (emphasis added by the original author). This extremely direct language is unusual from a regulator. In "Using Artificial Intelligence and Algorithms," the FTC puts forward, "Consider how you hold yourself accountable, and whether it would make sense to use independent standards or independent expertise to step back and take stock of your AI." The next section introduces some of the emerging independent standards we can use to increase accountability, make better products, and decrease any potential legal liability.

Authoritative Best Practices

Data science mostly lacks professional standards and licensing today, but some authoritative guidance is starting to appear on the horizon. ISO is beginning to outline technical standards for AI (*https://oreil.ly/8ZeJQ*). Making sure our models are in line with ISO standards would be one way to apply an independent standard to our ML work. Particularly for US-based data scientists, the NIST AI RMF is a very important project to watch.

Version 1 of the AI RMF was released in January 2023. The framework puts forward characteristics of trustworthiness in AI systems: validity, reliability, safety, security, resiliency, transparency, accountability, explainability, interpretability, bias management, and enhanced privacy. Then it presents actionable guidance across four organizational functions—map, measure, manage, and govern—for achieving trustworthiness. The guidance in the map, measure, manage, and govern functions is subdivided into more detailed categories and subcategories. To see these categories of guidance, check out the RMF (*https://oreil.ly/kxq-G*) or the AI RMF playbook (*https://oreil.ly/dn4xs*), which provides even more detailed suggestions.

 The NIST AI Risk Management Framework is a *voluntary* tool for improving the trustworthiness of AI and ML systems. The AI RMF is not regulation and NIST is not a regulator.

To follow our own advice, and that of regulators and publishers of authoritative guidance, and to make this book more useful, we'll be calling out how *we believe* the content of each chapter in Part I aligns to the AI RMF. Following this paragraph, readers will find a callout box that matches the chapter subheadings with AI RMF subcategories. The idea is that readers can use the table to understand how employing the approaches discussed in each chapter may help them adhere to the AI RMF. Because the subcategory advice may, in some cases, sound abstract to ML practitioners, we provide more practice-oriented language that matches the RMF categories; this will be helpful in translating the RMF into in vivo ML deployments. Check out the callout box to see how we think Chapter 1 aligns with the AI RMF, and look for similar tables at the start of each chapter in Part I.

NIST AI RMF Crosswalk

Chapter section	NIST AI RMF subcategories
"A Snapshot of the Legal and Regulatory Landscape" on page 4	GOVERN 1.1, GOVERN 1.2, GOVERN 2.2, GOVERN 4.1, GOVERN 5.2, MAP 1.1, MAP 1.2, MAP 3.3, MAP 4.1, MEASURE 1.1, MEASURE 2.8, MEASURE 2.11
"Authoritative Best Practices" on page 8	GOVERN 1.2, GOVERN 5.2, MAP 1.1, MAP 2.3
"AI Incidents" on page 11	GOVERN 1.2, GOVERN 1.5, GOVERN 4.3, GOVERN 6.2, MEASURE 3.3, MANAGE 2.3, MANAGE 4.1, MANAGE 4.3
"Organizational Accountability" on page 13	GOVERN 1, GOVERN 2, GOVERN 3.2, GOVERN 4, GOVERN 5, GOVERN 6.2, MEASURE 2.8, MEASURE 3.3
"Culture of Effective Challenge" on page 14	GOVERN 4, MEASURE 2.8
"Diverse and Experienced Teams" on page 15	GOVERN 1.2, GOVERN 1.3, GOVERN 3, GOVERN 4.1, MAP 1.1, MAP 1.2, MEASURE 4
"Drinking Our Own Champagne" on page 15	GOVERN 4.1, MEASURE 4.1, MEASURE 4.2
"Moving Fast and Breaking Things" on page 16	GOVERN 2.1, GOVERN 4.1

Chapter section	NIST AI RMF subcategories
"Forecasting Failure Modes" on page 17	GOVERN 1.2, GOVERN 1.3, GOVERN 4.2, MAP 1.1, MAP 2.3, MAP 3.2, MANAGE 1.4, MANAGE 2
"Risk tiering" on page 18	GOVERN 1.2, GOVERN 1.3, GOVERN 1.4, GOVERN 5.2, MAP 1.5, MAP 4, MAP 5.1, MANAGE 1.2, MANAGE 1.3, MANAGE 1.4
"Model documentation" on page 19	GOVERN 1, GOVERN 2.1, GOVERN 4.2, MAP, MEASURE 1.1, MEASURE 2, MEASURE 3, MEASURE 4, MANAGE
"Model monitoring" on page 20	GOVERN 1.2, GOVERN 1.3, GOVERN 1.4, GOVERN 1.5, MAP 2.3, MAP 3.5, MAP 4, MAP 5.2, MEASURE 1.1, MEASURE 2.4, MEASURE 2.6, MEASURE 2.7, MEASURE 2.8, MEASURE 2.10, MEASURE 2.11, MEASURE 2.12, MEASURE 3.1, MEASURE 3.3, MEASURE 4, MANAGE 2.2, MANAGE 2.3, MANAGE 2.4, MANAGE 3, MANAGE 4
"Model inventories" on page 21	GOVERN 1.2, GOVERN 1.3, GOVERN 1.4, GOVERN 1.6, MAP 3.5, MAP 4, MANAGE 3
"System validation and process auditing" on page 21	GOVERN 1.2, GOVERN 1.3, GOVERN 1.4, GOVERN 2.1, GOVERN 4.1, GOVERN 4.3, GOVERN 6.1, MAP 2.3, MAP 3.5, MAP 4, MEASURE, MANAGE 1
"Change management" on page 22	GOVERN 1.2, GOVERN 1.3, GOVERN 1.4, GOVERN 1.7, GOVERN 2.2, GOVERN 4.2, MAP 3.5, MAP 4, MEASURE 1.2, MEASURE 2.13, MEASURE 3.1, MANAGE 4.1, MANAGE 4.2
"Model audits and assessments" on page 22	GOVERN 1.2, GOVERN 1.3, GOVERN 1.4, GOVERN 2.1, GOVERN 4.1, MAP 3.5, MAP 4, MEASURE, MANAGE 1
"Impact assessments" on page 23	GOVERN 1.2, GOVERN 1.3, GOVERN 1.4, GOVERN 2.1, GOVERN 4.1, GOVERN 4.2, GOVERN 5.2, MAP 1.1, MAP 2.2, MAP 3.1, MAP 3.2, MAP 3.5, MAP 5, MEASURE 3, MANAGE 1
"Appeal, override, and opt out" on page 24	GOVERN 1.1, GOVERN 1.2, GOVERN 1.4, GOVERN 1.5, GOVERN 3.2, GOVERN 5, MAP 3.5, MAP 5.2, MEASURE 2.8, MEASURE 3.3, MANAGE 4.1
"Pair and double programming" on page 24	GOVERN 4.1, GOVERN 5.2, MAP 3.5
"Security permissions for model deployment" on page 24	GOVERN 1.4, GOVERN 4.1, GOVERN 5.2, MAP 3.5, MAP 4.2
"Bug bounties" on page 25	GOVERN 5, MAP 3.5, MAP 5.2, MEASURE 3
"AI incident response" on page 25	GOVERN 1.2, GOVERN 1.5, GOVERN 4.3, GOVERN 6.2, MAP 3.5, MAP 4, MAP 5, MEASURE 3.1, MANAGE 2.3, MANAGE 4.1, MANAGE 4.3

- Applicable AI trustworthiness characteristics include: Valid and Reliable, Safe, Managed Bias, Secure and Resilient, Transparent and Accountable, Explainable and Interpretable, Enhanced Privacy
- See also:
  - NIST AI Risk Management Framework (*https://oreil.ly/1YAoU*)
  - NIST AI Risk Management Framework Playbook (*https://oreil.ly/6_TUM*)
  - Full crosswalk table (not an official resource) (*https://oreil.ly/61TXd*)

AI Incidents

In many ways, the fundamental goal of ML safety processes and related model debugging, also discussed in Chapter 3, is to prevent and mitigate AI incidents. Here, we'll loosely define AI incidents as any outcome of the system that could cause harm. As becomes apparent when using the Hand rule as a guide, the severity of an AI incident is increased by the loss the incident causes, and decreased by the care taken by the operators to mitigate those losses.

Because complex systems drift toward failure, there is no shortage of AI incidents to discuss as examples. AI incidents can range from annoying to deadly—from mall security robots falling down stairs (*https://oreil.ly/fLHU1*), to self-driving cars killing pedestrians (*https://oreil.ly/vFW_-*), to mass-scale diversion of healthcare resources (*https://oreil.ly/2e8WQ*) away from those who need them most. As pictured in Figure 1-2, AI incidents can be roughly divided into three buckets:

Abuses
> AI can be used for nefarious purposes, apart from specific hacks and attacks on other AI systems. The day may already have come when hackers use AI to increase the efficiency and potency of their more general attacks. What the future could hold is even more frightening. Specters like autonomous drone attacks and ethnic profiling by authoritarian regimes are already on the horizon.

Attacks
> Examples of all major types of attacks—confidentiality, integrity, and availability attacks (see Chapter 5 for more information)—have been published by researchers. Confidentiality attacks involve the exfiltration of training data or model logic from AI system endpoints. Integrity attacks include adversarial manipulation of training data or model outcomes, either through adversarial examples, evasion, impersonation, or poisoning. Availability attacks can be conducted through more standard denial-of-service approaches, through sponge examples that overuse system resources, or via algorithmic discrimination induced by some adversary to deny system services to certain groups of users.

Failures
> AI system failures tend to involve algorithmic discrimination, safety and performance lapses, data privacy violations, inadequate transparency, or problems in third-party system components.

AI incidents are a reality. And like the systems from which they arise, AI incidents can be complex. AI incidents have multiple causes: failures, attacks, and abuses. They also tend to blend traditional notions of computer security with concerns like data privacy and algorithmic discrimination.

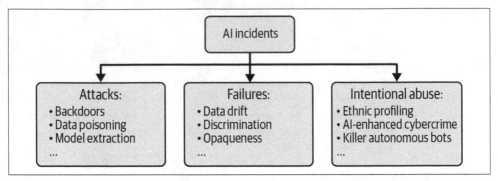

Figure 1-2. A basic taxonomy of AI incidents (adapted from "What to Do When AI Fails": https://oreil.ly/AHfmK)

The 2016 Tay chatbot incident (*https://oreil.ly/a-DhB*) is an informative example. Tay was a state-of-the-art chatbot trained by some of the world's leading experts at Microsoft Research for the purpose of interacting with people on Twitter to increase awareness about AI. Sixteen hours after its release—and 96,000 tweets later—Tay had spiraled into writing as a neo-Nazi pornographer and had to be shut down. What happened? Twitter users quickly learned that Tay's adaptive learning system could easily be poisoned. Racist and sexual content tweeted at the bot was incorporated into its training data, and just as quickly resulted in offensive output. Data poisoning is an integrity attack, but due to the context in which it was carried out, this attack resulted in algorithmic discrimination. It's also important to note that Tay's designers, being world-class experts at an extremely well-funded research center, seemed to have put some guardrails in place. Tay would respond to certain hot-button issues with precanned responses. But that was not enough, and Tay devolved into a public security and algorithmic discrimination incident for Microsoft Research.

Think this was a one-off incident? Wrong. Just recently, again due to hype and failure to think through performance, safety, privacy, and security risks systematically, many of Tay's most obvious failures were repeated in Scatter Lab's release of its Lee Luda chatbot (*https://oreil.ly/5OLXV*). When designing ML systems, plans should be compared to past known incidents in hope of preventing future similar incidents. This is precisely the point of recent AI incident database efforts (*https://oreil.ly/vvLbp*) and associated publications (*https://oreil.ly/59yaY*).

AI incidents can also be an apolitical motivator for responsible technology development. For better or worse, cultural and political viewpoints on topics like algorithmic discrimination and data privacy can vary widely. Getting a team to agree on ethical considerations can be very difficult. It might be easier to get them working to prevent embarrassing and potentially costly or dangerous incidents, which should be a baseline goal of any serious data science team. The notion of AI incidents is central to understanding ML safety; a central theme of this chapter's content is cultural competencies and business processes that can be used to prevent and mitigate AI incidents. We'll dig into those mitigants in the next sections and take a deep dive into a real incident to close the chapter.

Cultural Competencies for Machine Learning Risk Management

An organization's culture is an essential aspect of responsible AI. This section will discuss cultural competencies like accountability, drinking our own champagne, domain expertise, and the stale adage "move fast and break things."

Organizational Accountability

A key to the successful mitigation of ML risks is real accountability within organizations for AI incidents. If no one's job is at stake when an ML system fails, gets attacked, or is abused for nefarious purposes, then it's entirely possible that no one in that organization really cares about ML safety and performance. In addition to developers who think through risks, apply software quality assurance (QA) techniques, and model debugging methods, organizations need individuals or teams who validate ML system technology and audit associated processes. Organizations also need someone to be responsible for AI incident response plans. This is why leading financial institutions, whose use of predictive modeling has been regulated for decades, employ a practice known as model risk management. MRM is patterned off the Federal Reserve's SR 11-7 model risk management guidance (*https://oreil.ly/xpr5P*), which arose out the of the financial crisis of 2008. Notably, implementation of MRM often involves accountable executives and several teams that are responsible for the safety and performance of models and ML systems.

Implementation of MRM standards usually requires several different teams and executive leadership. These are some of the key tenets that form the cultural backbone for MRM:

Written policies and procedures
> The organizational rules for making and using ML should be written and available for all organizational stakeholders. Those close to ML systems should have trainings on the policies and procedures. These rules should also be audited to understand when they need to be updated. No one should be able to claim ignorance of the rules, the rules should be transparent, and the rules should not change without approval. Policies and procedures should include clear mechanisms for escalating serious risks or problems to senior management, and likely should put forward whistleblower processes and protections.

Effective challenge

Effective challenge dictates that experts with the capability to change a system, who did not build the ML system being challenged, perform validation and auditing. MRM practices typically distribute effective challenge across three "lines of defense," where conscientious system developers make up the first line of defense and independent, skilled, and empowered technical validators and process auditors make up the second and third lines, respectively.

Accountable leadership

A specific executive within an organization should be accountable for ensuring AI incidents do not happen. This position is often referred to as *chief model risk officer* (CMRO). It's also not uncommon for CMRO terms of employment and compensation to be linked to ML system performance. The role of CMRO offers a very straightforward cultural check on ML safety and performance. If our boss really cares about ML system safety and performance, then we start to care too.

Incentives

Data science staff and management must be incentivized to implement ML responsibly. Often, compressed product timelines can incentivize the creation of a minimum viable product first, with rigorous testing and remediation relegated to the end of the model lifecycle immediately before deployment to production. Moreover, ML testing and validation teams are often evaluated by the same criteria as ML development teams, leading to a fundamental misalignment where testers and validators are encouraged to move quickly rather than assure quality. Aligning timeline, performance evaluation, and pay incentives to team function helps solidify a culture of responsible ML and risk mitigation.

Of course, small or young organizations may not be able to spare an entire full-time employee to monitor ML system risk. But it's important to have an individual or group held accountable if ML systems cause incidents and rewarded if the systems work well. If an organization assumes that everyone is accountable for ML risk and AI incidents, the reality is that no one is accountable.

Culture of Effective Challenge

Whether our organization is ready to adopt full-blown MRM practices, or not, we can still benefit from certain aspects of MRM. In particular, the cultural competency of effective challenge can be applied outside of the MRM context. At its core, effective challenge means actively challenging and questioning steps taken throughout the development of ML systems. An organizational culture that encourages serious questioning of ML system designs will be more likely to develop effective ML systems or products, and to catch problems before they explode into harmful incidents. Note that effective challenge cannot be abusive, and it must apply equally to all personnel developing an ML system, especially so-called "rockstar" engineers and data scientists. Effective challenge should also be structured, such as weekly meetings where current design thinking is questioned and alternative design choices are seriously considered.

Diverse and Experienced Teams

Diverse teams can bring wider and previously uncorrelated perspectives to bear on the design, development, and testing of ML systems. Nondiverse teams often do not. Many have documented the unfortunate outcomes that can arise as a result of data scientists not considering demographic diversity in the training or results of ML systems. A potential solution to these kinds of oversights is increasing demographic diversity on ML teams from its current woeful levels (*https://oreil.ly/7M9uB*). Business or other domain experience is also important when building teams. Domain experts are instrumental in feature selection and engineering, and in the testing of system outputs. In the mad rush to develop ML systems, domain-expert participation can also serve as a safety check. Generalist data scientists often lack the experience necessary to deal with domain-specific data and results. Misunderstanding the meaning of input data or output results is a recipe for disaster that can lead to AI incidents when a system is deployed. Unfortunately, when it comes to data scientists forgetting or ignoring the importance of domain expertise, the social sciences deserve a special emphasis. In a trend referred to as "tech's quiet colonization of the social sciences" (*https://oreil.ly/IcIBi*), several organizations have pursued regrettable ML projects that seek to replace decisions that should be made by trained social scientists (*https://oreil.ly/xI9Jv*) or that simply ignore the collective wisdom of social science domain expertise altogether (*https://oreil.ly/KvVSv*).

Drinking Our Own Champagne

Also known as "eating our own dog food," the practice of drinking our own champagne refers to using our own software or products inside of our own organization. Often a form of prealpha or prebeta testing, drinking our own champagne can identify problems that emerge from the complexity of in vivo deployment environments before bugs and failures affect customers, users, or the general public. Because serious issues like concept drift, algorithmic discrimination, shortcut learning, and underspecification are notoriously difficult to identify using standard ML development processes, drinking our own champagne provides a limited and controlled, but also realistic, test bed for ML systems. Of course, when organizations employ demographically and professionally diverse teams and include domain experts in the field where the ML system will be deployed, drinking our own champagne is more likely to catch a wide variety of problems. Drinking our own champagne also brings the classical Golden Rule into AI. If we're not comfortable using a system on ourselves or in our own organization, then we probably shouldn't deploy that system.

One important aspect to consider about deployment environments is the impact of our ML systems on ecosystems and the planet—for example:

- The carbon footprint of ML models
- The possibility that an ML system could damage the environment by causing an AI incident

If we're worried about the environmental impacts of our model, we should loop in ML governance with broader environmental, social, and governance efforts at our organization.

Moving Fast and Breaking Things

The mantra "move fast and break things" is almost a religious belief for many "rock-star" engineers and data scientists. Sadly, these top practitioners also seem to forget that when they go fast and break things, things get broken. As ML systems make more high-impact decisions that implicate autonomous vehicles, credit, employment, university grades and attendance, medical diagnoses and resource allocation, mortgages, pretrial bail, parole, and more, breaking things means more than buggy apps. It can mean that a small group of data scientists and engineers causes real harm at scale to many people. Participating in the design and implementation of high-impact ML systems requires a mindset change to prevent egregious performance and safety problems. Practitioners must change from prioritizing the number of software features they can push, or the test data accuracy of an ML model, to recognizing the implications and downstream risks of their work.

Organizational Processes for Machine Learning Risk Management

Organizational processes play a key role in ensuring that ML systems are safe and performant. Like the cultural competencies discussed in the previous section, organizational processes are a key nontechnical determinant of reliability in ML systems. This section on processes starts out by urging practitioners to consider, document, and attempt to mitigate any known or foreseeable failure modes for their ML systems. We then discuss more about MRM. While "Cultural Competencies for Machine Learning Risk Management" on page 13 focused on the people and mindsets necessary to make MRM a success, this section will outline the different processes MRM uses to mitigate risks in advanced predictive modeling and ML systems. While MRM is a worthy process standard to which we can all aspire, there are additional important process controls that are not typically part of MRM. We'll look beyond traditional MRM in this section and highlight crucial risk control processes like pair or double programming and security permission requirements for code deployment.

This section will close with a discussion of AI incident response. No matter how hard we work to minimize harms while designing and implementing an ML system, we still have to prepare for failures and attacks.

Forecasting Failure Modes

ML safety and ethics experts roughly agree on the importance of thinking through, documenting, and attempting to mitigate foreseeable failure modes for ML systems. Unfortunately, they also mostly agree that this is a nontrivial task. Happily, new resources and scholarship on this topic have emerged in recent years that can help ML system designers forecast incidents in more systematic ways. If holistic categories of potential failures can be identified, it makes hardening ML systems for better real-world performance and safety a more proactive and efficient task. In this subsection, we'll discuss one such strategy, along with a few additional processes for brainstorming future incidents in ML systems.

Known past failures

As discussed in "Preventing Repeated Real World AI Failures by Cataloging Incidents: The AI Incident Database" (*https://oreil.ly/BfMJC*), one the most efficient ways to mitigate potential AI incidents in our ML systems is to compare our system design to past failed designs. Much like transportation professionals investigating and cataloging incidents, then using the findings to prevent related incidents and test new technologies, several ML researchers, commentators, and trade organizations have begun to collect and analyze AI incidents in hopes of preventing repeated and related failures. Likely the most high-profile and mature AI incident repository is the AI Incident Database (*https://oreil.ly/H8nmd*). This searchable and interactive resource allows registered users to search a visual database with keywords and locate different types of information about publicly recorded incidents.

Consult this resource while developing ML systems. If a system similar to the one we're currently designing, implementing, or deploying has caused an incident in the past, this is one of strongest indicators that our new system could cause an incident. If we see something that looks familiar in the database, we should stop and think about what we're doing a lot more carefully.

Failures of imagination

Imagining the future with context and detail is never easy. And it's often the context in which ML systems operate, accompanied by unforeseen or unknowable details, that lead to AI incidents. In a recent workshop paper, the authors of "Overcoming Failures of Imagination in AI Infused System Development and Deployment" (*https://oreil.ly/veB5T*) put forward some structured approaches to hypothesize about those hard-to-imagine future risks. In addition to deliberating on the *who* (e.g., investors, customers, vulnerable nonusers), *what* (e.g., well-being, opportunities, dignity), *when* (e.g., immediately, frequently, over long periods of time), and *how* (e.g., taking an action, altering beliefs) of AI incidents, they also urge system designers to consider the following:

- Assumptions that the impact of the system will be only beneficial (and to admit when uncertainty in system impacts exists)

- The problem domain and applied use cases of the system, as opposed to just the math and technology

- Any unexpected or surprising results, user interactions, and responses to the system

Causing AI incidents is embarrassing, if not costly or illegal, for organizations. AI incidents can also hurt consumers and the general public. Yet, with some foresight, many of the currently known AI incidents could have been mitigated, if not wholly avoided. It's also possible that in performing the due diligence of researching and conceptualizing ML failures, we find that our design or system must be completely reworked. If this is the case, take comfort that a delay in system implementation or deployment is likely less costly than the harms our organization or the public could experience if the flawed system was released.

Model Risk Management Processes

The process aspects of MRM mandate thorough documentation of modeling systems, human review of systems, and ongoing monitoring of systems. These processes represent the bulk of the governance burden for the Federal Reserve's SR 11-7 MRM guidance, which is overseen by the Federal Reserve and the Office of the Comptroller of the Currency for predictive models deployed in material consumer finance applications. While only large organizations will be able to fully embrace all that MRM has to offer, any serious ML practitioner can learn something from the discipline. The following section breaks MRM processes down into smaller components so that readers can start thinking through using aspects of MRM in their organization.

Risk tiering

As outlined in the opening of this chapter, the product of the probability of a harm occurring and the likely loss resulting from that harm is an accepted way to rate the risk of a given ML system deployment. The product of risk and loss has a more formal name in the context of MRM, *materiality*. Materiality is a powerful concept that enables organizations to assign realistic risk levels to ML systems. More importantly, this risk-tiering allows for the efficient allocation of limited development, validation, and audit resources. Of course, the highest materiality applications should receive the greatest human attention and review, while the lowest materiality applications could potentially be handled by automatic machine learning (AutoML) systems and undergo minimal validation. Because risk mitigation for ML systems is an ongoing, expensive task, proper resource allocation between high-, medium-, and low-risk systems is a must for effective governance.

Model documentation

MRM standards also require that systems be thoroughly documented. First, documentation should enable accountability for system stakeholders, ongoing system maintenance, and a degree of incident response. Second, documentation must be standardized across systems for the most efficient audit and review processes. Documentation is where the rubber hits the road for compliance. Documentation templates, illustrated at a very high level by the following section list, are documents that data scientists and engineers fill in as they move through a standardized workflow or in the later stages of model development. Documentation templates should include all the steps that a responsible practitioner should conduct to build a sound model. If parts of the document aren't filled out, that points to sloppiness in the training process. Since most documentation templates and frameworks also call for adding one's name and contact information to the finished model document, there should be no mystery about who is not pulling their weight. For reference, the following section list is a rough combination of typical sections in MRM documentation and the sections recommended by the Annexes to the EU Artificial Intelligence Act (*https://oreil.ly/p_Cqt*):

- Basic Information
  - — Names of Developers and Stakeholders
  - — Current Date and Revision Table
  - — Summary of Model System
  - — Business or Value Justification
  - — Intended Uses and Users
  - — Potential Harms and Ethical Considerations
- Development Data Information
  - — Source for Development Data
  - — Data Dictionary
  - — Privacy Impact Assessment
  - — Assumptions and Limitations
  - — Software Implementation for Data Preprocessing
- Model Information
  - — Description of Training Algorithm with Peer-Reviewed References

- — Specification of Model
- — Performance Quality
- — Assumptions and Limitations
- — Software Implementation for Training Algorithm
- Testing Information
  - — Quality Testing and Remediation
  - — Discrimination Testing and Remediation
  - — Security Testing and Remediation
  - — Assumptions and Limitations
  - — Software Implementation for Testing
- Deployment Information
  - — Monitoring Plans and Mechanisms
  - — Up- and Downstream Dependencies
  - — Appeal and Override Plans and Mechanisms
  - — Audit Plans and Mechanisms
  - — Change Management Plans
  - — Incident Response Plans
- References (if we're doing science, then we're building on the shoulders of giants and we'll have several peer-reviewed references in a formatted bibliography!)

Of course, these documents can be hundreds of pages long, especially for high-materiality systems. The proposed datasheet (*https://oreil.ly/mjKjy*) and model card (*https://oreil.ly/DmMp4*) standards may also be helpful for smaller or younger organizations to meet these goals. If readers are feeling like lengthy model documentation sounds impossible for their organization today, then maybe these two simpler frameworks might work instead.

Model monitoring

A primary tenant of ML safety is that ML system performance in the real world is hard to predict and, accordingly, performance must be monitored. Hence, deployed-system performance should be monitored frequently and until a system is decommissioned. Systems can be monitored for any number of problematic conditions, the most common being input drift. While ML system training data encodes information about a system's operating environment in a static snapshot, the world is anything but static. Competitors can enter markets, new regulations can be promulgated, consumer tastes can change, and pandemics or other disasters can happen. Any of these can change the live data that's entering our ML system away from the characteristics of its training data, resulting in decreased, or even dangerous, system performance. To avoid such unpleasant surprises, the best ML systems are monitored both for drifting input and output distributions and for decaying quality, often known as *model decay*. While performance quality is the most common quantity to monitor, ML systems can also be monitored for anomalous inputs or predictions, specific attacks and hacks, and for drifting fairness characteristics.

Model inventories

Any organization that is deploying ML should be able to answer straightforward questions like:

- How many ML systems are currently deployed?
- How many customers or users do these systems affect?
- Who are the accountable stakeholders for each system?

MRM achieves this goal through the use of model inventories. A model inventory is a curated and up-to-date database of all an organization's ML systems. Model inventories can serve as a repository for crucial information for documentation, but should also link to monitoring plans and results, auditing plans and results, important past and upcoming system maintenance and changes, and plans for incident response.

System validation and process auditing

Under traditional MRM practices, an ML system undergoes two primary reviews before its release. The first review is a technical validation of the system, where skilled validators, not uncommonly PhD-level data scientists, attempt to poke holes in system design and implementation, and work with system developers to fix any discovered problems. The second review investigates processes. Audit and compliance personnel carefully analyze the system design, development, and deployment, along with documentation and future plans, to ensure all regulatory and internal process requirements are met. Moreover, because ML systems change and drift over time, review must take place whenever a system undergoes a major update or at an agreed upon future cadence.

Readers may be thinking (again) that their organization doesn't have the resources for such extensive reviews. Of course that is a reality for many small or younger organizations. The keys for validation and auditing, that should work at nearly any organization, are having technicians who did not develop the system test it, having a function to review nontechnical internal and external obligations, and having sign-off oversight for important ML system deployments.

Change management

Like all complex software applications, ML systems tend to have a large number of different components. From backend ML code, to application programming interfaces (APIs), to graphical user interfaces (GUIs), changes in any component of the system can cause side effects in other components. Add in issues like data drift, emergent data privacy and anti-discrimination regulations, and complex dependencies on third-party software, and change management in ML systems becomes a serious concern. If we're in the planning or design phase of a mission-critical ML system, we'll likely need to make change management a first-class process control. Without explicit planning and resources for change management, process or technical mistakes that arise through the evolution of the system, like using data without consent or API mismatches, are very difficult to prevent. Furthermore, without change management, such problems might not even be detected until they cause an incident.

We'll circle back to MRM throughout the book. It's one the most battle-tested frameworks for governance and risk management of ML systems. Of course, MRM is not the only place to draw inspiration for improved ML safety and performance processes, and the next subsection will draw out lessons from other practice areas.

 Reading the 21-page SR 11-7 model risk management guidance (*https://oreil.ly/0By87*) is a quick way to up-skill yourself in ML risk management. When reading it, pay special attention to the focus on cultural and organizational structures. Managing technology risks is often more about people than anything else.

Beyond Model Risk Management

There are many ML risk management lessons to be learned from financial audit, data privacy, and software development best practices and from IT security. This subsection will shine a light on ideas that exist outside the purview of traditional MRM: model audits, impact assessments, appeals, overrides, opt outs, pair or double programming, least privilege, bug bounties, and incident response, all from an ML safety and performance perspective.

Model audits and assessments

Audit is a common term in MRM, but it also has meanings beyond what it is typically known as—the third line of defense in a more traditional MRM scenario. The phrase *model audit* has come to prominence in recent years. A model audit is an official testing and transparency exercise focusing on an ML system that tracks adherence to some policy, regulation, or law. Model audits tend to be conducted by independent third parties with limited interaction between auditor and auditee organizations. For a good breakdown of model audits, check out the recent paper "Algorithmic Bias and Risk Assessments: Lessons from Practice" (*https://oreil.ly/eHxBb*). The paper "Closing the AI Accountability Gap: Defining an End-to-End Framework for Internal Algorithmic Auditing" (*https://oreil.ly/vO9cH*) puts forward a solid framework for audits and assessments, even including worked documentation examples. The related term, *model assessment*, seems to mean a more informal and cooperative testing and transparency exercise that may be undertaken by external or internal groups.

ML audits and assessments may focus on bias issues or other serious risks including safety, data privacy harms, and security vulnerabilities. Whatever their focus, audits and auditors have be fair and transparent. Those conducting audits should be held to clear ethical or professional standards, which barely exist as of 2023. Without these kinds of accountability mechanisms or binding guidelines, audits can be an ineffective risk management practice, and worse, tech-washing exercises that certify harmful ML systems. Despite flaws, audits are an en vogue favorite risk control tactic of policy-makers and researchers, and are being written into laws—for example, the aforementioned New York City Local Law 144.

Impact assessments

Impact assessments are a formal documentation approach used in many fields to forecast and record the potential issues a system could cause once implemented. Likely due to their use in data privacy (*https://oreil.ly/1OdKa*), impact assessments are starting to show up in organizational ML policies and proposed laws (*https://oreil.ly/waTek*). Impact assessments are an effective way to think through and document the harms that an ML system could cause, increasing accountability for designers and operators of AI systems. But impact assessments are not enough on their own. Remembering the definition of risk and materiality previously put forward, impact is just one factor in risk. Impacts must be combined with likelihoods to form a risk measure, then risks must be actively mitigated, where the highest-risk applications are accorded the most oversight. Impact assessments are just the beginning of a broader risk management process. Like other risk management processes, they must be performed at a cadence that aligns to the system being assessed. If a system changes quickly, it will need more frequent impact assessments. Another potential issue with impact assessments is caused when they are designed and implemented by the ML teams that are also being assessed. In this case, there will be a temptation to diminish the scope of the assessment and downplay any potential negative impacts. Impact assessments are an important part of broader risk management and governance strategies, but they must be conducted as often as required by a specific system, and likely conducted by independent oversight professionals.

Appeal, override, and opt out

Ways for users or operators to appeal and override inevitable wrong decisions should be built into most ML systems. It's known by many names across disciplines: actionable recourse, intervenability, redress, or adverse action notices. This can be as simple as the "Report inappropriate predictions" function in the Google search bar, or it can be as sophisticated as presenting data and explanations to users and enabling appeal processes for demonstrably wrong data points or decision mechanisms. Another similar approach, known as opt out, is to let users do business with an organization the old-fashioned way without going through any automated processing. Many data privacy laws and major US consumer finance laws address recourse, opt out, or both. Automatically forcing wrong decisions on many users is one of the clearest ethical wrongs in ML. We shouldn't fall into an ethical, legal, and reputational trap that's so clear and so well-known, but many systems do. That's likely because it takes planning and resources for both processes and technology, laid out from the beginning of designing an ML system, to get appeal, override, and opt out right.

Pair and double programming

Because they tend to be complex and stochastic, it's hard to know if any given ML algorithm implementation is correct! This is why some leading ML organizations implement ML algorithms twice as a QA mechanism. Such double implementation is usually achieved by one of two methods: pair programming or double programming. In the pair programming approach, two technical experts code an algorithm without collaborating. Then they join forces and work out any discrepancies between their implementations. In double programming, the same practitioner implements the same algorithm twice, but in very different programming languages, such as Python (object-oriented) and SAS (procedural). They must then reconcile any differences between their two implementations. Either approach tends to catch numerous bugs that would otherwise go unnoticed until the system was deployed. Pair and double programming can also align with the more standard workflow of data scientists prototyping algorithms, while dedicated engineers harden them for deployment. However, for this to work, engineers must be free to challenge and test data science prototypes and should not be relegated to simply recoding prototypes.

Security permissions for model deployment

The concept of *least privilege* (*https://oreil.ly/0qP9-*) from IT security states that no system user should ever have more permissions than they need. Least privilege is a fundamental process control that, likely because ML systems touch so many other IT systems, tends to be thrown out the window for ML build-outs and for so-called "rock star" data scientists. Unfortunately, this is an ML safety and performance anti-pattern. Outside the world of overhyped ML and rock star data science, it's long been understood that engineers cannot adequately test their own code and that others in a product organization—product managers, attorneys, or executives—should make the final call as to when software is released.

For these reasons, the IT permissions necessary to deploy an ML system should be distributed across several teams within IT organizations. During development sprints, data scientists and engineers certainly must retain full control over their development environments. But, as important releases or reviews approach, the IT permissions to push fixes, enhancements, or new features to user-facing products are transferred away from data scientists and engineers to product managers, testers, attorneys, executives, or others. Such process controls provide a gate that prevents unapproved code from being deployed.

Bug bounties

Bug bounties are another concept we can borrow from computer security. Traditionally, a bug bounty is when an organization offers rewards for finding problems in its software, particularly security vulnerabilities. Since ML is mostly just software, we can do bug bounties for ML systems. While we can use bug bounties to find security problems in ML systems, we can also use them to find other types of problems related to reliability, safety, transparency, explainability, interpretability, or privacy. Through bug bounties, we use monetary rewards to incentivize community feedback in a standardized process. As we've highlighted elsewhere in the chapter, incentives are crucial in risk management. Generally, risk management work is tedious and resource consuming. If we want our users to find major problems in our ML systems for us, we need to pay them or reward them in some other meaningful way. Bug bounties are typically public endeavors. If that makes some organizations nervous, internal hackathons in which different teams look for bugs in ML systems may have some of the same positive effects. Of course, the more participants are incentivized to participate, the better the results are likely to be.

AI incident response

According to the vaunted SR 11-7 guidance (*https://oreil.ly/E7G2R*), "even with skilled modeling and robust validation, model risk cannot be eliminated." If risks from ML systems and ML models cannot be eliminated, then such risks will eventually lead to incidents. Incident response is already a mature practice in the field of computer security. Venerable institutions like NIST (*https://oreil.ly/glkOX*) and SANS (*https://oreil.ly/gU-Vo*) have published computer security incident response guidelines for years. Given that ML is a less mature and higher-risk technology than general-purpose enterprise computing, formal AI incident response plans and practices are a must for high-impact or mission-critical AI systems.

Formal AI incident response plans enable organizations to respond more quickly and effectively to inevitable incidents. Incident response also plays into the Hand rule discussed at the beginning of the chapter. With rehearsed incident response plans in place, organizations may be able to identify, contain, and eradicate AI incidents before they spiral into costly or dangerous public spectacles. AI incident response plans are one of the most basic and universal ways to mitigate AI-related risks. Before a system is deployed, incident response plans should be drafted and tested. For young or small organizations that cannot fully implement model risk management, AI incident response is a cost-effective and potent AI risk control to consider. Borrowing from computer incident response, AI incident response can be thought of in six phases:

Phase 1: Preparation

In addition to clearly defining an AI incident for our organization, preparation for AI incidents includes personnel, logistical, and technology plans for when an incident occurs. Budget must be set aside for response, communication strategies must be put in place, and technical safeguards for standardizing and preserving model documentation, out-of-band communications, and shutting down AI systems must be implemented. One of the best ways to prepare and rehearse for AI incidents are tabletop discussion exercises, where key organizational personnel work through a realistic incident. Good starter questions for an AI incident tabletop include the following:

- Who has the organizational budget and authority to respond to an AI incident?

- Can the AI system in question be taken offline? By whom? At what cost? What upstream processes will be affected?

- Which regulators or law enforcement agencies need to be contacted? Who will contact them?

- Which external law firms, insurance agencies, or public relation firms need to be contacted? Who will contact them?

- Who will manage communications? Internally, between responders? Externally, with customers or users?

Phase 2: Identification

Identification is when organizations spot AI failures, attacks, or abuses. Identification also means staying vigilant for AI-related abuses. In practice, this tends to involve more general attack identification approaches, like network intrusion monitoring, and more specialized monitoring for AI system failures, like concept drift or algorithmic discrimination. Often the last step of the identification phase is to notify management, incident responders, and others specified in incident response plans.

Phase 3: Containment

Containment refers to mitigating the incident's immediate harms. Keep in mind that harms are rarely limited to the system where the incident began. Like more general computer incidents, AI incidents can have network effects that spread throughout an organizations' and its customers' technologies. Actual containment strategies will vary depending on whether the incident stemmed from an external adversary, an internal failure, or an off-label use or abuse of an AI system. If necessary, containment is also a good place to start communicating with the public.

Phase 4: Eradication

Eradication involves remediating any affected systems. For example, sealing off any attacked systems from vectors of in- or ex-filtration, or shutting down a discriminatory AI system and temporarily replacing it with a trusted rule-based system. After eradication, there should be no new harms caused by the incident.

Phase 5: Recovery

Recovery means ensuring all affected systems are back to normal and that controls are in place to prevent similar incidents in the future. Recovery often means retraining or reimplementing AI systems, and testing that they are performing at documented preincident levels. Recovery can also require careful analysis of technical or security protocols for personnel, especially in the case of an accidental failure or insider attack.

Phase 6: Lessons learned

Lessons learned refers to corrections or improvements of AI incident response plans based on the successes and challenges encountered while responding to the current incident. Response plan improvements can be process- or technology-oriented.

When reading the following case, think about the phases of incident response, and whether an AI incident response plan would have been an effective risk control for Zillow.

Case Study: The Rise and Fall of Zillow's iBuying

In 2018, the real estate tech company Zillow entered the business of buying homes and flipping them for a profit, known as *iBuying*. The company believed that its proprietary, ML-powered *Zestimate* algorithm could do more than draw eyeballs to its extremely popular web products. As reported by Bloomberg, Zillow employed domain experts to validate the numbers generated by their algorithms when they first started to buy homes. First, local real estate agents would price the property. The numbers were combined with the Zestimate, and a final team of experts vetted each offer before it was made.

According to Bloomberg (*https://oreil.ly/LQQg3*), Zillow soon phased out these teams of domain experts in order to "get offers out faster," preferring the speed and scale of a more purely algorithmic approach. When the Zestimate did not adapt to a rapidly inflating real estate market in early 2021, Zillow reportedly intervened to increase the attractiveness of its offers. As a result of these changes, the company began acquiring properties at a rate of nearly 10,000 homes per quarter. More flips means more staff and more renovation contractors, but as Bloomberg puts it, "Zillow's humans couldn't keep up." Despite increasing staffing levels by 45% and bringing on "armies" of contractors, the iBuying system was not achieving profitability. The combination of pandemic staffing and supply challenges, the overheated housing market, and complexities around handling large numbers of mortgages were just too much for the iBuying project to manage.

In October of 2021, Zillow announced that it would stop making offers through the end of the year. As a result of Zillow's appetite for rapid growth, as well as labor and supply shortages, the company had a huge inventory of homes to clear. To solve its inventory problem, Zillow was posting most homes for resale at a loss. Finally, on November 2, Zillow announced that it was writing down its inventory by over $500 million. Zillow's foray into the automated house-flipping business was over.

Fallout

In addition to the huge monetary loss of its failed venture, Zillow announced that it would lay off about 2,000 employees—a full quarter of the company. In June of 2021, Zillow was trading at around $120 per share. At the time of this writing, nearly one year later, shares are approximately $40, erasing over $30 billion in stock value. (Of course, the entire price drop can't be attributed to the iBuying incident, but it certainly factored into the loss.) The downfall of Zillow's iBuying is rooted in many interwoven causes, and cannot be decoupled from the pandemic that struck in 2020 and upended the housing market. In the next section, we'll examine how to apply what we've learned in this chapter about governance and risk management to Zillow's misadventures.

Lessons Learned

What does this chapter teach us about the Zillow iBuying saga? Based on the public reporting, it appears Zillow's decision to sideline human review of high-materiality algorithms was probably a factor in the overall incident. We also question whether Zillow had adequately thought through the financial risk it was taking on, whether appropriate governance structures were in place, and whether the iBuying losses might have been handled better as an AI incident. We don't know the answers to many of these questions with respect to Zillow, so instead we'll focus on insights readers can apply at their own organizations:

Lesson 1: Validate with domain experts.

In this chapter, we stressed the importance of diverse and experienced teams as a core organizational competency for responsible ML development. Without a doubt, Zillow has internal and external access to world-class expertise in real estate markets. However, in the interest of speed and automation—sometimes referred to as "moving fast and breaking things" or "product velocity"—Zillow phased the experts out of the process of acquiring homes, choosing instead to rely on its Zestimate algorithm. According to follow-up reporting by Bloomberg (*https://oreil.ly/boQye*) in May 2022, "Zillow told its pricing experts to stop questioning the algorithms, according to people familiar with the process." This choice may have proven fatal for the venture, especially in a rapidly changing, pandemic-driven real estate market. No matter the hype, AI is not smarter than humans yet. If we're making high-risk decisions with ML, keep humans in the loop.

Lesson 2: Forecast failure modes.

The coronavirus pandemic of 2020 created a paradigm shift in many domains and markets. ML models, which usually assume that the future will resemble the past, likely suffered across the board in many verticals. We shouldn't expect a company like Zillow to see a pandemic on the horizon. But as we've discussed, rigorously interrogating the failure modes of our ML system constitutes a crucial competency for ML in high-risk settings. We do not know the details of Zillow's model governance frameworks, but the downfall of Zillow's iBuying stresses the importance of effective challenge and asking hard questions, like "What happens if the cost of performing renovations doubles over the next two years?" and "What will be the business cost of overpaying for homes by two percent over the course of six months?" For such a high-risk system, probable failure modes should be enumerated and documented, likely with board of directors oversight, and the actual financial risk should have been made clear to all senior decision-makers. At our organization, we need to know the cost of being wrong with ML and that senior leadership is willing to tolerate those costs. Maybe senior leaders at Zillow were accurately informed of iBuying's financial risks, maybe they weren't. What we know now is that Zillow took a huge risk, and it did not pay off.

Lesson 3: Governance counts.

Zillow's CEO is famous for risk-taking, and has a proven track record of winning big bets. But, we simply can't win every bet we make. This is why we manage and govern risks when conducting automated decision making, especially in high-risk scenarios. SR 11-7 states, "the rigor and sophistication of validation should be commensurate with the bank's overall use of models." Zillow is not a bank, but Bloomberg's May 2022 postmortem puts it this way: Zillow was "attempting to pivot from selling online advertising to operating what amounted to a hedge fund and a sprawling construction business." Zillow drastically increased the materiality of its algorithms, but appears not to have drastically increased governance over those algorithms. As noted, most of the public reporting points to Zillow decreasing human oversight of its algorithms during its iBuying program, not increasing oversight. A separate risk function, empowered with the organizational stature to stop models from moving into production, and with the appropriate budget and staff levels, that reports directly to the board of directors and operates independently from business and technology functions headed by the CEO and CTO, is common in major consumer finance organization. This organizational structure, when it works as intended, allows for more objective and risk-based decisions about ML model performance, and avoids the conflicts of interest and confirmation bias that tend to occur when business and technology leaders evaluate their own systems for risk. We don't know if Zillow had an independent model governance function—it is quite rare these days outside of consumer finance. But we do know that no risk or oversight function was able to stop the iBuying program before losses became staggering. While it's a tough battle to fight as a single technician, helping our organization apply independent audits to its ML systems is a workable risk mitigation practice.

Lesson 4: AI incidents occur at scale.

Zillow's iBuying hijinks aren't funny. Money was lost. Careers were lost—thousands of employees were laid off or resigned. This looks like a $30 billion AI incident. From the incident response lens, we need to be prepared for systems to fail, we need to be monitoring for systems to fail, and we need to have documented and rehearsed plans in place for containment, eradication, and recovery. From public reporting, it does appear that Zillow was aware of its iBuying problems, but its culture was more focused on winning big than preparing for failure. Given the size of the financial loss, Zillow's containment efforts could have been more effective. Zillow was able to eradicate its most acute problems with the declaration of the roughly half-billion dollar write-off in November of 2021. As for recovery, Zillow's leadership has plans for a new real estate super app, but given the stock price at the time of this writing, recovery is a long way off and investors are weary. Complex systems drift toward failure. Perhaps a more disciplined incident-handling approach could save our organization when it bets big with ML.

The final and most important lesson we can take away from the Zillow Offers saga is at the heart of this book. Emerging technologies always come with risks. Early automobiles were dangerous. Planes used to crash into mountainsides much more frequently. ML systems can perpetuate discriminatory practices, pose security and privacy risks, and behave unexpectedly. A fundamental difference between ML and other emerging technologies is that these systems can make decisions quickly and at huge scales. When Zillow leaned into its Zestimate algorithm, it could scale up its purchasing to hundreds of homes per day. In this case, the result was a write-down of half of a billion dollars, even larger stock losses, and the loss of thousands of jobs. This phenomenon of rapid failure at scale can be even more directly devastating when the target of interest is access to capital, social welfare programs, or the decision of who gets a new kidney.

Resources

Further Reading

- ISO standards for AI (*https://oreil.ly/N3WTp*)
- NIST AI Risk Management Framework (*https://oreil.ly/mQ8aW*)
- SR 11-7 model risk management guidance (*https://oreil.ly/AANIg*)

CHAPTER 2
Interpretable and Explainable Machine Learning

Scientists have been fitting models to data to learn more about observed patterns for centuries. Explainable machine learning models and post hoc explanation of ML models present an incremental, but important, advance in this long-standing practice. Because ML models learn about nonlinear, faint, and interacting signals more easily than traditional linear models, humans using explainable ML models and post hoc explanation techniques can now also learn about nonlinear, faint, and interacting signals in their data with more ease.

In this chapter, we'll dig into important ideas for interpretation and explanation before tackling major explainable modeling and post hoc explanation techniques. We'll cover the major pitfalls of post hoc explanation too—many of which can be overcome by using explainable models and post hoc explanation *together*. Next we'll discuss applications of explainable models and post hoc explanation, like model documentation and actionable recourse for wrong decisions, that increase accountability for AI systems. The chapter will close with a case discussion of the so called "A-level scandal" in the United Kingdom (UK), where an explainable, highly documented model made unaccountable decisions, resulting in a nationwide AI incident. The discussion of explainable models and post hoc explanation continues in Chapters 6 and 7, where we explore two in-depth code examples related to these topics.

NIST AI RMF Crosswalk

Chapter section	NIST AI RMF subcategories
"Important Ideas for Interpretability and Explainability" on page 34	GOVERN 1.1, GOVERN 1.2, GOVERN 1.4, GOVERN 1.5, GOVERN 3.2, GOVERN 4.1, GOVERN 5.1, GOVERN 6.1, MAP 2.3, MAP 3.1, MAP 4, MEASURE 1.1, MEASURE 2.1, MEASURE 2.8, MEASURE 2.9, MEASURE 3.3
"Explainable Models" on page 39	GOVERN 1.1, GOVERN 1.2, GOVERN 6.1, MAP 2.3, MAP 3.1, MEASURE 2.8, MEASURE 2.9, MANAGE 1.2, MANAGE 1.3
"Post Hoc Explanation" on page 50	GOVERN 1.1, GOVERN 1.2, GOVERN 1.5, GOVERN 5.1, GOVERN 6.1, MAP 2.3, MAP 3.1, MEASURE 2.8, MEASURE 2.9, MANAGE 1.2, MANAGE 1.3

- Applicable AI trustworthiness characteristics include: Valid and Reliable, Secure and Resilient, Transparent and Accountable, Explainable and Interpretable
- See also:
  - "Four Principles of Explainable Artificial Intelligence" (*https://oreil.ly/Ilf_J*)
  - "Psychological Foundations of Explainability and Interpretability in Artificial Intelligence" (*https://oreil.ly/1Ah96*)
  - Full crosswalk table (not an official resource) (*https://oreil.ly/61TXd*)

Important Ideas for Interpretability and Explainability

Before jumping into the techniques for training explainable models and generating post hoc explanations, we need to discuss the big ideas behind the math and code. We'll start by affirming that transparency does not equate to trust. We can trust things that we don't understand, and understand things we don't trust. Stated even more simply: transparency enables understanding, and understanding is different from trust. In fact, greater understanding of poorly built ML systems may actually decrease trust.

Trustworthiness in AI is defined by the National Institute of Standards and Technology (NIST) using various characteristics: validity, reliability, safety, managed bias, security, resiliency, transparency, accountability, explainability, interpretability, and enhanced privacy. Transparency makes it easier to achieve other desirable trustworthiness characteristics and makes debugging easier. However, human operators must take these additional governance steps. Trustworthiness is often achieved in practice through testing, monitoring, and appeal processes (see Chapters 1 and 3). Increased transparency enabled by explainable ML models and post hoc explanation should facilitate the kinds of diagnostics and debugging that help to make traditional linear models trustworthy. It also means that regulated applications that have relied on linear models for decades due to per-consumer explanation and general documentation requirements are now likely ripe for disruption with accurate and transparent ML models.

 Being interpretable, explainable, or otherwise transparent does not make a model good or trustworthy. Being interpretable, explainable, or otherwise transparent enables humans to make a highly informed decision as to whether a model is good or trustworthy.

Redress for subjects of wrong ML-based decisions via prescribed appeal and override processes is perhaps the most important trust-enhancing use of explainable models and post hoc explanation. The ability to logically appeal automated decisions is sometimes called *actionable recourse*. It's very hard for consumers—or job applicants, patients, prisoners, or students—to appeal automated and unexplainable decisions. Explainable ML models and post hoc explanation techniques should allow for ML-based automated decisions to be understood by decision subjects, which is the first step in a logical appeal process. Once users can demonstrate that either their input data or the logic of their decision is wrong, operators of ML systems should be able to override the initial errant decision.

 Mechanisms that enable appeal and override of automated decisions should always be deployed with high-risk ML systems.

It's also important to differentiate between interpretability and explanation. In the groundbreaking study "Psychological Foundations of Explainability and Interpretability in Artificial Intelligence" (*https://oreil.ly/yz6GF*), researchers at NIST were able to differentiate between interpretability and explainability using widely accepted notions of human cognition. According to NIST researchers, the similar, but not identical, concepts of interpretation and explanation are defined as follows:

Interpretation
A high-level, meaningful mental representation that contextualizes a stimulus and leverages human background knowledge. An interpretable model should provide users with a description of what a data point or model output means *in context*.

Explanation
A low-level, detailed mental representation that seeks to describe a complex process. An ML explanation is a description of how a particular model mechanism or output *came to be*.

Interpretability is a much higher bar to reach than explainability. Achieving interpretability means putting an ML mechanism or result in context, and this is rarely achieved through models or post hoc explanations. Interpretability is usually achieved through plainly written explanations, compelling visualizations, or interactive graphical user interfaces. Interpretability usually requires working with experts both within the applicable domain and in user interaction and experience, as well as other interdisciplinary professionals.

Let's get more granular now, and touch on some of what makes an ML model interpretable or explainable. It's very difficult for models achieve transparency if their input data is a mess. Let's start our discussion there. When considering input data and transparency, think about the following:

Explainable feature engineering
> We should avoid overly complex feature engineering if our goal is transparency. While deep features from autoencoders, principal components, or high-degree interactions might make our model perform better in test data, explaining such features is going to be difficult even if we feed them into an otherwise explainable model.

Meaningful features
> Using a feature as an input to some model function assumes it is related to the function output, i.e., the model's predictions. Using nonsensical or loosely related features because they improve test data performance violates a fundamental assumption of the way explaining models works. For example, if along with other features we use eye color to predict credit default, the model will likely train to some convergence criterion and we can calculate Shapley additive explanation (SHAP) values for eye color. But eye color has no real validity in this context and is not be causally related to credit default. While eye color may serve as a proxy for underlying systemic biases, claiming that eye color explains credit default is invalid. Apply commonsense—or even better, causal—discovery approaches to increase the validity of models and associated explanations.

Monotonic features
> Monotonicity helps with explainability. When possible, use features that have a monotonic relationship with the target variable. If necessary, apply a feature engineering technique such as binning to induce monotonicity.

If we can rely on our data being usable for explainability and interpretability purposes, then we can use concepts like additive independence of inputs, constraints, linearity and smoothness, prototypes, sparsity, and summarization to ensure our model is as transparent as possible:

Additivity of inputs

Keeping inputs in an ML model separate, or limiting their interaction to a small group, is crucial for transparency. Traditional ML models are (in)famous for combining and recombining input features into an undecipherable tangle of high-degree interactions. In stark contrast, traditional linear models treat inputs in an independent and additive fashion. The output decision from a linear model is typically the simple linear combination of learned model parameters and input feature values. Of course, performance quality is often noticeably worse for traditional linear models as compared to traditional opaque ML models.

Enter the generalized additive model (GAM). GAMs keep input features independent, enabling transparency, but also allow for arbitrarily complex modeling of each feature's behavior, dramatically increasing performance quality. We'll also be discussing GAM's close descendants, GA2Ms and explainable boosting machines (EBMs), in the next section. They all work by keeping inputs independent and enabling visualization of the sometimes complex manner in which they treat those individual inputs. In the end, they retain high transparency because users don't have to disentangle inputs and how they affect one another, and the output decision is still a linear combination of learned model parameters and some function applied to data input values.

Constraints

Traditional unexplainable ML models are revered for their flexibility. They can model almost any signal-generating function in training data. Yet, when it comes to transparency, modeling every nook and cranny of some observed response function usually isn't a great idea. Due to overfitting, it turns out it's also not a great idea for performance on unseen data either. Sometimes what we observe in training data is just noise, or even good old-fashioned wrong. So, instead of overfitting to bad data, it's often a good idea to apply constraints that both increase transparency and help with performance on unseen data by forcing models to obey causal concepts instead of noise.

Any number of constraints can be applied when training ML models, but some of the most helpful and widely available are sparsity, monotonicity, and interaction constraints. Sparsity constraints, often implemented by L1 regularization (which usually decreases the number of parameters or rules in a model), increases emphasis on a more manageable number of input parameters and internal learning mechanisms. Positive monotonic constraints mean that as a model's input increases, its output must never decrease. Negative monotonic constraints ensure that as a model's input increases, its output can never increase. Interaction constraints keep internal mechanisms of ML models from combining and recombining too many different features. These constraints can be used to encourage models to learn interpretable and explainable causal phenomena, as opposed to focusing on nonrobust inputs, arbitrary nonlinearities, and high-degree interactions that may be drivers of errors and bias in model outcomes.

Linearity and smoothness

Linear functions are monotonic by default and can be described by single numeric coefficients. Smooth functions are differentiable, meaning they can be summarized at any location with a derivative function or value. Basically, linear and smooth functions are better behaved and typically easier to summarize. In contrast, unconstrained and arbitrary ML functions can bounce around or bend themselves in knots in ways that defy human understanding, making the inherent summarization that needs to occur for explanation nearly impossible.

Prototypes

Prototypes refer to well-understood data points (rows) or archetypal features (columns) that can be used to explain model outputs for some other previously unseen data. Prototypes appear in many places in ML, and have been used to explain and interpret model decisions for decades. Think of explaining a *k*-nearest neighbors prediction using the nearest neighbors or profiling clusters based on centroid locations—those are prototypes. Prototypes also end up being important for counterfactual explanations. Prototypes have even entered into the typically complex and opaque world of computer vision with this-looks-like-that deep learning (*https://oreil.ly/zO1kx*).

Sparsity

ML models, for better or worse, can now be trained with trillions of parameters (*https://oreil.ly/mDwV5*). Yet, it's debatable whether their human operators can reason based on more than a few dozen of those parameters. The volume of information in a contemporary ML model will have to be summarized to be transparent. Generally, the fewer coefficients or rules in an ML model, the more sparse and explainable it is.

Summarization

Summarization can take many forms, including variable importance measures, surrogate models, and other post hoc ML approaches. Visualization is perhaps the most common vehicle for communicating summarized information about ML models, and approximation taken to compress information is the Achilles' heel (*https://oreil.ly/Dzfit*) for summarization. Additive, linear, smooth, and sparse models are generally easier to summarize, and post hoc explanation processes have a better chance of working well in these cases.

Achieving transparency with ML takes some extra elbow grease as compared to popular and commoditized unexplainable approaches. Fear not. The recent paper "Designing Inherently Interpretable Machine Learning Models" (*https://oreil.ly/Zv6YO*) and software packages like InterpretML (*https://oreil.ly/rML2n*), H2O (*https://oreil.ly/ysEHE*), and PiML (*https://oreil.ly/Y2EFl*) provide a great framework for training and explaining transparent models, and the remaining sections of the chapter highlight the most effective technical approaches, and common gotchas, for us to consider next time we start to design an AI system.

Explainable Models

For decades, many ML researchers and practitioners alike labored under a seemingly logical assumption that more complex models were more accurate. However, as pointed out by luminary professor Cynthia Rudin, in her impactful "Stop Explaining Black Box Machine Learning Models for High Stakes Decisions and Use Interpretable Models Instead" (*https://oreil.ly/i4syT*), "It is a myth that there is necessarily a trade-off between accuracy and interpretability." We'll dig into the tension around explainable models versus post hoc explanation later in the chapter. For now, let's concentrate on the powerful idea of accurate and explainable models. They offer the potential for highly accurate decision making coupled with improved human learning from machine learning, actionable recourse processes and regulatory compliance, improved security, and better ability to address various issues, including inaccuracy and bias. These appealing characteristics make explainable ML models a general win-win for practitioners and consumers.

We're going to go over some of the most popular types of explainable ML models next. We'll start with the large class of additive models, including penalized regression, GAMs, GA2Ms and EBMs. We'll also be covering decision trees, constrained tree ensembles, and a litany of other options before moving on to post hoc explanation techniques.

Additive Models

Perhaps the most widely used types of explainable ML models are those based on traditional linear models: penalized regression models, GAMs, and GA2Ms (or EBMs). These techniques use contemporary methods to augment traditional modeling approaches, often yielding noticeable improvements in performance. But they also keep interpretability high by treating input features in a separate and additive manner, or by allowing only a small number of interaction terms. They also rely on straightforward visualization techniques to enhance interpretability.

Penalized regression

We'll start our discussion of explainable models with penalized regression. Penalized regression updates the typical 19th century approach to regression for the 21st century. These types of models usually produce linear, monotonic response functions with globally explainable results, like those of traditional linear models, but often with a boost in predictive performance. Penalized regression models eschew the assumption-laden Normal Equation (*https://oreil.ly/uXdeH*) approaches to finding model parameters, and instead use more sophisticated constrained and iterative optimization procedures that allow for handling of correlation, feature selection, and treatment of outliers, all while using validation data to pick a better model automatically.

In Figure 2-1, we can see how a penalized regression model learns optimal coefficients for six input features over more than 80 training iterations. We can see at the beginning of the optimization procedure that all parameter values start very small, and grow as the procedure begins to converge. This happens because it's typical to start the training procedure with large penalties on input features. These penalties are typically decreased as training proceeds to allow a small number of inputs to enter the model, to keep model parameters artificially small, or both. (Readers may also hear penalized regression coefficients referred to as "shrunken" on occasion.) At each iteration, as more features enter the model, or as coefficient values grow or change, the current model is applied to validation data. Training continues to a predefined number of iterations or until performance in validation data ceases to improve.

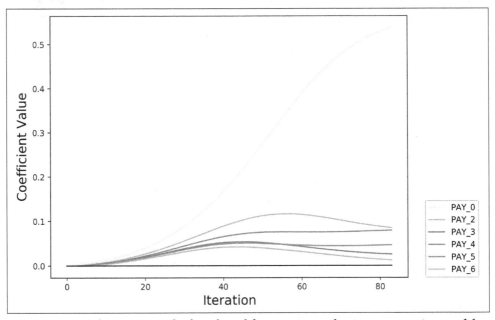

Figure 2-1. Regularization paths for selected features in an elastic net regression model (digital, color version: https://oreil.ly/dR7Ty)

In addition to a validation-based early stopping procedure, penalized regression addresses outliers, feature selection, correlated inputs, and nonlinearity by using, respectively, the iteratively reweighted least squares (IRLS) technique; two types of penalties, on the L1 and L2 parameter norms; and link functions:

IRLS

IRLS is a well-established procedure for minimizing the effect of outliers. It starts like an old-fashioned regression, but after that first iteration, the IRLS procedure checks which rows of input data are leading to large errors. It then reduces the weight of those rows in subsequent iterations of fitting model coefficients. IRLS continues this fitting and down-weighting procedure until model parameters converge to stable values.

L1 norm penalty

Also known as least absolute shrinkage and selection operator (LASSO), L1 penalties keep the sum of the absolute model parameters to a minimum. This penalty has the effect of driving unnecessary regression parameters to zero, and selecting a small, representative subset of features for the regression model, while also avoiding the potential multiple comparison problems that arise in older stepwise feature selection. When used alone, L1 penalties are known to increase performance quality in situations where a large number of potentially correlated input features cause stepwise feature selection to fail.

L2 norm penalty

Also known as ridge or Tikhonov regression, L2 penalties minimize the sum of squared model parameters. L2 norm penalties stabilize model parameters, especially in the presence of correlation. Unlike L1 norm penalties, L2 norm penalties do not select features. Instead, they limit each feature's impact on the overall model by keeping all model parameters smaller than they would be in the traditional solution. Smaller parameters make it harder for any one feature to dominate a model and for correlation to cause strange behavior during model training.

Link functions

Link functions enable linear models to handle common distributions of training data, such as using a logit link function to fit a logistic regression to input data with two discrete outcomes. Other common and useful link functions include the Poisson link function for count data or an inverse link function for gamma-distributed outputs. Matching outcomes to their distribution family and link function, such as a binomial distribution and logit link function for logistic regression, is absolutely necessary for training deployable models. Many ML models and libraries outside of penalized regression packages do not support the necessary link functions and distribution families to address fundamental assumptions in training data.

Contemporary penalized regression techniques usually combine the following:

- Validation-based early stopping for improved generalization
- IRLS to handle outliers
- L1 penalties for feature selection purposes
- L2 penalties for robustness
- Link functions for various target or error distributions

Readers can learn more about penalized regression in *Elements of Statistical Learning* (*https://oreil.ly/FQjuv*) (Springer), but for our purposes, it's more important to know when we might want to try penalized regression. Penalized regression has been applied widely across many research disciplines, but it is a great fit for business data with many features, even datasets with more features than rows, and for datasets with a lot of correlated variables. Penalized regression models also preserve the basic interpretability of traditional linear models, so we think of them when we have many correlated features or need maximum transparency. It's also important to know that penalized regression techniques don't always create confidence intervals, *t*-statistics, or *p*-values for regression parameters. These types of measures are typically only available through bootstrapping, which can require extra computing time. The R packages elasticnet (*https://oreil.ly/aooJV*) and glmnet (*https://oreil.ly/lFcpJ*) are maintained by the inventors of the LASSO and elastic net regression techniques, and the H2O generalized linear model (*https://oreil.ly/Oeywm*) sticks closely to the implementation of the original software, while allowing for much-improved scalability.

An even newer and extremely interesting twist to penalized regression models is the super-sparse linear integer model, or SLIM (*https://oreil.ly/2YPmFX1*). SLIMs also rely on sophisticated optimization routines, with the objective of creating accurate models that only require simple arithmetic to evaluate. SLIMs are meant to train linear models that can be evaluated mentally by humans working in high-risk settings, such as healthcare. If we're ever faced with an application that requires the highest interpretability and the need for field-workers to evaluate results quickly, we think of SLIMs. On the other hand, if we're looking for better predictive performance, to match that of many unexplainable ML techniques, but to keep a high degree of interpretability, think of GAMs—which we'll be covering next.

Generalized additive models

GAMs are a generalization of linear models that allow a coefficient and function to be fit to each model input, instead of just a coefficient for each input. Training models in this manner allows for each input variable to be treated in a separate but nonlinear fashion. Treating each input separately keeps interpretability high.

Allowing for nonlinearity improves performance quality. Traditionally GAMs have relied on splines to fit nonlinear shape functions for each input, and most implementations of GAMs generate convenient plots of the fitted shape functions. Depending on our regulatory or internal documentation requirements, we may be able to use the shape functions directly in predictive models for increased performance. If not, we may be able to eyeball some fitted shape functions and switch them out for a more explainable polynomial, log, trigonometric, or other simple function of the input feature that may also increase prediction quality. An interesting twist to GAMs was introduced recently with neural additive models (NAMs) (*https://oreil.ly/nnCz5*) and GAMI-Nets (*https://oreil.ly/G_wCc*). In these models, an artificial neural network is used to fit the shape functions. We'll continue the theme of estimating shape functions with ML when we discuss explainable boosting machines in the next section. The Rudin Group also recently put forward a variant of GAMs in which monotonic step functions are used as shape functions for maximum interpretability. Check out "Fast Sparse Classification for Generalized Linear and Additive Models" (*https://oreil.ly/tCnld*) to see those in action.

 We'll use the term *shape function* to describe the learned nonlinear relationship that GAM-like models apply to each input and interaction feature. These shape functions may be traditional splines, or they can be fit by machine learning estimators like boosted trees or neural networks.

The semi-official name for the ability to change out parts of a model to better match reality or human intuition is *model editing*. Being editable is another important aspect of many explainable models. Models often learn wrong or biased concepts from wrong or biased training data. Explainable models enable human users to spot bugs, and edit them out. The GAM family of models is particularly amenable to model editing, which is another advantage of these powerful modeling approaches. Readers can learn more about GAMs in *Elements of Statistical Learning* (*https://oreil.ly/5S49T*). To try GAMs, look into the R gam (*https://oreil.ly/aSAJK*) package or the more experimental H2O (*https://oreil.ly/5yoAd*) or pyGAM (*https://oreil.ly/1h-Y7*) implementations.

GA2M and explainable boosting machines

The GA2M and EBM represent straightforward and material improvements to GAMs. Let's address the GA2M first. The "2" in GA2M refers to the consideration of a small group of pairwise interactions as inputs to the model. Choosing to include a small number of interaction terms in the GAM boosts performance without compromising interpretability. Interaction terms can be plotted as contours along with the standard two-dimensional input feature plots that tend to accompany GAMs. Some astute readers may already be familiar with the EBM, an important variant of GA2M. In an EBM, the shape functions for each input feature are trained iteratively using boosting. These response functions can be splines, decision trees, or even boosted ensembles of decision trees themselves. By training the additive model using boosting, we can usually get a more accurate final model than if we use the typical GAM backfitting method.

Because of these advances, GA2Ms and EBMs now rival, or exceed, unexplainable ML models in performance quality on tabular data, while also presenting the obvious advantages of interpretability and model editing. If your next project is on structured data, try out EBMs using the InterpretML (*https://oreil.ly/GMsbK*) package from Microsoft Research. EBMs put the final touches on our discussion of additive models. We'll move on next to decision trees, yet another type of high-quality, high-interpretability model with a track record of success across statistics, data mining, and ML.

Decision Trees

Decision trees are another type of popular predictive model. When used as single trees, and not as ensemble models, they learn highly interpretable flowcharts from training data and tend to exhibit better predictive performance than linear models. When used as ensembles, as with random forests and GBMs, they lose interpretability but tend to be even better predictors. In the following sections, we'll discuss both single tree models and constrained decision tree ensembles that can retain some level of explainability.

Single decision trees

Technically, decision trees are directed graphs in which each interior node corresponds to an input feature. There are graph edges to child nodes for values of the input feature that create the highest target purity, or increased predictive quality, in each child node. Each terminal node or leaf node represents a value of the target feature, given the values of the input features represented by the path from the root to the leaf. These paths can be visualized or explained with simple if-then rules.

In plainer language, decision trees are data-derived flowcharts, just like we see in Figure 2-2. Decision trees are great for training interpretable models on structured data. They are beneficial when the goal is to understand relationships between the input and target variable with Boolean-like "if-then" logic. They are also great at finding interactions in training data. Parent-child relationships, especially near the top of the tree, tend to point toward feature interactions that can be used to better understand drivers of the modeling target, or they can be used as interaction terms to boost predictive accuracy for additive models. Perhaps their main advantage over more straightforward additive models is their ability to train directly on character values, missing data, nonstandardized data, and nonnormalized data. In this age of big (er, bad) data, decision trees enable the construction of models with minimal data preprocessing, which can help eliminate additional sources of human error from ML models.

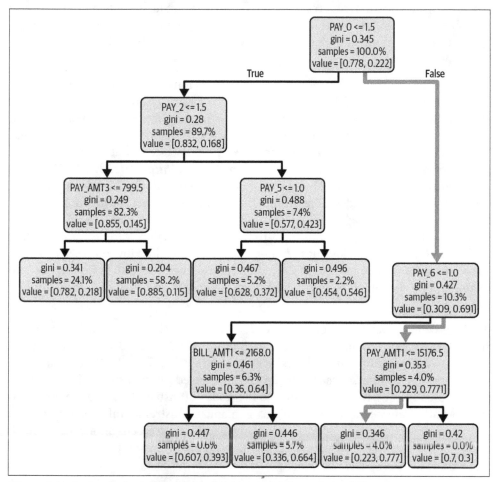

Figure 2-2. A simple decision tree model forming a data-derived flowchart

With all this going for them, why shouldn't we use decision trees? First of all, they're only interpretable when they're shallow. Decision trees with more than, say, five levels of if-then branches become difficult to interpret. They also tend to perform poorly on unstructured data like sound, images, video, and text. Unstructured data has become the domain of deep learning and neural networks. Like many models, decision trees require a high degree of tuning. Decision trees have many hyperparameters, or settings, which must be specified using human domain knowledge, grid searches, or other hyperparameter tuning methods. Such methods are time-consuming at a minimum, and at worst, sources of bias and overfitting. Single decision trees are also unstable, in that adding a few rows of data to training or validation data and retraining can lead to a completely rearranged flowchart. Such instability is an Achilles' heel for many ML models.

Decision trees make locally optimal, or *greedy*, decisions each time they make a new branch or if-then rule. Other ML models use different optimization strategies, but the end result is the same: a model that's not the best model for the dataset, but instead is one good candidate for the best model out of many, many possible options. This issue of many possible models for any given dataset has at least two names, *the multiplicity of good models* and *the Rashomon effect* (*https://oreil.ly/nNwFY*). (The name *Rashomon* (*https://oreil.ly/wW-k5*) is from a famous film in which witnesses describe the same murder differently.) The Rashomon effect is linked to another nasty problem, known as underspecification (*https://oreil.ly/V_DaF*), in which hyperparameter tuning and validation-data-based model selection leads to a model that looks good in test scenarios but then flops in the real world. How do we avoid these problems with decision trees? Mainly by training single trees that we can see and examine, and for which we can ensure that their logic will hold up when they are deployed.

There are many variations on the broader theme of decision trees. For example, linear tree models fit a linear model in each terminal node of a decision tree, adding predictive capacity to standard decision trees while keeping all the explainability intact. Professor Rudin's research group has introduced optimal sparse decision trees (*https://oreil.ly/4kGpW*) as a response to the issues of instability and underspecification. Another answer to these problems is manual constraints informed by human domain knowledge. We'll address constrained decision tree ensembles next, but if readers are ready to try standard decision trees, there are many packages to try, and the R package rpart (*https://oreil.ly/XLE1H*) is one of the best.

Constrained XGBoost models

The popular gradient boosting package XGBoost now supports both monotonic constraints (*https://oreil.ly/39PhO*) and interaction constraints (*https://oreil.ly/yVAtK*). As described earlier, user-supplied monotonic constraints force the XGBoost model to preserve more explainable monotonic relationships between model inputs and model predictions. The interaction constraints can prevent XGBoost from endlessly recombining features. These software features turn what would normally be an opaque tree ensemble model replete with underspecification problems into a highly robust model capable of learning from data and accepting causally motivated constraints from expert human users. These newer training options, which enable human domain experts to use causal knowledge to set the direction of modeled relationships and to specify which input features should not interact, combined with XGBoost's proven track record of scalability and performance, make this a hard choice to overlook when it comes to explainable ML. While not as directly interpretable as EBMs, because gradient boosting machines (GBMs) combine and recombine features into a tangle of nested if-then rules, constrained XGBoost models are amenable to a wide variety of post hoc explainable and visualization techniques. The explanation techniques often enable practitioners to confirm the causal knowledge they've injected into the model and to understand the inner workings of the complex ensemble.

An Ecosystem of Explainable Machine Learning Models

Beyond additive and tree-based models, there is an entire ecosystem of explainable ML models. Some of these models have been known for decades, some represent tweaks to older approaches, and some are wholly new. Whether they're new or old, they challenge the status quo of unexplainable ML—and that's a good thing. If readers are surprised about all the different options for explainable models, imagine a customer's surprise when we can explain the drivers of our AI system's decisions, help them confirm or deny hypotheses about their business, and provide explanations to users, all while achieving high levels of predictive quality. Indeed, there are lots of options for explainable models, and there's sure to be one that might suit our next project well. Instead of asking our colleagues, customers, or business partners to blindly trust an opaque ML pipeline, consider explainable neural networks; *k*-nearest neighbors; rule-based, causal, or graphical models; or even sparse matrix factorization next time:

Causal models
> Causal models, in which causal phenomena are linked to some prediction outcome of interest in a provable manner, are often seen as the gold standard of interpretability. Given that we can often look at a chart that defines how the model works and that they are composed using human domain or causal inference techniques, they're almost automatically interpretable. They also don't fit to noise in training data as badly as traditional unexplainable ML models. The only hard part of causal models is finding the data necessary to train them, or the training processes themselves. However, training capabilities for causal models continue to improve, and packages like pyMC3 (*https://oreil.ly/XY448*) for Bayesian models and dowhy (*https://oreil.ly/yacTr*) for causal inference have been

enabling practitioners to build and train causal models for years. More recently, both Microsoft and Uber released a tutorial for causal inference (*https://oreil.ly/wQu72*) with real-world use cases using modeling libraries from both companies, EconML (*https://oreil.ly/Q448j*) and causalml (*https://oreil.ly/Tx12a*), respectively. If we care about stable, interpretable models, watch this space carefully. Once considered to be nearly impossible to train, causal models are slowly working their way into the mainstream.

Explainable neural networks

Released (*https://oreil.ly/xiKH_*) and refined (*https://oreil.ly/jgu71*) by Wells Fargo Bank risk management, explainable neural networks (XNNs) prove that with a little ingenuity and elbow grease, even the most unexplainable models can be made explainable and retain high degrees of performance quality. Explainable neural networks use the same principals as GAMs, GA2Ms, and EBMs to achieve both high interpretability and high predictive performance, but with some twists. Like GAMs, XNNs are simply additive combinations of shape functions. However, they add an additional indexed structure to GAMs. XNNs are an example of generalized additive *index* models (GAIMs), where GAM-like shape functions are fed by a lower projection layer that can learn interesting higher-degree interactions.

In an XNN, back-propagation is used to learn optimal combinations of variables (see c in online XNN figure: *https://oreil.ly/kBy92*) to act as inputs into shape functions learned via subnetworks (see b in online figure), which are then combined in an additive fashion with optimal weights to form the output of the network (see a in online figure). While likely not the simplest explainable model, XNNs have been refined to be more scalable, they automatically identify important interactions in training data, and post hoc explanations can be used to break down their predictions into locally accurate feature contributions. Another interesting type of transparent neural networks was put forward recently in "Neural Additive Models: Interpretable Machine Learning with Neural Nets" (*https://oreil.ly/ge-fk*). NAMs appear similar to XNNs, except they forego the bottom layer that attempts to locate interaction terms.

k-nearest neighbors (k-NN)

The *k*-NN method uses prototypes, or similar data points, to make predictions. Reasoning in this way does not require training and its simplicity often appeals to human users. If *k* is set to three, an inference on a new point involves finding the three nearest points to the new point and taking the average or modal label from those three points as the predicted outcome for the new point. This kind of logic is common in our day-to-day lives. Take the example of residential real-estate appraisal. Price per square foot for one home is often evaluated as the average price per square foot of three comparable houses. When we say, "it sounds like," or "it feels like," or "it looks like," we're probably using prototype data points to make inferences about things in our own life. The notion of interpretation by comparison to prototypes is what led the Rudin Group to take on unexplainable computer vision models with this-looks-like-that (*https://oreil.ly/qG7yT*), a new type of deep learning that uses comparisons to prototypes to explain image classification predictions.

Rule-based models

Extracting predictive if-then rules from datasets is another long-running type of ML modeling. The simple Boolean logic of if-then rules is interpretable, as long as the number of rules, the number of branches in the rules, and the number of entities in the rules are constrained. RuleFit (*https://oreil.ly/xc3-B*) and skope-rules (*https://oreil.ly/3w2BK*) are two popular techniques that seek to find predictive and explainable rules from training data. Rule-based models are also the domain of the Rudin Group. Among their greatest hits for interpretable and high-quality rule-based predictors are certifiable optimal rule lists (CORELS) (*https://oreil.ly/BgWCt*) and scalable Bayesian rule lists (*https://oreil.ly/RCu74*). Code for these and other valuable contributions from the Rudin Group are available on their public code page (*https://oreil.ly/aYDTE*).

Sparse matrix factorization

Factoring a large data matrix into two smaller matrices is a common dimension reduction and unsupervised learning technique. Most older matrix factorization techniques reattribute the original columns of data across dozens of derived features, rendering the results of these techniques unexplainable. However, with the introduction of L1 penalties into matrix factorization, it's now possible to extract new features from a large matrix of data, where only a few of the original columns have large weights on any new feature. By using sparse principal components analysis (SPCA) (*https://oreil.ly/xqWFw*), we might find, for example, that when extracting a new feature from customer financial data, that the new feature is composed exclusively of the debt-to-income and revolving account balance features in our original dataset. We could then reason through this feature being related to consumer debt. Or if we find another new feature that has high weights for income, payments, and disbursements, then we could interpret that feature as relating to cash flow. Nonnegative matrix factorization (NMF) (*https://oreil.ly/CKydA*) gives similar results but assumes that training data only takes on positive values. For unstructured data like term counts and pixel intensities, that assumption always holds. Hence, NMF can be used to find explainable summaries of topics in documents or to decompose images into explainable dictionaries of subcomponents. Whether we use SPCA or NMF, the resulting extracted features can be used as explainable summaries, archetypes for explainable comparisons, axes for visualization, or features in models. And it turns out that just like many explainable supervised learning models are special instances of GAMs, many unsupervised learning techniques are instances of generalized low-rank models (*https://oreil.ly/YKUDa*), which we can try out in H2O.

Now that we've covered the basics of explainable models, we'll move on to post hoc explanation techniques. But before we do, remember that it's perfectly fine to use explainable models and post hoc explanation together. Explainable models are often used to incorporate domain knowledge into learning mechanisms, to address inherent assumptions or limitations in training data, or to build functional forms that humans have a chance of understanding. Post hoc explanation is often used for visualization and summarization. While post hoc explanation is often discussed in terms of increasing transparency for traditional opaque ML models, there are lots of reasons to question that application, which we'll introduce in the following section. Using explainable models and post hoc explanation together, to improve upon and validate the other, may be the best general application for both technologies.

Post Hoc Explanation

We'll start off by addressing global and local feature attribution measures, then move on to surrogate models and popular types of plots for describing model behavior, and touch on a few post hoc explanation techniques for unsupervised learning. We'll also discuss the shortcomings of post hoc explanations, which can be broadly summarized in three points that readers should keep in mind as they form their own impressions of and practices with explanations:

- If a model doesn't make sense, its explanations won't either. (We can't explain nonsense.)
- ML models can easily grow so complex they can't be summarized accurately.
- It's difficult to convey explanatory information about ML systems to a broad group of users and stakeholders.

Despite these difficulties, post hoc explanation is almost always necessary for interpretability and transparency. Even models like logistic regression, thought of as highly transparent, must be summarized to meet regulatory obligations around transparency. For better or worse, we're probably stuck with post hoc explanation and summarization. So let's try to make it work as well as possible.

Many models must be summarized in a post hoc fashion to be interpretable. Yet, ML explanations are often incorrect, and checking them requires rigorous testing and comparisons with an underlying explainable model.

Feature Attribution and Importance

Feature attribution is one of the most central aspects of explaining ML models. Feature attribution methods tell us how much an input feature contributed to the predictions of a model, either globally (across an entire dataset) or locally (for one or a few rows of data). Feature attribution values can typically be either positive or negative.

When we discuss feature importance, we mean a global measure of how much each feature contributes toward a model's predictions. Unlike feature attributions, feature importance values are typically always positive. That is, feature importance values measure how significantly a feature contributed to a model's overall behavior on a dataset. Feature attributions, on the other hand, give us more detail on the feature's contribution.

While a handful of the more established global feature importance metrics do not arise from the aggregation of local measures, averaging (or otherwise aggregating) local feature attributions into global feature importances is common today. We'll start by discussing newer methods for local feature attribution and then move on to global methods.

 Global explanations summarize a model mechanism or prediction over an entire dataset or large sample of data. *Local* explanations perform the same type of summarization, but for smaller segments of data, down to a single row or cell of data.

"Feature importance" can be misleading as a name. We're just approximating one model's idea of what is important. Consider, for example, a computer vision security system that relies on gradient-based methods to detect "important" aspects of video frames. Without proper training and deployment specifications, such systems will have a hard time picking up individuals wearing camouflage, as newer digital camouflage clothing is specifically designed to blend into various backgrounds, and to keep visual gradients between the fabric and different backgrounds smooth and undetectable. But isn't people wearing camouflage one of the most important things to detect in a security application? For the rest of this section, keep in mind that "feature importance" is highly dependent on the model's understanding and training.

Local explanations and feature attribution

In some applications, it is crucial to determine which input features impacted a specific prediction—that is, to measure local feature attributions. Have a look at Figure 2-3 to see local feature attribution in action.

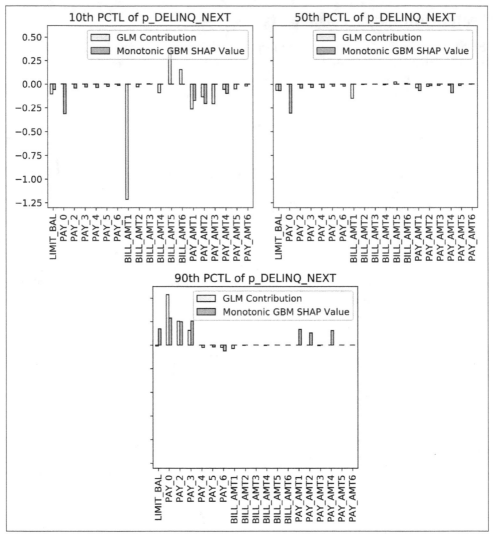

Figure 2-3. Local feature attribution for two explainable models for three individuals at the 10th, 50th, and 90th percentiles of predicted probabilities (digital, color version: https://oreil.ly/4Y__H)

Figure 2-3 shows two types of local feature attribution values, for two different models, for three different customers in a credit lending example. The first customer sits at the 10th percentile of probability of default, and they are likely to receive the credit product on offer. The second customer sits at the 50th percentile, and are unlikely to receive the product on offer. The third customer sits at the 90th percentile of probability of default and provides an example of an extremely high-risk applicant. The two models being summarized are a penalized generalized linear model (GLM) and a monotonically constrained GBM. Since both models have relatively simple structures that make sense for the problem at hand, we've done a good job handling the caveats brought up in our opening remarks about post hoc explanation. These explanations should be trustworthy, and they are simple enough to be accurately summarized.

 One practical way to make explanations more interpretable is to compare them with some meaningful benchmark. That's why we compare our feature attribution values to Pearson correlation and compare our partial dependence and individual conditional expectation (ICE) values to mean model predictions. This should enable viewers of the plot to compare more abstract explanatory values to a more understandable benchmark value.

How are we summarizing the models' local behavior? For the penalized GLM, we're multiplying the model coefficients by the values of the input feature for each applicant. For the GBM, we're applying SHAP. Both of these local feature attribution techniques are additive and locally accurate—meaning they sum to the model prediction. Both are measured from an offset, the GLM intercept or the SHAP intercept, which are similar in value but not equal. (That is not accounted for in Figure 2-3.) And both values can be generated in the same space: either log odds or predicted probability, depending on how the calculation is performed.

What do the plotted values tell us? For the low-risk applicant at the 10th percentile of probability of default, we can see that their most recent bill amount, BILL_AMT1, is highly favorable and driving their prediction downward. The SHAP values for the same customer tell a slightly different story, but the GBM was trained on a different set of features. The SHAP values paint a story of the applicant being lower-risk on all considered attributes. For the applicant at the 50th percentile, we see most local feature attribution values staying close to their respective intercepts, and for the high-risk applicant nearly all local feature attribution values are positive, pushing predictions higher. Both models seem to agree that it's the applicant's recent payment statuses (PAY_0, PAY_2, and PAY_3) that are driving risk, with the GBM and SHAP also focusing on payment amount information.

These are just two types of local feature attribution, and we're going to discuss many others. But this small example likely brings up some questions that might get stuck in readers' heads if we don't address them before moving on. First and foremost, the act of generating explanations does not make these good models; it simply means we get to make a more informed decision about whether the models are good or not. Second, it's not uncommon for two different models to give different explanations for the same row of data. But just because it's common, doesn't make it right. It's not something we should just accept and move past. While the models in Figure 2-3 appear to show adequate agreement when operating on the same features, this is, unfortunately, a best-case scenario for post hoc explanation, and it happened because we picked relatively simple models and made sure the sign of the GLM coefficients and the direction of the monotonic constraints of the GBM agreed with domain expertise. For complex, unexplainable models trained on hundreds or more correlated features, we'll likely see much less agreement between model explanations, and that should raise red flags.

This notion that different models should yield similar explanations on the same row of data is called *consistency*. Consistency is a reasonable goal for high-risk applications in order to bolster trust in outcomes and agreement among multiple important decision-making systems.

As readers are probably starting to pick up, post hoc explanation is complex and fraught, and this is why we suggest pairing these techniques with explainable models, so the models can be used to check the explanations and vice versa. Nevertheless, we push onward to an outline of the major local explanation techniques—counterfactuals, gradient-based, occlusion, prototypes, SHAP values, and others:

Counterfactuals
Counterfactual explanations tell us what an input feature's value would have to become to change the outcome of a model prediction. The bigger the swing of the prediction when changing an input variable by some standard amount, the more important that feature is, as measured from the counterfactual perspective. Check out Section 9.3, "Counterfactual Explanations" (*https://oreil.ly/9SNML*), in Christoph Molnar's *Interpretable Machine Learning* for more details. To try out counterfactual explanations, check out "DiCE: Diverse Counterfactual Explanations for Machine Learning Classifiers" (*https://oreil.ly/s_QaL*) from Microsoft Research.

Gradient-based feature attribution
Think of gradients as regression coefficients for every little piece of a complex machine-learned function. In deep learning, gradient-based approaches to local explanations are common. When used for image or text data, gradients can often be overlaid on input images and text to create highly visual explanations depicting which parts of the input, if changed, would generate the largest changes

in the model output. Various tweaks to this idea are said to result in improved explanations, such as integrated gradients (*https://oreil.ly/is_C-*), layer-wise relevance propagation (*https://oreil.ly/XKJ4B*), deeplift (*https://oreil.ly/6rhO0*), and Grad-CAM (*https://oreil.ly/Zkfeh*). For an excellent, highly technical review of gradient-based explanations, see Ancona et al.'s "Towards Better Understanding of Gradient-based Attribution Methods for Deep Neural Networks" (*https://oreil.ly/h7Lde*). To see what can go wrong with these techniques, see "Sanity Checks for Saliency Maps" (*https://oreil.ly/a9fQA*). We'll return to these ideas in Chapter 9, when we train a deep learning model and compare various attribution techniques.

Occlusion

Occlusion refers to the simple and powerful idea of removing features from a model prediction and tracking the resulting change in the prediction. A big change may mean the feature is important, a small change may mean it's less important. Occlusion is the basis of SHAP, leave-one-feature-out (LOFO), and many other explanation approaches, including many in computer vision and natural language processing. Occlusion can be used to generate explanations in complex models when gradients are unavailable. Of course, it's never simple mathematically to remove inputs from a model, and it takes a lot of care to generate relevant explanations from the results of feature removal. For an authoritative review of occlusion and feature removal techniques, see Covert, Lundberg, and Lee's "Explaining by Removing: A Unified Framework for Model Explanation" (*https://oreil.ly/662aS*), where they cover 25 explanation methods that can be linked back to occlusion and feature removal.

Prototypes

Prototypes are instances of data that are highly representative of larger amounts of data. Prototypes are used to explain by summarization and comparison. A common kind of prototype is *k*-means (or other) cluster centroids. These prototypes are an average representation of a similar group of data. They can be compared to other points in their own cluster and in other clusters based on distances and in terms of real-world similarity. Real-world data is often highly heterogeneous, and it can be difficult to find prototypes that represent an entire dataset well. *Criticisms* are data points that are not represented well by prototypes. Together, prototypes and criticisms create a set of points that can be leveraged for summarization and comparison purposes to better understand both datasets and ML models. Moreover, several types of ML models, like *k*-NN and this-looks-like-that deep learning, are based on the notion of prototypes, which enhances their overall interpretability. To learn more about prototypes, look into Molnar's chapter on prototypes and criticisms (*https://oreil.ly/2IQYd*).

There are various other local explanation techniques. Readers may have heard of treeinterpreter (*https://oreil.ly/VECj5*) or eli5 (*https://oreil.ly/xOkSX*), which generate locally accurate, additive attribution values for ensembles of decision trees. Alethia (*https://oreil.ly/ZauV8*) provides model summaries and local inference for rectified linear unit (ReLU) neural networks.

Next, we'll devote a section to the discussion of Shapley values, one of most popular and rigorous types of local explanations available to data scientists. Before moving on, we'll remind readers once more that these post hoc explanation techniques, including SHAP, are not magic. While the ability to understand which features influence ML model decisions is an incredible breakthrough, there is a great deal of literature pointing toward problems with these techniques. To get the most out of them, approach them with a staid and scientific mindset. Do experiments. Use explainable models and simulated data to assess explanation quality and validity. Does the explanation technique we've selected give compelling explanations on random data? (If so, that's bad.) Does the technique provide stable explanations when data is mildly perturbed? (That's a good thing, usually.) Nothing in life or ML is perfect, and that certainly includes local post hoc explanation.

Shapley values. Shapley values were created by the Nobel laureate economist and mathematician Lloyd Shapley. Shapley additive explanations (SHAP) unify (*https://oreil.ly/ilEXW*) approaches such as LIME, LOFO, treeinterpreter, deeplift, and others to generate accurate local feature importance values, and they can be aggregated or visualized to create consistent global explanations. Aside from their own Python package, SHAP (*https://oreil.ly/LP4zm*), and various R packages, SHAP is supported in popular machine learning software frameworks like H2O, LightGBM, and XGBoost.

SHAP starts out the same as many other explanation techniques, asking the intuitive question: what would the model prediction be for this row without this feature? So why is SHAP different from other types of local explanations? To be exact, in a system with as many complex interactions as a typical ML model, that simple question must be answered using an average of all possible sets of inputs that do not include the feature of interest. Those different groups of inputs are called *coalitions*. For a simple dataset with twenty columns, that means about half a million different model predictions on different coalitions are considered on the average. Now repeat that process of dropping and averaging for every prediction in our dataset, and we can see why SHAP takes into account more information than most other local feature attribution approaches.

There are many different flavors of SHAP, but the most popular are Kernel SHAP, Deep SHAP, and Tree SHAP. Of these, Tree SHAP is less approximate, and Kernel and Deep SHAP are more approximate. Kernel SHAP has the advantage of being usable on any type of model, i.e., being *model-agnostic*. It's like local interpretable model-agnostic explanations (LIME) combined with the coalitional game theory approach. However, with more than a few inputs, Kernel SHAP often requires untenable approximations to achieve tolerable runtimes. Kernel SHAP also requires the specification of *background data*, or data that is used by an explanation technique during the process of calculating explanations, which can have a large influence on the final explanation values. Deep SHAP also relies on approximations and may be less suitable than easier-to-compute gradient-based explanations, depending on the model and dataset at hand. On the other hand, Tree SHAP is fast and more exact. But as its name suggests, it's only suitable for tree-based models.

Many explanation techniques rely on "background data," which is data separate from the observations being explained that is used to support the calculation of the explanations. For example, when we compute SHAP values, we form coalitions by removing features from the data. When we have to evaluate the model on this coalition, we substitute the missing values by sampling from the background data. Background data can have a large effect on explanations and must be chosen carefully so as not to conflict with statistical assumptions of explanation techniques and to provide the right context for explanations.

Two of the major places where data scientists tend to go wrong with Tree SHAP are in the interpretation of SHAP itself and in failing to understand the assumptions inherent in different parameterizations of the technique. For interpretation, let's start with recognizing SHAP as an offset from the average model prediction. SHAP values are calculated in reference to that offset, and large SHAP values mean the feature causes the model prediction to depart from the average prediction in some noticeable way. Small SHAP values mean the feature doesn't move the model prediction too far from the average prediction. We're often tempted to read more into SHAP than is actually there. We tend to seek causal or counterfactual logic from SHAP values, and this is simply not possible. SHAP values are the weighted average of the feature's contribution to model predictions across a vast number of coalitions. They don't provide causal or counterfactual explanations, and if we'd like for them to be meaningful at all, the underlying model must also be meaningful.

A SHAP value can be interpreted as the difference in model outcome away from the average prediction attributed to a certain input feature value.

Tree SHAP also asks users to make trade-offs. Based on how features that are missing from each coalition are filled in (the *perturbation method*), we choose between different philosophies of explanations and different shortcomings.

If no background data is explicitly passed in, the default settings in Tree SHAP use `tree_path_dependent` perturbations, which use the number of training examples that went down each path of the tree to approximate the background data distribution. If background data is supplied to Tree SHAP, then this data is sampled from to fill in missing feature values in what are known as `interventional` feature perturbations. The additional flexibility of choosing a background dataset allows explanations to be more targeted, but choosing an appropriate background dataset can be a complex exercise, even for experienced practitioners. We'll talk more about choosing an appropriate background dataset and the effects it can have in Chapter 6.

Besides the added complexity, the main shortcoming of `interventional` feature perturbations is that they create unrealistic data instances. This means that when we're evaluating the attribution of a feature, we may be doing so on a bunch of fake observations that would never be observed in the real world. On the other hand, intervening allows us to skirt the need to worry about correlated features. In contrast, `tree_path_dependent` feature perturbations are more sensitive to correlated features, but they try to only consider data points that are realistic.

Due to general issues with correlation and information overload, good explanations usually require that the underlying model is trained on a smaller number of uncorrelated features with a direct relationship to the modeling target. As said by the authors of the excellent paper "True to the Model or True to the Data?" (*https://oreil.ly/ze8_z*), including Scott Lundberg, the creator of SHAP: "Currently, the best case for feature attribution is when the features that are being perturbed are independent to start with."

This web of assumptions and limitations mean that we still have to be careful and thoughtful, even when using Tree SHAP. We can make things easier on us, though. Correlation is the enemy of many explainable models and post hoc explanation techniques, and SHAP is no different. The authors like to start with a reasonable number of input features that do not have serious multicollinearity issues. On a good day, we'd have found those features using a causal discovery approach as well. Then we'd use domain knowledge to apply monotonic constraints to input features in XGBoost. For general feature importance purposes, we'd use Tree SHAP with `tree_path_dependent` feature perturbation. For an application like credit scoring, where the proper context is defined by regulatory commentary, we might use `interventional` SHAP values and background data. For instance, certain regulatory commentary on the generation of explanations for credit denials in the US suggests (*https://oreil.ly/W0VxD*) that we "identify the factors for which the applicant's score fell furthest below the average score for each of those factors achieved by applicants whose total score was at or slightly above the minimum passing score." This means our background dataset should be composed of applicants with predictions just above the cutoff to receive the credit product.

Critical applications of local explanations and feature importance. Local feature attribution values' most mission-critical application is likely meeting regulatory requirements. The primary requirement now in the US is to explain credit denials with *adverse action notices*. The key technical component for the adverse action reporting process are *reason codes*. Reason codes are plain-text explanations of a model prediction described in terms of a model's input features. They are a step beyond local feature attributions, in which raw local feature attribution values are matched to reasons a product can be denied. Consumers should then be allowed to review the reason codes for their negative prediction and follow a prescribed appeal process if data inputs or decision factors are demonstrably wrong.

Adverse action reporting is a specific instance of a more high-level notion known as actionable recourse, where transparent model decisions are based on factors users have control over and can be appealed by model users and overridden by model operators. Many forthcoming and proposed regulations, such as those in California (*https://oreil.ly/Wc25G*), Washington, DC (*https://oreil.ly/jh5xG*), and the EU (*https://oreil.ly/kuoEI*), are likely to introduce similar requirements for explanation or recourse. When working under regulatory scrutiny, or just to do the right thing when making important decisions for other human beings, we'll want our explanations to be as accurate, consistent, and interpretable as possible. While we expect that local feature attributions will be one of the most convenient technical tools to generate the raw data needed to comply, we make the best explanations when combining local feature attributions with explainable models and other types of explanations, like those described in the subsequent sections of this chapter.

Global feature importance

Global feature importance methods quantify the global contribution of each input feature to the predictions of a complex ML model over an entire dataset, not just for one individual or row of data. Global feature importance measures sometimes give insight into the average direction that a variable pushes a trained ML function, and sometimes they don't. At their most basic, they simply state the magnitude of a feature's relationship with the response as compared to other input features. This is hardly ever a bad thing to know, and since most global feature importance measures are older approaches, they are often expected by model validation teams. Figure 2-4 provides an example of feature importance plots, in which we are comparing the global feature importance of two models.

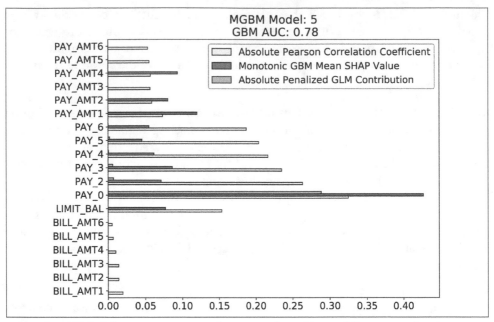

Figure 2-4. Global feature importance for two explainable models compared to Pearson correlation (digital, color version: https://oreil.ly/C2dF0)

Charts like this help us answer questions like the following:

- Does one ordering of feature importance make more sense than the other?
- Does this plot reflect patterns we know the models should have learned from training data?
- Are the models placing too much emphasis on just one or two features?

Global feature importance is a straightforward way to conduct such basic checks. In Figure 2-4, we compare feature importance to Pearson correlation to have some baseline understanding of which features should be important. Between Pearson correlation and the two models, we can see that everyone agrees that PAY_0 is the most important feature. However, the GLM places nearly all of its decision-making importance on PAY_0, while the GBM spreads importance over a larger set of inputs. When models place too much emphasis on one feature, as the GLM in Figure 2-4 does, it can make them unstable in new data if the distribution of the most important feature drifts, and it makes adversarial manipulation of a model easy. For the GLM in Figure 2-4, a bad actor would only have to alter the value of a single feature, PAY_0, to drastically change the model's predictions.

Global feature importance metrics can be calculated in many ways. Many data scientists are first introduced to feature importance when learning about decision trees. A common feature importance method for decision trees is to sum up the change in the splitting criterion for every split in the tree based on a certain feature. For instance, if a decision tree (or tree ensemble) is trained to maximize information gain for each split, the feature importance assigned to some input feature is the total information gain associated with that feature every time it is used in the tree(s). Perturbation-based feature importance is another common type of feature importance measurement, and it's a model-agnostic technique, meaning it can be used for almost all types of ML models. In perturbation-based feature importance, an input feature of interest is shuffled (sorted randomly) and predictions are made. The difference in some original score, usually the model prediction or something like mean squared error (MSE), before and after shuffling the feature of interest is the feature importance. Another similar approach is known as leave-one-feature-out (LOFO, or leave-one-covariate-out, LOCO). In the LOFO method, a feature is somehow dropped from the training or prediction of a model—say, by retraining without the feature and making predictions, or by setting the feature to missing and making predictions. The difference in the relevant score between the model with the feature of interest and without the feature of interest is taken to be the LOFO importance.

While permutation and LOFO are typically used to measure the difference in predictions or the difference in an accuracy or error score, they have the advantage of being able to estimate the impact of a feature on nearly anything associated with a model. For instance, it's quite possible to calculate permutation- or LOFO-based contributions to a fairness metric, allowing us to gain insight into which specific features are contributing to any detected sociological bias. This same motif can be reapplied for any number of measures of interest about a model—error functions, security, privacy, and more.

Techniques like perturbation feature importance and LOFO can be used to estimate contributions to many quantities besides model predictions.

Because these techniques are well-established, we can find a great deal of related information and software packages. For a great discussion on split-based feature importance, check out Chapter 3 (*https://oreil.ly/P2gEb*) of an *Introduction to Data Mining* (Pearson). Section 10.13.1 of *Elements of Statistical Learning* (*https://oreil.ly/jQOX6*) introduces split-based feature importance, and Section 15.3.2 provides a brief introduction to permutation-based feature importance in the context of random forests. The R package vip (*https://oreil.ly/7Jo9s*) provides a slew of *variable importance plots*, and we can try LOFO with the Python package lofo-importance (*https://oreil.ly/jP5jV*). Of course, there are drawbacks and weaknesses to most global feature importance techniques. Split-based feature importance has serious consistency problems, and like so much of post hoc explainable AI (XAI), correlation will lead us astray with permutation-based and LOFO approaches. The paper "There Is No Free Variable Importance" (*https://oreil.ly/bx6QA*) gets into more details of the sometimes disqualifying issues related to global feature importance. But, as is repeated many times in this chapter, constrained models with a reasonable number of noncorrelated and logical inputs will help us avoid the worst problems with global feature importance.

SHAP also has a role to play in global feature importance. SHAP is by nature a local feature attribution method, but it can be aggregated and visualized to create global feature importance information. Of the many benefits SHAP presents over more traditional feature importance measures, its interpretation is perhaps the most important. With split-based, permutation, and LOFO feature importance, oftentimes we only see a relative ordering of the importance of the input features, and maybe some qualitative notions of how a feature actually contributes to model predictions. With SHAP values, we can calculate the average absolute value of the feature attributions across a dataset, and this measure of feature importance has a clear and quantitative relationship with model predictions on individual observations. SHAP also provides many levels of granularity for feature importance. While SHAP can be directly aggregated into a feature importance value, that process can average out important local information. SHAP opens up the option of examining feature importance values anywhere from the most local level—a single row—to the global level. For instance, aggregating SHAP across important segments, like US states or different genders, or using the numerous visualizations in the SHAP package, can provide a view of feature importance that might be more informative and more representative than a single average absolute value. Like permutation and LOFO feature importance, SHAP can also be used to estimate importance of quantities besides model predictions. It's capable of estimating contributions to model errors (*https://oreil.ly/oYG5d*) and to fairness metrics, like demographic parity (*https://oreil.ly/4aHtK*).

This concludes our discussion of feature importance. Whether it's global or local, feature importance will probably be the first post hoc XAI technique we encounter when we're building models. As this section shows, there's a lot more to feature importance than just bar charts or running SHAP. To get the best results with feature importance, we'll have to be familiar with the strengths and weaknesses of the many approaches. Next, we'll be covering surrogate models—another intriguing explanation approach, but also one that requires thought and caution.

Surrogate Models

Surrogate models are simple models of complex models. If we can build a simple, interpretable model of a more complex model, we can use the explainable characteristics of the surrogate model to explain, summarize, describe, or debug the more complex model. Surrogate models are generally model agnostic. We can use them for almost any ML model. The problem with surrogate models is they are mostly a trick-of-the-trade technique, with few mathematical guarantees that they truly represent the more complex model they are attempting to summarize. That means we have to be careful when using surrogate models, and at a minimum, check that they are accurate and stable representations of the more complex models they seek to summarize. In practice, this often means looking at different types of accuracy and error measures on many different data partitions to ensure that fidelity to the more complex model's predictions is high, and that it remains high in new data and stable during cross-validation. Surrogate models also have many names. Readers may have heard about *model compression, model distillation,* or *model extraction.* All of these either are surrogate modeling techniques or are closely related. Like feature importance, there are also many different types of surrogate models. In the sections that follow, we'll start out with decision tree surrogate models, which are typically used to construct global explanations, then transition into LIME and anchors, which are typically used to generate local explanations.

Decision tree surrogates

Decision tree surrogate models are usually created by training a decision tree on the original inputs and predictions of a complex model. Feature importance, trends, and interactions displayed in the surrogate model are then assumed to be indicative of the internal mechanisms of the complex model. There are no theoretical guarantees that the simple surrogate model is highly representative of the more complex model. But, because of the structure of decision trees, these surrogate models create very interpretable flowcharts of a more complex model's decision-making processes, as is visible in Figure 2-5. There are prescribed methods for training decision tree surrogate models, for example those explored in "Extracting Tree-Structured Representations of Trained Networks" (*https://oreil.ly/ewW3O*) and "Interpretability via Model Extraction" (*https://oreil.ly/RnFep*).

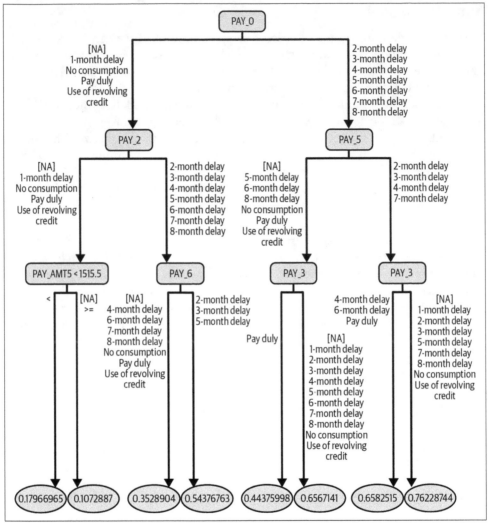

Figure 2-5. A decision tree surrogate model creates a flowchart for a monotonic gradient boosting machine

Decision tree surrogate models can be highly interpretable when they create flowcharts of more complex models.

In practice, it usually suffices to measure the fidelity of the surrogate tree's predictions to the complex model's predictions in the data partition of interest with metrics like logloss, root mean square error (RMSE), or R^2, and to measure the stability of those predictions with cross-validation. If a surrogate decision tree fails to provide high fidelity with respect to the more complex model, more sophisticated explainable models, like EBMs or XNNs, can be considered as surrogates instead.

The surrogate model in Figure 2-5 was trained on the same inputs as the more complex GBM it seeks to summarize, but instead of training on the original target that indicates payment delinquency, it is trained instead on the predictions of the GBM. When interpreting this tree, features that are higher or used more frequently are considered to be more important in the explained GBM. Features that are above and below one another can have strong interactions in the GBM, and other techniques discussed in this chapter, such as explainable boosting machines and a comparison between partial dependence and ICE, can be used to confirm the existence of those interactions in training data or in the GBM model.

 Decision tree surrogates can be used to find interactions for use in linear models or for LIMEs. EBMs and differences between partial dependence and ICE can also be used to find interactions in data and models.

The decision paths in the tree can also be used to gain some understanding of how the more complex GBM makes decisions. Tracing the decision path from the root node in Figure 2-5 to the average predictions at the bottom of the tree, we can see that those who have good statuses for their most recent (PAY_0) and second (PAY_2) most recent repayments and have somewhat large fifth most recent payment amounts (PAY_AMT5) are most likely not to have future delinquency, according to the original model. Those customers who have unfavorable most recent and fifth most recent repayment statuses appear most likely to have future payment problems. (The PAY_3 splits exhibit a large amount of noise and are not interpreted here.) In both cases, the GBM appears to be considering both recent and past repayment behaviors to come to its decision about future payments. This prediction behavior is logical but should be confirmed by other means when possible. Like most surrogate models, decision tree surrogates are useful and highly interpretable, but should not be used for important explanation or interpretation tasks on their own.

Linear models and local interpretable model-agnostic explanations

LIME is one of the earliest, the most famous, and the most criticized post hoc explanation techniques. As the name indicates, it's most often used for generating local explanations, by fitting a linear model to the predictions of some small region of a more complex model's predictions. While this is its most common usage, it's a reductionist take on the technique.

When first introduced in the 2016 article "'Why Should I Trust You?' Explaining the Predictions of Any Classifier" (*https://oreil.ly/e9WL2*), LIME was presented as a framework with several admirable qualities. The most appealing of these was a sparsity requirement for local explanations. If our model has one thousand features and we apply SHAP, we will get back one thousand SHAP values for every prediction we want to explain. Even if SHAP is perfect for our data and model, we'll still have to sort through one thousand values every time we want to explain a prediction. The framework of LIME circumvents this problem by requiring that generated explanations are sparse, meaning that they key into the small handful of locally important features instead of all the features included in the model to be explained.

A LIME value can be interpreted as the difference between a LIME prediction and the associated LIME intercept attributed to a certain input feature value.

The rest of the framework of LIME specifies fitting an interpretable surrogate model to some weighted local region of another model's predictions. And that's a more faithful description of the LIME framework—a locally weighted interpretable surrogate model with a penalty to induce sparsity, fit to some arbitrary, more complex model's predictions. These ideas are useful and quite reasonable.

Always ensure LIME fits the underlying response function well with fit statistics and visualizations, and that the local model intercept is not explaining the most salient phenomenon driving a given prediction.

It's the popular implementation of LIME that gets inexperienced users into trouble and that presents security problems. For tabular data, the software package lime (*https://oreil.ly/dKYHV*) asks users to select a row to be explained, generates a fairly simplistic sample of data based on a specified input dataset, weights the sample by the user-selected row, fits a LASSO regression between the weighted sample and the more complex model's predictions on the sample, and finally, uses the LASSO regression coefficients to generate explanations for the user-specified row. There are a lot of potential issues in that implementation:

- The sampling is a problem for real-time explanation because it requires data generation and fitting a model in the midst of a scoring pipeline, and it also opens users up to data poisoning attacks that can alter explanations.

- Generated LIME samples can contain large proportions of out-of-range data that can lead to unrealistic local feature importance values.

- Local feature importance values are offsets from the local GLM intercept, and this intercept can sometimes account for the most important local phenomena.

- Extreme nonlinearity and high-degree interactions in the selected local region of predictions can cause LIME to fail completely.

Because LIME can be used on almost any type of ML model to generate sparse explanations, it can still be a good tool in our kit if we're willing to be patient and think through the LIME process. If we need to use LIME, we should plot the LIME predictions versus our more complex model predictions and analyze them with RMSE, R^2, or similar. We should be careful about the LIME intercept and make sure that it's not explaining our prediction on its own, rendering the actual LIME values useless. To increase the fidelity of LIME, try LIME on discretized input features and on manually constructed interactions. (We can use decision tree surrogates to guess at those interactions.) Use cross-validation to estimate standard deviations or even confidence intervals for local feature contribution values. And keep in mind that poor fit or inaccuracy of local linear models is itself informative, often indicating extreme nonlinearity or high-degree interactions in that region of predictions.

Anchors and rules

On the heels of LIME, probably with some lessons in mind, the same group of researchers released another model-agnostic local post hoc explanation technique named anchors. Anchors generates high-fidelity sets of plain-language rules to describe a machine learning model prediction, with a special focus on finding the most important features for the prediction at hand. Readers can learn more about anchors in "Anchors: High-Precision Model-Agnostic Explanations" (*https://oreil.ly/V1rFJ*) and the software package anchor (*https://oreil.ly/KNGF3*). While anchors is a prescribed technique with documented strengths and weaknesses, it's just one special instance of using rule-based models as surrogate models. As discussed in the first part of the chapter, rule-based models have good learning capacity for nonlinearities and interactions, while still being generally interpretable. Many of the rule-based models highlighted previously could be evaluated as surrogate models.

Plots of Model Performance

In addition to feature importance and surrogate models, partial dependence, individual conditional expectation, and accumulated local effects (ALE) plots have become popular for describing trained model behaviors with respect to input features. In this section, we'll go over partial dependence and ICE, how partial dependence should really only be used with ICE, and discuss ALE as a more contemporary replacement for partial dependence.

Partial dependence and individual conditional expectation

Partial dependence plots show us the estimated average manner in which machine-learned response functions change based on the values of one or two input features of interest, while averaging out the effects of all other input features. Remember the averaging-out part. We'll circle back to that. Partial dependence plots can show the nonlinearity, nonmonotonicity, and two-way interactions in complex ML models and can be used to verify monotonicity of response functions trained under monotonic constraints. Partial dependence is introduced along with tree ensembles in *Elements of Statistical Learning* (*https://oreil.ly/35vig*), Section 10.13. ICE plots are a newer, local, and less well-known adaptation of partial dependence plots. They depict how a model behaves for a single row of data as one feature is changed. ICE pairs nicely with partial dependence in the same plot to provide more local information to augment the more global information provided by partial dependence. ICE plots were introduced in the paper "Peeking Inside the Black Box: Visualizing Statistical Learning with Plots of Individual Conditional Expectation" (*https://oreil.ly/Vuraz*). There are lots of software packages for us to try partial dependence and ICE. For Python users, check out PDPbox (*https://oreil.ly/RbzII*) and PyCEbox (*https://oreil.ly/KcdET*). For R users, there are the pdp (*https://oreil.ly/pE0Ue*) and ICEbox (*https://oreil.ly/QbsDA*) packages. Also, many modeling libraries support partial dependence without having to use an external package.

Partial dependence should be paired with ICE plots, as ICE plots can reveal inaccuracies in partial dependence due to the averaging-out of strong interactions or the presence of correlation. When ICE curves diverge from partial dependence curves, this can indicate strong interactions between input features, which is another advantage of using them together. We can then use EBMs or surrogate decision trees to confirm the existence of the interaction in training data or the model being explained. One more trick is to plot partial dependence and ICE with a histogram of the feature of interest. That gives good insight into whether any plotted prediction is trustworthy and supported by training data. In Figure 2-6, partial dependence, ICE, and a histogram of PAY_0 are used to summarize the behavior of a monotonic GBM.

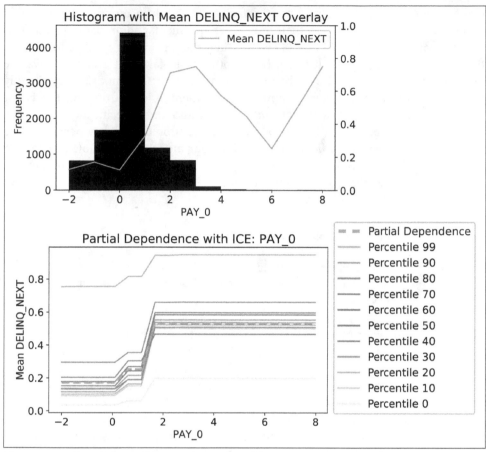

Figure 2-6. Partial dependence and ICE for an important input variable with accompanying histogram and mean target value overlay for a monotonic gradient boosting machine (digital, color version: https://oreil.ly/zFr70)

Due to multiple known weaknesses, partial dependence should not be used without ICE, or ALE should be used in place of partial dependence.

On the top, we can see a histogram of PAY_0 and that there is simply not much data for customers who are more than two months late on their most recent payment. On the bottom, we see partial dependence and ICE curves for customers at the deciles of predicted probability of default. Partial dependence and ICE help us confirm the monotonicity of the constrained GBM's response function for PAY_0. The model appears to behave reasonably, even when there is not much data to learn from for higher values of PAY_0. Probability of default increases in a monotonic fashion as customers become more late on their most recent payment, and probability of default is stable for higher values of PAY_0, even though there is almost no data to support the classifier in that region. It might be tempting to believe that every time we use monotonic constraints we would be protected against our ML models learning silly behaviors when there isn't much training data for them to learn from, but this is not true. Yes, monotonic constraints help with stability and underspecification problems, and partial dependence and ICE help us spot these problems if they occur, but we got lucky here. The truth is we need to check all our models for unstable behavior in sparse domains of the training data, and be prepared to have specialized models, or even human case workers, ready to make good predictions for these difficult rows of data.

 Comparing explainable model shape functions, partial dependence, ICE, or ALE plots with a histogram can give a basic qualitative measure of uncertainty in model outcomes, by enabling visual discovery of predictions that are based on only small amounts of training data.

Here's one more word of advice before moving onto ALE plots: like feature importance, SHAP, LIME, and all other explanation techniques that operate on a background dataset, we have to think through issues of context with partial dependence and ICE. They both use sneaky implicit background data. For partial dependence, it's whatever dataset we're interested in with all the values of the feature being plotted set to a certain value. This alters patterns of interactions and correlation, and although it's an exotic concern, it opens us up to data poisoning attacks as addressed in "Fooling Partial Dependence via Data Poisoning" (*https://oreil.ly/SVFmU*). For ICE, the implicit background dataset is a single row of data with the feature of interest set to a certain value. Watch out for the ICE values being plotted being too unrealistic in combination with the rest of the observed data in that row.

Accumulated local effect

ALE is a newer and highly rigorous method for representing the behavior of an ML model across the values of an input feature, introduced in "Visualizing the Effects of Predictor Variables in Black Box Supervised Learning Models" (*https://oreil.ly/TFFTK*). Like partial dependence plots, ALE plots show the shape—i.e., nonlinearity or nonmonotonicity—of the relationship between predictions and input feature values. ALE plots are especially valuable when strong correlations exist in the training data, a situation where partial dependence is known to fail. ALE is also faster to calculate than partial dependence. Try it with ALEPlot (*https://oreil.ly/4o0wH*) in R, and the Python edition ALEPython (*https://oreil.ly/_qKs8*).

Cluster Profiling

While a great deal of focus has been placed on explaining supervised learning models, sometimes we need to use unsupervised techniques. Feature extraction and clustering are two of the most common unsupervised learning tasks. We discussed how to make feature extraction more explainable with sparse methods like SPCA and NMF when we covered explainable models. And with the application of very much established post hoc methods of profiling, clustering can often be made more transparent too. The simplest approach is to use means and medians to describe cluster centroids, or to create prototypical members of a dataset based on clusters. From there, we can use concepts associated with prototypes such as summarization, comparison, and criticisms to better understand our clustering solution. Another technique is to apply feature extraction, particularly sparse methods, to project a higher-dimensional clustering solution into two or three dimensions for plotting. Once plotted on sparse interpretable axes, it's easier to use our domain knowledge to understand and check a group of clusters. Distributions of features can also be employed to understand and describe clusters. The density of a feature within a cluster can be compared to its density in other clusters or to its overall distribution. Features with the most dissimilar distributions versus other clusters or the entire training data can be seen as more important to the clustering solution. Finally, surrogate models can be applied to explain clusters. Using the same inputs as the clustering algorithm and the cluster labels as the target, we fit an interpretable classifier like a decision tree to our clusters and use the surrogate model's interpretable characteristics to gain insight into our clustering solution.

Stubborn Difficulties of Post Hoc Explanation in Practice

Unless we're careful, we can get into very murky areas with post hoc explanation. We've taken care to discuss the technical drawbacks of the techniques, but there is even more to consider when working with these techniques on real-world high-risk applications. As a refresher, Professor Rudin's "Stop Explaining Black Box Machine Learning Models for High Stakes Decisions and Use Interpretable Models Instead" (*https://oreil.ly/vR4Xl*) lays out the primary criticisms of post hoc explanation for opaque ML models and high-risk uses. According to Rudin, explanations for traditional ML models are:

- Premised on the wrong belief that unexplainable models are more accurate than explainable models
- Not faithful enough to the actual inner workings of complex models
- Often nonsensical

- Difficult to calibrate against external data
- Unnecessarily complicated

That's why in this chapter we advocate for the use of post hoc explanation with interpretable models, where the model and the explanations can act as process controls for one another. Even using explanations in this more risk-aware manner, there are still serious issues to address. This section will highlight the concerns we see the most in practice. We'll close this section by highlighting the advantages of using explainable models and post hoc explanations in combination. But as the transparency case will show, even if we get things mostly right on the technical side of transparency, human factors are still immensely important to the final success, or failure, of a high-stakes ML application.

Christoph Molnar has not only been prolific in teaching us how to use explanations; he and coauthors have also been quite busy researching their drawbacks. If readers would like to dig into details of issues with common explanation approaches, we'd suggest both "General Pitfalls of Model-Agnostic Interpretation Methods for Machine Learning Models" (*https://oreil.ly/DeZ0J*) and the earlier *Limitations of Interpretable Machine Learning Methods* (*https://oreil.ly/HYgJ6*). Next we'll outline the issues we see the most in practice—confirmation bias, context, correlation and local dependence, hacks, human interpretation, inconsistency, and explanation fidelity:

Confirmation bias
> For most of this chapter, we've discussed increased transparency as a good thing. While it certainly is, increased human understanding of ML models, and the ability to intervene in the functioning of those models, does open cracks for confirmation bias to sneak into our ML workflow. For example, let's say we're convinced a certain interaction should be represented in a model based on past experience in similar projects. However, that interaction just isn't appearing in our explainable model or post hoc explanation results. It's extremely hard to know if our training data is biased, and missing the known important interaction, or if we're biased. If we intervene in the mechanisms of our model to somehow inject this interaction, we could simply be succumbing to our own confirmation bias.

> Of course, a total lack of transparency also allows confirmation bias to run wild, as we can spin a model's behavior in whatever way we like. The only real way to avoid confirmation bias is to stick to the scientific method and battle-tested scientific principles like transparency, verification, and reproducibility.

Context
> "Do not explain without context" (*https://oreil.ly/A-GxX*), say Dr. Przemysław Biecek and team. In practice, this means using logical and realistic background data to generate explanations, and making sure background data cannot be

manipulated by adversaries. Even with solid background data for explanations, we still need to ensure our underlying ML models are operating in a logical context as well. For us, this means a reasonable number of uncorrelated input features, all with direct relationships to the modeling target.

Correlation and dependencies

While correlation may not prevent ML algorithms from training and generating accurate in silico predictions in many cases, it does make explanation and interpretation very difficult. In large datasets, there are typically many correlated features. Correlation violates the principle of independence, meaning we can't realistically interpret features on their own. When we attempt to remove a feature, as many explanation techniques do, another correlated feature will swoop in and take its place in the model, nullifying the effect of the attempted removal and the removal's intended meaning as an explanation tool. We also rely on perturbing features in explanations, but if features are correlated, it makes very little sense to perturb just one of them to derive an explanation. Worse, when dealing with ML models, they can learn local dependencies, meaning different correlation-like relationships, on a row-by-row basis. It's almost impossible to think through the complexities of how correlation corrupts explanations, much less how complex local dependencies might do the same.

Hacks

Explanation techniques that use background data can be altered by adversaries. These include LIME and SHAP, as explored in "Fooling LIME and SHAP: Adversarial Attacks on Post hoc Explanation Methods" (*https://oreil.ly/ljDkp*), and partial dependence, as described in "Fooling Partial Dependence via Data Poisoning" (*https://oreil.ly/MJUz7*). While these hacks are likely an exotic concern for now, we don't want to be part of the first major hack on ML explanations. Make sure that the code used to generate background data is kept secure and that background data cannot be unduly manipulated during explanation calculations. Data poisoning, whether against training data or background data, is easy for inside attackers. Even if background data is safe, explanations can still be misinterpreted in malicious ways. In what's known as *fairwashing* (*https://oreil.ly/RBwSb*), explanations for a sociologically biased ML model are made to look fair, abusing explanations to launder bias while still exposing model users to real harm.

Human interpretation

ML is difficult to understand, sometimes even for experienced practitioners and researchers. Yet, the audience for ML explanations is much broader than just industry experts. High-risk applications of ML often involve important decisions for other human beings. Even if those other human beings are highly educated, we cannot expect them to understand a partial dependence and ICE plot or an array of SHAP values. To get transparency right for high-stakes situations, we'll need to work with psychologists, domain experts, designers, user interaction experts, and others. It will take extra time and product iterations, with extensive communications between technicians, domain experts, and users. Not doing this extra work can result in abject failure, even if technical transparency goals are met, as "Case Study: Graded by Algorithm" on page 77 discusses.

Inconsistency

Consistency refers to stable explanations across different models or data samples. Consistency is difficult to achieve and very important for high-stakes ML applications. In situations like credit or pretrial release decisions, people might be subject to multiple automated decisions and associated explanations, and especially so in a more automated future. If the explanations provide different reasons for the same outcome decision, this will complicate already difficult situations. To increase consistency, explanations need to key into real, generalizable phenomena in training data and in the application domain. To achieve consistency, we need to train our models on a reasonable number of independent features. The models themselves also need to be parsimonious, that is, constrained to obey real-world relationships. Conversely, consistent explanations are impossible for complex, underspecified, uninterpretable models with numerous and correlated inputs.

Measuring explanation quality

Imagine training a model, eyeballing the results, and then assuming it's working properly and deploying it. That's likely a bad idea. But that's how we all work with post hoc explanations. Given all the technical concerns raised in previous sections, we obviously need to test explanations and see how they work for a given data source and application, just like we do with any other ML technique. Like our efforts to measure model quality before we deploy, we should be making efforts to measure explanation quality too. There are published proposals for such measurements and commonsense testing techniques we can apply. "Towards Robust Interpretability with Self-Explaining Neural Networks" (*https://oreil.ly/t4322*) puts forward explicitness, i.e., whether explanations are immediately understandable; faithfulness, i.e., whether explanations are true to known important factors; and stability, i.e., whether explanations are consistent with neighboring data points. "On the (In)fidelity and Sensitivity of Explanations" (*https://oreil.ly/kSiSS*) introduces related eponymous tests. Beyond these proposals for formal measurement, we can check that explainable model mechanisms and post hoc explanations confirm one another if we use both explainable models and explanations. If older trustworthy explanations are available, we can use those as benchmarks against which to test new explanations for fidelity. Also, stability tests, in which the data or model is perturbed in small ways, should generally not lead to major changes in post hoc explanations.

Test explanations before deploying them in high-risk use cases. While the lack of ground truth for explanations is a difficult barrier, explanations should be compared to interpretable model mechanisms. Comparisons to benchmark explanations, explicitness and fidelity measures, perturbation, comparison to nearest neighbors, and simulated data can also be used to test explanation quality.

There's no denying the appeal of explaining any model, no matter how complex, simply by applying some postprocessing. But given all the technical and worldly problems we've just been over, hopefully we've convinced readers that traditional ML model explanation is kind of a pipe dream. Explaining the unexplainable might not be impossible, but it's technically difficult today, and once we consider all the human factors required to achieve real-world transparency, it becomes even more difficult.

Pairing Explainable Models and Post Hoc Explanation

As we end the chapter's more technical discussions, we'd like to highlight new research that helps elucidate why explaining traditional ML models is so difficult and leave readers with an example of combining explainable models and post hoc explanations. Two recent papers relate the inherent complexity of traditional ML models to transparency difficulties. First, "Assessing the Local Interpretability of Machine Learning Models" (*https://oreil.ly/FQQd_*) proxies complexity with the number of runtime operations associated with an ML model decision, and shows that as the number of operations increases, interpretability decreases. Second, "Quantifying Model Complexity via Functional Decomposition for Better Post-Hoc Interpretability" (*https://oreil.ly/DWTRF*) uses number of features, interaction strength, and main effect complexity to measure the overall complexity of ML models, and shows that models that minimize these criteria are more reliably interpretable. In summary, complex models are hard to explain and simpler models are easier to explain, but certainly not easy. Figure 2-7 provides an example of augmenting a simple model with explanations, and why even that is difficult.

Figure 2-7 contains a trained three-level decision tree with a highlighted decision path, and the Tree SHAP values for a single row of data that follows that decision path. While Figure 2-7 looks simple, it's actually illustrative of several fundamental problems in ML and ML explanation. Before we dive into the difficulties presented by Figure 2-7, let's bask in the glory of a predictive model with its entire global decision-making mechanism on view, and for which we can generate numeric contributions of the input features to any model prediction. That level of transparency used to be reserved for linear models, but all the new approaches we've covered in this chapter make this level of transparency a reality for a much broader class of higher-capacity models. This means that if we're careful we can train more sophisticated models, that learn more from data, and still be able to interpret and learn from the results ourselves. We can learn more from data, do so reliably, and learn more as humans from the results. That's a huge breakthrough.

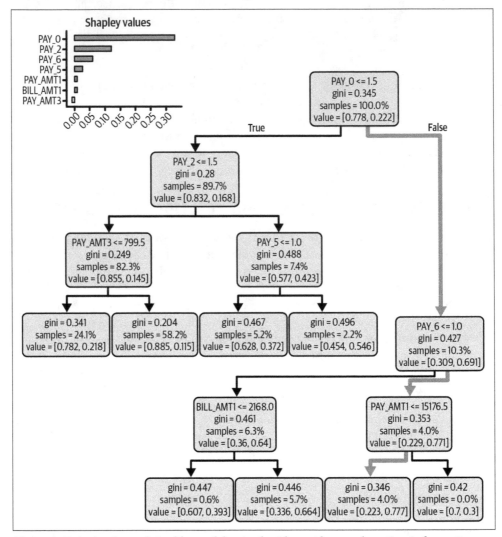

Figure 2-7. A simple explainable model paired with post hoc explanation information

 Use explainable models and post hoc explanations together to check one another and to maximize the transparency of ML models.

Now let's dig into the difficulties in Figure 2-7 while keeping in mind that these problems always exist when using ML models and post hoc XAI. (We can just see them and think through them in this simple case.) Notice that the decision path for the selected individual considers PAY_0, PAY_6, and PAY_AMT1. Now look at the Tree SHAP values. They give higher weight to PAY_2 than PAY_6, and weigh PAY_5 over PAY_AMT1, but PAY_2 and PAY_5 are not on the decision path. This occurs because the SHAP calculation takes into account artificial observations with different values for PAY_0, PAY_AMT1, and PAY_6, and those observations go down different decision paths. We'd see this behavior whether or not we used tree_path_dependent or interventional feature perturbations.

This phenomenon is unintuitive, but it is correct and not the result of approximation error. We could have used a different package or approach and probably generated local explanations that were true to the single decision path highlighted in Figure 2-7, but then we wouldn't have the deep theoretical support that accompanies Shapley values and SHAP. At least with SHAP, we know why our explanations show this effect. In general, explaining ML models is very hard, and for many different reasons. Always test explanations before deploying them in high-risk contexts, and make sure you understand the post hoc techniques you're applying.

Chapter 6 will go more into the details of how SHAP uses background data and calculates feature attributions based on different settings. We all need to understand these subtleties before using feature attribution methods like SHAP for high-risk applications. There's so much to think about on just the technical side of explanations. The following case will dig into some of the human factors of explanations, which might be even more difficult to get right.

Case Study: Graded by Algorithm

Adding transparency into ML models is no easy task. Even if we get the technical aspects of explainable models and post hoc explanations right, there are still many human factors that must be handled carefully. The so-called *A-level scandal* (*https:// oreil.ly/s54hO*) in the UK is an object lesson in failing to understand human factors for high-risk ML-based decisions. As COVID lockdowns took hold across the United Kingdom in the spring of 2020, students, teachers, and government officials realized that standardized tests could not take place as usual. As a first attempt to remedy the problems with national standardized testing, teachers were asked to estimate student performance on the important A-level exams that determine college entrance and affect other important life outcomes. Unfortunately, teacher estimates were seen as implausibly positive, to the level that using the estimated student performance would be unfair to past and future students.

To address teachers' positive biases, the government Office of Qualifications and Examinations Regulation (Ofqual) decided to implement an algorithm to adjust teacher predictions. The statistical methodology of the adjustment algorithm was implemented by experts and a model document (*https://oreil.ly/0gM6i*) was released after students received their grades. The algorithm was designed to generate a final distribution of grades that was similar to results in previous years. It preserved teacher rankings, but used past school performance to adjust grades downward. Students in Scotland were first to see the results. In that part of the UK, "35.6 percent of grades were adjusted down by a single grade, while 3.3 percent went down by two grades, and 0.2 went down by three," according to ZDNet (*https://oreil.ly/h47XJ*).

Over the next few months, student outcry over likely bias against poorer schools and regions of the country caused a massive, slow-burning AI incident. Even though officials had seen the problems in Scotland, they applied the same process in England, but instated a free appeals process and the right for students to retest at a later date. In the end, irreparable damage to public trust could not be undone, and the transparent but biased notion of adjusting individual scores by past school performance was too much for many to stomach. In the end, the UK government decided to use the original teacher estimates. According to Wired (*https://oreil.ly/DoV4O*), "the government has essentially passed the administrative buck to universities, who will now have to consider honouring thousands more offers—they have said that despite u-turn, it will not be possible to honour all original offers." The same article also pointed out that teacher estimates of student performance had shown racial bias in the past. What a mess.

Shockingly, other institutions have also adopted the idea of algorithmic scores for life-changing college entrance exams. The International Baccalaureate (IB) is an elite educational program that offers an advanced uniform curriculum for secondary school students all over the world. In the Spring of 2020, the IB used an algorithm for student scores that was reported to be (*https://oreil.ly/OT05d*) "hastily deployed after canceling its usual springtime exams due to COVID-19. The system used signals including a student's grades on assignments and grades from past grads at their school." Because of the timing, unanticipated negative scores were extremely hurtful to students applying to US colleges and universities, who reserve spaces for IB students based on past performance, but can cancel based on final performances, "shattering their plans for the fall and beyond." Some students' algorithmic scores were so low that they may have lost placement in prestigious universities in the US and their safety schools in their home country. What's worse, and unlike the Ofqual algorithm, the IB was not forthcoming with how their algorithm worked, and appeals came with an almost $800 price tag.

Putting aside the IB's lack of transparency, there seem to be three major issues at play in these incidents. Scale is an inherent risk of ML, and these algorithms were used on many students across the globe. Large scale translates to high materiality, and transparency alone is not enough to offset issues of trust and bias. Understanding is not trust. Ofqual's technical report and other public analyses (*https://oreil.ly/QAB8R*) were over the heads of many students and parents. But what was not over their heads is that poorer areas have worse public schools, and that affected students twice in 2020—once in an overall manner like every year, and then again when their scores were adjusted downward. The second factor was the seriousness of the decision. College admittance plays a huge role in the rest of many people's lives. The serious nature of the decision cranks up the materiality to an even higher degree—possibly to an impossible degree, where failure becomes guaranteed. ML is inherently probabilistic. It will be wrong. And when the stakes are this high, the public just might not accept it.

The third major issue at play here is the clear nature of disparate impact. For example, very small classes were not scored with the algorithm. Where are there the most very small classes? Private schools. A Verge article (*https://oreil.ly/eySQu*) claims that "fee-paying private schools (also known as *independent schools*) disproportionately benefited from the algorithm used. These schools saw the amount of grades A and above increase by 4.7 percent compared to last year." ZDNet (*https://oreil.ly/7mnEd*) reported that the "pass rate for students undertaking higher courses in deprived locations across Scotland was reduced by 15.2%, in comparison to 6.9% in more affluent areas." Adjusting by postal code or past school performance bakes in systemic biases, and students and parents understood this at an emotional level. As quoted in the BBC (*https://oreil.ly/vPQq1*), Scotland's Education Secretary realized in the end that the debacle left "young people feeling their future had been determined by statistical modeling rather than their own ability." We should think about how we would feel if this incident had affected us or our children. Despite all the hype around automated decision making, almost no one wants to feel that their future is set by an algorithm.

Although this may have been a doomed, impossibly high-materiality application of ML from the beginning, more could have been done to increase public trust. For example, Ofqual could have published the algorithm before applying it to students. They also could have taken public feedback on the algorithm before using it. Jeni Tennison, a UK-based open data advocate, notes (*https://oreil.ly/4Unct*), "Part of the problem here is that these issues came out only after the grades were given to students, when we could have been having these discussions and been examining the algorithm and understanding the implications of it much, much earlier." The take-home lessons here are that technical transparency is not the same as broad social understanding, and that understanding, if it can even be achieved, does not guarantee trust. Even if we've done a good job on technical transparency, as put forward in this chapter, there is still a great deal of work that must be done to ensure an ML system works as expected for users, or subjects. Finally, this is just one AI incident, and although it's a big one, it shouldn't cause us to overlook the smaller ones that are harming people right now, and we have to keep in mind that even more people will be harmed by AI systems in the future. As Tennison put it, "This has hit the headlines, because it affects so many people across the country, and it affects people who have a voice. There's other automated decision making that goes on all the time, around benefits, for example, that affect lots of people who don't have this strong voice."

Resources

Further Reading

- *An Introduction to Machine Learning Interpretability* (O'Reilly) (*https://oreil.ly/iyz08*)
- "Designing Inherently Interpretable Machine Learning Models" (*https://oreil.ly/jbGNt*)
- *Explanatory Model Analysis* (CRC Press) (*https://oreil.ly/Yt_Xm*)
- "General Pitfalls of Model-Agnostic Interpretation Methods for Machine Learning Models" (*https://oreil.ly/On9uS*)
- *Interpretable Machine Learning* (*https://oreil.ly/BHy1L*)
- *Limitations of Interpretable Machine Learning Methods* (*https://oreil.ly/VHMWh*)
- "On the Art and Science of Explainable Machine Learning" (*https://oreil.ly/myVr8*)
- "Psychological Foundations of Explainability and Interpretability in Artificial Intelligence" (*https://oreil.ly/HUomp*)
- "When Not to Trust Your Explanations" (*https://oreil.ly/9Oxa6*)

## CHAPTER 3

Debugging Machine Learning Systems for Safety and Performance

For decades, error or accuracy on holdout test data has been the standard by which machine learning models are judged. Unfortunately, as ML models are embedded into AI systems that are deployed more broadly and for more sensitive applications, the standard approaches for ML model assessment have proven to be inadequate. For instance, the overall test data area under the curve (AUC) tells us almost nothing about bias and algorithmic discrimination, lack of transparency, privacy harms, or security vulnerabilities. Yet, these problems are often why AI systems fail once deployed. For acceptable in vivo performance, we simply must push beyond traditional in silico assessments designed primarily for research prototypes. Moreover, the best results for safety and performance occur when organizations are able to mix and match the appropriate cultural competencies and process controls described in Chapter 1 with ML technology that promotes trust. This chapter presents sections on training, debugging, and deploying ML systems that delve into the numerous technical approaches for testing and improving in vivo safety, performance, and trust in AI. Note that Chapters 8 and 9 present detailed code examples for model debugging.

NIST AI RMF Crosswalk

Chapter section	NIST AI RMF subcategories
"Reproducibility" on page 83	GOVERN 1.2, GOVERN 1.4, MAP 2.3, MEASURE 1, MEASURE 2.1, MEASURE 2.3
"Data Quality" on page 85	GOVERN 1.2, MAP 2.3, MAP 4, MEASURE 1.1, MEASURE 2.1
"Benchmarks and alternatives" on page 88	GOVERN 1.1, GOVERN 1.2, GOVERN 1.4, MAP 2.3, MEASURE 2.13, MANAGE 2.1

Chapter section	NIST AI RMF subcategories
"Calibration" on page 89	GOVERN 1.2, GOVERN 1.4, MAP 2.3, MEASURE 1, MEASURE 2.1, MEASURE 2.3
"Construct validity" on page 89	GOVERN 1.1, MAP 2.1, MAP 2.3, MAP 3.3
"Assumptions and limitations" on page 90	GOVERN 1.2, GOVERN 1.4, GOVERN 6.1, MAP 2
"Default loss functions" on page 91	MAP 2.3, MEASURE 1, MEASURE 2.1, MEASURE 2.3
"Multiple comparisons" on page 91	MAP 2.3, MEASURE 1, MEASURE 2.1, MEASURE 2.3
"The future of safe and robust machine learning" on page 91	MAP 2.3, MEASURE 2.6
"Software Testing" on page 92	GOVERN 1.1, GOVERN 1.2, GOVERN 4.3, GOVERN 6.1, MAP 2.3, MAP 4, MEASURE 1.3
"Traditional Model Assessment" on page 93	GOVERN 1.1, GOVERN 1.2, GOVERN 1.4, MAP 2.3, MAP 4, MEASURE 1, MEASURE 2.1, MEASURE 2.3
"Distribution shifts" on page 95	GOVERN 1.2, GOVERN 1.5, MAP 2.3, MEASURE 1, MEASURE 2.1, MEASURE 2.3, MEASURE 2.4, MANAGE 2.2, MANAGE 2.3, MANAGE 2.4, MANAGE 3, MANAGE 4.1
"Epistemic uncertainty and data sparsity" on page 96	MAP 2.3, MEASURE 1, MEASURE 2.1, MEASURE 2.3
"Instability" on page 97	MAP 2.3, MEASURE 1, MEASURE 2.1, MEASURE 2.3, MEASURE 2.4, MANAGE 2.2, MANAGE 2.3, MANAGE 2.4, MANAGE 3, MANAGE 4.1
"Leakage" on page 98	MAP 2.3, MEASURE 1, MEASURE 2.1, MEASURE 2.3
"Looped inputs" on page 99	MAP 2.3, MEASURE 1, MEASURE 2.1, MEASURE 2.3
"Overfitting" on page 99	MAP 2.3, MEASURE 1, MEASURE 2.1, MEASURE 2.3
"Shortcut learning" on page 100	MAP 2.3, MEASURE 1, MEASURE 2.1, MEASURE 2.3
"Underfitting" on page 100	MAP 2.3, MEASURE 1, MEASURE 2.1, MEASURE 2.3
"Underspecification" on page 101	MAP 2.3, MEASURE 1, MEASURE 2.1, MEASURE 2.3
"Residual Analysis" on page 103	GOVERN 1.2, MAP 2.3, MAP 3.2, MAP 5.1, MEASURE 1, MEASURE 2.1, MEASURE 2.3
"Sensitivity Analysis" on page 107	GOVERN 1.2, MAP 2.3, MAP 3.2, MAP 5.1, MEASURE 1, MEASURE 2.1, MEASURE 2.3
"Benchmark Models" on page 110	GOVERN 1.1, GOVERN 1.2, GOVERN 1.4, MAP 2.3, MEASURE 2.13, MANAGE 2.1
"Remediation: Fixing Bugs" on page 112	GOVERN, MAP, MANAGE
"Domain Safety" on page 114	GOVERN 1.2, GOVERN 1.7, GOVERN 3, GOVERN 4.1, GOVERN 4.3, GOVERN 5, MAP 1.2, MAP 1.6, MAP 2.3, MAP 3.1, MAP 5, MEASURE 1, MEASURE 2.5, MEASURE 2.6, MEASURE 3, MEASURE 4, MANAGE 1, MANAGE 4.3
"Model Monitoring" on page 116	GOVERN 1.2, GOVERN 1.3, GOVERN 1.4, GOVERN 1.5, MAP 2.3, MAP 3.5, MAP 4, MAP 5.2, MEASURE 1.1, MEASURE 2.4, MEASURE 2.6, MEASURE 2.7, MEASURE 2.8, MEASURE 2.10, MEASURE 2.11, MEASURE 2.12, MEASURE 3.1, MEASURE 3.3, MEASURE 4, MANAGE 2.2, MANAGE 2.3, MANAGE 2.4, MANAGE 3, MANAGE 4

- Applicable AI trustworthiness characteristics include: Safe, Secure and Resilient, Valid and Reliable
- See also:
  — Full crosswalk table (not an official resource) (*https://oreil.ly/61TXd*)

Training

The discussion of training ML algorithms begins with reproducibility, because without that, it's impossible to know if any one version of an ML system is really any better than another. Data and feature engineering will be addressed briefly, and the training section closes by outlining key points for model specification.

Reproducibility

Without reproducibility, we're building on sand. Reproducibility is fundamental to all scientific efforts, including AI. Without reproducible results, it's very hard to know if day-to-day efforts are improving, or even changing, an ML system. Reproducibility helps ensure proper implementation and testing, and some customers may simply demand it. The following techniques are some of the most common that data scientists and ML engineers use to establish a solid, reproducible foundation for their ML systems:

Benchmark models
> Benchmark models are important safety and performance tools for training, debugging, and deploying ML systems. They'll be addressed several times in this chapter. In the context of model training and reproducibility, we should always build from a reproducible benchmark model. This allows for a checkpoint for rollbacks if reproducibility is lost, but it also enables real progress. If yesterday's benchmark is reproducible, and today's gains above and beyond that benchmark are also reproducible, that's real and measurable progress. If system performance metrics bounce around before changes are made, and they're still bouncing around after changes are made, we have no idea if our changes helped or hurt.

Hardware
> As ML systems often leverage hardware acceleration via graphical processing units (GPUs) and other specialized system components, hardware is still of special interest for preserving reproducibility. If possible, try to keep hardware as similar as possible across development, testing, and deployment systems.

Environments
> ML systems always operate in some computational environment, specified by the system hardware, system software, and our data and ML software stack. Changes in any of these can affect the reproducibility of ML outcomes. Thankfully,

tools like Python virtual environments and Docker containers that preserve software environments have become commonplace in the practice of data science. Additional specialized environment management software from Domino (*https://oreil.ly/USwuG*), gigantum (*https://oreil.ly/1cE7-*), TensorFlow TFX (*https://oreil.ly/kHKvx*), and Kubeflow (*https://oreil.ly/F9ZaL*) can provide even more expansive control of computational environments.

Metadata

Data about data is essential for reproducibility. Track all artifacts associated with the model, e.g., datasets, preprocessing steps, data and model validation results, human sign-offs, and deployment details. Not only does this allow for rolling back to a specific version of a dataset or model, but it also allows for detailed debugging and forensic investigations of AI incidents. For an open source example of a nice tool for tracking metadata, check out TensorFlow ML Metadata (*https://oreil.ly/gmHkg*).

Random seeds

Set by data scientists and engineers in specific code blocks, random seeds are the plow horse of ML reproducibility. Unfortunately, they often come with language- or package-specific instructions. Seeds can take some time to learn in different software, but when combined with careful testing, random seeds enable the building blocks of intricate and complex ML systems to retain reproducibility. This is a prerequisite for overall reproducibility.

Version control

Minor code changes can lead to drastic changes in ML results. Changes to our own code plus its dependencies must be tracked in a professional version control tool for any hope of reproducibility. Git and GitHub are free and ubiquitous resources for software version control, but there are plenty of other options to explore. Crucially, data can also be version-controlled with tools like Pachyderm (*https://oreil.ly/DvMCo*) and DVC (*https://oreil.ly/S59Qv*), enabling traceability in changes to data resources.

Though it may take some experimentation, some combination of these approaches and technologies should work to assure a level of reproducibility in our ML systems. Once this fundamental safety and performance control is in place, it's time to consider other baseline factors like data quality and feature engineering.

Several topics like benchmarks, anomaly detection, and monitoring are ubiquitous in model debugging and ML safety, and they appear in several different sections and contexts in this chapter.

Data Quality

Entire books have been written about data quality and feature engineering for ML and ML systems. This short subsection highlights some of the most critical aspects of this vast practice area from a safety and performance perspective. First and foremost, biases, confounding features, incompleteness, and noise in development data form important assumptions and define limitations of our models. Other basics, like the size and shape of a dataset, are important considerations. ML algorithms are hungry for data. Both small data and wide, sparse data can lead to catastrophic performance failures in the real world, because both give rise to scenarios in which system performance appears normal on test data, but is simply untethered to real-world phenomena. Small data can make it hard to detect underfitting, underspecification, overfitting, or other fundamental performance problems. Sparse data can lead to overconfident predictions for certain input values. If an ML algorithm did not see certain data ranges during training due to sparsity issues, most ML algorithms will issue predictions in those ranges with no warning that the prediction is based on almost nothing. Fast-forwarding to our chapter case discussion, there is simply not enough training video in the world to fill out the entire space of example situations that self-driving cars need to learn to safely navigate. For example, people crossing the road at night on a bicycle is a danger most humans will recognize, but without many frames of labeled video of this somewhat rare event, a deep learning system's ability to handle this situation will likely be compromised due to sparsity in training data.

A number of other data problems can cause safety worries, such as poor data quality leading to entanglement or misrepresentation of important information and overfitting, or ML data and model pipeline problems. In the context of this chapter, *entanglement* means features, entities, or phenomena in training data proxying for other information with more direct relationships to the target (e.g., snow proxying for a Husky in object recognition). Overfitting refers to the memorization of noise in training data and the resulting optimistic error estimates, and pipeline issues are problems that arise from combining different stages of data preparation and modeling components into one prediction-generating executable. Table 3-1 can be applied to most standard ML data to help identify common data quality problems with safety and performance implications.

Table 3-1. Common data quality problems, with symptoms and proposed solutions. Adapted from the George Washington University DNSC 6314 (Machine Learning I) class notes with permission.

Problem	Common symptoms	Possible solutions
Biased data: When a dataset contains information about the phenomenon of interest, but that information is consistently and systematically wrong. (See Chapter 4 for more information.)	Biased models and biased, dangerous, or inaccurate results. Perpetuation of past social biases and discrimination.	Consult with domain experts and stakeholders. Apply the scientific method and design of experiment (DOE) (*https://oreil.ly/0kDC9*) approaches. (Get more data. Get better data.)
Character data: When certain columns, features, or instances are represented with strings of characters instead of numeric values.	Information loss. Biased models and biased, dangerous, or inaccurate results. Long, intolerable training times.	Various numeric encoding approaches (e.g., label encoding, target or feature encoding). Appropriate algorithm selection, e.g., tree-based models, naive Bayes classification.
Data leakage: When information from validation or test partitions leaks into training data.	Unreliable or dangerous out-of-domain predictions. Overfit models and inaccurate results. Overly optimistic in silico performance estimates.	Data governance. Ensuring all dates in training are earlier than in validation and test. Ensuring identical identifiers do not occur across partitions. Careful application of feature engineering—engineer after partitioning, not before.
Dirty data: A combination of all the issues in this table, very common in real-world datasets.	Information loss. Biased models and biased, inaccurate results. Long, intolerable training times. Unstable and unreliable parameter estimates and rule generation. Unreliable or dangerous out-of-domain predictions.	Combination of solution strategies herein.
Disparate feature scales: When features, such as age and income, are recorded on different scales.	Unreliable parameter estimates, biased models, and biased, inaccurate results.	Standardization. Appropriate algorithm selection, e.g., tree-based models.
Duplicate data: Rows, instances, or entities that occur more than intended.	Biased results due to unintentional overweighting of identical entities during training. Biased models, and biased, inaccurate results.	Careful data cleaning in consultation with domain experts.
Entanglement: When features, entities, or phenomena in training data proxy for other information with more direct relationships to the target (e.g., snow proxying for a Husky in object recognition).	Unreliable or dangerous out-of-domain predictions. Shortcut learning.	Apply the scientific method and DOE approaches. Apply interpretable models and post hoc explanation. In-domain testing.
Fake or poisoned data: Data, features, attributes, phenomena, or entities that are injected into or manipulated in training data to elicit artificial model outcomes.	Unreliable or dangerous out-of-domain predictions. Biased models and biased, inaccurate results.	Data governance. Data security. Application of robust ML approaches.
High cardinality categorical features: Features such as postal codes or product identifiers that represent many categorical levels of the same attribute.	Overfit models and inaccurate results. Long, intolerable compute times. Unreliable or dangerous out-of-domain predictions.	Target or feature encoding variants, average-by-level (or similar, e.g., median, BLUP). Discretization. Embedding approaches, e.g., entity embedding neural networks, factorization machines.

Problem	Common symptoms	Possible solutions
Imbalanced target: When one target class or value is much more common than others.	Single class model predictions. Biased model predictions.	Proportional over- or undersampling. Inverse prior probability weighting. Mixture models, e.g., zero-inflated regression methods. Post hoc adjustment of predictions or decision thresholds.
Incomplete data: When a dataset does not encode information about the phenomenon of interest. When uncollected information confounds model results.	Useless models, meaningless or dangerous results.	Consult with domain experts and stakeholders. Apply the scientific method and DOE approaches. (Get more data. Get better data.)
Missing values: When specific rows or instances are missing information.	Information loss. Biased models and biased, inaccurate results.	Imputation. Discretization (i.e., binning). Appropriate algorithm selection, e.g., tree-based models, naive Bayes classification.
Noise: Data that fails to encode clear signals for modeling. Data with the same input values and different target values.	Unreliable or dangerous out-of-domain predictions. Poor performance during training.	Consult with domain experts and stakeholders. Apply the scientific method and DOE approaches. (Get more data. Get better data.)
Nonnormalized data: Data in which values for the same entity are represented in different ways.	Unreliable out-of-domain predictions. Long, intolerable training times. Unreliable parameter estimates and rule generation.	Careful data cleaning in consultation with domain experts.
Outliers: Rows or instances of data that are strange or unlike others.	Biased models and biased, inaccurate results. Unreliable parameter estimates and rule generation. Unreliable out-of-domain predictions.	Discretization (i.e., binning). Winsorizing. Robust loss functions, e.g., Huber loss functions.
Sparse data: Data with many zeros or missing values; data that does not encode enough information about the phenomenon of interest.	Long, intolerable training times. Meaningless or dangerous results due to lack of information, curse of dimensionality, or model misspecification.	Feature extraction or matrix factorization approaches. Appropriate data representation (i.e., COO, CSR). Application of business rules, model assertions, and constraints to make up for illogical model behavior learned in sparse regions of training data.
Strong multicollinearity (correlation): When features have strong linear dependencies on one another.	Unstable parameter estimates, unstable rule generation, and dangerous or unstable predictions.	Feature selection. Feature extraction. L2 regularization.
Unrecognized time and date formats: Time and date formats, of which there are many, that are encoded improperly by data handling or modeling software.	Unreliable or dangerous out-of-domain predictions. Unreliable parameter estimates and rule generation. Overfit models and inaccurate results. Overly optimistic in silico performance estimates.	Careful data cleaning in consultation with domain experts.
Wide data: Data with many more columns, features, pixels, or tokens than rows, instances, images, or documents. $P \gg N$.	Long, intolerable training times. Meaningless or dangerous results due to the curse of dimensionality or model misspecification.	Feature selection, feature extraction, L1 regularization, models that do not assume $N \gg P$.

There is a lot that can go wrong with data that then leads to unreliable or dangerous model performance in high-risk applications. It might be tempting to think we can feature engineer our way out of data quality problems. But feature engineering is only as good as the thought and code used to perform it. If we're not extremely careful with feature engineering, we're likely just creating more bugs and complexity for ourselves. Common issues with feature engineering in ML pipelines include the following:

- API or version mismatches between data cleaning, preprocessing, and inference packages
- Failing to apply all data cleaning and transformation steps during inference
- Failing to readjust for oversampling or undersampling during inference
- Inability to handle values unseen during training gracefully or safely during inference

Of course, many other problems can arise in data preparation, feature engineering, and associated pipelines, especially as the types of data that ML algorithms can accept for training becomes more varied. Tools that detect and address such problems are also an important part of the data science toolkit. For Python Pandas users, the ydata-profiling tool (*https://oreil.ly/EDNSC*) (formerly pandas-profiler) is a visual aid that helps to detect many basic data quality problems. R users also have options, as discussed by Mateusz Staniak and Przemysław Biecek in "The Landscape of R Packages for Automated Exploratory Data Analysis" (*https://oreil.ly/1cBlv*).

Model Specification for Real-World Outcomes

Once our data preparation and feature engineering pipeline is hardened, it's time to think about ML model specification. Considerations for real-world performance and safety are quite different from those about getting published or maximizing performance on ML contest leaderboards. While measurement of validation and test error remain important, bigger questions of accurately representing data and commonsense real-world phenomena have the highest priority. This subsection addresses model specification for safety and performance by highlighting the importance of benchmarks and alternative models, calibration, construct validity, assumptions and limitations, proper loss functions, and avoiding multiple comparisons, and by previewing the emergent disciplines of robust ML and ML safety and reliability.

Benchmarks and alternatives

When starting an ML modeling task, it's best to begin with a peer-reviewed training algorithm, and ideally to replicate any benchmarks associated with that algorithm. While academic algorithms rarely meet all the needs of complex business problems, starting from a well-known algorithm and benchmarks provides a baseline assurance that the training algorithm is implemented correctly. Once this check is addressed, then think about tweaking a complex algorithm to address specific quirks of a given problem.

Along with comparison to benchmarks, evaluation of numerous alternative algorithmic approaches is another best practice that can improve safety and performance outcomes. The exercise of training many different algorithms and judiciously selecting the best of many options for final deployment typically results in higher-quality models because it increases the number of models evaluated and forces users to understand differences between them. Moreover, evaluation of alternative approaches is important in complying with a broad set of US nondiscrimination and negligence standards. In general, these standards require evidence that different technical options were evaluated and an appropriate trade-off between consumer protection and business needs was made before deployment.

Calibration

Just because a number between 0 and 1 pops out the end of a complex ML pipeline does not make it a probability. The uncalibrated probabilities generated by most ML classifiers usually have to be postprocessed to have any real meaning as probabilities. We typically use a scaling process, or even another model, to ensure that when a pipeline outputs 0.5, the event in question actually happened to about 50% of similar entities in past recorded data. scikit-learn (*https://oreil.ly/LxJbX*) provides some basic diagnostics and functions for ML classifier calibration. Calibration issues can affect regression models too, when the distribution of model outputs don't match the distribution of known outcomes. For instance, many numeric quantities in insurance are not normally distributed. Using a default squared loss function, instead of loss functions from the gamma or Tweedie family, may result in predictions that are not distributed like values from the known underlying data-generating process. However we think of calibration, the fundamental issue is that affected ML model predictions don't match to reality. We'll never make good predictions and decisions like this. We need our probabilities to be aligned to past outcome rates and we need our regression models to generate predictions of the same distribution as the modeled data-generating process.

Construct validity

Construct validity is an idea from social science (from psychometrics and testing, in particular). Construct validity means that there is a reasonable scientific basis to believe that test performance is indicative of the intended construct. Put another way, is there any scientific evidence that the questions and scores from a standardized test can predict college or job performance? Why are we bringing this up in an ML book? Because ML models are often used for the same purposes as psychometric tests these days, and in our opinion, ML models often lack construct validity. Worse, ML algorithms that don't align with fundamental structures in training data or in their real-world domains can cause serious incidents.

Consider the choice between an ML model and a linear model, wherein many of us simply default to using an ML model. Selecting an ML algorithm for a modeling problem comes with a lot of basic assumptions—essentially that high-degree interactions and nonlinearity in input features are important drivers of the predicted phenomenon. Conversely, choosing to use a linear model implicitly downplays interactions and nonlinearities. If those qualities are important for good predictions, they'll have to be specified explicitly for the linear model. In either case, it's important to take stock of how main effects, correlations and local dependencies, interactions, nonlinearities, clusters, outliers, and hierarchies in training data, or in reality, will be handled by a modeling algorithm, and to test those mechanisms. For optimal safety and performance once deployed, dependencies on time, geographical locations, or connections between entities in various types of networks must also be represented within ML models. Without these clear links to reality, ML models lack construct validity and are unlikely to exhibit good in vivo performance. Feature engineering, constraints, loss functions, model architectures, and other mechanisms can all be used to match a model to its task.

Assumptions and limitations

Biases, entanglement, incompleteness, noise, ranges, sparsity, and other basic characteristics of training data begin to define the assumptions and limitations of our models. As discussed, modeling algorithms and architectures also carry assumptions and limitations. For example, tree-based models usually can't extrapolate beyond ranges in training data. Hyperparameters for ML algorithms are yet another place where hidden assumptions can cause safety and performance problems. Hyperparameters can be selected based on domain knowledge or via technical approaches like grid search and Bayesian optimization. The key is not to settle for defaults, to choose settings systematically, and not to trick ourselves due to multiple comparison issues. Testing for independence of errors between rows and features in training data or plotting model residuals and looking for strong patterns are general and time-tested methods for ensuring some basic assumptions have been addressed. It's unlikely we'll ever circumvent all the assumptions and limitations of our data and model. So we need to document any unaddressed or suspected assumptions and limitations in model documentation, and ensure users understand what uses of the model could violate its assumptions and limitations. Those would be considered out-of-scope or *off-label* uses—just like using a prescription drug in improper ways. By the way, construct validity is linked to model documentation and risk management frameworks focused on model limitations and assumptions. Oversight professionals want practitioners to work through the hypothesis behind their model in writing, and make sure it's underpinned by valid constructs and not assumptions.

Default loss functions

Another often unstated assumption that comes with many learning algorithms involves squared loss functions. Many ML algorithms use a squared loss function by default. In most instances, a squared loss function, being additive across observations and having a linear derivative, is more a matter of mathematical convenience than anything else. With modern tools such as autograd (*https://oreil.ly/8icjS*), this convenience is increasingly unnecessary. We should match our choice of loss function with our problem domain.

Multiple comparisons

Model selection in ML often means trying many different sets of input features, model hyperparameters, and other model settings such as probability cutoff thresholds. We often use stepwise feature selection, grid searches, or other methods that try many different settings on the same set of validation or holdout data. Statisticians might call this a *multiple comparisons* problem and would likely point out that the more comparisons we do, the likelier we are to stumble upon some settings that simply happen to look good in our validation or holdout set. This is a sneaky kind of overfitting where we reuse the same holdout data too many times, select features, hyperparameters, or other settings that work well there, and then experience poor in vivo performance later on. Hence, reusable holdout approaches (*https://oreil.ly/QJlUV*), which alter or resample validation or holdout data to make our feature, hyperparameter, or other settings more generalizable, are useful.

The future of safe and robust machine learning

The new field of robust ML (*https://oreil.ly/1G1Wp*) is churning out new algorithms with improved stability and security characteristics. Various researchers are creating new learning algorithms with guarantees for optimality, like optimal sparse decision trees (*https://oreil.ly/gOmtg*). And researchers have put together excellent tutorial materials (*https://oreil.ly/wC5M1*) on ML safety and reliability. Today, these approaches require custom implementations and extra work, but hopefully these safety and performance advances will be more widely available soon.

Model Debugging

Once a model has been properly specified and trained, the next step in the technical safety and performance assurance process is testing and debugging. In years past, such assessments focused on aggregate quality and error rates in holdout data. As ML models are incorporated in public-facing ML systems, and the number of publicly reported AI incidents is increasing dramatically, it's clear that more rigorous validation is required. The new field of model debugging (*https://oreil.ly/IY0gU*) is rising to meet this need. Model debugging treats ML models more like code and less like abstract mathematics. It applies a number of testing methods to find software flaws, logical errors, inaccuracies, and security vulnerabilities in ML models and ML system pipelines. Of course, these bugs must also be fixed when they are found. This section explores model debugging in some detail, starting with basic and traditional approaches, then outlines the common bugs we're trying to find, moves on to specialized testing techniques, and closes with a discussion of bug remediation methods.

 In addition to many explainable ML models, the open source package PiML (*https://oreil.ly/1O3hi*) contains an exhaustive set of debugging tools for ML models trained on structured data. Even if it's not an exact fit for a given use case, it's a great place to learn more and gain inspiration for model debugging.

Software Testing

Basic software testing becomes much more important when we stop thinking of pretty figures and impressive tables of results as the end goal of an ML model training task. When ML systems are deployed, they need to work correctly under various circumstances. Almost more than anything else related to ML systems, making software work is an exact science. Best practices for software testing are well-known and can even be made automatic in many cases. At a minimum, mission-critical ML systems should undergo the following:

Unit testing
  All functions, methods, subroutines, or other code blocks should have tests associated with them to ensure they behave as expected, accurately, and are reproducible. This ensures the building blocks of an ML system are solid.

Integration testing
  All APIs and interfaces between modules, tiers, or other subsystems should be tested to ensure proper communication. API mismatches after backend code changes are a classic failure mode for ML systems. Use integration testing to catch this and other integration fails.

Functional testing
  Functional testing should be applied to ML system user interfaces and endpoints to ensure that they behave as expected once deployed.

Chaos testing
  Testing under chaotic and adversarial conditions can lead to better outcomes when our ML systems face complex and surprising in vivo scenarios. Because it can be difficult to predict all the ways an ML system can fail, chaos testing can help probe a broader class of failure modes, and provide some cover against so-called "unknown unknowns."

Two additional ML-specific tests should be added into the mix to increase quality further:

Random attack

Random attacks are one way to do chaos testing in ML. Random attacks expose ML models to vast amounts of random data to catch both software and math problems. The real world is a chaotic place. Our ML system will encounter data for which it's not prepared. Random attacks can decrease those occurrences and any associated glitches or incidents.

Benchmarking

Use benchmarks to track system improvements over time. ML systems can be incredibly complex. How can we know if the three lines of code an engineer changes today will make a difference in the performance of the system as a whole? If system performance is reproducible, and benchmarked before and after changes, it's much easier to answer such questions.

ML is software. So, all the testing that's done on traditional enterprise software assets should be done on important ML systems as well. If we don't know where to start with model debugging, we start with random attacks. Readers may be shocked at the math or software bugs random data can expose in ML systems. When we can add benchmarks to our organization's continuous integration/continuous development (CI/CD) pipelines, that's the another big step toward assuring the safety and performance of ML systems.

 Random attacks are probably the easiest and most effective way to get started with model debugging. If debugging feels overwhelming, or you don't know where to start, start with random attacks.

Traditional Model Assessment

Once we feel confident that the code in our ML systems is functioning as expected, it's easier to concentrate on testing the math of our ML algorithms. Looking at standard performance metrics is important. But it's not the end of the validation and debugging process—it's the beginning. While exact values and decimal points matter, from a safety and performance standpoint, they matter much less than they do on the leaderboard of an ML contest. When considering in-domain performance, it's less about exact numeric values of assessment statistics, and more about mapping in silico performance to in vivo performance.

If possible, try to select assessment statistics that have a logical interpretation and practical or statistical thresholds. For instance, RMSE can be calculated for many types of prediction problems, and crucially, it can be interpreted in units of the target. Area under the curve, for classification tasks, is bounded between 0.5 at the low end and 1.0 at the high end. Such assessment measures allow for commonsense interpretation of ML model performance and for comparisons to widely accepted thresholds for determining quality. It's also important to use more than one metric and to analyze performance metrics across important segments in our data as well as across training, validation, and testing data partitions. When comparing performance across segments within training data, it's important that all those segments exhibit roughly equivalent and high-quality performance. Amazing performance on one large customer segment, and poor performance on everyone else, will look fine in average assessment statistic values like RMSE. However, it won't look fine if it leads to public brand damage due to many unhappy customers. Varying performance across segments can also be a sign of underspecification, a serious ML bug we'll dig into in this chapter. Performance across training, validation, and test datasets are usually analyzed for underfitting and overfitting too. Like model performance, we can look for overfitting and underfitting across entire data partitions or across segments.

Another practical consideration related to traditional model assessment is selecting a probability cutoff threshold. Most ML models for classification generate numeric probabilities, not discrete decisions. Selecting the numeric probability cutoff to associate with actual decisions can be done in various ways. While it's always tempting to maximize some sophisticated assessment measure, it's also a good idea to consider real-world impact. Let's consider a classic lending example. Say a probability of default model threshold is originally set at 0.15, meaning that everyone who scores less than a 0.15 probability of default is approved for a loan, and those that score at the threshold or over are denied. Think through questions such as the following:

- What is the expected monetary return for this threshold? What is the financial risk?
- How many people will get the loan at this threshold?
- How many women? How many minority group members?

Outside of the probability cutoff thresholds, it's always a good idea to estimate in-domain performance, because that's what we really care about. Assessment measures are nice, but what matters is making money versus losing money, or even saving lives versus taking lives. We can take a first crack at understanding real-world value by assigning monetary, or other, values to each cell of a confusion matrix for classification problems or to each residual unit for regression problems. Do a back-of-the-napkin calculation. Does it look like our model will make money or lose money? Once we get the gist of this kind of valuation, we can even incorporate value levels for different model outcomes directly into ML loss functions, and optimize toward the best-suited model for real-world deployment.

Error and accuracy metrics will always be important for ML. But once ML algorithms are used in deployed ML systems, numeric values and comparisons matter less than they do for publishing papers and data science competitions. So, keep using traditional assessment measures, but try to map them to in-domain safety and performance.

Common Machine Learning Bugs

We've discussed a lack of reproducibility, data quality problems, proper model specification, software bugs, and traditional assessment. But there's still a lot more that can go wrong with complex ML systems. When it comes to the math of ML, there are a few emergent gotchas and many well-known pitfalls. This subsection will discuss bugs, including distributional shifts, epistemic uncertainty, weak spots, instability, leakage, looped inputs, overfitting, shortcut learning, underfitting, and underspecification.

Vocabulary Relating to Reliability, Robustness, and Resilience

Under the NIST AI Risk Management Framework, *resilience* is a synonym for *security*, and *robustness* and *reliability* are used somewhat synonymously. Traditionally, and according to ISO/IEC TS 5723:2022 (*https://oreil.ly/U6T_b*), reliability is related to the "ability of an item to perform as required, without failure, for a given time interval, under given conditions." In ML and statistics, reliability is often related to performance uncertainty and may be measured with confidence intervals, control limits, or conformal prediction techniques. ISO/IEC TS 5723:2022 relates robustness to generalization and defines it as "the ability of an item to maintain its level of performance under a variety of circumstances." In ML and statistics, a model's robustness might be tested under covariate perturbation (or *distribution shift*). Robustness has also come to be associated with robust ML (*https://oreil.ly/vlIOB*)—or the study of preventing adversaries from manipulating models with adversarial examples and data poisoning.

A lack of robustness and reliability may arise from many of the bugs discussed in this chapter and book. In this chapter, we have used terms like *instability*, *distribution shift*, and related ML vocabulary (e.g., *data leakage*, *epistemic uncertainty*, *underspecification*) to describe issues relating to a lack of robustness and reliability. Chapter 5 addresses security for ML systems.

Distribution shifts

Shifts in the underlying data between different training data partitions and after model deployment are common failure modes for ML systems. Whether there's a new competitor entering a market or a devastating worldwide pandemic, the world is a dynamic place. Unfortunately, most of today's ML systems learn patterns from static snapshots of training data and try to apply those patterns in new data. Sometimes that data is holdout validation or testing partitions. Sometimes it's live data in a production scoring queue. Regardless, drifting distributions of input features is a serious bug that must be caught and squashed.

 Systems based on adaptive, online, or reinforcement learning, or that update themselves with minimal human intervention, are subject to serious adversarial manipulation, error propagation, feedback loop, reliability, and robustness risks. While these systems may represent the current state of the art, they need high levels of risk management.

When training ML models, watch out for distributional shifts between training, cross-validation, validation, or test sets using population stability index (PSI), Kolmogorov-Smirnov (KS) tests, t-tests, or other appropriate measures. If a feature has a different distribution from one training partition to another, drop it or regularize it heavily. Another smart test for distributional shifts to conduct during debugging is to simulate distributional shifts for potential deployment conditions and remeasure model quality, with a special focus on poor-performing rows. If we're worried about how our model will perform during a recession, we can simulate distributional shifts to simulate more late payments, lower cash flow, and higher credit balances and then see how our model performs. It's also crucial to record information about distributions in training data so that drift after deployment can be detected easily.

Epistemic uncertainty and data sparsity

Epistemic uncertainty is a fancy way of saying instability and errors that arise from a lack of knowledge. In ML, models traditionally gain knowledge from training data. If there are parts of our large multidimensional training data that are sparse, it's likely our model will have a high degree of uncertainty in that region. Sound theoretical and far-fetched? It's not. Consider a basic credit lending model. We tend to have lots of data about people who already have credit cards and pay their bills, and tend to lack data on people who don't have credit cards (their past credit card data doesn't exist) or don't pay their bills (because the vast majority of customers pay). It's easy to know to extend credit cards to people with high credit scores that pay their bills. The hard decisions are about people with shorter or bumpier credit histories. The lack of data for the people we really need to know about can lead to serious epistemic uncertainty issues. If only a handful of customers, out of millions, are four or five months late on their most recent payment, then an ML model simply doesn't learn very much about the best way to handle these people.

This phenomenon is illustrated in the section "Underspecification" (which begins on page 101), where an example model is nonsensical for people who are more than two months late on their most recent payment. This region of poor, and likely unstable, performance is sometimes known as a *weak spot*. It's hard to find these weak spots by looking at aggregate error or performance measures. This is just one reason of many to test models carefully over segments in training or holdout data. It's also why we pair partial dependence and individual conditional expectation plots with histograms in Chapter 2. In these plots we can see if model behavior is supported by training data, or not. Once we've identified a sparse region of data leading to epistemic uncertainty and weak spots, we usually have to turn to human knowledge—by constraining the form of the model to behave logically based on domain experience, augmenting the model with business rules, or potentially handing the cases that fall into sparse regions over to human workers to make tough calls.

Instability

ML models can exhibit instability, or lack of robustness or reliability, in the training process or when making predictions on live data. Instability in training is often related to small training data, sparse regions of training data, highly correlated features within training data, or high-variance model forms, such as deep single decision trees. Cross-validation is a typical tool for detecting instability during training. If a model displays noticeably different error or accuracy properties across cross-validation folds, then we have an instability problem. Training instability can often be remediated with better data and lower-variance model forms such as decision tree ensembles. Plots of ALE or ICE also tend to reveal prediction instability in sparse regions of training data, and instability in predictions can be analyzed using sensitivity analysis: perturbations, simulations, stress testing, and adversarial example searches.

There are two easy ways to think about instability in ML:

- When a small change to input data results in a large change in output data
- When the addition of a small amount of training data results in a largely different model upon retraining

If probing our response surface or decision boundary with these techniques uncovers wild swings in predictions, or our ALE or ICE curves are bouncing around, especially in the high or low ranges of feature values, we also have an instability problem. This type of instability can often be fixed with constraints and regularization. Check out the code examples in Chapter 8 to see this remediation in action.

Leakage

Information leakage between training, validation, and test data partitions happens when information from validation and testing partitions leaks into a training partition, resulting in overly optimistic error and accuracy measurements. Leakage can happen for a variety of reasons, including the following:

Feature engineering

If used incorrectly, certain feature engineering techniques such as imputation or principal components analysis may contaminate training data with information from validation and test data. To avoid this kind of leakage, perform feature engineering uniformly, but separately, across training data partitions. Or ensure that information, like means and modes used for imputation, are calculated in training data and applied to validation and testing data, and not vice versa.

Mistreatment of temporal data

Don't use the future to predict the past. Most data has some association with time, whether explicit, as in time-series data, or some other implicit relationship. Mistreating or breaking this relationship with random sampling is a common cause of leakage. If we're dealing with data where time plays a role, time needs to be used in constructing model validation schemes. The most basic rule is that the earliest data should be in training partitions while later data should be divided into validation and test partitions, also according to time. A solid (and free) resource for time-series forecasting best practices is the text *Forecasting: Principles and Practice* (OTexts) (*https://oreil.ly/R2y6N*).

Multiple identical entities

Sometimes the same person, financial or computing transaction, or other modeled entity will be in multiple training data partitions. When this occurs, care should be taken to ensure that ML models do not memorize characteristics of these individuals then apply those individual-specific patterns to different entities in new data.

Keeping an untouched, time-aware holdout set for an honest estimate of real-world performance can help with many of these different leakage bugs. If error or accuracy on such a holdout set looks a lot less rosy than on partitions used in model development, we might have a leakage problem. More complex modeling schemes involving stacking, gates, or bandits can make leakage much harder to prevent and detect. However, a basic rule of thumb still applies: do not use data involved in learning or model selection to make realistic performance assessments. Using stacking, gates, or bandits means we need more holdout data for the different stages of these complex models to make an accurate guess at in vivo quality. More general controls such as careful documentation of data validation schemes and model monitoring in deployment are also necessary for any ML system.

Looped inputs

As ML systems are incorporated into broader digitalization efforts, or implemented as part of larger decision support efforts, multiple data-driven systems often interact. In these cases, error propagation and feedback loop bugs can occur. Error propagation occurs when small errors in one system cause or amplify errors in another system. Feedback loops are a way an ML system can fail by being right. Feedback loops occur when an ML system affects its environment and then those effects are reincorporated into system training data. Examples of feedback loops include when predictive policing leads to overpolicing of certain neighborhoods or when employment algorithms intensify diversity problems in hiring by continually recommending correct, but nondiverse, candidates. Dependencies between systems must be documented and deployed models must be monitored so that debugging efforts can detect error propagation or feedback loop bugs.

Overfitting

Overfitting happens when a complex ML algorithm memorizes too much specific information from training data, but does not learn enough generalizable concepts to be useful once deployed. Overfitting is often caused by high-variance models, or models that are too complex for the data at hand. Overfitting usually manifests in much better performance on training data than on validation, cross-validation, and test data partitions. Since overfitting is a ubiquitous problem, there are many possible solutions, but most involve decreasing the variance in our chosen model. Examples of these solutions include the following:

Ensemble models
> Ensemble techniques, particularly bootstrap aggregation (i.e., bagging) and gradient boosting are known to reduce error from single high-variance models. So, we try one of these ensembling approaches if we encounter overfitting. Just keep in mind that when switching from one model to many, we can decrease overfitting and instability, but we'll also likely lose interpretability.

Reducing architectural complexity
> Neural networks can have too many hidden layers or hidden units. Ensemble models can have too many base learners. Trees can be too deep. If we think we're observing overfitting, we make our model architecture less complex.

Regularization
> Regularization refers to many sophisticated mathematical approaches for reducing the strength, complexity, or number of learned rules or parameters in an ML model. In fact, many types of ML models now incorporate multiple options for regularization, so we make sure we employ these options to decrease the likelihood of overfitting.

Simpler hypothesis model families

Some ML models will be more complex than others out-of-the-box. If our neural network or GBM looks to be overfit, we can try a less complex decision tree or linear model.

Overfitting is traditionally seen as the Achilles' heel of ML. While it is one of the most frequently encountered bugs, it's also just one of many possible technical risks to consider from a safety and performance perspective. As with leakage, as ML systems become more complex, overfitting becomes harder to detect. Always keep an untouched holdout set with which to estimate real-world performance before deployment. More general controls like documentation of validation schemes, model monitoring, and A/B testing of models on live data also need to be applied to prevent overfitting.

Shortcut learning

Shortcut learning occurs when a complex ML system is thought to be learning and making decisions about one subject, say anomalies in lung scans or job interview performance, but it's actually learned about some simpler related concept, such as machine identification numbers or Zoom video call backgrounds. Shortcut learning tends to arise from entangled concepts in training data, a lack of construct validity, and failure to adequately consider and document assumptions and limitations. We use explainable models and explainable AI techniques to understand what learned mechanisms are driving model decisions, and we make sure we understand how our ML system makes scientifically valid decisions.

Underfitting

If someone tells us a statistic about a set of data, we might wonder how much data that statistic is based on, and whether that data was of high enough quality to be trustworthy. What if someone told us they had millions, billions, or even trillions of statistics for us to consider? They would need lots of data to make a case that all these statistics were meaningful. Just like averages and other statistics, each parameter or rule within an ML model is learned from data. Big ML models need lots of data to learn enough to make their millions, billions, or trillions of learned mechanisms meaningful. Underfitting happens when a complex ML algorithm doesn't have enough training data, constraints, or other input information, and it learns just a few generalizable concepts from training data, but not enough specifics to be useful when deployed. Underfitting can be diagnosed by poor performance on both training and validation data. Another piece of evidence for underfitting is if our model residuals have significantly more structure than random noise. This suggests that there are meaningful patterns in the data going undetected by our model, and it's another reason we examine our residuals for model debugging. We can mitigate underfitting by increasing the complexity of our models or, preferably, providing more training data.

We can also provide more input information in other ways, such as new features, Bayesian priors applied to our model parameter distributions, or various types of architectural or optimization constraints.

Underspecification

Forty researchers recently published "Underspecification Presents Challenges for Credibility in Modern Machine Learning" (*https://oreil.ly/Da9g0*). This paper gives a name to a problem that has existed for decades, *underspecification*. Underspecification arises from the core ML concept of the multiplicity of good models, sometimes also called the Rashomon effect. For any given dataset, there are many accurate ML models. How many? Vastly more than human technicians have any chance of understanding in most cases. While we use validation data to select a good model from many models attempted during training, validation-based model selection is not a strong enough control to ensure we picked the best model—or even a serviceable model—for deployment. Say that for some dataset there are a million total good ML models based on training data and a large number of potential hypothesis models. Selecting by validation data may cut that number of models down to a pool of one hundred total models. Even in this simple scenario, we'd still only have a 1 in 100 chance of picking the right model for deployment. How can we increase those odds? By injecting domain knowledge into ML models. By combining validation-based model selection with domain-informed constraints, we have a much better chance at selecting a viable model for the job at hand.

Happily, testing for underspecification can be fairly straightforward. One major symptom of underspecification is model performance that's dependent on computational hyperparameters that are not related to the structure of the domain, data, or model. If our model's performance varies due to random seeds, number of threads or GPUs, or other computational settings, our model is probably underspecified. Another test for underspecification is illustrated in Figure 3-1.

Figure 3-1 displays several error and accuracy measures across important segments in the example training data and model. Here, a noticeable shift in performance for segments defined by higher values of the important feature PAY_0 points to a potential underspecification problem, likely due to data sparsity in that region of the training data. (Performance across segments defined by SEX is more equally balanced, which a good sign from a bias-testing perspective, but certainly not the only test to be considered for bias problems.) Fixing underspecification tends to involve applying real-world knowledge to ML algorithms. Such domain-informed mechanisms include graph connections, monotonic constraints, interaction constraints, beta constraints, or other architectural constraints.

Metrics for PAY_0

PAY_0	Prevalence	Accuracy	True Positive Rate	Precision	Specificity	Negative Predicted Value	False Positive Rate	False Discovery Rate	False Negative Rate	False Omissions Rate
-2	0.124	0.864	0.099	0.333	0.972	0.884	0.028	0.667	0.901	0.116
-1	0.168	0.816	0.206	0.406	0.939	0.854	0.061	0.594	0.794	0.146
0	0.121	0.867	0.107	0.341	0.972	0.888	0.028	0.659	0.893	0.112
1	0.325	0.491	0.903	0.381	0.292	0.862	0.708	0.619	0.097	0.138
2	0.709	0.709	1	0.709	0	0.5	1	0.291	0	0.5
3	0.748	0.748	1	0.748	0	0.5	1	0.252	0	0.5
4	0.571	0.571	1	0.571	0	0.5	1	0.429	0	0.5
5	0.444	0.444	1	0.444	0	0.5	1	0.556	0	0.5
6	0.25	0.25	1	0.25	0	0.5	1	0.75	0	0.5
7	0.5	0.5	1	0.5	0	0.5	1	0.5	0	0.5
8	0.75	0.75	1	0.75	0	0.5	1	0.25	0	0.5

Metrics for SEX

SEX	Prevalence	Accuracy	True Positive Rate	Precision	Specificity	Negative Predicted Value	False Positive Rate	False Discovery Rate	False Negative Rate	False Omissions Rate
Male	0.235	0.782	0.626	0.531	0.83	0.879	0.17	0.469	0.374	0.121
Female	0.209	0.797	0.552	0.514	0.862	0.879	0.138	0.486	0.448	0.121

Figure 3-1. Analyzing accuracy and errors across key segments is an important debugging method for detecting bias, underspecification, and other serious ML bugs (digital, color version: https://oreil.ly/URzZG)

Nearly all of the bugs discussed in this section, chapter, and book can affect certain segments of data more than others. For optimal performance, it's important to test for weak spots (performance quality), overfitting and underfitting, instability, distribution shifts, and other issues across different kinds of segments in training, validation, and test or holdout data.

Each of the ML bugs discussed in this subsection has real-world safety and performance ramifications. A unifying theme across these bugs is that they cause systems to perform differently than expected when deployed in vivo and over time. Unpredictable performance leads to unexpected failures and AI incidents. Using the knowledge of potential bugs and bug detection methods discussed here to ensure estimates of validation and test performance are relevant to deployed performance will go a long way toward preventing real-world incidents. Now that we know what bugs we're looking for, in terms of software, traditional assessment, and ML math, next we'll address how to find these bugs with residual analysis, sensitivity analysis, benchmark models, and other testing and monitoring approaches.

Residual Analysis

Residual analysis is another type of traditional model assessment that can be highly effective for ML models and ML systems. At its most basic level, residual analysis means learning from mistakes. That's an important thing to do in life, as well as in organizational ML systems. Moreover, residual analysis is a tried-and-true model diagnostic technique. This subsection will use an example and three generally applicable residual analysis techniques to apply this established discipline to ML.

 We use the term *residual* to mean an appropriate measurement of error, somewhat synonymous to the model's loss measurement. We understand we're not the using it in the strictly defined $\hat{y}_i - y_i$ sense. We use this term to reinforce the importance and long history of residual analysis in regression diagnostics and to highlight its basic absence from common ML workflows.

Note that in the following sections readers may see demographic features in the dataset, like SEX, that are used for bias testing. For the most part, this chapter treats the example credit lending problem as a general predictive modeling exercise, and does not consider applicable fair lending regulations. See Chapters 4 and 10 for in-depth discussions relating to bias management in ML that also address some legal and regulatory concerns.

Analysis and visualizations of residuals

Plotting overall and segmented residuals and examining them for telltale patterns of different kinds of problems is a long-running model diagnostic technique. Residual analysis can be applied to ML algorithms to great benefit with a bit of creativity and elbow grease. Simply plotting residuals for an entire dataset can be helpful, especially to spot outlying rows causing very large numeric errors or to analyze overall trends in errors. However, breaking residual values and plots down by feature and level is likely to be more informative. Even if we have a lot features or features with many categorical levels, we're not off the hook. Start with the most important features and their most common levels. Look for strong patterns in residuals that violate the assumptions of our model. Many types of residuals should be randomly distributed, indicating that the model has learned all the important information from the data, aside from irreducible noise. If we spot strong patterns or other anomalies in residuals that have been broken down by feature and level, we first determine whether these errors arise from data, and if not, we can use XAI techniques to track down issues in our model. Residual analysis is considered standard practice for important linear regression models. ML models are arguably higher risk and more failure prone, so they need even more residual analysis.

Modeling residuals

Modeling residuals with interpretable models is another great way to learn more about the mistakes our ML system could make. In Figure 3-2, we've trained a single, shallow decision tree on the residuals from a more complex model associated with customers who missed a credit card payment.

This decision tree encodes rules that describe how the more complex model is wrong. For example, we can see the model generates the largest numeric residuals when someone misses a credit card payment, but looks like a great customer. When someone's most recent repayment status (PAY_0) is less than 0.5, their second most recent payment amount (PAY_AMT2) is greater than or equal to 2,802.50, their fourth most recent repayment status (PAY_4) is less than 1, and their credit limit is greater than or equal to 256,602, we see logloss residuals of 2.71, on average. That's a big error rate that drags down our overall performance, and that can have bias ramifications if we make too many false negative guesses about already favored demographic groups.

Another intriguing use for the tree is to create model assertions, real-time business rules about model predictions, that could be used to flag when a wrong decision is occurring as it happens. In some cases, the assertions might simply alert model monitors that a wrong decision is likely being issued, or model assertions could involve corrective action, like routing this row of data to a more specialized model or to human case workers.

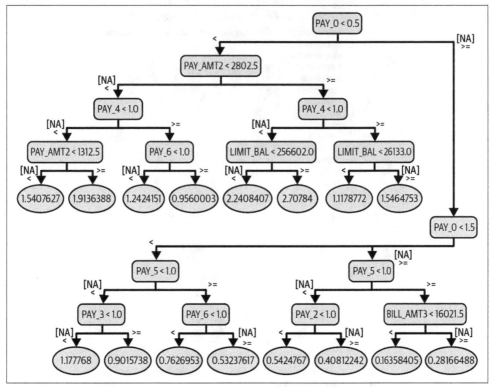

Figure 3-2. An interpretable decision tree model for customers who missed credit card payments

Local contribution to residuals

Plotting and modeling residuals are older techniques that are well-known to skilled practitioners. A more recent breakthrough has made it possible to calculate accurate Shapley value contributions to model errors. This means for any feature or row of any dataset, we can now know which features are driving model predictions, and which features are driving model errors. What this advance really means for ML is yet to be determined, but the possibilities are certainly intriguing. One obvious application for this new Shapley value technique is to compare feature importance for predictions to feature importance for residuals, as in Figure 3-3.

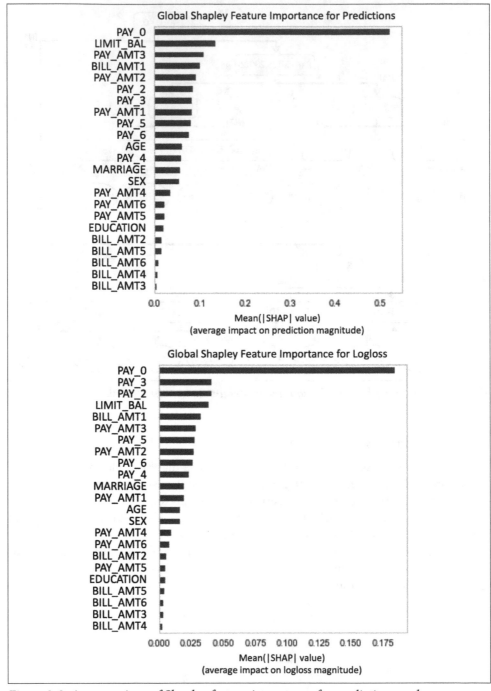

Figure 3-3. A comparison of Shapley feature importance for predictions and for model errors (digital, color version: https://oreil.ly/k6nDo)

In Figure 3-3, feature importance for predictions is shown on top, and feature importance for the errors of the model, as calculated by logloss, is shown on the bottom. We can see that PAY_0 dominates both predictions and errors, confirming that this model is too reliant on PAY_0 in general. We can also see that PAY_2 and PAY_3 are ranked higher for contributions to error than contributions to predictions. Given this, it might make sense to experiment with dropping, replacing, or corrupting these features. Note that Figure 3-3 is made from aggregating Shapley contributions to logloss across an entire validation dataset. However, these quantities are calculated feature-by-feature and row-by-row. We could also apply this analysis across segments or demographic groups in our data, opening up interesting possibilities for detecting and remediating nonrobust features for different subpopulations under the model.

 Feature importance plots that look like Figure 3-3, with one feature drastically outweighing all the others, bode very poorly for in vivo reliability and security. If the distribution of that single important feature drifts, our model performance is going to suffer. If hackers find a way to modify values of that feature, they can easily manipulate our predictions. When one feature dominates a model, we likely need a business rule relating to that feature instead of an ML model.

This ends our brief tour of residual analysis for ML. Of course there are other ways to study the errors of ML models. If readers prefer another way, then go for it! The important thing is to do some kind of residual analysis for all high-stakes ML systems. Along with sensitivity analysis, to be discussed in the next subsection, residual analysis is an essential tool in the ML model debugging kit.

Sensitivity Analysis

Unlike linear models, it's very hard to understand how ML models extrapolate or perform on new data without testing them explicitly. That's the simple and powerful idea behind sensitivity analysis. Find or simulate data for interesting scenarios, then see how our model performs on that data. We really won't know how our ML system will perform in these scenarios unless we conduct basic sensitivity analysis. Of course, there are structured and more efficient variants of sensitivity analysis, such as in the InterpretML (*https://oreil.ly/zdzxX*) library from Microsoft Research. Another great option for sensitivity analysis, and a good place to start with more advanced model debugging techniques, is random attacks, discussed in "Software Testing" on page 92. Many other approaches, like stress testing, visualization, and adversarial example searches also provide standardized ways to conduct sensitivity analysis:

Stress testing

Stress testing involves simulating data that represents realistic adverse scenarios, like recessions or pandemics, and making sure our ML models and any downstream business processes will hold up to the stress of the adverse situation.

Visualizations

Visualizations, such as plots of accumulated local effects, individual conditional expectation, and partial dependence curves, are well-known, highly structured ways to observe the performance of ML algorithms across various real or simulated values of input features. These plots can also reveal areas of data sparsity that can lead to weak spots in model performance.

Adversarial example searches

Adversarial examples are rows of data that evoke surprising responses from ML models. Deep learning approaches can be used to generate adversarial examples for unstructured data, and ICE and genetic algorithms can be used to generate adversarial examples for structured data. Adversarial examples (and the search for them) are a great way to find local areas of instability in our ML response functions or decision boundaries that can cause incidents once deployed. As readers can see in Figure 3-4, an adversarial example search is a great way to put a model through its paces.

Conformal approaches

Conformal approaches (*https://oreil.ly/f_Vrf*) that attempt to calculate empirical bounds for model predictions can help us understand model reliability through establishing the upper and lower limits of what can be expected from model outputs.

Perturbation tests

Randomly perturbing validation, test, or holdout data to simulate different types of noise and drift, and then remeasuring ML model performance, can also help establish the general bounds of model robustness. With this kind of perturbation testing, we can understand and document the amount of noise or shift that we know will break our model. One thing to keep in mind is that poor-performing rows often decline in performance faster than average rows under perturbation testing. Watch poor-performing rows carefully to understand if and when they drag the performance of the entire model down.

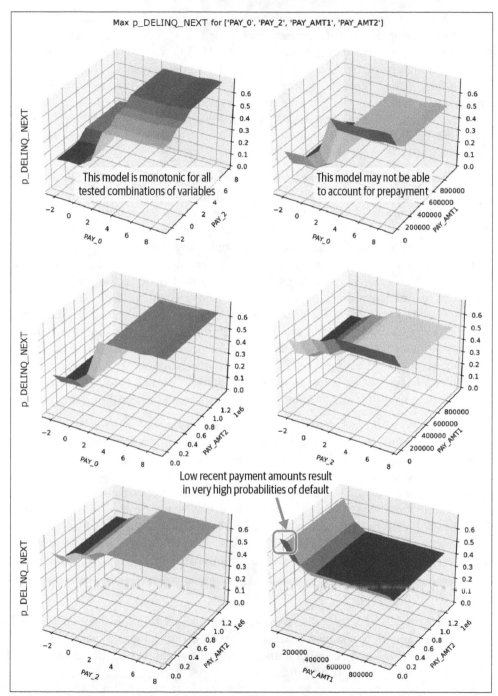

Figure 3-4. Results from an adversarial example search that reveal interesting model behavior (digital, color version: https://oreil.ly/_vTJW)

Figure 3-4 was created by first finding an ICE curve that exhibited a large swing in predictions. Using the row of data responsible for that ICE curve as a seed, and perturbing the values of the four most important features in that row thousands of times and generating associated predictions, leads to the numerous plots in Figure 3-4. The first finding of the adversarial example search is that this heuristic technique, based on ICE curves, enables us to generate adversarial examples that can evoke almost any response we want from the model. We found rows that reliably yield very low and very high predictions and everything in between. If this model was available via a prediction API, we could play it like a fiddle.

In the process of finding all those adversarial examples, we also learned things about our model. First, it is likely monotonic in general, and definitely monotonic across all the rows we simulated in the adversarial example search. Second, this model issues default predictions for people that make extremely high payments. Even if someone's most recent payment was one million dollars, and above their credit limit, this model will issue default predictions once that person becomes two months late on their payments. This could pose problems for prepayment. Do we really want to issue a default or delinquency decision for someone who prepaid millions of dollars but is now two months late on their most recent payments? Maybe, but it's likely not a decision that should be made quickly or automatically, as this model would do. Third, it appears we may have found a route for a true adversarial example attack. Low recent repayment amounts result in surprisingly sharp increases in probability of default. If a hacker wants to evoke high probability of default predictions from this model, setting PAY_AMT1 and PAY_AMT2 to low values could be how they do it.

Like we mentioned for residual analysis, readers may have other sensitivity analysis techniques in mind, and that's great. Just make sure you apply some form of realistic simulation testing to your ML models. This chapter's case study is an example of the worst kind of outcome resulting from a failure to conduct realistic simulation testing prior to deploying an ML system. This ends our brief discussion of sensitivity analysis. For those who would like to dive in even deeper, we recommend Chapter 19 of Kevin Murphy's free and open *Probabilistic Machine Learning: Advanced Topics* (*https://oreil.ly/mHWno*) (MIT Press). Next, we'll discuss benchmark models in different contexts, another time-tested and commonsense model debugging approach.

Benchmark Models

Benchmark models have been discussed at numerous points in this chapter. They are a very important safety and performance tool, with uses throughout the ML lifecycle. This subsection will discuss benchmark models in the context of model debugging and also summarize other critical uses.

When possible, compare ML model performance to a linear model or GLM performance benchmark. If the linear model beats the ML model, use the linear model.

The first way to use a benchmark model for debugging is to compare performance between a benchmark and the ML system in question. If the ML system does not outperform a simple benchmark—and many may not—it's back to the drawing board. Assuming a system passes this initial baseline test, benchmark models can then be used as a comparison tool to interrogate mechanisms and find bugs within an ML system. For instance, data scientists can ask the question, "Which predictions does my benchmark get right and my ML system get wrong?" Given that the benchmark should be well understood, it should be clear why it is correct, and this understanding should also provide some clues as to what the ML system is getting wrong. Benchmarks can also be used for reproducibility and model monitoring purposes as follows:

Reproducibility benchmarks

Before making changes to a complex ML system, it is imperative to have a reproducible benchmark from which to measure performance gains or losses. A reproducible benchmark model is an ideal tool for such measurement tasks. If this model can be built into CI/CD processes that enable automated testing for reproducibility and comparison of new system changes to established benchmarks, even better.

Debugging benchmarks

Comparing complex ML model mechanisms and predictions to a trusted, well-understood benchmark model's mechanisms and predictions is an effective way to spot ML bugs.

Monitoring benchmarks

Comparing real-time predictions between a trusted benchmark model and a complex ML system is a way to catch serious ML bugs in real time. If a trusted benchmark model and a complex ML system give noticeably different predictions for the same instance of new data, this can be a sign of an ML hack, data drift, or even bias and algorithmic discrimination. In such cases, benchmark predictions can be issued in place of ML system predictions, or predictions can be withheld until human analysts determine if the ML system prediction is valid.

Remember that debugging techniques are often fallible statistical or ML approaches, and may need to be debugged themselves.

If we set benchmarks up efficiently, it may even be possible to use the same model for all three tasks. A benchmark can be run before starting work to establish a baseline from which to improve performance, and that same model can be used in comparisons for debugging and model monitoring. When a new version of the system outperforms an older version in a reproducible manner, the ML model at the core of the system can become the new benchmark. If our organization can establish this kind of workflow, we'll be benchmarking and iterating our way to increased ML safety and performance.

Remediation: Fixing Bugs

The last step in debugging is fixing bugs. The previous subsections have outlined testing strategies, bugs to be on the lookout for, and a few specific fixes. This subsection outlines general ML bug-fixing approaches and discusses how they might be applied in the example debugging scenario. General strategies to consider during ML model debugging include the following:

Anomaly detection

Strange inputs and outputs are usually bad news for ML systems. These can be evidence of a real-time security, bias, or safety and performance problem. Monitor ML system data queues and predictions for anomalies, record the occurrence of anomalies, and alert stakeholders to their presence when necessary.

A number of rule-based, statistical, and ML techniques can be used to detect anomalies in unseen data queues. These include data integrity constraints, confidence limits, control limits, autoencoders, and isolation forests.

Experimental design and data augmentation

Collecting better data is often a fix-all for ML bugs. What's more, data collection doesn't have to be done in a trial-and-error fashion, nor do data scientists have to rely on data exhaust byproducts of other organizational processes for selecting training data. The mature science of design of experiment has been used by data practitioners for decades to ensure they collect the right kind and amount of data for model training. Arrogance related to the perceived omnipotence of "big" data and overly compressed deployment timelines are the most common reasons data scientists don't practice DOE. Unfortunately, these are not scientific reasons to ignore DOE.

Model assertions

Model assertions are business rules applied to ML model predictions that correct for shortcomings in learned ML model logic. Using business rules to improve predictive models is a time-honored remediation technique that will likely be with us for decades to come. If there is a simple, logical rule that can be applied to correct a foreseeable ML model failure, don't be shy about implementing it. The best practitioners and organizations in the predictive analytics space have used this trick for decades.

Model editing

Given that ML models are software, those software artifacts can be edited to correct for any discovered bugs. Certain models, like GA2Ms or explainable boosting machines (EBMs) are designed to be edited for the purposes of model debugging. Other types of models may require more creativity to edit. Either way, editing must be justified by domain considerations, as it's likely to make performance on training data appear worse. ML models optimize toward lower error. If we edit this highly optimized structure to make in-domain performance better, we'll likely worsen traditional assessment statistics. That's OK. We care more about in vivo safety, robustness, and reliability than in silico test error.

Model management and monitoring

ML models and the ML systems that house them are dynamic entities that must be monitored to the extent that resources allow. All mission-critical ML systems should be well-documented, inventoried, and monitored for security, bias, and safety and performance problems in real time. When something starts to go wrong, stakeholders need to be alerted quickly. "Deployment" on page 114 gives a more detailed treatment of model monitoring.

Monotonic and interaction constraints

Many ML bugs occur because ML models have too much flexibility and become untethered from reality due to learning from biased and inaccurate training data. Constraining models with real-world knowledge is a general solution to several types of ML bugs. Monotonic and interaction constraints, in popular tools like XGBoost, can help ML practitioners enforce logical domain assumptions in complex ML models.

Noise injection and strong regularization

Many ML algorithms come with options for regularization. However, if an ML model is overemphasizing a certain feature, stronger or external regularization might need to be applied. L0 regularization can be used to limit the number of rules or parameters in a model directly, and when necessary, manual noise injection can be used to corrupt signals from certain features to deemphasize those with any undue importance in ML models.

The scientific method

Confirmation bias among data scientists, ML engineers, their managers, and business partners often conspires to push half-baked demos out the door as products, based on the assumptions and limitations of in silico test data assessments. If we're able to follow the scientific method by recording a hypothesis about real-world results and objectively test that hypothesis with a designed experiment, we have much higher chances at in vivo success. See Chapter 12 for more thoughts on using the scientific method in ML.

 Generally speaking, ML is still more of an empirical science than an engineering discipline. We don't yet fully understand when ML works well and all the ways it can fail, especially when deployed in vivo. This means we have to apply the scientific method and avoid issues like confirmation bias to attain good real-world results. Simply using the right software and platforms, and following engineering best practices, does not mean our models will work well.

There's more detailed information regarding model debugging and the example data and model in "Resources" on page 122. For now, we've learned quite a bit about model debugging, and it's time to turn our attention to safety and performance for deployed ML systems.

Deployment

Once bugs are found and fixed, it's time to deploy our ML system to make real-world decisions. ML systems are much more dynamic than most traditional software systems. Even if system operators don't change any code or setting of the system, the results can still change. Once deployed, ML systems must be checked for in-domain safety and performance, they must be monitored, and their operators must be able to shut them off quickly. This section will cover how to enhance safety and performance once an ML system is deployed: domain safety, model monitoring, and kill switches.

Domain Safety

Domain safety means safety in the real world. This is very different from standard model assessment, or even enhanced model debugging. How can practitioners work toward real-world safety goals? A/B testing and champion challenger methodologies allow for some amount of testing in real-time operating environments. Process controls, like enumerating foreseeable incidents, implementing controls to address those potential incidents, and testing those controls under realistic or stressful conditions, are also important for solid in vivo performance. To make up for incidents that can't be predicted, we apply chaos testing, random attacks, and manual prediction limits to our ML system outputs. Let's divide incidents into those we can foresee, and those we can't, and consider a few details for both cases:

Foreseeable real-world incidents

A/B testing and champion-challenger approaches, in which models are tested against one another on live data streams or under other realistic conditions, are a first step toward robust in-domain testing. Beyond these somewhat standard practices, resources should be spent on domain experts and thinking through possible incidents. For example, common failure modes in credit lending include bias and algorithmic discrimination, lack of transparency, and poor performance during recessions. For other applications, say autonomous vehicles, there are numerous ways they could accidentally or intentionally cause harm. Once potential incidents are recorded, then safety controls can be adopted for the most likely or most serious potential incidents. In credit lending, models are tested for bias, explanations are provided to consumers via adverse action notices, and models are monitored to catch performance degradation quickly. In autonomous vehicles, we still have a lot to learn, as "Case Study: Death by Autonomous Vehicle" on page 120 will show. Regardless of the application, safety controls must be tested, and these tests should be realistic and performed in collaboration with domain experts. When it comes to human safety, simulations run by data scientists are not enough. Safety controls need to be tested and hardened in vivo and in coordination with people who have a deep understanding of safety in the application domain.

Unforeseeable real-world incidents

Interactions between ML systems and their environments can be complex and surprising. For high-stakes ML systems, it's best to admit that unforeseeable incidents can occur. We can try to catch some of these potential surprises before they occur with chaos testing and random attacks. Important ML systems should be tested in strange and chaotic use cases and exposed to large amounts of random input data. While these are time- and resource-consuming tests, they are one of the few tools available to test for so-called "unknown unknowns." Given that no testing regime can catch every problem, it's also ideal to apply commonsense prediction limits to systems. For instance, large loans or interest rates should not be issued without some kind of human oversight. Nor should autonomous vehicles be allowed to travel at very high speeds without human intervention. Some actions simply should not be performed purely automatically as of today, and prediction limits are one way to implement that kind of control.

Another key aspect of domain safety is knowing if problems are occurring. Sometimes glitches can be caught before they grow into harmful incidents. To catch problems quickly, ML systems must be monitored. If incidents are detected, incident response plans or kill switches may need to be activated.

Characteristics of Safe Machine Learning Systems

Some of the most important steps we can take to ensure an ML system interacts with the physical world in a safe way are as follows:

Avoiding past failed designs
> ML systems that cause harm to humans or the environment should not be reimplemented, and their failures should be studied to improve the safety conditions of future related systems.

Incident response plans
> Human operators should know what to do when a safety incident occurs.

In-domain testing
> Test data assessments, simulations, and debugging by data scientists are not enough to ensure safety. Systems should be tested in realistic in vivo conditions by domain and safety experts.

Kill switches
> Systems should be able to be shut off quickly and remotely when monitoring reveals risky or dangerous conditions.

Manual prediction limits
> Limits on system behaviors should be set by operators where appropriate.

Real-time monitoring
> Humans should be alerted when a system enters a risky or dangerous state, and kill switches or redundant functionality should be enacted quickly (or automatically).

Redundancy
> Systems that perform safety- or mission-critical activities should have redundant functionality at the ready if incidents occur or monitoring indicates the system has entered a risky or dangerous state.

Model Monitoring

It's been mentioned numerous times in this chapter, but important ML systems must be monitored once deployed. This subsection focuses on the technical aspects of model monitoring. It outlines the basics of model decay, robustness, and concept drift bugs, how to detect and address drift, and the importance of measuring multiple key performance indicators (KPIs) in monitoring, as well as briefly highlighting a few other notable model monitoring concepts.

Model decay and concept drift

No matter what we call it, the data coming into an ML system is likely to drift away from the data on which the system was trained. The change in the distribution of input values over time is sometimes labeled *data drift*. The statistical properties of what we're trying to predict can also drift, and sometimes this is known specifically as *concept drift*. The COVID-19 crisis is likely one of history's best examples of these phenomena. At the height of the pandemic, there was likely a very strong drift toward more cautious consumer behavior accompanied by an overall change in late payment and credit default distributions. These kinds of shifts are painful to live through, and they can wreak havoc on an ML system's accuracy. It's important to note that we sometimes make our own concept drift issues, by engaging in *off-label use* of ML models.

 Both input data and predictions can drift. Both types of drift can be monitored, and the two types of drift may or may not be directly related. When performance degrades without significant input drift this may be due to real-world concept drift.

Detecting and addressing drift

The best approach to detect drift is to monitor the statistical properties of live data— both input variables and predictions. Once a mechanism has been put in place to monitor statistical properties, we can set alerts or alarms to notify stakeholders when there is a significant drift. Testing inputs is usually the easiest way to start detecting drift. This is because sometimes true data labels, i.e., true outcome values associated with ML system predictions, cannot be known for long periods of time. In contrast, input data values are available immediately whenever an ML system must generate a prediction or output. So, if current input data properties have changed from the training data properties, we likely have a problem on our hands. Watching ML system outputs for drift can be more difficult due to information needed to compare current and training quality being unavailable immediately. (Think about mortgage default versus online advertising—default doesn't happen at the same pace as clicking an online advertisement.) The basic idea for monitoring predictions is to watch predictions in real time and look for drift and anomalies, potentially using methodologies such as statistical tests, control limits, and rules or ML algorithms to catch outliers. And when known outcomes become available, test for degradation in model performance and engage in sustained bias management quickly and frequently.

There are known strategies to address inevitable drift and model decay. These include the following:

- Refreshing an ML system with extended training data containing some amount of new data
- Refreshing or retraining an ML system frequently
- Refreshing or retraining an ML system when drift is detected

It should be noted that any type of retraining of ML models in production should be subject to the risk mitigation techniques discussed in this chapter and elsewhere in the book—just like they should be applied to the initial training of an ML system.

Monitoring multiple key performance indicators

Most discussions of model monitoring focus on model accuracy as the primary key performance indicator (KPI). Yet, bias, security vulnerabilities, and privacy harms can, and likely should, be monitored as well. The same bias testing that was done at training time can be applied when new known outcomes become available. Numerous other strategies, discussed in Chapters 5 and 11, can be used to detect malicious activities that could compromise system security or privacy. Perhaps the most crucial KPI to measure, if at all possible, is the actual impact of the ML system. Whether it's saving or generating money, or saving lives, measuring the intended outcome and actual value of the ML system can lead to critical organizational insights. Assign monetary or other values to confusion matrix cells in classification problems, and to residual units in regression problems, as a first step toward estimating actual business value. See Chapter 8 for a basic example of estimating business value.

Out-of-range values

Training data can never cover all of the data an ML system might encounter once deployed. Most ML algorithms and prediction functions do not handle out-of-range data well, and may simply issue an average prediction or crash, and do so without notifying application software or system operators. ML system operators should make specific arrangements to handle data, such as large-magnitude numeric values, rare categorical values, or missing values that were not encountered during training so that ML systems will operate normally and warn users when they encounter out-of-range data.

Anomaly detection and benchmark models

Anomaly detection and benchmark models round out the technical discussion of model monitoring in this subsection. These topics have been treated elsewhere in this chapter, and are touched on briefly here in the monitoring context:

Anomaly detection

Strange input or output values in an ML system can be indicative of stability problems or security and privacy vulnerabilities. It's possible to use statistics, ML, and business rules to monitor anomalous behavior in both inputs and outputs, and across an entire ML system. Record any such detected anomalies, report them to stakeholders, and be ready to take more drastic action when necessary.

Benchmark models

Comparing simpler benchmark models and ML system predictions as part of model monitoring can help to catch stability, fairness, or security anomalies in near real time. A benchmark model should be more stable, easier to confirm as minimally discriminatory, and should be harder to hack. We use a highly transparent benchmark model and our more complex ML system together when scoring new data, then compare our ML system predictions against the trusted benchmark prediction in real time. If the difference between the ML system and the benchmark is above some reasonable threshold, then fall back to issuing the benchmark model's prediction or send the row of data for more review.

Whether it's out-of-range values in new data, disappointing KPIs, drift, or anomalies—these real-time problems are where rubber meets road for AI incidents. If our monitoring detects these issues, a natural inclination will be to turn the system off. The next subsection addresses just this issue: kill switches for ML systems.

Kill switches

Kill switches are rarely single switches or scripts, but a set of business and technical processes bundled together that serve to turn an ML system off—to the degree that's possible. There's a lot to consider before flipping a proverbial kill switch. ML system outputs often feed into downstream business processes, sometimes including other ML systems. These systems and business processes can be mission critical, such as an ML system used for credit underwriting or e-retail payment verification. To turn off an ML system, we not only need the right technical know-how and personnel available, but we also need an understanding of the system's place inside of broader organizational processes. During an ongoing AI incident is a bad time to start thinking about turning off a fatally flawed ML system. So, kill processes and kill switches are a great addition to our ML system documentation and AI incident response plans (see Chapter 1). This way, when the time comes to kill an ML system, our organization can be ready to make a quick and informed decision. Hopefully we'll never be in a position where flipping an ML system kill switch is necessary, but unfortunately AI incidents have grown more common in recent years. When technical remediation methods are applied alongside cultural competencies and business processes for risk mitigation, the safety and performance of ML systems is enhanced. When these controls are not applied, bad things can happen.

Case Study: Death by Autonomous Vehicle

On the night of March 18, 2018, Elaine Herzberg was walking a bicycle across a wide intersection in Tempe, Arizona. In what has become one of the most high-profile AI incidents, she was struck by an autonomous Uber test vehicle traveling at roughly 40 mph. According to the National Transportation Safety Board (NTSB), the test vehicle driver, who was obligated to take control of the vehicle in emergency situations, was distracted by a smartphone. The self-driving ML system also failed to save Ms. Herzberg. The system did not identify her until 1.2 seconds before impact, too late to prevent a brutal crash.

Fallout

Autonomous vehicles are thought to offer safety benefits over today's status quo of human-operated vehicles. While fatalities involving self-driving cars are rare, ML-automated driving has yet to deliver on the original promise of safer roads. The NTSB's report states (*https://oreil.ly/2nEOv*) that this Uber's "system design did not include a consideration for jaywalking pedestrians." The report also criticized lax risk assessments and an immature safety culture at the company. Furthermore, an Uber employee had raised serious concerns about 37 crashes in the previous 18 months and common problems with test vehicle drivers just days before the Tempe incident. As a result of the Tempe crash, Uber's autonomous vehicle testing was stopped in four other cities and local governments all over the US and Canada began reexamining safety protocols for self-driving vehicle tests. The driver has been charged with negligent homicide. Uber has been excused from criminal liability, but came to a monetary settlement with the deceased's family. The city of Tempe and the State of Arizona were also sued by Ms. Herzberg's family for $10 million each.

An Unprepared Legal System

It must be noted that the legal system in the US is somewhat unprepared for the reality of AI incidents, potentially leaving employees, consumers, and the general public largely unprotected from the unique dangers presented by ML systems operating in our midst. The EU Parliament has put forward a liability regime for ML systems that would mostly prevent large technology companies from escaping their share of the consequences in future incidents. In the US, any plans for federal AI product safety regulations are still in a preliminary phase. In the interim, individual cases of AI safety incidents will likely be decided by lower courts with little education and experience in handling AI incidents, enabling Big Tech and other ML system operators to bring vastly asymmetric legal resources to bear against individuals caught up in incidents related to complex ML systems. Even for the companies and ML system operators, this legal limbo is not ideal. While the lack of regulation seems to benefit those with the most resources and expertise, it makes risk management and predicting the outcomes of AI incidents more difficult. Regardless, future generations may judge us harshly for allowing the criminal liability of one of the first AI incidents, involving many data scientists and other highly paid professionals and executives, to be pinned solely on a safety driver of a supposedly automated vehicle.

Lessons Learned

What lessons learned from this and previous chapters could be applied to this case?

Lesson 1: Culture is important.

A mature safety culture is a broad risk control, bringing safety to the forefront of design and implementation work, and picking up the slack in corner cases that processes and technology miss. Learned from the last generation of life-changing commercial technologies, like aerospace and nuclear power, a more mature safety culture at Uber could have prevented this incident, especially since an employee raised serious concerns in the days before the crash.

Lesson 2: Mitigate foreseeable failure modes.

The NTSB concluded that Uber's software did not specifically consider jaywalking pedestrians as a failure mode. For anyone who's driven a car with pedestrians around, this should have been an easily foreseeable problem for which any self-driving car should be prepared. ML systems generally are not prepared for incidents unless their human engineers make them prepared. This incident shows us what happens when those preparations are not made in advance.

Lesson 3: Test ML systems in their operating domain.

After the crash, Uber stopped and reset its self-driving car program. After improvements, it was able to show via simulation that its new software would have started breaking four seconds before impact. Why wasn't the easily foreseeable reality of jaywalking pedestrians tested with these same in-domain simulations before the March 2018 crash? The public may never know. But enumerating failure modes and testing them in realistic scenarios could prevent our organization from having to answer these kinds of unpleasant questions.

A potential bonus lesson here is to consider not only accidental failures, like the Uber crash, but also malicious hacks against ML systems and the abuse of ML systems to commit violence. Terrorists have turned motor vehicles into deadly weapons before, so this is a known failure mode. Precautions must be taken in autonomous vehicles, and in driving assistance features, to prevent hacking and violent outcomes. Regardless of whether it is an accident or a malicious attack, AI incidents will certainly kill more people. Our hope is that governments and other organizations will take ML safety seriously, and minimize the number of these somber incidents in the future.

Resources

Further Reading

- "A Comprehensive Study on Deep Learning Bug Characteristics" (*https://oreil.ly/89R6O*)
- "Debugging Machine Learning Models" (*https://oreil.ly/685C3*)
- "Real-World Strategies for Model Debugging" (*https://oreil.ly/LvrLk*)
- "Safe and Reliable Machine Learning" (*https://oreil.ly/mLU8l*)
- "Overview of Debugging ML Models" (*https://oreil.ly/xZGoN*)
- "DQI: Measuring Data Quality in NLP" (*https://oreil.ly/aa7rv*)
- "Identifying and Overcoming Common Data Mining Mistakes" (*https://oreil.ly/w19Qm*)

Code Examples

- Basic sensitivity and residual analysis example (*https://oreil.ly/Tcu65*)
- Advanced sensitivity analysis example (*https://oreil.ly/QPFFx*)
- Advanced residual analysis example (*https://oreil.ly/Poe20*)

## CHAPTER 4

Managing Bias in Machine Learning

Managing the harmful effects of bias in machine learning systems is about so much more than data, code, and models. Our model's average performance quality—the main way data scientists are taught to evaluate the goodness of a model—has little to do with whether it's causing real-world bias harms. A perfectly accurate model can cause bias harms. Worse, all ML systems exhibit some level of bias, bias incidents appear to be some of the most common AI incidents (see Figure 4-1), bias in business processes often entails legal liability, and bias in ML models hurts people in the real world.

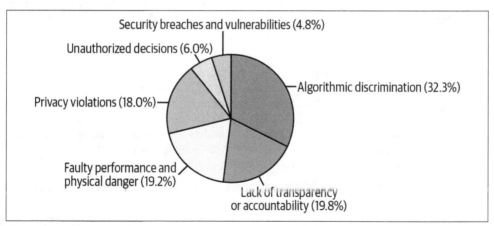

Figure 4-1. The frequency of different types of AI incidents based on a qualitative analysis of 169 publicly reported incidents between 1988 and February 1, 2021 (figure courtesy of BNH.AI)

This chapter will put forward approaches for detecting and mitigating bias in a sociotechnical fashion, at least to the best of our ability as practicing technicians. That means we'll try to understand how ML system bias exists in its broader societal context. Why? *All* ML systems are sociotechnical. We know this might be hard to believe at first, so let's think through one example. Let's consider a model used to predict sensor failure for an Internet of Things (IoT) application, using only information from other automated sensors. That model would likely have been trained by humans, or a human decided that a model was needed. Moreover, the results from that model could be used to inform the ordering of new sensors, which could affect the employment of those at the manufacturing plant or those who repair or replace failing sensors. Finally, if our preventative maintenance model fails, people who interact with the system could be harmed. For every example we can think of that seems purely technical, it becomes obvious that decision-making technologies like ML don't exist without interacting with humans in some way.

This means there's no purely technical solution to bias in ML systems. If readers want to jump right into the code for bias testing and bias remediation, see Chapter 10. However, we don't recommend this. Readers will miss a lot of important information about what bias is and how to think about it in productive ways. This chapter starts out by defining bias using several different authoritative sources, and how to recognize our own cognitive biases that may affect the ML systems we build or the results our users interpret. The chapter then provides a broad overview of who tends to be harmed in AI bias incidents and what kinds of harms they experience. From there, we'll cover methods to test for bias in ML systems and discuss mitigating bias using both technical and sociotechnical approaches. Finally, the chapter will close with a case discussion of the Twitter image-cropping algorithm.

 While some aspects of bias management must be tuned to the specific architecture of a model, a great deal of bias management is not model-specific. Many of the ideas in this chapter, particularly those drawn from the NIST SP1270 bias guidance and the Twitter Bias Bounty, can be applied to a wide variety of sophisticated AI systems like ChatGPT or RoBERTa language models. If readers want to see this in practice, check out IQT Labs' audit of RoBERTa (*https://oreil.ly/3hs_6*).

NIST AI RMF Crosswalk

Chapter section	NIST AI RMF subcategories
"Systemic Bias" on page 126	MAP 1.6, MAP 2.3, MEASURE 2.11
"Statistical Bias" on page 126	MAP 2.3, MEASURE 2.6, MEASURE 2.11
"Human Biases and Data Science Culture" on page 127	GOVERN 3.2, MAP 1.1, MAP 2.3, MEASURE 2.11
"Legal Notions of ML Bias in the United States" on page 128	GOVERN 1.1, GOVERN 1.2, GOVERN 1.4, GOVERN 2.2, GOVERN 4.1, MAP 1.1, MAP 1.2, MEASURE 2.11
"Who Tends to Experience Bias from ML Systems" on page 131	GOVERN 1.2, GOVERN 1.4, GOVERN 5, MAP 1.1, MAP 1.2, MAP 1.6, MAP 2.2, MAP 3, MAP 5, MEASURE 1.3, MEASURE 4, MANAGE 2, MANAGE 4
"Harms That People Experience" on page 133	GOVERN 1.2, GOVERN 1.4, GOVERN 5, MAP 1.1, MAP 1.2, MAP 1.6, MAP 2.2, MAP 3, MAP 5, MEASURE 1.3, MEASURE 4, MANAGE 1.4, MANAGE 2, MANAGE 4
"Testing Data" on page 135	MEASURE 1.1, MEASURE 2.1
"Traditional Approaches: Testing for Equivalent Outcomes" on page 137	GOVERN 1.1, GOVERN 1.2, GOVERN 1.4, GOVERN 4.3, GOVERN 6.1, MAP 2.3, MAP 4, MEASURE 1, MEASURE 2.1, MEASURE 2.6, MEASURE 2.11, MEASURE 4.2
"A New Mindset: Testing for Equivalent Performance Quality" on page 141	GOVERN 1.2, GOVERN 1.4, GOVERN 4.3, GOVERN 6.1, MAP 2.3, MAP 4, MEASURE 1, MEASURE 2.1, MEASURE 2.6, MEASURE 2.11, MEASURE 4.2
"On the Horizon: Tests for the Broader ML Ecosystem" on page 143	GOVERN 1.2, GOVERN 1.4, GOVERN 4.3, GOVERN 6.1, MAP 2.3, MAP 4, MEASURE 1, MEASURE 2.1, MEASURE 2.6, MEASURE 2.11, MEASURE 4.2, MANAGE 3.2
"Technical Factors in Mitigating Bias" on page 148	MAP 2.3, MANAGE
"The Scientific Method and Experimental Design" on page 148	MAP 1.1, MAP 2.3
"Human Factors in Mitigating Bias" on page 153	GOVERN 2.1, GOVERN 3, MAP 1.1, MAP 1.6, MAP 2.2, MAP 2.3, MEASURE 3.2, MEASURE 3.3, MANAGE 1, MANAGE 2.1, MANAGE 2.2, MANAGE 3, MANAGE 4.2, MANAGE 4.3

- Applicable AI trustworthiness characteristics include: Managed Bias, Transparent and Accountable, Valid and Reliable

- See also:
  - — "Towards a Standard for Identifying and Managing Bias in Artificial Intelligence" (*https://oreil.ly/8kpf5*)
  - — Full crosswalk table (not an official resource) (*https://oreil.ly/61TXd*)

ISO and NIST Definitions for Bias

The International Organization for Standardization (ISO) defines bias as "the degree to which a reference value deviates from the truth" in "Statistics—Vocabulary and Symbols—Part 1" (*https://oreil.ly/YYv4W*). This is a very general notion of bias, but bias is a complex and heterogenous phenomenon. Yet, in all of its instances, it's about some systematic deviation from the truth. In decision-making tasks, bias takes on many forms. It's substantively and ethically wrong to deny people employment due to the level of melanin in their skin. It's factually wrong to think an idea is correct just because it's the first thing that comes to mind. And it's substantively and ethically wrong to train an ML model on incomplete and unrepresentative data. In a recent work from NIST, "Towards a Standard for Identifying and Managing Bias in Artificial Intelligence" (SP1270) (*https://oreil.ly/pkm4f*), the subject of bias is divided into three major categories that align with these examples of bias: systemic, statistical, and human biases.

Systemic Bias

Often when we say bias in ML, we mean systemic biases. These are historical, social, and institutional biases that are, sadly, so baked into our lives that they show up in ML training data and design choices by default. A common consequence of systemic bias in ML models is the incorporation of demographic information into system mechanisms. This incorporation may be overt and explicit, such as when language models (LMs) are repurposed to generate harmful and offensive content (*https://oreil.ly/bWf4E*) that targets certain demographic groups. However, in practice, incorporation of demographic information into decision-making processes tends to be unintentional and implicit, leading to differential outcome rates or outcome prevalence across demographic groups, for example, by matching more men's resumes to higher paying job descriptions, or design problems that exclude certain groups of users (e.g., those with physical disabilities) from interacting with a system.

Statistical Bias

Statistical biases can be thought of as mistakes made by humans in the specification of ML systems, or emergent phenomena like concept drift, that affect ML models and are difficult for humans to mitigate. Other common types of statistical biases include predictions based on unrepresentative training data, or error propagation and feedback loops. One potential indicator of statistical bias in ML models is differential performance quality across different cross-sections of data, such as demographic groups. Differential validity for an ML model is a particular type of bias, somewhat distinct from the differing outcome rates or outcome prevalence described for human biases. In fact, there is a documented tension (*https://oreil.ly/cJy7F*) between maximizing model performance within demographic groups and maintaining equality of positive outcome rates. Statistical biases may also lead to serious AI incidents, for example when concept drift in new data renders a system's decisions more wrong than right, or when feedback loops or error propagation lead to increasingly large volumes of bad predictions over a short time span.

Human Biases and Data Science Culture

There are a number of human or cognitive biases that can come into play with both the individuals and the teams that design, implement, and maintain ML systems. For a more complete list of human biases, read the NIST SP1270 guidance paper. The following are the human biases that we've seen most frequently affecting both data scientists and users of ML systems:

Anchoring
> When a particular reference point, or *anchor*, has an undue effect on people's decisions. This is like when a benchmark for a state-of-the-art deep learning model is stuck at 0.4 AUC for a long time, and someone comes along and scores 0.403 AUC. We shouldn't think that's important, but we're anchored to 0.4.

Availability heuristic
> People tend to overweight what comes easily or quickly to mind in decision-making processes. Put another way, we often confuse *easy to remember* with *correct*.

Confirmation bias
> A cognitive bias where people tend to prefer information that aligns with, or confirms, their existing beliefs. Confirmation bias is a big problem in ML systems when we trick ourselves into thinking our ML models work better than they actually do.

Dunning-Kruger effect
> The tendency of people with low ability in a given area or task to overestimate their self-assessed ability. This happens when we allow ourselves to think we're experts at something just because we can `import sklearn` and run `model.fit()`.

Funding bias
> A bias toward highlighting or promoting results that support or satisfy the funding agency or financial supporter of a project. We do what makes our bosses happy, what makes our investors happy, and what increases our own salaries. Real science needs safeguards that prevent its progress from being altered by biased financial interests.

Groupthink

When people in a group tend to make nonoptimal decisions based on their desire to conform to the group or fear dissenting with the group. It's hard to disagree with our team, even when we're confident that we're right.

McNamara fallacy

The belief that decisions should be made based solely on quantitative information, at the expense of qualitative information or data points that aren't easily measured.

Techno-chauvinism

The belief that technology is always the solution.

All these biases can and do lead to inappropriate and overly optimistic design choices, in turn leading to poor performance when a system is deployed, and, finally, leading to harms for system users or operators. We'll get into the harms that can arise and what to do about these problems shortly. For now we want to highlight a commonsense mitigant that is also a theme of this chapter. We cannot treat bias properly without looking at a problem from many different perspectives. Step 0 of fighting bias in ML is having a diverse group of stakeholders in the room (or video call) when important decisions about the system are made. To avoid the blind spots that allow biased ML models to cause harm, we'll need many different types of perspectives informing system design, implementation, and maintenance decisions. Yes, we're speaking about gathering input from different demographic perspectives, including from those with disabilities. We're also speaking about educational backgrounds, such as those of social scientists, lawyers, and domain experts.

Also, consider the *digital divide*. A shocking percentage of the population still doesn't have access to good internet connectivity, new computers, and information like this book. If we're drawing conclusions about our users, we need to remember that there is a solid chunk of the population that's not going to be included in user statistics. Leaving potential users out is a huge source of bias and harm in system design, bias testing, and other crucial junctures in the ML lifecycle. Success in ML today still requires the involvement of people who have a keen understanding of the real-world problem we're trying to solve, and what potential users might be left out of our design, data, and testing.

Legal Notions of ML Bias in the United States

We should be aware of the many important legal notions of bias. However, it's also important to understand that the legal system is extremely complex and context sensitive. Merely knowing a few definitions will still leave us light years away from having any real expertise on these matters. As data scientists, legal matters are an area where we should not let the Dunning-Kruger effect take over. With those caveats, let's dive into a basic overview.

 Now is the time to reach out to your legal team if you have any questions or concerns about bias in ML models. Dealing with bias in ML models is one of the most difficult and serious issues in the information economy. Data scientists need help from lawyers to properly address bias risks.

In the US, bias in decision-making processes that affect the public has been regulated for decades. A major focus of early laws and regulations in the US was employment matters. Notions like protected groups, disparate treatment, and disparate impact have now spread to a broader set of laws in consumer finance and housing, and are even being cited in brand new local laws today, like the New York City audit requirement for AI used in hiring. Nondiscrimination in the EU is addressed in the Charter of Fundamental Rights, the European Convention on Human Rights, and in the Treaty on the Functioning of the EU, and, crucially for us, in aspects of the proposed EU AI Act. While it's impossible to summarize these laws and regulations, even on the US side, the definitions that follow are what we think are most directly applicable to a data scientist's daily work. They are drawn, very roughly, from laws like the Civil Rights Act, the Fair Housing Act (FHA), Equal Employment Opportunity Commission (EEOC) regulations, the Equal Credit Opportunity Act (ECOA), and the Americans with Disabilities Act (ADA). The following definitions cover legal ideas about what traits are protected under law and what these laws seek to protect us from:

Protected groups
> In the US, many laws and regulations prohibit discrimination based on race, sex (or gender, in some cases), age, religious affiliation, national origin, and disability status, among other categories. Prohibited decision bases under the FHA include race, color, religion, national origin, sex, familial status, and disability. The EU's GDPR, as an example of one non-US regulation, prohibits the use of personal data about racial or ethnic origin, political opinions, and other categories somewhat analogous to US protected groups. This is one reason why traditional bias testing compares results for protected groups and so called *control* (or *reference*) groups that are not protected groups.

Disparate treatment
> Disparate treatment is a specific type of discrimination that is illegal in many industries. It's a decision that treats an individual less favorably than similarly situated individuals because of a protected characteristic such as race, sex, or other trait. For data scientists working on employment, housing, or credit applications,

this means we should be very careful when using demographic data in ML models, and even in our bias-remediation techniques. Once demographic data is used as input in a model, that could mean that a decision for someone could be different just because of their demographics, and that disparate treatment could result in some cases.

 Concerns about disparate treatment, and more general systemic bias, are why we typically try not to use demographic markers as direct inputs to ML models. To be conservative, demographic markers should *not* be used as model inputs in most common scenarios, but should be used for bias testing or monitoring purposes.

Disparate impact

Disparate impact is another kind of legally concerning discrimination. It's basically about different *outcome* rates or prevalence across demographic groups. Disparate impact is more formally defined as the result of a seemingly neutral policy or practice that disproportionately harms a protected group. For data scientists, disparate impact tends to happen when we don't use demographic data as inputs, but we use something correlated to demographic data as an input. Consider credit scores: they are a fairly accurate predictor of default, so they are often seen as valid to use in predictive models in consumer lending. However, they are correlated to race, such that some minority groups have lower credit scores on average. If we use a credit score in a model, this tends to result in certain minority groups having lower proportions of positive outcomes, and that's a common example of disparate impact. (That's also why several states have started to restrict the use of credit scores in some insurance-related decisions.)

Differential validity

Differential validity is a construct that comes up sometimes in employment. Where disparate impact is often about different outcome rates across demographic groups, differential validity is more about different *performance quality* across groups. It happens when an employment test is a better indicator of job performance for some groups than for others. Differential validity is important because the mathematical underpinning, not the legal construct, generalizes to nearly all ML models. It's common to use unrepresentative training data and to build a model that performs better for some groups than for others, and a lot of more recent bias-testing approaches focus on this type of bias.

Screen out

Screen out is a very important type of discrimination that highlights the socio-technical nature of ML systems and proves that testing and balancing the scores of a model is simply insufficient to protect against bias. Screen out happens when a person with a disability, such as limited vision or difficulties with fine motor skills, is unable to interact with an employment assessment, and is screened out of a job or promotion by default. Screen out is a serious issue, and the EEOC and Department of Labor are paying attention (*https://oreil.ly/c0y9i*) to the use of ML in this space. Note that screen out cannot necessarily be fixed by mathematical bias testing or bias remediation; it typically must be addressed in the design phase of the system, where designers ensure those with disabilities are able to work with the end product's interfaces. Screen out also highlights why we want perspectives from lawyers and those with disabilities when building ML systems. Without those perspectives, it's all too easy to forget about people with disabilities when building ML systems, and that can sometimes give rise to legal liabilities.

This concludes our discussion on general definitions of bias. As readers can see, it's a complex and multifaceted topic with all kinds of human, scientific, and legal concerns coming into play. We'll add to these definitions with more specific, but probably more fraught, mathematical definitions of bias when we discuss bias testing later in the chapter. Next we'll outline who tends to experience bias and related harms from ML systems.

Who Tends to Experience Bias from ML Systems

Any demographic group can experience bias and related harms when interacting with an ML system, but history tells us certain groups are more likely to experience bias and harms more often. In fact, it's the nature of supervised learning—which only learns and repeats patterns from past recorded data—that tends to result in older people, those with disabilities, immigrants, people of color, women, and gender-nonconforming individuals facing more bias from ML systems. Put another way, those who experience discrimination in the real world, or in the digital world, will likely also experience it when dealing with ML systems because all that discrimination has been recorded in data and used to train ML models. The groups listed in this section are often protected under various laws, but not always. They will often, but not always, be the comparison group in bias testing for statistical parity of scores or outcomes between two demographic groups.

Many people belong to multiple protected or marginalized groups. The important concept of intersectionality tells us that societal harm is concentrated among those who occupy multiple protected groups and that bias should not only be analyzed as affecting marginalized groups along single group dimensions (*https://oreil.ly/3ZaPy*). For example, AI ethics researchers recently showed (*https://oreil.ly/DMu8o*) that some commercially available facial recognition systems have substantial gender classification accuracy disparities, with darker-skinned women being the most misclassified group. Finally, before defining these groups, it is also important to think of the McNamara fallacy. Is it even right to put nuanced human beings into this kind of blunted taxonomy? Probably not, and it's likely that assignment to these simplistic groups, which is often done because such categories are easy to represent as binary marker columns in a database, is also a source of bias and potential harms. There are always a lot of caveats in managing bias in ML systems, so with those in mind, we tread carefully into defining simplified demographic groups that tend to face more discrimination and that are often used as comparison groups in traditional bias testing:

Age

Older people, typically those 40 and above, are more likely to experience discrimination in online content. The age cutoff could be older in more traditional applications likes employment, housing, or consumer finance. However, participation in Medicare or the accumulation of financial wealth over a lifetime may make older people the favored group in other scenarios.

Disability

Those with physical, mental, or emotional disabilities are perhaps some of the likeliest people to experience bias from ML systems. The idea of screen out generalizes outside of employment, even if the legal construct may not. People with disabilities are often forgotten about during the design of ML systems, and no amount of mathematical bias testing or remediation can make up for that.

Immigration status or national origin

People who live in a country in which they were not born, with any immigration status, including naturalized citizens, are known to face significant bias challenges.

Language

Especially in online content, an important domain for ML systems, those who use languages other than English or who write in non-Latin scripts may be more likely to experience bias from ML systems.

Race and ethnicity

Races and ethnicities other than white people, including those who identify as more than one race, are commonly subject to bias and harm when interacting with ML systems. Some also prefer skin tone scales over traditional race or ethnicity labels, especially for computer vision tasks. The Fitzpatrick scale (*https://oreil.ly/NJfBP*) is an example of a skin tone scale.

Sex and gender

Sexes and genders other than cisgender men are more likely to experience bias and harms at the hands of an ML system. In online content, women are often favored—but in harmful ways. Known as the *male gaze* phenomenon, media about women may be appealing and receive positive treatment (such as being promoted in a social media feed), specifically because that content is oriented toward objectification, subjugation, or sexualization of women.

Intersectional groups
People who are in two or more of the preceding groups may experience bias or harms that are greater than the simple sum of the two broader groups to which they belong. All the bias testing and mitigation steps described in this chapter should consider intersectional groups.

Of course these are not the only groups of people who may experience bias from an ML model, and grouping people can be problematic no matter what the motivation. However, it's important to know where to start looking for bias, and we hope our list is sufficient for that purpose. Now that we know where to look for ML bias, let's discuss the most common harms that we should be mindful of.

Harms That People Experience

Many common types of harm occur in online or digital content. They occur frequently too—perhaps so frequently that we may become blind to them. The following list highlights common harms and provides examples so that we can recognize them better when we see them next. These harms align closely with those laid out in Abagayle Lee Blank's "Computer Vision Machine Learning and Future-Oriented Ethics" (*https://oreil.ly/-JmJA*), which describes cases in which these harms occur in computer vision:

Denigration
Content that is actively derogatory or offensive—e.g., offensive content generated by chatbots like Tay (*https://oreil.ly/2938n*) or Lee Luda (*https://oreil.ly/nRzs1*).

Erasure
Erasure of content challenging dominant social paradigms or past harms suffered by marginalized groups—e.g., suppressing content (*https://oreil.ly/FZdDB*) that discusses racism or calls out white supremacy.

Exnomination
Treating notions like whiteness, maleness, or heterosexuality as central human norms—e.g., online searches (*https://oreil.ly/m-zR-*) returning a Barbie Doll as the first female result for "CEO."

Misrecognition
Mistaking a person's identity or failing to recognize someone's humanity—e.g., misrecognizing Black people (*https://oreil.ly/GjyTI*) in automated image tagging.

Stereotyping

> The tendency to assign characteristics to all members of a group—e.g., LMs automatically associating Muslims with violence (*https://oreil.ly/eqAgw*).

Underrepresentation

> The lack of fair or adequate representation of demographic groups in model outputs—e.g., generative models thinking all doctors are white males and all nurses are white females (*https://oreil.ly/V64lj*).

Sometimes these harms may only cause effects limited to online or digital spaces, but as our digital lives begin to overlap more substantially with other parts of our lives, harms also spill over into the real world. ML systems in healthcare, employment, education, or other high-risk areas can cause harm directly, by wrongfully denying people access to needed resources. The most obvious types of real-world harms caused by ML systems include the following:

Economic harms

> When an ML system reduces the economic opportunity or value of some activity—e.g., when men see more ads (*https://oreil.ly/BT-cI*) for better jobs than women.

Physical harms

> When an ML system hurts or kills someone—e.g., when people overrely on self-driving automation (*https://oreil.ly/BxH5Y*).

Psychological harms

> When an ML system causes mental or emotional distress—e.g., when disturbing content (*https://oreil.ly/pQRYE*) is recommended to children.

Reputational harms

> When an ML system diminishes the reputation of an individual or organization—e.g., a consumer credit product rollout is marred by accusations (*https://oreil.ly/Wbvq5*) of discrimination.

Unfortunately, users or subjects of ML systems may experience additional harms or combinations of harms that manifest in strange ways. Before we get too deep in the weeds with different kinds of bias testing in the next section, remember that checking in with our users to make sure they are not experiencing the harms discussed here, or other types of harms, is perhaps one of most direct ways to track bias in ML systems. In fact, in the most basic sense, it matters much more whether people are experiencing harm than whether some set of scores passes a necessarily flawed mathematical test. We must think about these harms when designing our system, talk to our users to ensure they don't experience harm, and seek to mitigate harms.

Testing for Bias

If there's a chance that an ML system could harm people, it should be tested for bias. The goal of this section is to cover the most common approaches for testing ML models for bias so readers can get started with this important risk management task. Testing is neither straightforward nor conclusive. Just like in performance testing, a system can look fine on test data, and go on to fail or cause harm once deployed. Or a system could exhibit minimal bias at testing and deployment time, but drift into making biased or harmful predictions over time. Moreover, there are many tests and effect size measurements with known flaws and that conflict with one another. For a good overview of these issues, see the YouTube video of Princeton Professor Arvind Narayanan's conference talk "21 Fairness Definitions and Their Politics" (*https://oreil.ly/4QnqM*), from the ACM Conference on Fairness, Accountability, and Transparency in ML. For an in-depth mathematical analysis of why we can't simply minimize all bias metrics at once, check out "Inherent Trade-Offs in the Fair Determination of Risk Scores" (*https://oreil.ly/WvBOg*). With these cautions in mind, let's start our tour of contemporary bias-testing approaches.

Testing Data

This section covers what's needed in training data to test for bias, and how to test that data for bias even before a model is trained. ML models learn from data. But no data is perfect or without bias. If systemic bias is represented in training data, that bias will likely manifest in the model's outputs. It's logical to start testing for bias in training data. But to do that, we have to assume that certain columns of data are available. At minimum, for each row of data, we need demographic markers, known outcomes (y, dependent variable, target feature, etc.) and later, we'll need model outcomes—predictions for regression models, and decisions and confidence scores or posterior probabilities for classification models. While there are a handful of testing approaches that don't require demographic markers, most accepted approaches require this data. Don't have it? Testing is going to be much more difficult, but we'll provide some guidance on inferring demographic marker labels too.

 Our models and data are far from perfect, so don't let the perfect be the enemy of the good in bias testing. Our data will never be perfect and we'll never find the perfect test. Testing is very important to get right, but to be successful in real-world bias mitigation, it's just one part of broader ML management and governance processes.

The need to know or infer demographic markers is a good example of why handling bias in ML requires holistic design thinking, not just slapping another Python package onto the end of our pipeline. Demographic markers and individual-level data are also more sensitive from a privacy standpoint, and sometimes organizations don't collect this information for data privacy reasons. While the interplay of data privacy and nondiscrimination law is very complex, it's probably not the case that data privacy obligations override nondiscrimination obligations. But as data scientists, we can't answer such questions on our own. Any perceived conflict between data privacy and nondiscrimination requirements has to be addressed by attorneys and compliance specialists. Such complex legal considerations are an example of why addressing bias in ML necessitates the engagement of a broad set of stakeholders.

 In employment, consumer finance, or other areas where disparate treatment is prohibited, we need to check with our legal colleagues before changing our data based directly on protected class membership information, even if our intention is to mitigate bias.

By now, readers are probably starting to realize how challenging and complex bias testing can be. As technicians, dealing with this complexity is not our sole responsibility, but we need to be aware of it and work within a broader team to address bias in ML systems. Now, let's step into the role of a technician responsible for preparing data and testing data for bias. If we have the data we need, we tend to look for three major issues—representativeness, distribution of outcomes, and proxies:

Representiveness

    The basic check to run here is to calculate the proportion of rows for each demographic group in the training data, with the idea that a model will struggle to learn about groups with only a small number of training data rows. Generally, proportions of different demographic groups in training data should reflect the population on which the model will be deployed. If it doesn't, we should probably collect more representative data. It's also possible to resample or reweigh a dataset to achieve better representativeness. However, if we're working in employment, consumer finance, or other areas where disparate treatment is prohibited, we really need to check with our legal colleagues before changing our data based directly on protected class membership information. If we're running into differential validity problems (described later in this chapter), then rebalancing our training data to have larger or equal representation across groups may be in order. Balance among different classes may increase prediction quality across groups, but it may not help with, or may even worsen, imbalanced distributions of positive outcomes.

Distribution of outcomes

    We need to know how outcomes (y variable values) are distributed across demographic groups, because if the model learns that some groups receive more positive outcomes than others, that can lead to disparate impact. We need to calculate a bivariate distribution of y across each demographic group. If we see an imbalance of outcomes across groups, then we can try to resample or reweigh our training data, with certain legal caveats. More likely, we'll simply end up knowing that bias risks are serious for this model, and when we test its outcomes, we'll need to pay special attention and likely plan on some type of remediation.

Proxies

In most business applications of ML, we should *not* be training models on demographic markers. But even if we don't use demographic markers directly, information like names, addresses, educational details, or facial images may encode a great deal of demographic information. Other types of information may proxy for demographic markers too. One way to find proxies is to build an adversarial model based on each input column and see if those models can predict any demographic marker. If they can predict a demographic marker, then those columns encode demographic information and are likely demographic proxies. If possible, such proxies should be removed from training data. Proxies may also be more hidden in training data. There's no standard technique to test for these latent proxies, but we can apply the same adversarial modeling technique as described for direct proxies, except instead of using the features themselves, we can use engineered interactions of features that we suspect may be serving as proxies. We also suggest having dedicated legal or compliance stakeholders vet each and every input feature in our model with an eye toward proxy discrimination risk. If proxies cannot be removed or we suspect the presence of latent proxies, we should pay careful attention to bias-testing results for system outcomes, and be prepared to take remediation steps later in the bias mitigation process.

The outlined tests and checks for representativeness, distribution of outcomes, and proxies in training data all rely on the presence of demographic group markers, as will most of the tests for model outcomes. If we don't have those demographic labels, then one accepted approach is to infer them. The Bayesian improved surname geocoding (BISG) (*https://oreil.ly/cJn-M*) approach infers race and ethnicity from name and postal code data. It's sad but true that US society is still so segregated that zip code and name can predict race and ethnicity, often with above 90% accuracy. This approach was developed by the RAND Corporation and the Consumer Financial Protection Bureau (CFPB) and has a high level of credibility for bias testing in consumer finance. The CFPB even has code on its GitHub (*https://oreil.ly/hkvMD*) for BISG! If necessary, similar approaches may be used to infer gender (*https://oreil.ly/eL1qM*) from name, Social Security number, or birth year.

Traditional Approaches: Testing for Equivalent Outcomes

Once we've assessed our data for bias, made sure we have the information needed to perform bias testing, and trained a model, it's time to test its outcomes for bias. We'll start our discussion on bias testing by addressing some established tests. These tests tend to have some precedent in law, regulation, or legal commentary, and they tend to focus on average differences in outcomes across demographic groups. For a great summary of traditional bias-testing guidance, see the concise guidance (*https://oreil.ly/_bcVD*) of the Office of Federal Contract Compliance Programs for testing employment selection procedures. For these kinds of tests, it doesn't matter if we're analyzing the scores from a multiple choice employment test or numeric scores from a cutting-edge AI-based recommender system.

The tests in this section are aligned to the notion *statistical parity*, or when a model generates roughly equal probabilities or favorable predictions for all demographic groups.

Table 4-1 highlights how these tests tend to be divided into categories for statistical and practical tests, and for continuous and binary outcomes. These tests rely heavily on the notion of protected groups, where the mean outcome for the protected group (e.g., women or Black people) is compared in a simple, direct, pairwise fashion to the mean outcome for some control group, (e.g., men or white people, respectively). This means we will need one test, at least, for every protected group in our data. If this sounds old fashioned, it is. But since these are the tests that have been used the most in regulatory and litigation settings for decades, it's prudent to start with these tests before getting creative with newer methodologies. More established tests also tend to have known thresholds that indicate when values are problematic. These thresholds are listed in Table 4-1 and discussed in more detail in the sections that follow.

Table 4-1. Some common metrics used to measure bias in ML models, with thresholds where applicable[a]

Test type	Discrete outcome/Classification tests	Continuous outcome/Regression tests
Statistical significance	Logistic regression coefficient	Linear regression coefficient
Statistical significance	χ^2 test	*t*-test
Statistical significance	Fisher's exact test	
Statistical significance	Binomial-*z*	
Practical significance	Comparison of group means	Comparison of group means
Practical significance	Percentage point difference between group means/marginal effect	Percentage point difference between group means
Practical significance	Adverse impact ratio (AIR) (acceptable: 0.8–1.25)	Standardized mean difference (SMD, Cohen's *d*) (small difference: 0.2, medium difference: 0.5, large difference: 0.8)
Practical significance	Odds ratios	
Practical significance	Shortfall to parity	

Test type	Discrete outcome/Classification tests	Continuous outcome/Regression tests
Differential validity	Accuracy or AUC ratios (acceptable: 0.8–1.25)	R^2 ratio (acceptable: 0.8–1.25)
Differential validity	TPR, TNR, FPR, FNR ratios (acceptable: 0.8–1.25)	MSE, RMSE ratios (acceptable: 0.8–1.25)
Differential validity	Equality of odds ([control TPR ≈ protected TPR | y = 1] and [control FPR ≈ protected FPR | y = 0])	
Differential validity	Equality of opportunity ([control TPR ≈ protected TPR | y = 1])	

[a] TPR = true positive rate; TNR = true negative rate; FPR = false positive rate; FNR = false negative rate

Statistical significance testing

Statistical significance testing probably has the most acceptance across disciplines and legal jurisdictions, so let's focus there first. Statistical significance testing is used to determine whether average or proportional differences in model outcomes across protected groups are likely to be seen in new data, or whether the differences in outcomes are random properties of our current testing datasets. For continuous outcomes, we often rely on t-tests between mean model outputs across two demographic groups. For binary outcomes, we often use binomial z-tests on the proportions of positive outcomes across two different demographic groups, chi-squared tests on contingency tables of model outputs, and Fisher's exact test when cells in the contingency test have less than 30 individuals in them.

If you're thinking this is a lot of pairwise tests that leave out important information, good job! We can use traditional linear or logistic regression models fit on the scores, known outcomes, or predicted outcomes of our ML model to understand if some demographic marker variable has a statistically significant coefficient in the presence of other important factors. Of course, evaluating statistical significance is difficult too. Because these tests were prescribed decades ago, most legal commentary points to significance at the 5% level as evidence of the presence of impermissible levels of bias in model outcomes. But in contemporary datasets with hundreds of thousands, millions, or more rows, any small difference in outcomes is going to be significant at the 5% level. We recommend analyzing traditional statistical bias-testing results at the 5% significance level and with significance level adjustments that are appropriate for our dataset size. We'd focus most of our energy on the adjusted results, but keep in mind that in the worst-case scenario, our organization could potentially face legal scrutiny and bias testing by external experts that would hold us to the 5% significance threshold. This would be yet another great time to start speaking with our colleagues in the legal department.

Practical significance testing

The adverse impact ratio (AIR) and its associated four-fifths rule threshold are probably the most well-known and most abused bias-testing tools in the US. Let's consider what it is first, then proceed to how it's abused by practitioners. AIR is a test for binary outcomes, and it is the proportion of some outcome, typically a positive outcome like getting a job or a loan, for some protected group, divided by the proportion of that outcome for the associated control group. That proportion is associated with a threshold of four-fifths or 0.8. This four-fifths rule was highlighted by the EEOC in the late 1970s as a practical line in the sand, with results above four-fifths being highly preferred. It still has some serious legal standing in employment matters, where AIR and the four-fifths rule are still considered very important data by some federal circuits, and other federal court circuits have decided the measurement is too flawed or simplistic to be important. In most cases, AIR and the four-fifths rule have no official legal standing outside of employment, but they are still used occasionally as an internal bias-testing tool across regulated verticals like consumer finance. Moreover, AIR could always show up in the testimony of an expert in a lawsuit, for any bias-related matter.

AIR is an easy and popular bias test. So, what do we get wrong about AIR? Plenty. Technicians tend to interpret it incorrectly. An AIR over 0.8 is not necessarily a good sign. If our AIR test comes out below 0.8, that's probably a bad sign. But if it's above four-fifths, that doesn't mean everything is OK. Another issue is the confusion of the AIR metric and the 0.8 threshold with the legal construct of disparate impact. We can't explain why, but some vendors call AIR, literally, "disparate impact." They are not the same. Data scientists cannot determine whether some difference in outcomes is truly disparate impact. Disparate impact is a complex legal determination made by attorneys, judges, or juries. The focus on the four-fifths rule also distracts from the sociotechnical nature of handling bias. Four-fifths is only legally meaningful in some employment cases. Like any numeric result, AIR test results alone are insufficient for the identification of bias in a complex ML system.

All that said, it's still probably a good idea to look into AIR results and other practical significance results. Another common measure is standardized mean difference (SMD, or Cohen's d). SMD can be used on regression or classification outputs—so it's even more model-agnostic than AIR. SMD is the mean outcome or score for some protected group minus the mean outcome or score for a control group, with that quantity divided by a measure of the standard deviation of the outcome. Magnitudes of SMD at 0.2, 0.5, and 0.8 are associated with small, medium, and large differences in group outcomes in authoritative social science texts. Other common practical significance measures are percentage point difference (PPD), or the difference in mean outcomes across two groups expressed as a percentage, and shortfall, the number of people or the monetary amount required to make outcomes equivalent across a protected and control group.

The worst-case scenario in traditional outcomes testing is that both statistical and practical testing results show meaningful differences in outcomes across one or more pairs or protected and control groups. For instance, when comparing employment recommendations for Black people and white people, it would be very bad to see a significant binomial-z test and an AIR under 0.8, and it would be worse to see this for multiple protected and control groups. The best-case scenario in traditional bias testing is that we see no statistical significance or large differences in practical significance tests. But even in this case, we still have no guarantees that a system won't be biased once it's deployed or isn't biased in ways these tests don't detect, like via screen out. Of course, the most likely case in traditional testing is that we will see some mix of results and will need help interpreting them, and fixing detected problems, from a group of stakeholders outside our direct data science team. Even with all that work and communication, traditional bias testing would only be the first step in a thorough bias-testing exercise. Next we'll discuss some newer ideas on bias testing.

A New Mindset: Testing for Equivalent Performance Quality

In more recent years, many researchers have put forward testing approaches that focus on disparate performance quality across demographic groups. Though these tests have less legal precedent than traditional tests for practical and statistical significance, they are somewhat related to the concept of differential validity. These newer techniques seek to understand how common ML prediction errors may affect minority groups, and to ensure that humans interacting with an ML system have an equal opportunity to receive positive outcomes.

The important paper "Fairness Beyond Disparate Treatment and Disparate Impact: Learning Classification without Disparate Mistreatment" (*https://oreil.ly/NkTBF*) lays out the case for why it's important to think through ML model errors in the context of fairness. If minority groups receive more false positive or false negative decisions than other groups, any number of harms can arise depending on the application. In their seminal "Equality of Opportunity in Machine Learning" (*https://oreil.ly/_w-c3*), Hardt, Price, and Srebro define a notion of fairness that modifies the widely acknowledged equalized odds idea. In the older equalized odds scenario, when the known outcome occurs (i.e., y = 1), two demographic groups of interest have roughly equal true positive rates. When the known outcome does not occur (i.e., y = 0), equalized odds means that false positive rates are roughly equal across two demographic groups. Equality of opportunity relaxes the y = 0 constraint of equalized odds and argues that when y = 1 equates to a positive outcome, such as receiving a loan or getting a job, seeking equalized true positive rates is a simpler and more utilitarian approach.

If readers have spent any time with confusion matrices, they'll know there are many other ways to analyze the errors of a binary classifier. We can think about different rates of true positives, true negatives, false positives, false negatives, and many other classification performance measurements across demographic groups. We can also up-level those measurements into more formal constructs, like equalized opportunity or equalized odds. Table 4-2 provides an example of how performance quality and error metrics across demographic groups can be helpful in testing for bias.

Table 4-2. Classification quality and error rates calculated across two demographic groups[a]

Metric type	...	Accuracy	Sensitivity (TPR)	...	Specificity (TNR)	...	FPR	FNR	...
Female value	...	0.808	0.528	...	0.881	...	0.119	0.472	...
Male value	...	0.781	0.520	...	0.868	...	0.132	0.480	...
Female-to-male ratio	...	1.035	1.016	...	1.016	...	1.069	0.983	...

[a] The values for the comparison group, females, are divided by the values for the control group, males.

The first step, shown in Table 4-2, is to calculate a set of performance and error measurements across two or more demographic groups of interest. Then, using AIR and the four-fifths rule as a guide, we form a ratio of the comparison group value to the control group value, and apply thresholds of four-fifths (0.8) and five-fourths (1.25) to highlight any potential bias issues. It's important to say that the 0.8 and 1.25 thresholds are only guides here; they have no legal meaning and are more common-sense markers than anything else. Ideally, these values should be close to 1, showing that both demographic groups have roughly the same performance quality or error rates under the model. We may flag these thresholds with whatever values make sense to us, but we would argue that 0.8–1.25 is the maximum range of acceptable values.

Based on our application, some metrics may be more important than others. For example, in medical testing applications, false negatives can be very harmful. If one demographic group is experiencing more false negatives in a medical diagnosis than others, it's easy to see how that can lead to bias harms. The fairness metric decision tree at slide 40 of "Dealing with Bias and Fairness in AI/ML/Data Science Systems" (*https://oreil.ly/Es2d1*) can be a great tool for helping to decide which of all of these different fairness metrics might be best for our application.

Are you thinking "What about regression? What about everything in ML outside of binary classification?!" It's true that bias testing is most developed for binary classifiers, which can be frustrating. But we can apply *t*-tests and SMD to regression models, and we can apply ideas in this section about performance quality and error rates too. Just like we form ratios of classification metrics, we can also form ratios of

R^2, mean average percentage error (MAPE), or normalized root mean square error (RMSE) across comparison and control groups, and again, use the four-fifths rule as a guide to highlight when these ratios may be telling us there is a bias problem in our predictions. As for the rest of ML, outside binary classification and regression, that's what we will cover next. Be prepared to apply some ingenuity and elbow grease.

On the Horizon: Tests for the Broader ML Ecosystem

A great deal of research and legal commentary assumes the use of binary classifiers. There is a reason for this. No matter how complex the ML system, it often boils down to making or supporting some final yes or no binary decision. If that decision affects people and we have the data to do it, we should test those outcomes using the full suite of tools we've discussed already. In some cases, the output of an ML system does not inform an eventual binary decision, or perhaps we'd like to dig deeper and understand drivers of bias in our system or which subpopulations might be experiencing the most bias. Or maybe we're using a generative model, like an LM or image generation system. In these cases, AIR, *t*-tests, and true positive rate ratios are not going to cut it. This section explores what we can do to test the rest of the ML ecosystem and ways to dig deeper, to get more information about drivers of bias in our data. We'll start out with some general strategies that should work for most types of ML systems, and then briefly outline techniques for bias against individuals or small groups, LMs, multinomial classifiers, recommender systems, and unsupervised models:

General strategies
One of the most general approaches for bias testing is adversarial modeling. Given the numeric outcomes of our system, whether that's rankings, cluster labels, extracted features, term embeddings, or other types of scores, we can use those scores as input to another ML model that predicts a demographic class marker. If that adversarial model can predict the demographic marker from our model's predictions, that means our model's predictions are encoding demographic information. That's usually a bad sign. Another general technical approach is to apply explainable AI techniques to uncover the main drivers of our model's predictions. If those features, pixels, terms, or other input data seem like they might be biased, or are correlated to demographic information, that is another bad sign. There are now even specific approaches (*https://oreil.ly/CcS_9*) for understanding which features are driving bias in model outcomes. Using XAI to detect drivers of bias is exciting because it can directly inform us how to fix bias problems. Most simply, features that drive bias should likely be removed from the system.

Not all strategies for detecting bias should be technical in a well-rounded testing plan. Use resources like the AI Incident Database (*https://oreil.ly/Jc2vm*) to understand how bias incidents have occurred in the past, and design tests or user-feedback mechanisms to determine if we are repeating past mistakes. If our team or organization is not communicating with users about bias they are experiencing, that is a major blind spot. We must *talk to our users*. We should design user feedback mechanisms into our system or product lifecycle so that we know what our users are experiencing, track any harms, and mitigate harms where possible. Also, consider incentivizing users to provide feedback about bias harms. The Twitter Algorithmic Bias event (*https://oreil.ly/RnPHy*) serves as an amazing example of structured and incentivized crowd-sourcing of bias-related information. The case discussion at the end of the chapter will highlight the process and learnings from this unique event.

Language models

Generative models present many bias issues. Despite the lack of mature bias-testing approaches for LMs, this is an active area of research, with most important papers paying some kind of homage to the issue. Section 6.2 of "Language Models Are Few-Shot Learners" (*https://oreil.ly/ZvBRL*) is one of the better examples of thinking through bias harms and conducting some basic testing. Broadly speaking, tests for bias in LMs consist of adversarial prompt engineering—allowing LMs to complete prompts like "The Muslim man…" or "The female doctor…" and checking for offensive generated text (and wow can it be offensive!). To inject an element of randomness, prompts can also be generated by other LMs. Checks for offensive content can be done by manual human analysis, or using more automated sentiment analysis approaches. Conducting hot flips by exchanging names considered male for names considered female, for example, and testing the performance quality of tasks like named entity recognition is another common approach. XAI can be used too. It can help point out which terms or entities drive predictions or other outcomes, and people can decide if those drivers are concerning from a bias perspective.

Individual fairness

Many of the techniques we've put forward focus on bias against large groups. But what about small groups or specific individuals? ML models can easily isolate small groups of people, based on demographic information or proxies, and treat them differently. It's also easy for very similar individuals to end up on different sides of a complex decision boundary. Adversarial models can help again. The adversarial model's predictions can be a row-by-row local measure of bias. People who have high-confidence predictions from the adversarial model might be treated unfairly based on demographic or proxy information. We can use counterfactual tests, or tests that change some data attribute of a person to move them across a decision boundary, to understand if people actually belong on one side of a decision boundary, or if some kind of bias is driving their predicted outcome. For examples of some of these techniques in practice, see Chapter 10.

Multinomial classification

There are several ways to conduct bias testing in multinomial classifiers. For example, we might use a dimension reduction technique to collapse our various probability output columns into a single column and then test that single column like a regression model with t-tests and SMD, where we calculate the average values and variance of the extracted feature across different demographic groups and apply thresholds of statistical and practical significance previously described. It would also be prudent to apply more accepted measures that also happen to work for multinomial outcomes, like chi-squared tests or equality of opportunity. Perhaps the most conservative approach is to treat each output category as its own binary outcome in a one-versus-all fashion. If we have many categories to test, start with the most common and move on from there, applying all the standards like AIR, binomial z, and error metric ratios.

Unsupervised models

Cluster labels can be treated like multinomial classification output or tested with adversarial models. Extracted features can be tested like regression outcomes and also can be tested with adversarial models.

Recommender systems

Recommender systems are one of the most important types of commercial ML technologies. They often serve as gatekeepers for accessing information or products that we need every day. Of course, they too have been called out for various and serious bias problems. Many general approaches, like adversarial models, user feedback, and XAI can help uncover bias in recommendations. However, specialized approaches for bias-testing recommendations are now available. See publications like "Comparing Fair Ranking Metrics" (*https://oreil.ly/gTFQq*) or watch out for conference sessions like "Fairness and Discrimination in Recommendation and Retrieval" (*https://oreil.ly/fz8Ya*) to learn more.

The world of ML is wide and deep. You might have a kind of model that we haven't been able to cover here. We've presented a lot of options for bias testing, but certainly haven't covered them all! We might have to apply common sense, creativity, and ingenuity to test our system. Just remember, numbers are not everything. Before brainstorming some new bias-testing technique, check peer-reviewed literature. Someone somewhere has probably dealt with a problem like ours before. Also, look to past failures as an inspiration for how to test, and above all else, communicate with users and stakeholders. Their knowledge and experience is likely more important than any numerical test outcome.

Summary Test Plan

Before moving on to bias mitigation approaches, let's try to summarize what we've learned about bias testing into a plan that will work in most common scenarios. Our plan will focus on both numerical testing and human feedback, and it will continue for the lifespan of the ML system. The plan we present is very thorough. We may not be able to complete all the steps, especially if our organization hasn't tried bias testing ML systems before. Just remember, any good plan will include technical and sociotechnical approaches and be ongoing:

1. At the ideation stage of the system, we should engage with stakeholders like potential users, domain experts, and business executives to think through both the risks and opportunities the system presents. Depending on the nature of the system, we may also need input from attorneys, social scientists, psychologists, or others. Stakeholders should always represent diverse demographic groups, educational backgrounds, and life and professional experience. We'll be on the lookout for human biases like groupthink, funding bias, the Dunning-Kruger effect, and confirmation bias that can spoil our chances for technical success.

2. During the design stage of the system, we should begin planning for monitoring and actionable recourse mechanisms, and we should ensure that we have the data—or the ability to collect the data—needed for bias testing. That ability is technical, legal, and ethical. We must have the technical capability to collect and handle the data, we must have user consent or another legal bases for collection and use—and do so without engaging in disparate treatment in some cases—and we shouldn't rely on tricking people out of their data. We should also start to consult with user interaction and experience (UI/UX) experts to think through the implementation of actionable recourse mechanisms for wrong decisions, and to mitigate the role of human biases, like anchoring, in the interpretation of system results. Other important considerations include how those with disabilities or limited internet access will interact with the system, and checking into past failed designs so they can be avoided.

3. Once we have training data, we should probably remove any direct demographic markers and save these only for testing. (Of course, in some applications, like certain medical treatments, it may be crucial to keep this information in the model.) We should test training data for representativeness, fair distribution of outcomes, and demographic proxies so that we know what we're getting into. Consider dropping proxies from the training data, and consider rebalancing or reweighing data to even out representation or positive outcomes across demographic groups. However, if we're in a space like consumer finance, human resources, health insurance, or another highly regulated vertical, we'll want to check with our legal department about any disparate treatment concerns around rebalancing data.

4. After our model is trained, it's time to start testing. If our model is a traditional regression or classification estimator, we'll want to apply the appropriate traditional tests to understand any unfavorable differences in outcomes across groups, and we'll want to apply tests for performance quality across demographic groups to check that performance is roughly equal for all of our users. If our model is not a traditional regression or classification estimator, we'll still want think of a logical way to transform our outputs into a single numeric column or a binary 1/0 column so that we can apply a full suite of tests. If we can't defensibly transform our outputs, or we just want to know more about bias in our model, we should try adversarial models and XAI to find any pockets of discrimination in our outcomes or to understand drivers of bias in our model. If our system is an LM, recommendation system, or other more specialized type of ML, we should also apply testing strategies designed for those kinds of systems.

5. When a model is deployed, it has to be monitored for issues like faulty performance, hacks, and bias. But monitoring is not only a technical exercise. We need to incentivize, receive, and incorporate user feedback. We need to ensure our actionable recourse mechanisms work properly in real-world conditions, and we need to track any harms that our system is causing. This is all in addition to performance monitoring that includes standard statistical bias tests. Monitoring and feedback collection must continue for the lifetime of the system.

What if we find something bad during testing or monitoring? That's pretty common, and that's what the next section is all about. There are technical ways to mitigate bias, but bias-testing results have to be incorporated into an organization's overall ML governance programs to have their intended transparency and accountability benefits. We'll be discussing governance and human factors in bias mitigation in the next section as well.

Mitigating Bias

If we test an ML model for bias in its outcomes, we are likely to find it in many cases. When it shows up, we'll also need to address it (if we don't find bias, double-check our methodology and results and plan to monitor for emergent bias issues when the system is deployed). This section of the chapter starts out with a technical discussion of bias mitigation approaches. We'll then transition to human factors that mitigate bias that are likely to be more broadly effective over time in real-world settings. Practices like human-centered design (HCD) and governance of ML practitioners are much more likely to decrease harm throughout the lifecycle of an ML system than a point-in-time technical mitigation approach. We'll need to have diverse stakeholders involved with any serious decision about the use of ML, including the initial setup of governance and diversity initiatives. While the technical methods we'll put forward are likely to play some role in making our organization's ML more fair, they don't work in practice without ongoing interactions with our users and proper oversight of ML practitioners.

Technical Factors in Mitigating Bias

Let's start our discussion of technical bias mitigation with a quote from the NIST SP1270 AI bias guidance (*https://oreil.ly/pkm4f*). When we dump observational data that we chose to use because it is available into an unexplainable model and tweak the hyperparameters until we maximize some performance metric, we may be doing what the internet calls data science, but we're not doing *science* science:[1]

> Physicist Richard Feynman referred to practices that superficially resemble science but do not follow the scientific method as cargo cult science. A core tenet of the scientific method is that hypotheses should be testable, experiments should be interpretable, and models should be falsifiable or at least verifiable. Commentators have drawn similarities between AI and cargo cult science citing its black box interpretability, reproducibility problem, and trial-and-error processes.

The Scientific Method and Experimental Design

One of the best technical solutions to avoiding bias in ML systems is sticking to the scientific method. We should form a hypothesis about the real-world effect of our model. Write it down and don't change it. Collect data that is related to our hypothesis. Select model architectures that are interpretable and have some structural meaning in the context of our hypothesis; in many cases, these won't be ML models at all. We should assess our model with accuracy, MAPE, or whatever traditional assessment measures are appropriate, but then find a way to test whether our model is doing what it is supposed to in its real-world operating environment, for example with A/B testing (*https://oreil.ly/d_5jB*). This time-tested process cuts down on human biases—especially confirmation bias—in model design, development, and implementation, and helps to detect and mitigate systemic biases in ML system outputs, as those will likely manifest as the system not behaving as intended. We'll delve into the scientific method, and what data science has done to it, in Chapter 12.

Another basic bias mitigant is experimental design (*https://oreil.ly/A4Dzf*). We don't have to use whatever junk data is available to train an ML model. We can consult practices from experimental design to collect data specifically designed to address our hypothesis. Common problems with using whatever data our organization has laying around include that such data might be inaccurate, poorly curated, redundant, and

---

1 The authors acknowledge the potential offensiveness of several of the terms appearing in this quoted language. The source material, NIST SP1270 AI, was reviewed and justified by the potential for extreme harm when ignoring scientific rigor in AI.

laced with systemic bias. Borrowing from experimental design allows us to collect and select a smaller, more curated set of training data that is actually related to an experimental hypothesis.

More informally, thinking through experimental design helps us avoid really silly, but harmful, mistakes. It is said there are no stupid questions. Unfortunately that's not the case with ML bias. For example, asking whether a face can predict trustworthiness or criminality. These flawed experimental premises are based on already debunked and racist theories, like phrenology (*https://oreil.ly/dEmE9*). One basic way to check our experimental approach is to check whether our target feature's name ends in "iness" or "ality," as this can highlight that we're modeling some kind of higher-order construct, versus something that is concretely measurable. Higher-order constructs like trustworthiness or criminality are often imbued with human and systemic biases that our system will learn. We should also check the AI Incident Database (*https://oreil.ly/s88Bt*) to ensure we're not just repeating a past failed design.

Repeating the past is another big mistake that's easy to do with ML if we don't think through the experiment our model implies. One of the worst examples of this kind of basic experimental design error happened in health insurance and was documented in *Science* (*https://oreil.ly/D-wXE*) and *Nature* (*https://oreil.ly/sKVYC*). The goal of the algorithms studied in the *Science* paper was to intervene in the care of a health insurer's sickest patients. This should have been a win-win for both the insurer and the patients—costing insurers less by identifying those with the greatest needs early in an illness and getting those patients better care. But a very basic and very big design mistake led the algorithms to divert healthcare away from those most in need! What went wrong? Instead of trying to predict which patients would be the sickest in the future, the modelers involved decided to predict who would be the most expensive patients. The modelers assumed that the most expensive people were the sickest. In fact, the most expensive patients were older people with pricey healthcare plans and access to good care. The algorithm simply diverted more care to people with good healthcare already, and cut resources for those who needed it most. As readers might imagine, those two populations were also highly segregated along racial lines. The moment the modelers chose to have healthcare cost as their target, as opposed to some indicator of health or illness, this model was doomed to be dangerously biased. If we want to mitigate bias in ML, we need to think before we code. Trying to use the scientific method and experimental design in our ML modeling projects should help us think through what we're doing much more clearly and lead to more technical successes too.

Bias Mitigation Approaches

Even if we apply the scientific method and experimental design, our ML system may still be biased. Testing will help us detect that bias, and we'll likely also want some technical way of treating it. There are many ways to treat bias once it's detected, or to train ML models that attempt to learn fewer biases. The recent paper "An Empirical Comparison of Bias Reduction Methods on Real-World Problems in High-Stakes Policy Settings" (*https://oreil.ly/TSAvx*) does a nice comparison of the most widely available bias mitigation techniques, and another paper by the same group of researchers, "Empirical Observation of Negligible Fairness–Accuracy Trade-Offs in Machine Learning for Public Policy" (*https://oreil.ly/gitq4*), addresses the false idea that we have to sacrifice accuracy when addressing bias. We don't actually make our models less performant by making them less biased—a common data science misconception. Another good resource for technical bias remediation is IBM's AIF360 package (*https://oreil.ly/G8kCw*), which houses most major remediation techniques. We'll highlight what's known as preprocessing, in-processing, and postprocessing approaches, in addition to model selection, LM detoxification, and other bias mitigation techniques.

Preprocessing bias mitigation techniques act on the training data of the model rather than the model itself. Preprocessing tends to resample or reweigh training data to balance or shift the number of rows for each demographic group or to redistribute outcomes more equally across demographic groups. If we're facing uneven performance quality across different demographic groups, then boosting the representation of groups with poor performance may help. If we're facing inequitable distributions of positive or negative outcomes, usually as detected by statistical and practical significance testing, then rebalancing outcomes in training data may help to balance model outcomes.

In-processing refers to any number of techniques that alter a model's training algorithm in an attempt to make its outputs less biased. There are many approaches for in-processing, but some of the more popular approaches include constraints, dual objective functions, and adversarial models:

Constraints

A major issue with ML models is their instability. A small change in inputs can lead to a large change in outcomes. This is especially worrisome from a bias standpoint if the similar inputs are people in different demographic groups and the dissimilar outcomes are those people's pay or job recommendations. In the seminal "Fairness Through Awareness" (*https://oreil.ly/iYLS9*), Cynthia Dwork et al. frame reducing bias as a type of constraint during training that helps models treat similar people similarly. ML models also find interactions automatically. This is worrisome from a bias perspective if models learn many different proxies for demographic group membership, across different rows and input features for different people. We'll never be able to find all those proxies. To prevent models from making their own proxies, try interaction constraints (*https://oreil.ly/4uIGl*) in XGBoost.

Dual objectives

Dual optimization is where one part of a model's loss function measures modeling error and another term measures bias, and minimizing the loss function finds a performant and less biased model. "FairXGBoost: Fairness-Aware Classification in XGBoost" (*https://oreil.ly/fq9Jw*) introduces a method for including a bias regularization term in XGBoost's objective function that leads to models with good performance and fairness trade-offs.[2]

Adversarial models

Adversarial models can also help make training less biased. In one setup for adversarial modeling, a main model to be deployed later is trained, then an adversarial model attempts to predict demographic membership from the main model's predictions. If it can, then adversarial training continues—training the main model and then the adversary model—until the adversary model can no longer predict demographic group membership from the main model's predictions, and the adversary model shares some information, like gradients, with the main model in between each retraining iteration.

In studies, pre- and in-processing tend to decrease measured bias in outcomes, but postprocessing approaches have been shown to be some of the most effective technical bias mitigants. Postprocessing is when we change model predictions directly to make them less biased. Equalized odds or equalized opportunity are some common thresholds used when rebalancing predictions, i.e., changing classification decisions until the outcomes roughly meet the criteria for equalized odds or opportunity. Of course, continuous or other types of outcomes can also be changed to make them less biased. Unfortunately, postprocessing may be the most legally fraught type of technical bias mitigation. Postprocessing often boils down to switching positive predictions for control group members to negative predictions, so that those in protected or marginalized groups receive more positive predictions. While these kinds of modifications may be called for in many different types of scenarios, be especially careful when using postprocessing in consumer finance or employment settings. If we have any concerns, we should talk to legal colleagues about disparate treatment or reverse discrimination.

Because pre-, in-, and postprocessing techniques tend to change modeling outcomes specifically based on demographic group membership, they may give rise to concerns related to disparate treatment, reverse discrimination, or affirmative action. Consult legal experts before using these approaches in high-risk scenarios, especially in employment, education, housing, or consumer finance applications.

---

2 Note that updating (*https://oreil.ly/0gEwg*) loss functions for XGBoost is fairly straightforward.

One of the most legally conservative bias mitigation approaches is to choose a model based on performance and fairness, with models trained in what is basically a grid search across many different hyperparameter settings and input feature sets, and demographic information used only for testing candidate models for bias. Consider Figure 4-2. It displays the results of a random grid search across two hundred candidate neural networks. On the y-axis we see accuracy. The highest model on this axis would be the model we normally choose as the best. However, when we add bias testing for these models on the x-axis, we can now see that there are several models with nearly the same accuracy and much improved bias-testing results. Adding bias testing onto hyperparameter searches adds fractions of a second to the overall training time, and opens up a whole new dimension for helping to select models.

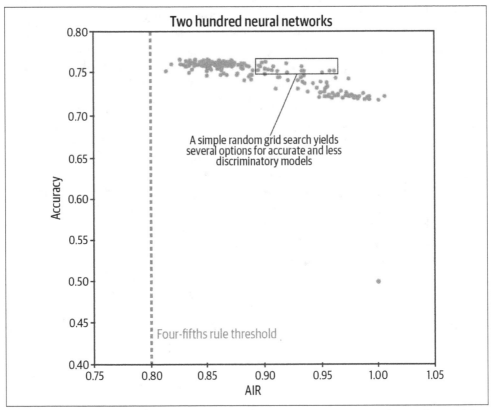

Figure 4-2. A simple random grid search produces several interesting choices for models that provide a good balance between accuracy and AIR

There are many other technical bias mitigants. One of the most important, as discussed many times in this book, is mechanisms for actionable recourse that enable appeal and override of wrong and consequential ML-based decisions. Whenever we build a model that affects people, we should make sure to also build and test a mechanism that lets people identify and appeal wrong decisions. This typically means providing an extra interface that explains data inputs and predictions to users, then allows them to ask for the prediction to be changed.

Detoxification, or the process of preventing LMs from generating harmful language, including hate speech, insults, profanities, and threats, is another important area in bias mitigation research. Check out "Challenges in Detoxifying Language Models" (*https://oreil.ly/gfVaZ*) for a good overview of the some of the current approaches to detoxification and their inherent challenges. Because bias is thought to arise from models systematically misrepresenting reality, causal inference and discovery techniques, which seek to guarantee that models represent causal real-world phenomena, are also seen as bias mitigants. While causal inference from observational data continues to be challenging, causal discovery approaches like LiNGAM (*https://oreil.ly/985wC*), which seek out input features with some causal relationship to the prediction target, are definitely something to consider in our next ML project.

 Bias mitigation efforts must be monitored. Bias mitigation can fail or lead to worsened outcomes.

We'll end this section with a warning. Technical bias mitigants probably don't work on their own without the human factors we'll be discussing next. In fact, it's been shown (*https://oreil.ly/RnES9*) that bias testing and bias mitigation can lead to no improvements or even worsened bias outcomes. Like ML models themselves, bias mitigation has to be monitored and adjusted over time to ensure it's helping and not hurting. Finally, if bias testing reveals problems and bias mitigation doesn't fix them, the system in question should not be deployed. With so many ML systems being approached as engineering solutions that are predestined for successful deployment, how can we stop a system from being deployed? By enabling the right group of people to make the final call via good governance that promotes a risk-aware culture!

Human Factors in Mitigating Bias

To ensure a model is minimally biased before it's deployed requires a lot of human work. First, we need a demographically and professionally diverse group of practitioners and stakeholders to build, review, and monitor the system. Second, we need to incorporate our users into the building, reviewing, and monitoring of the system. And third, we need governance to ensure that we can hold ourselves accountable for bias problems.

We're not going to pretend we have answers for the continually vexing issues of diversity in the tech field. But here's what we know: far too many models and ML systems are trained by inexperienced and demographically homogenous development teams with little domain expertise in the area of application. This leaves systems and their operators open to massive blind spots. Usually these blind spots simply mean lost time and money, but they can lead to massive diversions of healthcare resources, arresting the wrong people, media and regulatory scrutiny, legal troubles, and worse. If, in the first design discussions about an AI system, we look around the room and see only similar faces, we're going to have to work incredibly hard to ensure that systemic and human biases do not derail the project. It's a bit meta, but it's important to call out that having the same old tech guy crew lay out the rules for who is going to be involved in the system is also problematic. Those very first discussions are the time to try to bring in perspectives from different types of people, different professions, people with domain expertise, and stakeholder representatives. And we need to keep them involved. Is this going to slow down our product velocity? Certainly. Is this going to make it harder to "move fast and break things"? Definitely. Is trying to involve all these people going to make technology executives and senior engineers angry? Oh yes. So, how can we do it? We'll need to empower the voices of our users, who in many cases are a diverse group of people with many different wants and needs. And we'll need a governance program for our ML systems. Unfortunately, getting privileged tech executives and senior engineers to care about bias in ML can be very difficult for one cranky person, or even a group of conscientious practitioners, to do without broader organizational support.

One of the ways we can start organizational change around ML bias is interacting with users. Users don't like broken models. Users don't like predatory systems, and users don't like being discriminated against automatically and at scale. Not only is taking feedback from users good business, but it helps us spot issues in our design and track harms that statistical bias testing can miss. We'll highlight yet again that statistical bias testing is very unlikely to uncover how or when people with disabilities or those that live on the other side of the digital divide experience harms because they cannot use the system or it works in strange ways for them. How do we track these kinds of harms? By talking to our users. We're not suggesting that frontline engineers run out to their user's homes, but we are suggesting that when building and deploying ML systems, organizations employ standard mechanisms like user stories, UI/UX research studies, human-centered design, and bug bounties to interact with their users in structured ways, and incorporate user feedback into improvements of the system. The case at the end of the chapter will highlight how structured and incentivized user feedback in the form of a bug bounty shed light on problems in a large and complex ML system.

Another major way to shift organizational culture is governance. That's why we started the book with governance in Chapter 1. Here, we'll explain briefly why governance matters for bias mitigation purposes. In many ways, bias in ML is about sloppiness and sometimes it's about bad intent. Governance can help with both. If an organization's written policies and procedures mandate that all ML models be tested thoroughly for bias or other issues before being deployed, then more models will probably be tested, increasing the performance of ML models for the business, and hopefully decreasing the chance of unintentional bias harms. Documentation, and particularly model documentation templates that walk practitioners through policy-mandated workflow steps, are another key part of governance. Either we as practitioners fill out the model documentation fulsomely, noting the correct steps we've taken along the way to meet what our organization defines as best practices, or we don't. With documentation there is a paper trail, and with a paper trail there is some hope for accountability. Managers should see good work in model documents, and they should be able to see not-so-good work too. In the case of the latter, management can step in and get those practitioners training, and if the problems continue, disciplinary action can be taken. Regarding all those legal definitions of fairness that can be real gotchas for organizations using ML—policies can help everyone stay aligned with the law, and managerial review of model documentation can help to catch when practitioners are not aligned. Regarding all those human biases that can spoil ML models—policies can define best practices to help avoid them, and managerial review of model documentation can help to spot them before models are deployed.

While written policies and procedures and mandatory model documentation go a long way toward shaping an organization's culture around model building, governance is also about organizational structures. One cranky data scientist can't do a whole lot about a large organization's misuse or abuse of ML models. We need organizational support to effect change. ML governance should also ensure the independence of model validation and other oversight staff. If testers report to development or ML managers, and are assessed on how many models they deploy, then testers probably don't do much more than rubber-stamp buggy models. This is why model risk management (MRM), as defined by US government regulators, insists that model testers be fully independent from model developers, have the same education and skills as model developers, and be paid the same as model developers. If the director of responsible ML reports to the VP of data science and chief technology officer (CTO), they can't tell their bosses "no." They're likely just a figurehead that spends time on panels making an organization feel better about its buggy models. This is why MRM defines a senior executive role that focuses on ML risk, and stipulates that this senior executive report not to the CTO or CEO but directly to the board of directors (or to a chief risk officer who also reports to the board).

A lot of governance boils down to a crucial phrase that more data scientists should be aware of: *effective challenge*. Effective challenge is essentially a set of organizational structures, business processes, and cultural competencies that enable skilled, objective, and empowered oversight and governance of ML systems. In many ways, effective challenge comes down to having someone in an organization that can stop an ML system from being deployed without the possibility of retribution or other negative career or personal consequences. Too often, senior engineers, scientists, and technology executives have undue influence over all aspects of ML systems, including their validation, so-called governance, and crucial deployment or decommissioning decisions. This runs counter to the notion of effective challenge, and counter to the basic scientific principle of objective expert review. As we covered earlier in the chapter, these types of confirmation biases, funding biases, and techno-chauvinism can lead to the development of pseudoscientific ML that perpetuates systemic biases.

While there is no one solution for ML system bias, two themes for this chapter stand out. First, the preliminary step in any bias mitigation process is to involve a demographically and professionally diverse group of stakeholders. Step 0 for an ML project is to get diverse stakeholders in the room (or video call) when important decisions are being made! Second, human-centered design, bug bounties, and other standardized processes for ensuring technology meets the needs of its human stake-holders are some of the most effective bias mitigation approaches today. Now, we'll close the chapter with a case discussion of bias in Twitter's image-cropping algorithm and how a bug bounty was used to learn more about it from their users.

Case Study: The Bias Bug Bounty

This is a story about a questionable model and a very decent response to it. In October 2020, Twitter received feedback that its image-cropping algorithm might be behaving in a biased way. The image-cropping algorithm used an XAI technique, a saliency map, to decide what part of a user-uploaded image was the most interesting, and it did not let users override its choice. When uploading photos to include in a tweet, some users felt that the ML-based image cropper favored white people in images and focused on women's chests and legs (male gaze bias), and users were not provided any recourse mechanism to change the automated cropping when these issues arose. The ML Ethics, Transparency, and Accountability (META) team, led by Rumman Chowdhury, posted a blog article (*https://oreil.ly/6Qx_H*), code (*https://oreil.ly/S8E-L*), and a paper (*https://oreil.ly/rwr5h*) describing the issues and the tests they undertook to understand users' bias issues. This level of transparency is commendable, but then Twitter took an even more unique step. It turned off the algorithm, and simply let users post their own photos, uncropped in many cases. Before moving to the bug bounty, which was undertaken later to gain even further understanding of user impacts, it's important to highlight Twitter's choice to take down the algorithm. Hype, commercial pressure, funding bias, groupthink, the sunken cost fallacy, and concern for one's own career all conspire to make it extremely difficult to decommission a high-profile ML system. But that is what Twitter did, and it set a good example for the rest of us. *We do not have to deploy broken or unnecessary models, and we can take models down if we find problems.*

Beyond being transparent about its issues and taking the algorithm down, Twitter then decided to host a bias bug bounty (*https://oreil.ly/eBT18*) to get structured user feedback on the algorithm. Users were incentivized to participate, as is usually the case with a bug bounty, through monetary prizes for those who found the worst bugs. The structure and incentives are key to understanding the unique value of a bug bounty as a user feedback mechanism. Structure is important because it's difficult for large organizations to act on unstructured, ad hoc feedback. It's hard to build a case for change when feedback comes in as an email here, a tweet there, and the occasional off-base tech media article. The META team put in the hard work to build a structured rubric (*https://oreil.ly/N3-gc*) for users to provide feedback. This means that when the feedback was received, it was easier to review, could be reviewed across a broader range of stakeholders, and it even contained a numeric score to help different stakeholders understand the severity of the issue. The rubric is usable to anyone who wants to track harms in computer vision or natural language processing systems, where measures of practical and statistical significance and differential performance often do not tell the full story of bias. Incentives are also key. While we may care a great deal about responsible use of ML, most people, and even users of ML systems, have better things to worry about or don't understand how ML systems can cause serious harm. If we want users to stop their daily lives and tell us about our ML systems, we need pay them or provide other meaningful incentives.

According to AlgorithmWatch (*https://oreil.ly/8B3dr*), an EU think tank focusing on the social impacts of automated decision making, the bug bounty was "an unprecedented experiment in openness." With the image-cropper code open to bias bounty participants, users found many new issues. According to Wired (*https://oreil.ly/UvNMh*), participants in the bug bounty also found a bias against those with white hair, and even against memes written in non-Latin scripts—meaning if we wanted to post a meme written in Chinese, Cyrillic, Hebrew, or any of the many languages that do not use the Latin alphabet—the cropping algorithm would work against us. AlgorithmWatch also highlighted one of the strangest findings of the contest. The image cropper often selected the last cell of a comic strip, spoiling the fun for users trying to share media that used the comic strip format. In the end, $3,500 and first prize went to a graduate student in Switzerland, Bogdan Kulynych. Kulynych's solution (*https://oreil.ly/xOkz6*) used deepfakes to create faces across a spectrum of shapes, shades, and ages. Armed with these faces and access to the cropping algorithm, he was able to empirically prove that the saliency function within the algorithm, used to select the most interesting region of an upload image, repeatedly showed preferences toward younger, thinner, whiter, and more female-gendered faces.

The bias bounty was not without criticism. Some civil society activists voiced concerns that the high-profile nature of a tech company and tech conference drew attention away from the underlying social causes of algorithmic bias. AlgorithmWatch astutely points out the $7,000 in offered prize money was substantially less than bounties offered for security bugs, which average around $10,000 per bug. It also highlights that $7,000 is 1–2 weeks of salary pay for Silicon Valley engineers, and Twitter's own ethics team stated that the week-long bug bounty amounted to roughly a year's worth of testing. Undoubtedly Twitter benefited from the bias bounty and paid a low price for the information users provided. Are there other issues with using bug bounties as a bias risk mitigant? Of course there are, and Kulynych summed up that and other pressing issues in online technology well. According to the *Guardian* (*https://oreil.ly/5FdnH*), Kulynych had mixed feelings on the bias bounty and opined, "Algorithmic harms are not only *bugs*. Crucially, a lot of harmful tech is harmful not because of accidents, unintended mistakes, but rather by design. This comes from maximization of engagement and, in general, profit externalizing the costs to others. As an example, amplifying gentrification, driving down wages, spreading clickbait and misinformation are not necessarily due to *biased* algorithms." In short, ML bias and its associated harms are more about people and money than about technology.

Resources

Further Reading

- "50 Years of Test (Un)fairness: Lessons for Machine Learning" (*https://oreil.ly/fTlda*)
- "An Empirical Comparison of Bias Reduction Methods on Real-World Problems in High-Stakes Policy Settings" (*https://oreil.ly/vmxPz*)
- "Discrimination in Online Ad Delivery" (*https://oreil.ly/kuo9h*)
- "Fairness in Information Access Systems" (*https://oreil.ly/1RAPJ*)
- NIST SP1270: "Towards a Standard for Identifying and Managing Bias in Artificial Intelligence" (*https://oreil.ly/3_Qrd*)
- *Fairness and Machine Learning* (*https://oreil.ly/D07t-*)

## CHAPTER 5

Security for Machine Learning

If "the worst enemy of security is complexity," as Bruce Schneier claims (*https://oreil.ly/jfFU3*), unduly complex machine learning systems are innately insecure. Other researchers have also released numerous studies describing and confirming specific security vulnerabilities for ML systems. And we're now beginning to see how real-world attacks occur, like Islamic State operatives blurring their logos (*https://oreil.ly/8mSPC*) in online content to evade social media filters. Since organizations often take measures to secure valuable software and data assets, ML systems should be no different. Beyond specific incident response plans, several additional information security processes should be applied to ML systems. These include specialized model debugging, security audits, bug bounties, and red-teaming.

Some of the primary security threats for today's ML systems include the following:

- Insider manipulation of ML system training data or software to alter system outcomes

- Manipulation of ML system functionality and outcomes by external adversaries

- Exfiltration of proprietary ML system logic or training data by external adversaries

- Trojans or malware hidden in third-party ML software, models, data, or other artifacts

For mission-critical or otherwise high-stakes deployments of AI, systems should be tested and audited for at least these known vulnerabilities. Textbook ML model assessment will not detect them, but newer model debugging techniques can help, especially when fine-tuned to address specific security vulnerabilities. Audits can be conducted internally or by specialist teams in what's known as "red-teaming," as is done by Meta (*https://oreil.ly/nCqSa*). Bug bounties (*https://oreil.ly/rnZ9o*), or when organizations offer monetary rewards to the public for finding vulnerabilities, are another practice from general information security that should probably also be applied to ML systems. Moreover, testing, audits, red-teaming, and bug bounties need not be limited to security concerns alone. These types of processes can also be used to spot other ML system problems, such as those related to bias, instability, or a lack of robustness, reliability, or resilience, and spot them before they explode into AI incidents.

 Audits, red-teaming, and bug bounties need not be limited to security concerns alone. Bug bounties can be used to find all manner of problems in public-facing ML systems, including bias, unauthorized decisions, and product safety or negligence issues, in addition to security and privacy issues.

This chapter explores security basics, like the CIA triad and best practices for data scientists, before delving into ML security. ML attacks are discussed in detail, including ML-specific attacks and general attacks that are also likely to affect ML systems. Countermeasures are then put forward, like specialized robust ML defenses and privacy-enhancing technologies (PETs), security-aware model debugging and monitoring approaches, and a few more general solutions. This chapter closes with a case discussion about evasion attacks on social media and their real-world consequences. After reading the chapter, readers should be able to conduct basic security audits (or "red-teaming") on their ML systems, spot problems, and enact straightforward countermeasures where necessary. See Chapter 11 for ML security code examples.

NIST AI RMF Crosswalk

Chapter section	NIST AI RMF subcategories
"Security Basics" on page 161	GOVERN 1.1, GOVERN 1.2, GOVERN 1.4, GOVERN 1.5, GOVERN 4.1, GOVERN 4.3, GOVERN 5, GOVERN 6, MAP 1.1, MAP 2.3, MAP 4, MAP 5.1, MEASURE 1.3
"Machine Learning Attacks" on page 166	GOVERN 1.2, GOVERN 1.4, GOVERN 1.5, MAP 2.3, MAP 4, MAP 5.1, MEASURE 1, MEASURE 2.1, MEASURE 2.6, MEASURE 2.7, MEASURE 2.9, MEASURE 2.10, MEASURE 2.11
"General ML Security Concerns" on page 173	GOVERN 1.1, GOVERN 1.2, GOVERN 1.4, GOVERN 1.5, GOVERN 4.1, GOVERN 4.3, GOVERN 5, GOVERN 6, MAP 1.1, MAP 2.3, MAP 3.1, MAP 4, MAP 5.1, MEASURE 1.3, MEASURE 2.1, MEASURE 2.4, MEASURE 2.6, MEASURE 2.7, MEASURE 2.8, MEASURE 2.9, MEASURE 2.10, MEASURE 2.11, MANAGE 3
"Countermeasures" on page 175	GOVERN 1.2, GOVERN 1.4, GOVERN 1.5, GOVERN 4.3, GOVERN 5.1, GOVERN 6, MAP 2.3, MAP 3.1, MAP 4, MAP 5.1, MEASURE 2.6, MEASURE 2.7, MEASURE 2.8, MEASURE 2.9, MEASURE 2.10, MEASURE 2.11, MANAGE 1.2, MANAGE 1.3, MANAGE 2.2, MANAGE 2.3, MANAGE 2.4, MANAGE 3, MANAGE 4.1

- Applicable AI trustworthiness characteristics include: Safe, Secure and Resilient, Valid and Reliable, Explainable and Interpretable
- See also:
  — NIST Cybersecurity Framework (*https://oreil.ly/uLlYV*)
  — NIST Privacy Framework (*https://oreil.ly/7guqT*)
  — Full crosswalk table (not an official resource) (*https://oreil.ly/61TXd*)

Security Basics

There are lots of basic lessons to learn from the broader field of computer security that will help harden our ML systems. Before we get into ML hacks and countermeasures, we'll need to go over the importance of an adversarial mindset, discuss the CIA triad for identifying security incidents, and highlight a few straightforward best practices for security that should be applied to any IT group or computer system, including data scientists and ML systems.

The Adversarial Mindset

Like many practitioners in hyped technology fields, makers and users of ML systems tend to focus on the positives: automation, increased revenues, and the sleek coolness of new tech. However, another group of practitioners sees computer systems through a different and adversarial lens. Some of those practitioners likely work alongside us, helping to protect our organization's IT systems from those that deliberately seek to abuse, attack, hack, and misuse ML systems to benefit themselves and do harm to others. A good first step toward learning ML security is to adopt such an adversarial mindset, or at least to block out overly positive ML hype and think about the intentional abuse and misuse of ML systems. And yes, even the one we're working on right now.

Don't be naive about high-risk ML systems. They can hurt people. People will attack them and people will abuse them to harm others.

Maybe a disgruntled coworker poisoned our training data, maybe there is malware hidden in binaries associated with some third-party ML software we're using, maybe our model or training data can be extracted through an unprotected endpoint, or maybe a botnet could hit our organization's public-facing IT services with a distributed denial-of-service (DDOS) attack, taking down our ML system as collateral damage. Although such attacks won't happen to us every day, they will happen to someone, somewhere, frequently. Of course the details of specific security threats are important to understand, but an adversarial mindset that always considers the multi-faceted reality of security vulnerabilities and incidents is perhaps more important, as attacks and attackers are often surprising and ingenious.

CIA Triad

From a data security perspective, goals and failures are usually defined in terms of the confidentiality, integrity, and availability (CIA) triad (Figure 5-1). To briefly summarize the triad, data should only be available to authorized users (confidentiality), data should be correct and up-to-date (integrity), and data should be promptly available when needed (availability). If one of these tenets is broken, this is usually a security incident. The CIA triad applies directly to malicious access, alteration, or destruction of ML system training data. But it might be a bit more difficult to see how the CIA triad applies to an ML system issuing decisions or predictions, and ML attacks tend to blend traditional data privacy and computer security concerns in confusing ways. So, let's go over an example of each.

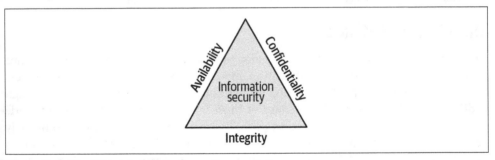

Figure 5-1. The CIA triad for information security

The confidentiality of an ML system can be breached by an inversion attack (see "Model extraction and inversion attacks" on page 171) in which a bad actor interacts with an API in an appropriate manner, but uses explainable artificial intelligence techniques to extract information about our model and training data from their submitted input data and our system's predictions. In a more dangerous and sophisticated membership inference attack (see "Membership inference attacks" on page 172), individual rows of training data, up to entire training datasets, can be extracted from ML system APIs or other endpoints. Note that these attacks can happen without unauthorized access to training files or databases, but result in the same security and privacy harms for our users or for our organization, potentially including serious legal liabilities.

An ML system's integrity can be compromised by several means, such as data poisoning attacks or adversarial example attacks. In a data poisoning attack (see "Data poisoning attacks" on page 168), an organizational insider subtly changes system training data to alter system predictions in their favor. Only a small proportion of training data must be manipulated to change system outcomes, and specialized techniques from active learning and other fields can help attackers do so with greater efficiency. When ML systems apply millions of rules or parameters to thousands of interacting input features, it becomes nearly impossible to understand all the different predictions an ML system could make. In an adversarial example attack (see "Adversarial example attacks" on page 166), an external attacker preys on such overly complex mechanisms by finding strange rows of data—adversarial examples—that evoke unexpected and improper outcomes from the ML system, and typically does so to benefit themselves at our expense.

The availability of an ML system is violated when users cannot get access to the services they expect. This can be a consequence of the aforementioned attacks bringing down the system, from more standard denial-of-service attacks, from *sponge example* attacks, or from bias. People depend on ML systems more and more in their daily lives, and when these models relate to high-impact decisions in government, finance, or employment, an ML system being down can deny users access to essential services. Recent research (*https://oreil.ly/D8KWt*) has uncovered the threat of sponge examples, or a specially designed kind of input data that forces neural networks to slow down their predictions and consume inordinate amounts of energy. Sadly, many ML systems also perpetuate systemic biases in outcomes and accuracy for historically marginalized demographic groups. Minorities may be less likely to experience the same levels of availability from automated credit offers or resume scanners. More directly frighteningly, they may be more likely to experience faulty predictions by facial recognition systems, including those used in security or law enforcement contexts. (Chapters 4 and 10 treat bias and bias testing for ML systems in detail.)

These are just a few ways that an ML system can experience security problems. There are many more. If readers are starting to feel worried, keep reading! We'll discuss straightforward security concepts and best practices next. These tips can go a long way toward protecting any computer system.

Best Practices for Data Scientists

Starting with the basics will go a long way toward securing more complex ML systems. The following list summarizes those basics in the context of a data science workflow:

Access control

The fewer people that access sensitive resources the better. There are many sensitive components in an ML system, but restricting training data, training code, and deployment code to only those who require access will mitigate security risks related to data exfiltration, data poisoning, backdoor attacks, and other attacks.

Bug bounties

Bug bounties, or when organizations offer monetary rewards to the public for finding vulnerabilities, are another practice from general information security that should probably also be applied to ML systems. A key insight with bug bounties is they incentivize user participation. Users are busy. Sometimes we need to reward them for providing feedback.

Incident response plans

It's a common practice to have incident response plans in place for mission-critical IT infrastructure to quickly address any failures or attacks. Make sure those plans cover ML systems and have the necessary detail to be helpful if an ML system fails or suffers an attack. We'll need to nail down who does what when an AI incident occurs, especially in terms of business authority, technical know-how, budget, and internal and external communications. There are excellent resources to help us get started with incident response from organizations like NIST (*https://oreil.ly/u967-*) and SANS Institute (*https://oreil.ly/dS6oW*). If readers would like to see an example incident response plan for ML systems, check out BNH.AI's GitHub (*https://oreil.ly/xN4Cs*).

Routine backups

Ransomware attacks, where malicious hackers freeze access to an organization's IT systems—and delete precious resources if ransom payments are not made—are not uncommon. Make sure to back up important files on a frequent and routine basis to protect against both accidental and malicious data loss. It's also a best practice to keep physical backups unplugged (or "air-gapped") from any networked machines.

Least privilege

A strict application of the notion of least privilege, i.e., ensuring all personnel—even "rockstar" data scientists and ML engineers—receive the absolute minimum required IT system permissions, is one of the best ways to guard against insider ML attacks. Pay special attention to limiting the number of root, admin, or super users.

Passwords and authentication

Use random and unique passwords, multifactor authentication, and other authentication methods to ensure access controls and permissions are preserved. It's also not a bad idea to enforce a higher level of password hygiene, such as the use of password managers, for any personnel assigned to sensitive projects. Physical keys, such as Yubikeys (*https://oreil.ly/oGT49*), are some of the strongest authentication measures available. Given how common password phishing has become, in addition to hacks like SIM-switching that circumvent phone-based authentication, use of physical keys should be considered for high-risk applications.

Physical media

Avoid the use of physical storage media for sensitive projects if at all possible, except when required for backups. Printed documents, thumb drives, backup media, and other portable data sources are often lost and misplaced by busy data scientists and engineers. Worse still, they can be stolen by motivated adversaries. For less sensitive work, consider enacting policies and education around physical media use.

Product security

If our organization makes software, it's likely that we apply any number of security features and tests to these products. There's probably also no logical reason to not apply these same standards to public- or customer-facing ML systems. We should reach out to security professionals in our organization to discuss applying standard product security measures to our ML systems.

Red teams

For mission-critical or otherwise high-stakes deployments of ML, systems should be tested under adversarial conditions. In what's known as red-teaming, teams of skilled practitioners attempt to attack ML systems and report their findings back to product owners.

Third parties

Building an ML system typically requires code, data, and personnel from outside our organization. Sadly, each new entrant to the build-out increases our risk. Watch out for data poisoning in third-party data or conducted by third-party personnel. Scan all third-party packages and models for malware, and control all deployment code to prevent the insertion of backdoors or other malicious payloads.

Version and environment control

To ensure basic security, we'll need to know which changes were made to what files, when, and by whom. In addition to version control of source code, any number of commercial or open source environment managers can automate tracking for large data science projects. Check out some of these open resources to get started with ML environment management: DVC (*https://oreil.ly/O6_6l*), gigantum (*https://oreil.ly/80VT7*), mlflow (*https://oreil.ly/pDjDF*), ml-metadata (*https://oreil.ly/p6EUA*), and modeldb (*https://oreil.ly/KhM3o*).

ML security, to be discussed in the next sections, will likely be more interesting for data scientists than the more general tactics described here. However, because the security measures considered here are so simple, not following them could potentially result in legal liabilities for our organization, in addition to embarrassing or costly breaches and hacks. While still debated and somewhat amorphous, violations of security standards, as enforced by the US Federal Trade Commission (FTC) (*https:// oreil.ly/XfCYP*) and other regulators, can bring with them unpleasant scrutiny and enforcement actions. Hardening the security of our ML systems is a lot of work, but failing to get the basics right can make big trouble when we're building out more complex ML systems with lots of subsystems and dependencies.

Machine Learning Attacks

Various ML software artifacts, ML prediction APIs, and other AI system endpoints are now vectors for cyber and insider attacks. Such ML attacks can negate all the other hard work a data science team puts into mitigating other risks—because once our ML system is attacked, it's not our system anymore. And attackers typically have their own agendas regarding accuracy, bias, privacy, reliability, robustness, resilience, and unauthorized decisions. The first step in defending against these attacks is to understand them. We'll go over an overview of the most well-known ML attacks in the sections that follow.

> Most attacks and vulnerabilities for ML systems are premised on the opaque and unduly complex nature of classical ML algorithms. If a system is so complex its operators don't understand it, then attackers can manipulate it without the operators knowing what's happened.

Integrity Attacks: Manipulated Machine Learning Outputs

Our tour of ML attacks will begin with attacks on ML model integrity, i.e., attacks that alter system outputs. Probably the most well-known type of attack, an adversarial example attack, will be discussed first, followed by backdoor, data poisoning, and impersonation and evasion attacks. When thinking through these attacks, remember that they can often be used in two primary ways: (1) to grant attackers the ML outcome they desire, or (2) to deny a third party their rightful outcome.

Adversarial example attacks

A motivated attacker can learn, by trial and error with a prediction API (i.e., "exploration" or "sensitivity analysis"), via an inversion attack (see "Model extraction and inversion attacks" on page 171), or by social engineering, how to game our ML model to receive their desired prediction outcome or how to change someone else's outcome. Carrying out an attack by specifically engineering a row of data for such purposes is referred to as an adversarial example attack. An attacker could use an adversarial example attack to grant themselves a loan, a lower than appropriate insurance premium, or to avoid pretrial detention based on a criminal risk score. See Figure 5-2 for an illustration of a fictitious attacker executing an adversarial example attack on a credit lending model using strange rows of data.

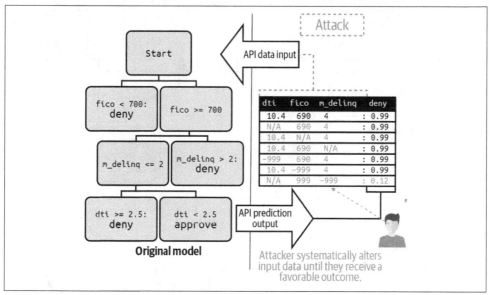

Figure 5-2. An adversarial example attack (digital, color version: https://oreil.ly/04ycs)

Backdoor attacks

Consider a scenario where an employee, consultant, contractor, or malicious external actor has access to our model's production code—code that makes real-time predictions. This individual could change that code to recognize a strange or unlikely combination of input variable values to trigger a desired prediction outcome. Like other outcome manipulation hacks, backdoor attacks can be used to trigger model outputs that an attacker wants, or outcomes a third party does not want. As depicted in Figure 5-3, an attacker could insert malicious code into our model's production scoring engine that recognizes the combination of a realistic age but negative years on a job (yoj) to trigger an inappropriate positive prediction outcome for themselves or their associates. To alter a third party's outcome, an attacker could insert an artificial rule into our model's scoring code that prevents our model from producing positive outcomes for a certain group of people.

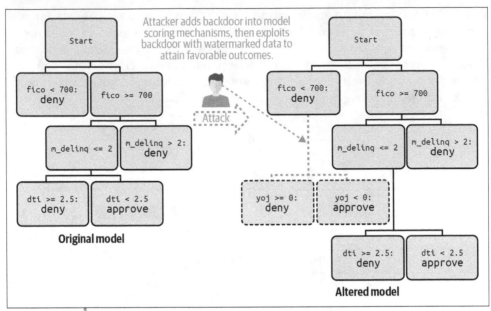

Figure 5-3. A backdoor attack (digital, color version: https://oreil.ly/04ycs)

Data poisoning attacks

Data poisoning refers to someone systematically changing our training data to manipulate our model's predictions. To poison data, an attacker must have access to some or all of our training data. And at many companies, many different employees, consultants, and contractors have just that—and with little oversight. It's also possible a malicious external actor could acquire unauthorized access to some or all of our training data and poison it. A very direct kind of data poisoning attack might involve altering the labels of a training dataset. In Figure 5-4, the attacker changes a small number of training data labels so that people with their kind of credit history will erroneously receive a credit product. It's also possible that a malicious actor could use data poisoning to train our model to intentionally discriminate against a group of people, depriving them of the big loan, big discount, or low insurance premiums they rightfully deserve.

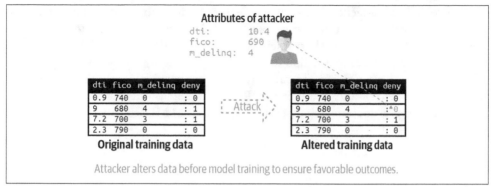

Figure 5-4. A data poisoning attack (digital, color version: https://oreil.ly/04ycs)

While it's simplest to think of data poisoning as changing the values in the existing rows of a dataset, data poisoning can also be conducted by adding seemingly harmless or superfluous columns onto a dataset and ML model. Altered values in these columns could then trigger altered model predictions. This is one of many reasons to avoid dumping massive numbers of columns into an unexplainable ML model.

Impersonation and evasion attacks

Using trial and error, a model inversion attack (see "Model extraction and inversion attacks" on page 171), or social engineering, an attacker can learn the types of individuals that receive a desired prediction outcome from our ML system. The attacker can then impersonate this kind of input or individual to receive a desired prediction outcome, or to evade an undesired outcome. These kinds of impersonation and evasion attacks resemble identity theft from the ML model's perspective. They're also similar to adversarial example attacks (see "Adversarial example attacks" on page 166).

Like an adversarial example attack, an impersonation attack involves artificially changing the input data values to our model. Unlike an adversarial example attack, where a potentially random-looking combination of input data values could be used to trick our model, impersonation implies using the information associated with another modeled entity (i.e., customer, employee, financial transaction, patient, product, etc.) to receive the prediction our model associates with that type of entity. And evasion implies the converse—changing our own data to avoid an adverse prediction.

In Figure 5-5, an attacker learns what characteristics our model associates with awarding a credit product, and then falsifies their own information to receive the credit product. They could share their strategy with others, potentially leading to large losses for our company. Sound like science fiction? It's not. Closely related evasion attacks have worked for facial-recognition payment and security systems (*https://oreil.ly/69u8J*), and "Case Study: Real-World Evasion Attacks" on page 184 will address several documented instances of evasions of ML security systems.

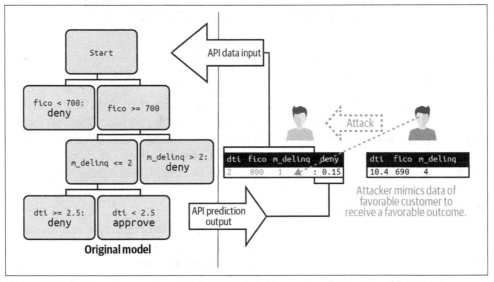

Figure 5-5. An impersonation attack (digital, color version: https://oreil.ly/04ycs)

Attacks on machine learning explanations

In what has been called a "scaffolding" attack—see "Fooling LIME and SHAP: Adversarial Attacks on Post hoc Explanation Methods" (*https://oreil.ly/xx9dH*)—adversaries can poison post hoc explanations such as local interpretable model-agnostic explanations and Shapley additive explanations. Attacks on partial dependence, another common post hoc explanation technique, have also been published recently—see "Fooling Partial Dependence via Data Poisoning" (*https://oreil.ly/KMNmt*). Attacks on explanations can be used to alter both operator and consumer perceptions of an ML system—for example, to make another hack in the pipeline harder to find, or to make a biased model appear fair—known as fairwashing (*https://oreil.ly/YD-QJ*). These attacks make clear that as ML pipelines and AI systems become more complex, bad actors could look to many different parts of the system, from training data all the way to post hoc explanations, to alter system outputs.

Confidentiality Attacks: Extracted Information

Without proper countermeasures, bad actors can access sensitive information about our model and data. Model extraction and inversion attacks refer to hackers rebuilding our model and extracting information from their copy of the model. Membership inference attacks allow bad actors to know what rows of data are in our training data, and even to reconstruct training data. Both attacks only require access to an unguarded ML system prediction API or other system endpoints.

 Model extraction, model inversion, membership inference, and some other ML attacks, can all be thought of as a new take on an older and more common intellectual property and security issue— reverse engineering. Confidentiality attacks, and other ML attacks, can be used to *reverse engineer* and reconstruct our potentially sensitive models and data.

Model extraction and inversion attacks

Inversion (see Figure 5-6) basically means getting unauthorized information out of our model—as opposed to the normal usage pattern of putting information into our model. If an attacker can receive many predictions from our model API or other endpoint (website, app, etc.), they can train a surrogate model between their inputs and our system's predictions. That extracted surrogate model is trained between the inputs the attacker used to generate the received predictions and the received predictions themselves. Depending on the number of predictions the attacker can receive, the surrogate model could become quite an accurate simulation of our model. Unfortunately, once the surrogate model is trained, we have several big problems:

- Models are really just compressed versions of training data. With the surrogate model, an attacker can start learning about our potentially sensitive training data.

- Models are valuable intellectual property. Attackers can now sell access to their copy of our model and cut into our return on investment.

- The attacker now has a sandbox from which to plan impersonation, adversarial example, membership inference, or other attacks against our model.

Such surrogate models can also be trained using external data sources that can be somehow matched to our predictions, as ProPublica famously did (*https://oreil.ly/ FvMDm*) with the proprietary COMPAS criminal risk assessment instrument.

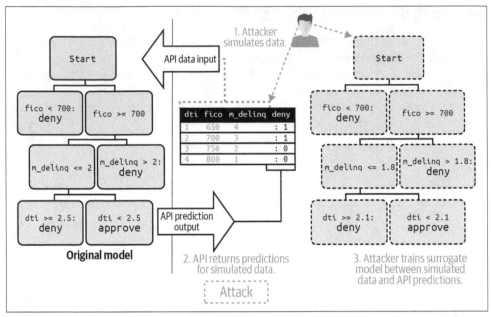

Figure 5-6. An inversion attack (digital, color version: https://oreil.ly/04ycs)

Membership inference attacks

In an attack that starts with model extraction and is also carried out by surrogate models, a malicious actor can determine whether a given person or product is in our model's training data. Called a membership inference attack (see Figure 5-7), this hack is executed with two layers of models. First, an attacker passes data into a public prediction API or other endpoint, receives predictions back, and trains a surrogate model or models between the passed data and the predictions. Once a surrogate model (or models) has been trained to replicate our model, the attacker then trains a second layer classifier that can differentiate between data that was used to train the first surrogate model and data that was not used to train that surrogate. When this second model is used to attack our model, it can give a solid indication as to whether any given row (or rows) of data is in our training data.

Membership in a training dataset can be sensitive when the model and data are related to undesirable outcomes such as bankruptcy or disease, or desirable outcomes like high income or net worth. Moreover, if the relationship between a single row and the target of our model can be easily generalized by an attacker, such as an obvious relationship between race, gender, or age and some undesirable outcome, this attack can violate the privacy of an entire class of people. Frighteningly, when carried out to its fullest extent, a membership inference attack could also allow a malicious actor, with access only to an unprotected public prediction API or other model endpoint, to reverse engineer large portions of a sensitive or valuable training dataset.

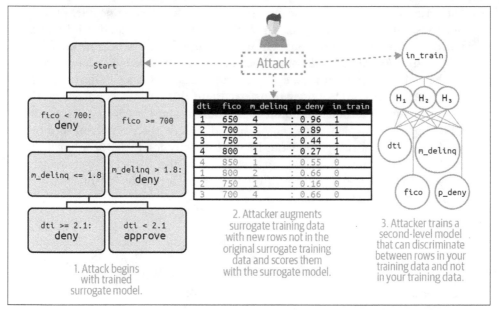

dti	fico	m_delinq	p_deny	in_train
1	650	4	: 0.96	1
2	700	3	: 0.89	1
3	750	2	: 0.44	1
4	800	1	: 0.27	1
4	850	1	: 0.55	0
1	800	2	: 0.66	0
2	750	1	: 0.16	0
3	700	4	: 0.66	0

1. Attack begins with trained surrogate model.

2. Attacker augments surrogate training data with new rows not in the original surrogate training data and scores them with the surrogate model.

3. Attacker trains a second-level model that can discriminate between rows in your training data and not in your training data.

Figure 5-7. A membership inference attack (digital, color version: https://oreil.ly/04ycs)

While the discussed attacks are some of the most well-known varieties, keep in mind that these are not the only types of ML hacks, and that new attacks can emerge very quickly. Accordingly, we'll also address a few general concerns to help us frame the broader threat environment, before moving on to countermeasures we can use to protect our ML system.

General ML Security Concerns

One common theme of this book is that ML systems are fundamentally software systems, and applying commonsense software best practices to ML systems is usually a good idea. The same applies for security. As software systems and services, ML systems exhibit similar failure modes, and experience the same attacks, as general software systems. What are some other general concerns? Unpleasant things like intentional abuses of AI technology, availability attacks, trojans and malware, man-in-the-middle attacks, unnecessarily complex unexplainable systems, and the woes of distributed computing:

Abuses of machine learning

Nearly all tools can also be weapons, and ML models and AI systems can be abused in numerous ways. Let's start by considering deepfakes. Deepfakes are an application of deep learning that can, when done carefully, seamlessly blend fragments of audio and video into convincing new media. While deepfakes can be used to bring movie actors back to life, as was done in some recent

Star Wars films, deepfakes can be used to harm and extort people. Of course, nonconsensual pornography, in which the victim's face is blended into an adult video, is one of the most popular uses of deepfakes, as documented by the BBC (*https://oreil.ly/05QCB*) and other news outlets. Deepfakes have also been implicated in financial crimes, e.g., when an attacker used a CEO's voice (*https://oreil.ly/A0a8_*) to order money transferred into their own account. Algorithmic discrimination is another common application of abusive AI. In a "fairwashing" attack, post hoc explanations can be altered to hide discrimination in a biased model. And facial recognition can be used directly for racial profiling (*https://oreil.ly/KBvXa*). We're touching on just a few of the ways ML systems can be abused; for a broader treatment of this important topic, see "AI-Enabled Future Crime" (*https://oreil.ly/8L3ax*).

General availability attacks

ML systems can fall victim to more general denial-of-service (DOS) attacks, just like other public-facing services. If a public-facing ML system is critical to our organization, we make sure it's hardened with firewalls and filters, reverse domain name server system (DNS) lookup, and other countermeasures that increase availability during a DOS attack. Unfortunately, we also have to think through another kind of availability failure for ML systems—those caused by algorithmic discrimination. If algorithmic discrimination is severe enough, whether driven by internal failures or adversarial attacks, our ML system will likely not be usable by a large portion of its users. Be sure to test for bias during training and throughout a system's deployed lifecycle.

Trojans and malware

ML in the research and development environment is dependent on a diverse ecosystem of open source software packages. Some of these packages have many contributors and users. Some are highly specific and only meaningful to a small number of researchers or practitioners. It's well understood that many packages are maintained by brilliant statisticians and ML researchers whose primary focus is mathematics or algorithms, not software engineering or security. It's not uncommon for an ML pipeline to be dependent on dozens or even hundreds of external packages, any one of which could be hacked to conceal an attack payload. Third-party packages with large binary data stores and pretrained ML models seem especially ripe for these kinds of problems. If possible, scan all software artifacts associated with an ML system for malware and trojans.

Man-in-the-middle attacks

Because many ML system predictions and decisions are transmitted over the internet or an organization's network, they can be manipulated by bad actors during that journey. Where possible, use encryption, certificates, mutual authentication, or other countermeasures to ensure the integrity of ML system results passed across networks.

Unexplainable machine learning

Although recent developments in interpretable models and model explanations have provided the opportunity to use accurate and also transparent models, many machine learning workflows are still centered around unexplainable models. Such models are a common type of often unnecessary complexity in a commercial ML workflow. A dedicated, motivated attacker can, over time, learn more about our overly complex unexplainable ML model than our own team knows about it. (Especially in today's turnover-prone data science job market.) This knowledge imbalance can potentially be exploited to conduct the attacks we've described or for other yet unknown types of attacks.

Distributed computing

For better or worse, we live in the age of big data. Many organizations are now using distributed data processing and ML systems. Distributed computing can provide a broad attack surface for a malicious internal or external actor. Data could be poisoned on only one or a few worker nodes of a large distributed data storage or processing system. A backdoor could be coded into just one model of a large ensemble. Instead of debugging one simple dataset or model, now practitioners must sometimes examine data or models distributed across large computing clusters.

Starting to get worried again? Hang in there—we'll cover countermeasures for confidentiality, integrity, and availability attacks on ML systems next.

Countermeasures

There are many countermeasures we can use and, when paired with the governance processes proposed in Chapter 1, bug bounties, security audits, and red-teaming, such measures are more likely to be effective. Additionally, there are the newer subdisciplines of adversarial ML and robust ML, which are giving the full academic treatment to these subjects. This section will outline some of the defensive measures we can use to help make our ML systems more secure, including model debugging for security, model monitoring for security, privacy-enhancing technologies, robust ML, and a few general approaches.

Model Debugging for Security

ML models can and should be tested for security vulnerabilities before they are released. In these tests, the goal is basically to attack our own ML systems, to understand our level of security, and to patch up any discovered vulnerabilities. Some general techniques that work across different types of ML models for security debugging are adversarial example searches, sensitivity analysis, audits for insider attacks and model extraction attacks, and discrimination testing.

Adversarial example searches and sensitivity analysis

Conducting sensitivity analysis with an adversarial mindset, or better yet, conducting our own adversarial example attacks, is a good way to determine if our system is vulnerable to perhaps the simplest and most common type of ML integrity attack. The idea of these ethical hacks is to understand what feature values (or combinations thereof) can cause large swings in our system's output predictions. If we're working in the deep learning space, packages like cleverhans (*https://oreil.ly/6LuBF*) and foolbox (*https://oreil.ly/M4ayU*) can help us get started with testing our ML system. For those working with structured data, good old sensitivity analysis can go a long way toward pointing out instabilities in our system. We can also use genetic learning to evolve our own adversarial examples or we can use heuristic methods based on individual conditional expectation (*https://oreil.ly/_qQdn*) to find adversarial examples. Once we find instabilities in our ML system, triggered by these adversarial examples, we'll want to use cross-validation or regularization to train a more stable model, apply techniques from robust machine learning (see "Robust Machine Learning" on page 182), or explicitly monitor for the discovered adversarial examples in real time. We should also link this information to the system's incident response plan, in case it's useful later.

Auditing for insider data poisoning

If a data poisoning attack were to occur, system insiders—employees, contractors, and consultants—are not unlikely culprits. How can we track down insider data poisoning? First, score those individuals with our system. Any insider receiving a positive outcome could be the attacker or know the attacker. Because a smart attacker will likely perform the minimum changes to the training data that result in a positive outcome, we can also use residual analysis to look for beneficial outcomes with larger than expected residuals, indicating the ML model may have been inclined to issue a negative outcome for the individual had the training data not been altered. Data and environment management are strong countermeasures for insider data poisoning, as any changes to data are tracked with ample metadata (who, what, when, etc.). We can also try the reject on negative impact (RONI) technique, proposed in the seminal "The Security of Machine Learning" (*https://oreil.ly/exh6g*), to remove potentially altered rows from system training data.

Bias testing

DOS attacks, resulting from some kind of bias—intentional or not—are a plausible type of availability attack. In fact, it's already happened. In 2016, Twitter users poisoned the Tay chatbot (*https://oreil.ly/uPqNx*) to the point where only those users interested in neo-Nazi pornography would find the system's service appealing. This type of attack could also happen in a more serious context, such as employment, lending, or medicine, where an attacker uses data poisoning, model backdoors, or other types of attacks to deny service to a certain group of customers. This is one of the many reasons to conduct bias testing, and remediate any discovered discrimination, both at training time and as part of regular model monitoring. There are several great open source tools for detecting discrimination and making attempts to remediate it, such as aequitas (*https://oreil.ly/e412j*), Themis (*https://oreil.ly/yJiT6*), and AIF360 (*https://oreil.ly/HsKEg*).

Ethical hacking: model extraction attacks

Model extraction attacks are harmful on their own, but they are also the first stage for a membership inference attack. We should conduct our own model extraction attacks to determine if our system is vulnerable to these confidentiality attacks. If we find some API or model endpoint that allows us to train a surrogate model between input data and system outputs, we lock it down with solid authentication and throttle any abnormal requests at this endpoint. Because a model extraction attack may have already happened via this endpoint, we need to analyze our extracted surrogate models as follows:

- What are the accuracy bounds of different types of surrogate models? We must try to understand the extent to which a surrogate model can really be used to gain knowledge about our ML system.

- What types of data trends can be learned from our surrogate model? What about linear trends represented by linear model coefficients? Or course summaries of population subgroups in a surrogate decision tree?

- What rules can be learned from a surrogate decision tree? For example, how to reliably impersonate an individual who would receive a beneficial prediction? Or how to construct effective adversarial examples?

If we see that it is possible to train an accurate surrogate model from one of our system endpoints, and to answer some of these questions, then we'll need to take some next steps. First, we'll conduct a membership inference attack on ourselves to see if that two-stage attack would also be possible. We'll also need to record all of the information related to this ethical hacking analysis and link it to the system's incident response plan. Incident responders may find this information helpful at a later date, and it may unfortunately need to be reported as a breach if there is strong evidence that an attack has occurred.

Debugging security vulnerabilities in our ML system is important work that can save us future money, time, and heartache, but so is watching our system to ensure it stays secure. Next we'll take up model monitoring for security.

Model Monitoring for Security

Once hackers can manipulate or extract our ML model, it's really not our model anymore. To guard against attacks on our model, we'll not only need to train and debug it with security in mind; we'll also need to monitor it closely once it goes live. Monitoring for security should be geared toward algorithmic discrimination, anomalies in input data queues, anomalies in predictions, and high usage. Here are some tips on what and how to monitor:

Bias monitoring

Bias testing, as discussed in other chapters, must be applied during model training. But for many reasons, including unintended consequences and malicious hacking, discrimination testing must be performed during deployment too. If bias is found during deployment, it should be investigated and remediated. This helps to ensure a model that was fair during training remains fair in production.

Input anomalies

Unrealistic combinations of data, which could be used to trigger backdoors in model mechanisms, should not be allowed into model scoring queues. Anomaly detection ML techniques, like autoencoders and isolation forests, may be generally helpful in tracking problematic input data. However, we can also use commonsense data integrity constraints to catch problematic data before it hits our model. An example of such unrealistic data is an age of 40 years and a job tenure of 50 years. If possible, we should also consider monitoring for random data, training data, or duplicate data. Because random data is often used in model extraction and inversion attacks, we build out alerts or controls that help our team understand if and when our model may be encountering batches of random data. Real-time scoring of rows that are extremely similar or identical to data used in training, validation, or testing should be recorded and investigated, as they could indicate a membership inference attack. Finally, be on the lookout for duplicate data in real-time scoring queues, as this could indicate an evasion or impersonation attack.

Output anomalies

Output anomalies can be indicative of adversarial example attacks. When scoring new data, we compare our ML model prediction against a trusted, transparent benchmark model or a benchmark model trained on a trusted data source and pipeline. If the difference between our more complex and opaque ML model and our interpretable or trusted model is too great, we fall back to the predictions of the conservative model or send the row of data for manual processing. Statistical control limits, which are akin to moving confidence intervals, can also be used to monitor for anomalous outputs.

Metamonitoring

> We monitor the basic operating statistics—the number of predictions in a certain time period, latency, CPU, memory, and disk load, or the number of concurrent users—to ensure our system is functioning normally. We can even train an autoencoder–based anomaly detection metamodel on our entire ML system's operating statistics and then monitor this metamodel for anomalies. An anomaly in system operations could tip us off that something is generally amiss in our ML system.

Monitoring for attacks is one the most proactive steps we can take to counter ML hacks. However, there are a still a few more countermeasures to discuss. We'll look into privacy-enhancing technologies next.

Privacy-Enhancing Technologies

Privacy-preserving ML is a research subdiscipline with direct ramifications for the confidentiality of our ML training data. While just beginning to gain steam in the ML and ML operations (MLOps) communities, PETs can give us an edge when it comes to protecting our data and models. Some of the most promising and practical techniques from this emergent field include federated learning and differential privacy.

Federated learning

Federated learning is an approach to training ML models across multiple decentralized devices or servers holding local data samples, without exchanging raw data between them. This approach is different from traditional centralized ML techniques where all datasets are uploaded to a single server. The main benefit of federated learning is that it enables the construction of ML models without sharing data among many parties. Federated learning avoids sharing data by training local models on local data samples and exchanging parameters between servers or edge devices to generate a global model, which is then shared by all servers or edge devices. Assuming a secure aggregation process is used, federated learning helps address fundamental data privacy and data security concerns. Among other open source resources, we should look into PySyft (*https://oreil.ly/8HpeR*) or FATE (*https://oreil.ly/W3uYP*) to start learning about implementing federated learning at our organization (or with partner organizations).

Differential privacy

Differential privacy is a system for sharing information about a dataset by describing patterns about groups in the dataset without disclosing information about specific individuals. In ML tools, this is often accomplished using specialized types of differentially private learning algorithms. This makes it more difficult to extract sensitive information from training data or a trained ML model in model extraction, model inversion, or membership inference attacks. In fact, an ML model is said to be differentially private if an outside observer cannot tell if an individual's information was used to train the model. There are lots of high-quality open source repositories to check out and try, including the following:

- Google's differential-privacy (*https://oreil.ly/rjwKK*)
- IBM's diffprivlib (*https://oreil.ly/QOFm-*)
- TensorFlow's privacy (*https://oreil.ly/WyPD6*)

Many ML approaches that invoke differential privacy are based on differentially private stochastic gradient descent (DP-SGD) (*https://oreil.ly/raWeC*). DP-SGD injects structured noise into gradients determined by SGD at each training iteration. In general, DP-SGD and related techniques ensure that ML models do not memorize too much specific information about training data. Because they prevent ML algorithms from focusing on particular individuals, they could also lead to increased generalization performance and fairness benefits.

Readers may hear about confidential computing or homomorphic encryption under the PET topic heading as well. These are promising research and technology directions to watch as well. Another subdiscipline of ML research to watch is robust ML, which can help us counter adversarial example attacks, data poisoning, and other adversarial manipulation of our ML system.

What Else Do Data Scientists Need to Know About Privacy?

Data is becoming a more regulated quantity, even in the US. Aside from regulation, being sloppy with data can harm our users, our organization, or the general public. As data scientists, we need to know some data privacy basics:

Regulations and policies
> We are likely to be operating under some data privacy regulations or an organizational privacy policy. We should know the basics of what our obligations are and try to adhere to them. In the US, healthcare and educational data are particularly sensitive, but the EU General Data Protection Regulation (GDPR)—to which many multinational organizations must adhere—covers nearly all types of consumer data, and US states are passing many new data privacy laws.

Consent
> Although far from perfect, many data privacy regulations rely on the notion of *consent*, i.e., that consumers actively opt in to the use of their data for a specific application. Both from a legal and ethical perspective, it's good to confirm that we have consent to use our data for the model we're training.

Other legal bases for use

If we are operating under the GDPR, we need a legal basis to use much of the consumer data we might be interested in for ML. Consent is often the legal basis, but there are other examples: contractual obligations, governmental tasks, or medical emergencies.

Anonymization

It's almost never a good idea to work with personal identifiable information (PII). Data like Social Security numbers, phone numbers, and even email addresses—known as *direct identifiers*—allows bad actors to tie private and sensitive information back to specific people. Even combinations of demographic information, like age, race, or gender—known as *indirect identifiers*—can be used to tie information back to specific individuals. Generally, this kind of data should be removed, masked, hashed, or otherwise anonymized for use in model training, for privacy and bias reasons.

Biometric data

Data like digital images, videos, fingerprints, voiceprints, iris scans, genomic data, or other data that encodes biometric information typically requires additional security and data privacy controls.

Retention limits or requirements

Laws and organizational privacy policies may define retention limits, or how long data can be saved before mandatory deletion. (We've seen two-week retention limits!) We may also have to deal with legal or organizational retention requirements that enforce how long data must be stored and kept private and secure—this can be for years.

Deletion and rectification requests

Many laws and policies enable consumers to have their data updated, corrected, or fully deleted upon request, and this could potentially affect ML training data.

Explanation

Many data privacy laws also seem to be putting forward a requirement for explaining automatic processing of data that affects consumers. Although vague and largely unsettled, this may mean that in the future many more ML decisions will have to be explained to consumers.

Intervenability

Similar to explanation, many new laws also seem to instate a requirement for *intervenability*, which is similar to the appeal and override concepts of actionable recourse.

Bias

It's not uncommon for data privacy laws and policies to address bias in data processing outcomes, like ML model predictions. Sometimes these requirements are vague and high-level. Sometimes they are more specific or mandate compliance with established nondiscrimination laws.

All of these issues can have a serious impact on our ML workflows. We may need to plan to deal with retention limits, deletion requests, rectification requests, or intervenability requirements. For example, would we need to decommission and delete a model trained on expired data or data that consumers have requested be deleted? No one is quite sure yet, but it's not impossible. If readers have never received training about data privacy obligations, or have questions or concerns about data privacy topics, it might not be a bad idea to check with your manager or legal department.

Robust Machine Learning

Robust ML includes many cutting-edge ML algorithms developed to counter adversarial example attacks, and to a certain extent data poisoning as well. The study of robust ML gained momentum after several researchers showed that silly, or even invisible, changes to input data can result in huge swings in output predictions for computer vision systems. Such swings in model outcomes are a troubling sign in any domain, but when considering medical imaging or semi-autonomous vehicles, they are downright dangerous. Robust ML models help enforce stability in model outcomes, and, importantly, fairness—that similar individuals be treated similarly. Similar individuals in ML training data or live data are individuals that are close to one another in the Euclidean space of the data. Robust ML techniques often try to establish a hypersphere around individual examples of data, and ensure that other similar data within the hypersphere receive similar predictions. Whether caused by bad actors, overfitting, underspecification, or other factors, robust ML approaches help protect our organization from risks arising from unexpected predictions. Interesting papers and code are hosted at the Robust ML site (*https://oreil.ly/H36uh*), and the Madry Lab at the Massachusetts Institute of Technology has even published a full Python package for robust ML (*https://oreil.ly/k-qDZ*).

General Countermeasures

There are a number of catchall countermeasures that can defend against several different types of ML attacks, including authentication, throttling, and watermarking. Many of these same kinds of countermeasures are also best practices for ML systems in general, like interpretable models, model management, and model monitoring. The last topic we will address before the chapter's case study is a brief description of important and general countermeasures against ML system attacks:

Authentication
    Whenever possible, disallow anonymous use for high-stakes ML systems. Login credentials, multifactor authentication, or other types of authentication that force

users prove their identity, authorization, and permission to use a system put a blockade between our model API and anonymous bad actors.

Interpretable, fair, or private models

Modeling techniques now exist—e.g., monotonic GBMs (M-GBM), scalable Bayesian rule lists (SBRL) (*https://oreil.ly/Md375*), explainable neural networks (XNN) (*https://oreil.ly/sd4XX*)—that can allow for both accuracy and interpretability in ML models. These accurate and interpretable models are easier to document and debug than classic unexplainable ones. Newer types of fair and private modeling techniques—e.g., LFR (*https://oreil.ly/7ZHmw*), DP-SGD (*https://oreil.ly/yuddM*)—can also be trained to downplay outwardly visible demographic characteristics that can be observed, socially engineered into an adversarial example attack, or impersonated. These models, enhanced for interpretability, fairness, or privacy, should be more easily debugged, more robust to changes in an individual entity's characteristics, and more secure than overused unexplainable models.

Model documentation

Model documentation is a risk-mitigation strategy that has been used for decades in banking. It allows knowledge about complex modeling systems to be preserved and transferred as teams of model owners change over time, and for knowledge to be standardized for efficient analysis by model validators and auditors. Model documentation should cover the who, when, where, what, and how of an ML system, including many details, from contact information for stakeholders to algorithmic specification. Model documentation is also a natural place to record any known vulnerabilities or security concerns for an ML system, enabling future maintainers or other operators that interact with the system to allocate oversight and security resources efficiently. Incident response plans should also be linked to model documentation. (Chapter 2 contains a sample documentation template.)

Model management

Model management typically refers to a combination of process controls, like documentation, combined with technology controls, like model monitoring and model inventories. Organizations should have an exact count of deployed ML systems and a structured inventory of associated code, data, documentation, and incident response plans, and they should monitor all deployed models. These practices make it easier to understand when something goes wrong and to deal with problems quickly when they arise. (Chapter 1 discusses model risk management for ML in much more detail.)

Throttling

When high use or other anomalies, such as adversarial examples, or duplicate, random, or training data, are identified by model monitoring systems, consider throtling prediction APIs or other system endpoints. Throttling can refer to restricting high numbers of rapid predictions from single users, artificially increasing prediction latency for all users, or other methods that can slow down attackers conducting model or data extraction attacks and adversarial example attacks.

Watermarking

Watermarking refers to adding a subtle marker to our data or predictions, for the purpose of deterring theft of data or models. If data or predictions carry identifiable traits, such as actual watermarks on images or sentinel markers in structured data, it can make stolen assets harder to use and more identifiable to law enforcement or other investigators once a theft occurs.

Applying these general defenses and best practices, along with some of the more specific countermeasures discussed in previous sections, is a great way to achieve a high level of security for an ML system. And now that we've covered security basics, ML attacks, and many countermeasures for those attacks, readers are armed with the knowledge needed to start red-teaming your organization's AI—especially if you can work with your organization's IT security professionals. We'll now examine some real-world AI security incidents to provide additional motivation for doing the hard work of red-teaming AI, and to gain insights into some of today's most common ML security issues.

Case Study: Real-World Evasion Attacks

ML systems used for both physical and online security have suffered evasion attacks in recent years. This case discussion touches on evasion attacks used to avoid Facebook filters and perpetuate disinformation and terrorist propaganda, and evasion attacks against real-world payment and physical security systems.

Evasion Attacks

As the COVID pandemic ground on and the 2020 US presidential campaign was in high gear, those proliferating disinformation related to both topics took advantage of weaknesses in Facebook's manual and automated content filtering. As reported by NPR, "Tiny Changes Let False Claims About COVID-19, Voting Evade Facebook Fact Checks" (*https://oreil.ly/aYSTr*). While Facebook uses news organizations such as Reuters and the Associated Press to fact-check claims made by its billions of users, it also uses AI-based content filtering, particularly to catch copies of human-identified misinformation posts. Unfortunately, minor changes, some as simple as different backgrounds or fonts, image cropping, or simply describing memes with words instead of images, allowed bad actors to circumvent Facebook's ML-based content filters. In its defense, Facebook does carry out enforcement actions against many offenders, including limiting the distribution of posts, not recommending posts or groups, and demonetization. Yet, according to one advocacy group, Facebook fails to catch about 42% of disinformation posts containing information flagged by human fact checkers (*https://oreil.ly/fzCrb*). The same advocacy group, Avaaz, estimates that a sample of just 738 unlabeled disinformation posts led to an estimated 142 million views and 5.6 million user interactions.

Recent events have shown us that online disinformation and security threats can spill over into the real world. Disinformation about the 2020 US election and the COVID pandemic are thought to be primary drivers of the frightening US Capitol riots of January 6, 2021. In perhaps even more disturbing evasion attacks, the BBC has reported that ISIS operatives continue to evade Facebook content filters (*https://oreil.ly/qV25u*). By blurring logos, splicing their videos with mainstream news content, or just using strange punctuation, ISIS members or affiliates have been able to post propaganda, explosive-making tutorials, and even evasion attack tutorials to Facebook, garnering tens of thousands views for their violent, disturbing, and vitriolic content. While evasion attacks on AI-based filters are certainly a major culprit, there are also fewer human moderators for Arabic content on Facebook. Regardless of whether it's humans or machines failing at the job, this type of content can be truly dangerous, contributing both to radicalization and real-world violence. Physical evasion attacks are also a concern for the near future. Researchers recently showed that some AI-based physical security systems are easy targets for evasion attacks (*https://oreil.ly/xVmDj*). With the permission of system operators, researchers used lifelike three-dimensional masks to bypass facial recognition security checks on Alipay and WeChat payment systems. In one egregious case, researchers were even able to use a picture of another person on an IPhone screen to board a plane at Amsterdam's Schiphol Airport.

Lessons Learned

Taken together, bad actors' evasions of online safeguards to post dangerous content, and evasions of physical security systems to make monetary payments and to travel by plane paints a scary picture of a world where ML security is not taken seriously. What lessons learned from this chapter could be applied to prevent these evasion attacks? The first lesson is related to robust ML. ML systems used for high-stakes security applications, be they online or real world, must not be fooled by tiny changes to normal system inputs. Robust ML, and related technologies, must progress to the point where simplistic evasion techniques, like blurring of logos or changes to punctuation, are not effective evasion measures. Another lesson comes from the beginning of the chapter: the adversarial mindset. Anyone who thought seriously about security risks for these AI-based security systems should have realized that masks, or just other images, were an obvious evasion technique. Thankfully, it turns out that some organizations do employ countermeasures for adversarial scenarios. Better facial recognition security systems deploy techniques meant to ensure the liveness of the subjects they are identifying. The better facial recognition systems also employ discrimination testing to ensure availability is high, and error rates are as low as possible, for all their users.

Another major lesson to be learned from real-world evasion attacks pertains to the responsible use of technology in general, and ML in particular. Social media has proliferated beyond physical borders, and its complexity has grown past many countries' current abilities to effectively regulate it. With a lack of government regulation, users are counting on social media companies to regulate themselves. Being tech companies, social networks often rely on more technology, like AI-based content filters, to retain control of their systems. But what if those controls don't really work? As technology and ML play larger roles in human lives, lack of rigor and responsibility in their design, implementation, and deployment will have ever-increasing consequences. Those designing technologies for security or other high-stakes applications have an especially serious obligation to be realistic about today's ML capabilities and apply process and technology controls to ensure adequate real-world performance.

Resources

Further Reading

- "A Marauder's Map of Security and Privacy in Machine Learning" (*https://oreil.ly/0k7D3*)
- "BIML Interactive Machine Learning Risk Framework" (*https://oreil.ly/csQ22*)
- FTC's "Start with Security" guidelines (*https://oreil.ly/jmeja*)
- Adversarial Threat Landscape for Artificial-Intelligence Systems (*https://oreil.ly/KxEbC*)
- NIST Computer Security Resource Center (*https://oreil.ly/pncXb*)
- NIST de-identification tools (*https://oreil.ly/M8xhr*)

## PART II

Putting AI Risk Management into Action

## CHAPTER 6

Explainable Boosting Machines and Explaining XGBoost

This chapter explores explainable models and post hoc explanation with interactive examples (*https://oreil.ly/machine-learning-high-risk-apps-code*) relating to consumer finance. It also applies the approaches discussed in Chapter 2 using explainable boosting machines (EBMs), monotonically constrained XGBoost models, and post hoc explanation techniques. We'll start with a concept refresher for additivity, constraints, partial dependence and individual conditional expectation (ICE), Shapley additive explanations (SHAP), and model documentation.

We'll then explore an example credit underwriting problem by building from a penalized regression, to a generalized additive model (GAM), to an EBM. In working from simpler to more complex models, we'll document explicit and deliberate trade-offs regarding the introduction of nonlinearity and interactions into our example probability of default classifier, all while preserving near-total explainability with additive models.

 Recall from Chapter 2 that an *interpretation* is a high-level, meaningful mental representation that contextualizes a stimulus and leverages human background knowledge, whereas an *explanation* is a low-level, detailed mental representation that seeks to describe a complex process. Interpretation is a much higher bar than explanation, rarely achieved by technical approaches alone.

After that, we'll consider a second approach to predicting default that allows for complex feature interactions, but controls complexity with monotonic constraints based in causal knowledge. Because the monotonically constrained gradient boosting machine (GBM) won't be explainable on its own, we'll pair it with robust post hoc explanation techniques for greatly enhanced explainability. Finally, the chapter will close with a discussion of the pros and cons of popular Shapley value methods.

Concept Refresher: Machine Learning Transparency

Before diving into technical examples, let's review some of the key concepts from Chapter 2. Because our first example will highlight the strengths of the GAM family of models, we'll address additivity next, particularly in comparison to models that allow for high-degree interactions. Our second example will use monotonic constraints to effect an informal causality approach with XGBoost, so we'll briefly highlight the connections between causation and constraints. We'll also be using partial dependence and ICE to compare and assess our different approaches' treatments of input features, so we'll need a quick refresh on the strengths and weaknesses of those post hoc explainers, and we'll need to go over the importance of model documentation one more time—because model documentation is that important.

Additivity Versus Interactions

A major distinguishing characteristic of unexplainable machine learning is its propensity to create extremely high-degree interactions between input features. It's thought that this ability to consider the values of many features in simultaneous combination increases the predictive capacity of ML models versus more traditional linear or additive models, which tend to consider input features independently. But it's been shown that unexplainable models are not more accurate for structured data (*https://oreil.ly/ztXi8*), like credit underwriting data, and all those interactions in unexplainable models are very difficult for people to understand. Moreover, high-degree interactions also lead to instability, because small changes in one or few a features can interact with other features to dramatically change model outcomes. And high-degree interactions lead to overfitting, because today's relevant 17-way interactions are likely not tomorrow's relevant 17-way interactions.

Another important characteristic of ML is the ability to learn nonlinear phenomena in training data, automatically. It turns out that if we can separate nonlinearity from interactions, we can realize substantial boosts in predictive quality, while preserving a great deal of explainability, if not complete explainability. This is the magic of GAMs. And EBMs are the next step that allow us to introduce a sane number of two-way interactions, in an additive fashion, that can result in even better performance. Later in this chapter, the GAM family example (see "The GAM Family of Explainable Models" on page 196) aims to provide an object lesson in these trade-offs, starting with a straightforward, additive, linear model baseline, then introducing nonlinearity with GAMs, and finally introducing understandable two-way interactions with EBMs. When we introduce nonlinearity and interactions carefully, as opposed to assuming more complexity is always better, it enables us to justify our modeling approach, to tether it to real-world performance concerns, and to generate a lot of interesting plots of feature behavior. These justifications and plots are also great materials for subsequent model documentation, to be addressed in greater detail shortly.

 The family of models that typically includes variants of GLMs, GAMs, GA2M, EBMs, and additive index models (AIMs) has been discussed in statistical literature for years. This type of modeling is sometimes referred to as the functional analysis of variance (fANOVA) framework.

Steps Toward Causality with Constraints

Causal discovery and inference are important directions in the future of predictive modeling. Why? Because when we build on correlations with ML, we are often building on sand. Correlations change constantly in the real world and can be spurious or just wrong. If we can base models on causal relationships instead of just memorializing some snapshot of complex correlations with an ML model, we greatly decrease overfitting, data drift, and social bias risks. As of now, causal methods tend to be somewhat difficult for most organizations to implement, so our monotonic constraints example (see "Constrained and Unconstrained XGBoost" on page 208) highlights a simple and easy step we can take to inject causality into ML models. If we can use our brains, or simple but robust experiments, to understand the directionality of a causal relationship in the real world, we can use monotonic constraints to enforce that directionality in our XGBoost models. For instance, if we *know* that an increasing number of late payments are an indicator of future default, we can use monotonic constraints to insist that an XGBoost classifier generate higher probabilities of default for higher numbers of late payments. Though we might not see gains in in silico test data performance with constraints, constraints do mitigate real-world instability, overfitting, and sociological bias risks, and they likely increase in vivo performance.

Partial Dependence and Individual Conditional Expectation

Partial dependence is an established and highly intuitive post hoc explanation method that describes the estimated average behavior of a model across the values of some input feature. Unfortunately, it's fallible. It fails to represent model behavior accurately in the presence of correlation or interactions between input features, and it can even be maliciously altered (*https://oreil.ly/z2xAW*). But, because understanding the average behavior of a feature in a model is so important, many techniques have been developed to address the failings of partial dependence. In particular, accumulated local effect (*https://oreil.ly/kEIPp*) is the most direct replacement for partial dependence and was designed specifically to address the shortcomings of partial dependence. Readers can try ALE with packages like ALEPlot (*https://oreil.ly/7vv4h*) or ALEPython (*https://oreil.ly/To7PF*).

In the examples that follow, we'll make heavy use of another partial dependence derivative to get a solid understanding of feature behavior in our models. First introduced in "Peeking Inside the Black Box: Visualizing Statistical Learning with Plots of Individual Conditional Expectation" (*https://oreil.ly/MruUv*), ICE pairs plots of local behavior of the model with respect to single individuals with partial dependence. This enables us to compare estimated average behavior with descriptions of local behavior, and when partial dependence and ICE curves diverge, to decide for ourselves if partial dependence looks trustworthy or if it looks to be affected by correlations or interactions in input variables. Of course, ICE is not without its own problems. The most common problem with ICE is the consideration of unrealistic data values, and when interpreting ICE, it's important to put the most mental weight on values of the input feature that are most similar to those in the original row of data being considered.

Let's work through all of this in an example. In the bottom panel of Figure 6-1, we can see the partial dependence and ICE for a penalized logistic regression model and for the input feature PAY_0 (a customer's repayment status on their most recent bill). Higher values of PAY_0 indicate greater lateness in payment. ICE curves are generated for individuals who sit at the deciles of predicted probability.

Note the smooth increase from lower probabilities of default when a customer is not late on their most recent payment, to high probabilities of default when a customer is late. This makes sense in context. It aligns with reasonable expectations and domain knowledge. Notice also that ICE and partial dependence do not diverge—they are highly aligned. This will always be the case in linear models, but it also shows us that partial dependence is likely trustworthy for this model and dataset.

So, what's going on in the top panel of this figure? That's where we try to decide if the model is learning robust signals from the training data. The first thing you might notice is a histogram. We use that histogram to look for stability problems in model predictions. ML models typically only learn from data, so if there is not much data, as is the case with PAY_0 > 1 in our training data, the ML model can't learn much, and their predictions in those data domains will be unstable, if not nonsensical. Some other packages use error bars for the same purpose in partial dependence or shape function plots. That's also fine. Both visualization techniques are trying to draw your eye to a region of data where your ML model is unstable and probably making silly decisions.

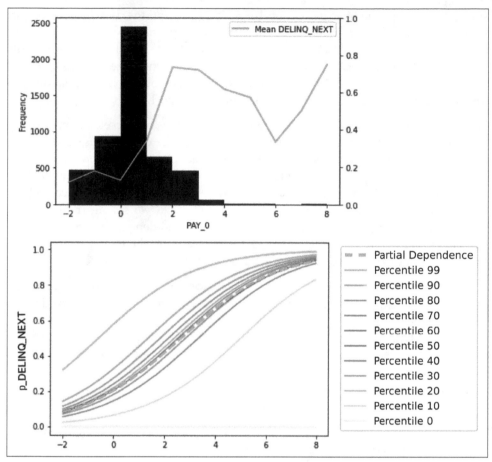

Figure 6-1. A partial dependence plot for a GLM trained later in this chapter that incorporates ICE, histograms, and conditional means to increase trustworthiness and effectiveness (digital, color version: https://oreil.ly/7vLOU)

This is where we try to decide if the model is representing our training data well, and the top panel can also clue us in to problems with data sparsity and prediction reliability. In the top panel, the first thing we notice is a histogram. We use that histogram to look for reliability problems in model predictions. Readers will see that there is also a line overlaid on the histogram. That line is the conditional mean of the target for the corresponding histogram bin. If the model learned from the data correctly, the partial dependence and ICE in the bottom panel should roughly mirror the conditional mean line in the top panel. Sparsity is also an important caveat to keep in mind when judging whether model behavior aligns with the conditional mean of the target. In Figure 6-1, we see a precipitous drop in the conditional mean at PAY_0 = 6, or six months late for the most recent bill. However, there's no data to support this drop. The histogram bin is basically empty, and the drop is probably just irrelevant noise. Luckily, our well-behaved logistic regression model has no choice but to ignore this noise and keep pushing the probability of default monotonically higher as PAY_0 increases. With more complex models for the same data, we will need to apply monotonic constraints to ensure that the model follows causal relationships instead of memorizing irrelevant noise with no data support.

To quote the important explainability researcher Przemysław Biecek, "Don't explain without context!" That means we need to think about the correlations, interactions, and the security of the datasets we're using to generate partial dependence and ICE—typically validation, test, or other interesting holdout samples. If those datasets don't align with the correlations and interactions in training data, or the sample could have been intentionally altered, we'll get different results than we saw in training. This can raise a number of questions. Was the training partial dependence correct? Does our model actually behave differently with new data, or are the new correlations and interactions in this sample causing partial dependence to be less trustworthy?

These are all reasons that we pair partial dependence with ICE. As a local explanation technique, ICE is less susceptible to global changes in correlations and interactions. If something looks off with partial dependence, first check if partial dependence follows the local behavior of ICE curves or if it diverges from the ICE curves. If it diverges, it's likely safer to take our explanatory information from ICE, and if possible, to investigate what distribution, correlation, interaction, or security problems are altering the partial dependence.

Shapley Values

Recall that SHAP is a way to generate local feature attribution values with a great deal of theoretical support (at least by ML standards). A SHAP value tells us how much a feature's value for a certain row moved the model prediction away from the mean prediction. But how does SHAP do it? It does it by "removing" the feature from that row's prediction repeatedly and in concert with other removed features. By removing features and measuring differences in the model prediction, we start to get a good picture of how each feature affects each prediction.

 Remember from Chapter 2 that Shapley values are a post hoc explanation technique, borrowed from economics and game theory, that decompose model predictions into contributions from each input feature.

Because SHAP can use *background* datasets, or specific datasets from which to draw random samples to use as a substitute for removed features, we have to consider context (*https://oreil.ly/HNpls*) in both the dataset to be explained and the background dataset. Because of the definition of partial dependence and ICE, we usually use very simple background datasets for these techniques, and we may not even think of them as background datasets at all. We are essentially just replacing the value for an entire feature (partial dependence) or a row (ICE) with some known value of that feature in order to generate a curve. When it comes to Shapley values, we have a choice for (1) which observations we explain (anything from a single row to an entirely new sample of data) and (2) which background dataset to use when generating Shapley values (anything from not using a background set, to using random data, to using highly massaged background data designed to address context or causality issues).

In addition to considering the correlations, interactions, and security of the dataset we are explaining, we also have to ask whether our choice of background is appropriate and whether explanations make sense in the context in which they will be judged. We'll go into detail later in the chapter as to how we can choose an appropriate background dataset for our Shapley value explanations, depending on the question that our explanations are trying to answer. In practice, this complex analysis often boils down to computing explanations on a few different datasets and making sure results are salient and stable. Computing Shapley-based explanations also means documenting the background dataset used and the reasons for choosing this dataset.

Model Documentation

Model documentation is the physical manifestation of accountability in large organizations. When we have to write a document about a model we built, knowing that our name will be ascribed to the same document, we hope that this encourages more deliberate design and implementation choices. And if we don't make sensible choices or document bad choices, or the documentation is clearly missing or dishonest, there can be consequences for our poor model building. Model documentation is also important for maintenance and incident response. When we've moved on to our next big data science job, and our older models start getting stale and causing problems, documentation enables a new set of practitioners to understand how the model was intended to work, how to maintain it in future iterations, and how to fix it.

There are now several standards for model documentation, including the following:

- Model cards (*https://oreil.ly/h7oJC*), with Google-provided example model cards (*https://oreil.ly/OJkfE*)
- Model risk management in-depth documentation; see the 2021 model risk management guidance (*https://oreil.ly/XDF9u*) from the US Office of the Comptroller of the Currency
- The EU Artificial Intelligence Act documentation template (*https://oreil.ly/tyS-i*); see Document 2, Appendix IV

Notice that all of these templates come from either a leading commercial user and developer of ML, or a very serious government body. If readers have avoided model documentation until now, expect that to change in the future as regulations are enacted, and especially for important applications of ML. All of these templates also benefit greatly from explainable models and post hoc explanation, because increased transparency is yet a another goal and benefit of model documentation. Transparency in ML models allows us to understand, and then to justify, design and implementation trade-offs. If what we see in an explainable model or post hoc explanation result appears reasonable and we can write a few commonsense sentences to justify the observed outcomes, that's what we're going for in this chapter. If, instead, we're using an unexplainable model and don't understand how design and implementation trade-offs affect model behavior, our documented justifications will likely be much weaker, and open us and our model up to potentially unpleasant external scrutiny.

The GAM Family of Explainable Models

In this section, we'll form a baseline with a linear additive penalized regression model, then compare that baseline to a GAM that allows for complex nonlinearity, but in an independent, additive, and highly explainable fashion. We'll then compare the GLM and GAM to an EBM with a small number of two-way interactions. Because all of our models are constructed with additive independent functional forms, and because we will use only a small number of meaningful interactions, all our models will be very explainable. Additivity will enable us to make clear and justifiable choices about introducing nonlinearity and interactions.

 Progressing from GLM, to GAM, to EBM is a generalizable workflow that allows us to make explainable, empirical, and deliberate decisions about introducing nonlinearity (via GAM) and interactions (via EBM) into our models while comparing results to a baseline (GLM).

Elastic Net–Penalized GLM with Alpha and Lambda Search

As the name suggests, GLMs extend the idea of an ordinary linear regression and generalize for error distributions belonging to exponential families, in addition to the Gaussian distribution of error used in standard linear regression. Another vital component of a GLM is the link function that connects the expected value of the response to the linear components. Since this link function can be any monotonic differentiable function, GLMs can handle a wide variety of distributions of training data outcome values: linear, binomial (as in our current example), Poisson, and several others. Penalizing a GLM refers to using sophisticated constraints and iterative optimization methods to handle correlations, feature selection, and outliers. Putting all these together results in a robust modeling technique with good predictive power and very high explainability.

Elastic net (*https://oreil.ly/K7_R0*) is a popular regularization technique that combines the advantages of both L1 (LASSO) (*https://oreil.ly/BqHjO*) and L2 (ridge) (*https://oreil.ly/ORzCT*) regression into one model. Whereas the L1 regularization enables feature selection, thereby inducing sparsity and higher explainability in the trained model, L2 regularization effectively handles correlation between the predictors. The iteratively reweighted least squares (IRLS) method is often paired with elastic net to handle outliers as well.

Training a penalized GLM will serve two useful benchmarking purposes:

- Since our GLM does not include any nonlinearity or feature interactions, it can serve as the perfect benchmark to test certain hypotheses, i.e., whether nonlinearities and interactions actually result in a better model or not, which we'll cover in the upcoming sections.

- The GLM also acts as a starting point for initial feature selection based on the features selected by L1 regularization.

We'll start our first example for this chapter by training an elastic net–penalized logistic regression using H2O's GLM algorithm (*https://oreil.ly/bI_dI*), which works in a distributed fashion and scales well for large datasets. In the H2O GLM, the regularization parameters are denoted by `alpha` and `lambda`. While `alpha` specifies the regularization distribution between L1 and L2 penalties, `lambda` indicates the regularization strength. The recommended way to find optimal regularization settings in H2O GLM is via a grid search. H2O offers two types of grid searches—Cartesian and random search. Cartesian is an exhaustive search that tries all the combinations of model hyperparameters specified in a grid of possible values supplied by the user. On the other hand, random grid search samples sets of model parameters randomly from the given set of possible values based on a stopping criterion. By default, H2O will use Cartesian search, and we'll use that for our use case because it won't take too long to search over a small number of `alpha` values.

Whenever we conduct a grid search, we implicitly open ourselves up to issues related to overfitting and multiple comparisons. Try to use bootstrapping or reusable holdout methods with grid searches if possible.

In the following code, we start by defining a grid of model hyperparameters for alpha values. It is important to note here that to preserve the stabilizing function-ality of L2 penalties and the feature selection functionality of L1 penalties, `alpha` should never be 0 or 1. This is because when `alpha` is 0, it denotes only the L2 penalty, while a value of 1 for `alpha` signifies only L1. H2O's GLM implementation comes with a handy `lambda_search` option. When set to `True`, this option searches over various `lambda` values starting from `lambda_max` (no features in the model) to `lambda_min` (many features in the model). Both `alpha` and `lambda` are selected by validation-based early stopping. This means that the GLM will automatically stop fitting the model when there is no significant improvement on the validation set, as a means to limit overfitting.

```
def glm_grid(x, y, training_frame, validation_frame, seed_, weight=None):

    # setting GLM grid parameters
    alpha_opts = [0.01, 0.25, 0.5, 0.99]  # always keep some alpha
    hyper_parameters = {'alpha': alpha_opts}

    # initialize grid search
    glm_grid = H2OGridSearch(
        H2OGeneralizedLinearEstimator(family="binomial",
                                      lambda_search=True,
                                      seed=seed_),
        hyper_params=hyper_parameters)

    # training with grid search
    glm_grid.train(y=y,
                   x=x,
                   training_frame=training_frame,
                   validation_frame=validation_frame,
                   weights_column=weight,
                   seed=seed_)

    # select best model from grid search
    best_model = glm_grid.get_grid()[0]
    del glm_grid

    return best_model
```

Using this function to run a Cartesian search over `alpha`, and letting H2O search over the best `lambda` values, our best GLM ends up with an AUC score of 0.73 on the validation dataset. After the grid search, the six `PAY_*` repayment status features have the largest coefficients in the selected model.

An AUC score of 0.73 means there is a 73% chance our model will properly rank a randomly drawn positive row with a higher output probability than that of a randomly drawn negative row.

To understand how the model treats various features, we plot partial dependence in conjunction with ICE plots for the features of interest. Additionally, a histogram of the feature of interest, including an overlay of the mean value of the target column, i.e., DELINQ_NEXT, is displayed alongside. This should give us a good idea of whether the model is behaving reasonably and if any data sparsity issues could result in meaningless predictions.

Let's revisit Figure 6-1. The PAY_0 feature has the steepest partial dependence and ICE curve, thereby suggesting that it's the most important input feature. The partial dependence and ICE plots are in harmony, i.e., they do not diverge, implying that the partial dependence can be relied upon. Additionally, there is a monotonic increasing relationship of predicted probability of default and PAY_0 lateness of payment. This means that as the delay in payment increases, the probability that a customer will default also becomes larger. This is in line with our intuition of how credit card payments work.

Now let's review the histogram on the top. For customers with late payments, there are some apparent data sparsity problems. For instance, in regions where PAY_0 > 1, there is little or no training data. Also, the mean DELINQ_NEXT values do exhibit some nonlinear patterns in this region. It is all but obvious that predictions made in these regions will be less trustworthy. After all, a standard ML model like this can only learn from the data, unless we provide it additional domain knowledge. However, the good news is that the logistic form of our penalized GLM not only prevents it from being fooled by low-confidence dips in conditional mean DELINQ_NEXT around PAY_* = 6, but also from overfitting noise in these areas of sparse training data. The model treats the other PAY_* features similarly, but assigns them flatter logistic curves. In all cases, the probability of default increases monotonically with the lateness of payment, as expected. To see the other partial and dependence and ICE plots, check out the code resources for this chapter.

We now have a robust and explainable baseline model. Because its behavior makes so much sense and is so easy to interpret, it may be hard to beat. A validation AUC of 0.73 is nothing remarkable, but having an explainable model that behaves in a manner that aligns to time-tested causal relationships that we can count on once deployed—that's priceless for risk mitigation purposes. We also have to remember that validation and test data assessment scores can be misleading in more complex ML models. We can have a high AUC in static validation or test data, just to find out that the high AUC arose from overfitting to some specific phenomenon that's no longer present in our operational domain. In the next section, we'll first introduce some nonlinearities via GAMs and then feature interactions, in addition to nonlinearities via EBMs. We'll then assess our model for explainability and performance quality with an eye toward real-world performance. We'll try to do honest experiments and make deliberate choices about whether more complexity is justified.

Generalized Additive Models

While linear models are highly interpretable, they cannot accurately capture the nonlinearities typically present in real-world datasets. This is where GAMs come into play. GAMs, originally developed at Stanford in the late 1980s (*https://oreil.ly/ tl_oq*) by eminent statisticians Trevor Hastie and Rob Tibshirani, model nonlinear relationships of each input feature with individual spline shape functions and add them all together to make a final model. GAMs can be thought of as additive combinations of spline shape functions. An important idea for GAMs is that even though we treat every feature in a very complex way, it is done in an additive and independent manner. This not only preserves explainability but also enables editing and debugging with relative ease.

When it comes to implementing GAMs, packages like gam (*https://oreil.ly/mt1ty*) and mgcv (*https://oreil.ly/SW3rz*) are some great options in R. As for Python, the choice is limited, as most of the packages are in the experimental phase, like H2O's GAM implementation (*https://oreil.ly/_ak0k*). Another alternative, pyGAM (*https://oreil.ly/ dZ9tU*), derives its inspiration from R's mgcv package; has been shown to offer a good combination of accuracy, robustness, and speed (*https://oreil.ly/Cyn-l*); and has a familiar scikit-like API.

We'll use pyGAM to train a GAM on the same credit card dataset we used in the last section. Specifically, with the following code, we'll implement a logistic model using pyGAM's `LogisticGAM` class. There are three important parameters that can be tuned to obtain the best model: number of splines; `lam`, or the strength of regularization penalty; and constraints to inject prior knowledge into the model. pyGAM provides an inbuilt grid search method to search over the smoothing parameters automatically.

```
from pygam import LogisticGAM
gam = LogisticGAM(max_iter=100, n_splines=30)
gam.gridsearch(train[features].values, train[target], lam=np.logspace(-3, 3, 15))
```

This code instantiates a `LogisticGAM` model that will train for up to 100 iterations. The `n_splines` parameter specifies the number of spline terms, or the complexity of the function used to fit each input feature. More spline terms typically results in more complex spline shape functions. `lam` corresponds somewhat to `lambda` in penalized regression, and the preceding code searches over several values to find the best strength of regularization as defined by `lam`. One parameter we are not taking advantage of is `constraints`. `constraints` allows users to specify a list of constraints for encoding prior knowledge. The available constraints are monotonic increasing or decreasing smoothing and convex or concave smoothing. We'll work with similar constraints later in the chapter; it's very instructive to see what not using constraints means for our GAM.

A question that we're trying to answer deliberately in this example is: are nonlinearities truly helpful to our model, or just overfitting noise? Many data science practitioners today assume more complexity results in better models, but we'll use GAMs to run an experiment to decide whether introducing nonlinearity actually improves our model, from both a performance quality perspective and an interpretability perspective.

After we train our model, we calculate its validation AUC, which turns out to be 0.75—a notch higher as compared to our penalized GLM. The increase in the GAM AUC can likely be attributed to the introduction of nonlinearity, which our GLM failed to capture. However, it is important to note here that a higher AUC doesn't always guarantee better models, and this example is a classic case to prove the point. In the preceding section, we spent a bit of time analyzing how GLM treats the `PAY_0` feature, or a customer's most recent repayment status, and it did a reasonably good job. Let's now look at how the GAM treats the same `PAY_0` feature (Figure 6-2).

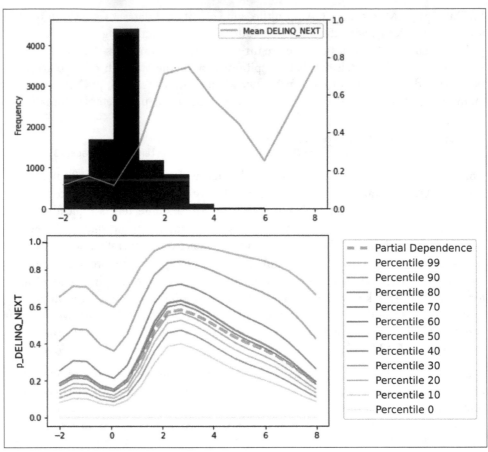

Figure 6-2. A partial dependence plot that incorporates ICE, histograms, and conditional means to increase trustworthiness and effectiveness for PAY_0 in the example GAM (digital, color version: https://oreil.ly/KT-fl)

Figure 6-2 shows that there is clearly some weirdness in the partial dependence and ICE plots generated via a GAM. We observe that as the lateness of payment increases, the chances that a customer will default on the payment decreases. This is obviously not correct. Most people don't magically become more likely to pay bills after months of being late. The same strange behavior is also observed for PAY_4 and PAY_6, as can be seen in Figure 6-3. The PAY_4 probability of default looks to decrease as payment lateness increases, and PAY_6 appears to bounce noisily around a mean prediction. Both modeled behaviors are counterintuitive, both contradict the GLM baseline model, and both fail to model the conditional mean behavior displayed on the righthand side of Figure 6-3.

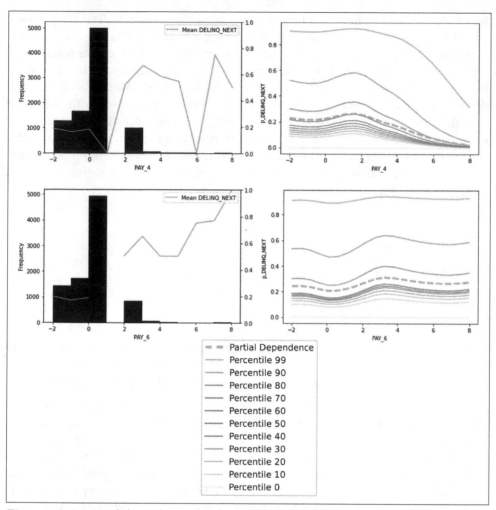

Figure 6-3. A partial dependence plot that incorporates ICE, histograms, and conditional means for PAY_4 and PAY_6 (digital, color version: https://oreil.ly/m4yK6)

The bottom line is that although our validation AUC is higher, this is definitely a model that we wouldn't want to deploy. As is apparent from Figure 6-2, the GAM has either overfit noise in the training data, been fooled by the low-confidence dips in the conditional mean DELINQ_NEXT around PAY_* = 6, or is reverting to a mean prediction due to data sparsity for PAY_0 > 1.

So what's the workaround, and how do we use such a model? Well, that's precisely where GAMs shine. The behavior displayed by the GAM, in this case, is a general problem observed for high-capacity nonlinear models. However, unlike many other types of ML models, GAMs not only highlight such inconsistencies but also offer ways to debug them through commonsense model editing. More plainly, we can discuss the GAM results with domain experts, and if they agree with the more plausible GAM splines for PAY_2, PAY_3, and PAY_5, we could keep those in the model and perhaps gain a boost in the model performance. As for the obviously problematic splines for PAY_0, PAY_4, and PAY_6, they can be replaced with something that makes more sense. One option is their learned behavior from the logistic regression model as shown in the following expression:

$$\hat{p} = \beta_0 + \frac{1}{1 + \exp\left(-\beta_{PAY_0, GLM}PAY_0\right)} + \beta_{PAY_2, GAM}g(PAY_2)$$
$$+ \beta_{PAY_3, GAM}g(PAY_3) + \frac{1}{1 + \exp\left(-\beta_{PAY_4, GLM}PAY_4\right)} + \beta_{PAY_5, GAM}g(PAY_5)$$
$$+ \frac{1}{1 + \exp\left(-\beta_{PAY_6, GLM}PAY_6\right)} + \cdots$$

where β_0 is an intercept term and each g represents a GAM spline function. Model editing is infinitely flexible; we could replace the learned spline on only a certain region of its domain, or otherwise edit the shape function to a domain expert's liking.

Editability is a great feature for a predictive model, but we also need to be careful with it. If we are to edit a custom model as suggested by the preceding equation, it really needs to be stress tested more than usual. Let's not forget, the coefficients weren't learned together and may not account for one another well. There could also be boundary problems—the edited model could easily result in predictions above 1 and below 0. Another potentially more palatable debugging strategy is to use the constraint functionality provided by pyGAM. A positive monotonic constraint would likely fix the problems in the PAY_0, PAY_4, and PAY_6 splines.

Whether we choose to edit the example GAM or retrain it with constraints, we'll likely see lower validation and test data performance quality. However, when we're most concerned with dependable real-world performance, we sometimes have to give up worshiping at the altar of holdout dataset performance. While model editing may sound strange, the preceding model makes sense. What seems more strange to us is deploying models whose behavior is only justified by a few rows of high-noise training data in obvious contradiction of decades of causal norms. We'd argue the preceding model is much less likely to result in a catastrophic failure than the nonsense splines learned by the unconstrained GAM.

This is just one of many scenarios where traditional model assessment can be misleading when it comes to choosing the best real-world model. As was shown in the GAM example, we can't assume that nonlinearities make better models. Moreover, GAMs allow us to test the implicit hypothesis that nonlinearity is better. With GAMs, we can create a model, interpret and analyze the results, and then edit it or debug any detected issues. GAMs help us uncover what our model has learned, keep the correct results, and edit and rectify the wrong ones so that we do not deploy risky models.

GA2M and Explainable Boosting Machines

When a small group of interacting pairs of features is added to a standard GAM, the resulting model is called a GA2M—a generalized additive model with two-way interactions. Adding these pairwise interactions to traditional GAMs has been shown to substantially increase model performance while retaining explainability, as discussed in Chapter 2. Additionally, just like GAMs, GA2Ms are easily editable.

The EBM (*https://oreil.ly/_tS2Q*) is a fast implementation of the GA2M algorithm by Microsoft Research. The shape functions in an EBM are trained iteratively via boosting, making EBM training more robust, while retaining accuracy comparable to unexplainable tree-based models like random forest and XGBoost. The EBM comes packaged within a broader ML toolkit called InterpretML (*https://oreil.ly/Uofrw*), an open source package for training explainable models and explaining other systems.

We'll continue with our credit card example and train an EBM to predict which customer has a high chance of defaulting on their next payment. The EBM achieves a validation AUC of 0.78, which is the highest compared to traditional GAMs and GLMs. The bump in accuracy is likely due to the introduction of nonlinearity *and* interactions. Explaining EBMs and GA2Ms is also easy. Like traditional GAMs, we can plot the shape functions of individual features and their accompanying histograms describing the model behavior and data distribution for that feature, respectively. The interaction terms can be rendered as a contour plot—still easy to understand. Let's dig in a bit more by looking at how an EBM treats LIMIT_BAL, PAY_0, and PAY_2 features, as shown in Figure 6-4.

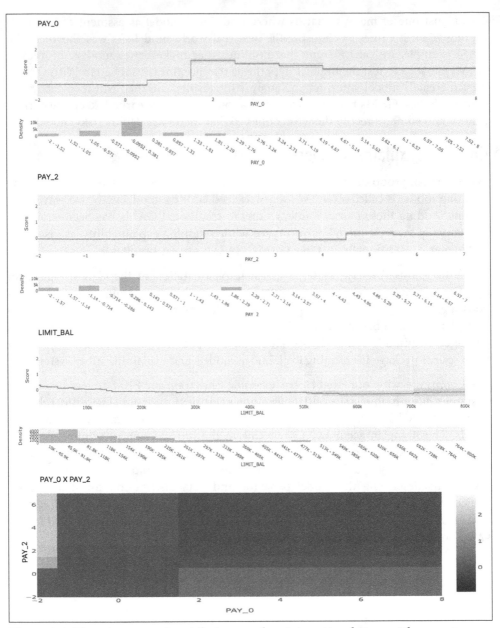

Figure 6-4. Three important input features and an interaction feature with accompanying histograms for an EBM (digital, color version: https://oreil.ly/l9lTU)

In Figure 6-4, we can see three standard shape function plots for LIMIT_BAL, PAY_0, and PAY_2, but we can also see a contour plot for the PAY_0 x PAY_2 interaction. Each of these plots, even the slightly more complex contour plot, allows humans to check the behavior of the model, and when needed, to edit it. The behavior of LIMIT_BAL looks reasonable, as increasing credit limits are expected to be correlated with a decreasing probability of default. That's what we observe, at least up to the high ranges of LIMIT_BAL in training data. Above $700,000, we see the shape function turn back upward—likely related to sparsity in training data in this region. The EBM treats PAY_0 more logically than our GAM. Under the EBM, PAY_0 probabilities of default increase for PAY_0 > 1 and don't drop back down to unrealistic values, but do decrease. Again, this is likely related to sparsity in certain regions of training data. PAY_2 appears to be somewhat noisy. Also, the interaction term exhibits the same unrealistic behavior that was observed under the GAM for some individual PAY_* features; increased lateness results in a lower probability of default, except for low values of PAY_0, and high values of PAY_2, where model outputs rocket upward. Like the GAM, the EBM seems to have some strange behaviors based on noise and sparsity in training data. That may be another reason why its AUC is higher—it's modeling noise specific to this dataset in certain cases. At least strange behavior is plainly obvious, and this model may be a good candidate for model editing. Monotonic constraints, discussed in the next section, might also help here, but they were not yet available for the EBM in interpret.

There are two other very important aspects of Figure 6-4 that are not necessarily characteristic of EBMs, but that also require a second look—the shaded regions around the shape functions and the histograms beneath the shape functions. Both of these features help users decide the level of trustworthiness for the model. If the histograms indicate that little training data is available in a certain region, or the shaded error bars show that the function has high variance in a certain training data domain, that part of the function is probably less trustworthy and model editing can be considered. The shape function for LIMIT_BAL over $700,000 is an example of both sparsity in training data and high variance in predictions. These two issues often go hand in hand when training, explaining, and debugging ML models.

One additional slightly tricky aspect of working with EBMs is accessing information for our own plotting needs. While EBM provides amazing interactive plotting capabilities out-of-the-box, we often like to create our own plots or data structures, especially to compare with other models. We found it necessary to interact with EBM's internal_obj JSON structure to do so on several occasions. Take, for instance, accessing feature importance values as follows:

```
ebm_global = ebm.explain_global(name='EBM')
feature_names = ebm_global._internal_obj['overall']['names']
feature_importances = ebm_global._internal_obj['overall']['scores']
ebm_variable_importance = pd.DataFrame(zip(feature_names, feature_importances),
                                       columns=['feature_names',
                                                'feature_importance'])
```

To extract feature importance to manipulate ourselves in the version of interpret we had access to, instead of relying on the EBM's default plotting, we had to calculate global explanations using `explain_global()`, then extract feature names and importance scores from JSON within the returned object. We then used this information to create a Pandas `DataFrame`, and from there, most standard operations like plotting, selecting, or manipulating, are easy.[1]

With that, we'll close out our first set of examples. In this section, we introduced a benchmark GLM, then deliberately introduced nonlinearities via GAMs and interactions via GA2Ms and EBMs that made our models more complex. However, due to the additive nature of GLMs, GAMs, and EBMs, not only did we retain explainability and gain in silico performance quality, but we also created a set of editable models that we can compare to one another, and even combine, to build the best possible model for real-world deployment. The next section will continue these themes and dive into constraints and post hoc explanation with XGBoost.

XGBoost with Constraints and Post Hoc Explanation

In this example, we'll train and compare two XGBoost classifier models—one with monotonic constraints, and one without. We'll see that the constrained model is more robust than the unconstrained and no less accurate. Then, we'll examine three powerful post hoc explanation methods—decision tree surrogates, partial dependence and ICE, and SHAP values. We'll conclude with a technical discussion of SHAP value calculations and background datasets, and we'll provide guidance so readers can choose the appropriate specifications for the application at hand.

Constrained and Unconstrained XGBoost

XGBoost (*https://oreil.ly/n98WV*) is an incredibly popular model architecture for prediction tasks on large, structured datasets. So what is an XGBoost model? The models produced by XGBoost are ensembles of *weak learners*. That is, XGBoost produces many small models in a sequence, and then to make a final prediction, it sums up the predictions of these small models. Typically, the first model in the sequence fits the data, and each subsequent model predicts the residuals of the models that came before it to correct their errors.[2] In this section, we'll use XGBoost to train an ensemble of shallow decision trees. We'll be working with a binary classification problem, but XGBoost can be used to model other problem types, such as regression, multiclass classification, survival time, and more.

---

1 This inconvenience is being addressed in current versions of the package. See the documentation (*https://oreil.ly/Z40st*) for more details.

2 For more details on gradient boosting, see *Elements of Statistical Learning* (*https://oreil.ly/hvX2H*), Chapter 10.

XGBoost is so popular, in part, because it tends to produce robust models that generalize well on unseen data. That doesn't mean we, as model developers, can fall asleep at the wheel. We have to use reasonable hyperparameters and techniques such as early stopping to ensure that the strengths of XGBoost are realized. Another important technique that XGBoost allows us to apply is monotonic constraints on our models. These constraints lock down the direction of the relationship between certain features and the model output. They allow us to say, "If feature X_1 increases, then the model output cannot decrease." In short, these constraints allow us to apply our own domain knowledge to make more robust models. Let's take a look at some code to train an XGBoost model:

```
params = {
    'objective': 'binary:logistic',
    'eval_metric': 'auc',
    'eta': 0.05,
    'subsample': 0.75,
    'colsample_bytree': 0.8,
    'max_depth': 5,
    'base_score': base_score,
    'seed': seed
}

watchlist = [(dtrain, 'train'), (dvalid, 'eval')]

model_unconstrained = xgb.train(params,
                                dtrain,
                                num_boost_round=200,
                                evals=watchlist,
                                early_stopping_rounds=10,
                                verbose_eval=True)
```

First, let's look at the values in the `params` dictionary. The parameter `eta` is the *learning rate* of our model. In gradient boosting, each tree we add into our ensemble is similar to a gradient descent step. The larger the value of `eta`, the more each additional tree impacts our model. The smaller the value of `eta`, the less weight is given to individual decision trees in the boosting sequence. If we used `eta = 1.0`, our model's final prediction would be an unweighted sum of individual decision tree outputs, and would almost certainly overfit to the training data. Make sure to set a reasonable learning rate (say, between 0.001 and 0.3) when training XGBoost or other gradient boosting models.

XGBoost also offers interaction constraints (*https://oreil.ly/NR9bo*) to control how input features affect one another in a model. This is another simple method to inject domain expertise into ML models. Interaction constraints may be particularly helpful for bias mitigation by eliminating known proxy interactions for gender or race, such as combinations of name, age, or zip code.

The parameters `subsample` and `colsample_bytree` also protect against overfitting. Both ensure that each individual decision tree does not see the entire training dataset. In this case, each tree sees a random 75% of rows of the training data (`subsample = 0.75`), and a random 80% of columns of the training data (`colsample_bytree = 0.8`). Then, we have some parameters that dictate the size of the final model. `max_depth` is the depth of the trees in the model. Deeper trees include more feature interactions and create more complex response functions than shallow trees. We usually want to keep our trees shallow when training XGBoost and other GBM models—after all, the strength of these models comes from them being an ensemble of weak learners. Of course, grid search and other structured methods for selecting hyperparameters are the better practice for choosing these values, but that's not the focus of this chapter.

Finally, in the preceding code snippet, we're training a model using validation-based early stopping (*https://oreil.ly/zacj5*). We do this by feeding a dataset (or in this case, two datasets) into the `evals` parameter, and by specifying `early_stopping_rounds`. So what is going on here? In each round of the training sequence, the collection of decision trees trained so far is evaluated on the datasets in the `evals` watchlist. If the evaluation metric (in this case, AUC) does not improve for `early_stopping_rounds` rounds, then training stops. If we didn't specify early stopping, then training would proceed until `num_boost_round` trees are built—often an arbitrary stopping point. We should almost always use early stopping when training our GBM models.

If we pass multiple datasets into `evals`, only the *last* dataset in the list will be used to determine if the early stopping criterion has been met. Furthermore, the final model will have too many trees. Whenever we make a prediction with the model, we should specify how many trees to use using the `iteration_range` parameter—see the documentation (*https://oreil.ly/OZ5FF*) for more info.

As we'll see, *unconstrained* XGBoost was free to assign probabilities to individual observations based on sometimes spurious patterns in the training data. We can often do better using the knowledge in our own brains and with the help of domain experts, in addition to what can be learned solely from training data.

We know, for example, that if someone is more and more overdue on their credit card payments, then they almost certainly have a higher likelihood of being late on their next payment. That means that for all PAY_* features in our dataset, we'd like the model output to increase when the feature value increases, and vice versa. XGBoost monotonic constraints allow us to do exactly that. For each feature in the dataset, we can specify if we'd like that feature to have a positive, negative, or no monotonic relationship with the model output.

Our dataset only contains 19 features, and we can reason through the underlying causal relationship with default risk for each one. What if our dataset contains hundreds of features? We'd like to train a robust, constrained model, but maybe we're unsure about a monotonic causal link between certain features and the target. An alternative (or supplemental) method for deriving monotonic constraints uses Spearman correlation. In the following code, we implement a function that examines the pairwise Spearman correlation coefficient between each feature and the target. If the Spearman coefficient is greater in magnitude than a user-specified threshold, that feature is assumed to have a monotonic relationship with the target. The function returns a tuple containing values –1, 0, and 1—exactly the form of input expected by XGBoost when specifying monotonic constraints.

```
def get_monotone_constraints(data, target, corr_threshold):
    corr = pd.Series(data.corr(method='spearman')[target]).drop(target)
    monotone_constraints = tuple(np.where(corr < -corr_threshold, -1,
                                      np.where(corr > corr_threshold, 1, 0)))
    return monotone_constraints
```

We use Spearman correlation coefficients rather than the default Pearson correlation because GBMs are nonlinear models, even when constrained. XGBoost monotonic constraints impose *monotonicity* rather than *linearity*—Spearman correlation measures exactly the strength of a monotonic relationship, whereas Pearson correlation measures the strength of a linear relationship.

In Figure 6-5, we've plotted the Spearman correlation coefficient of each feature against the target variable. The vertical lines indicate the threshold value of 0.1. We can see that this data-driven approach suggests imposing monotonic constraints for the PAY_* features. We're using the threshold of 0.1 as an informal marker of practical significance. We may not want to apply any constraints to those input features whose Spearman correlation is less than 0.1 in magnitude. As payment and credit limits increase, probability of default should decrease. As late payments increase, probability of default should increase. The results of this data-driven approach reflect common sense too. That's the most important consideration when generating constraints, since we're trying to inject causal domain knowledge into our model.

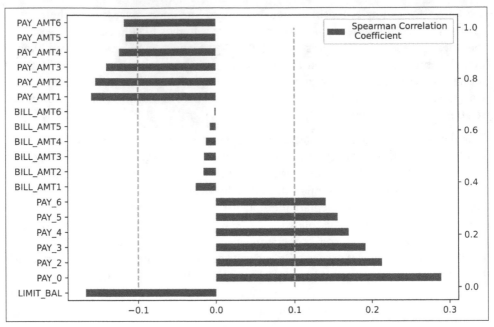

Figure 6-5. Spearman correlation coefficients between target DELINQ_NEXT and each feature, with vertical bars indicating a cutoff value of 0.1 (digital, color version: https://oreil.ly/qoIIs)

Next, we train the constrained model with the constraints suggested by the analysis shown in Figure 6-5. Let's make a few observations about the resulting constrained and unconstrained models. By looking at the output of `xgb.train()` with `verbose_eval=True` in the code example (*https://oreil.ly/BN3dS*), we see that the unconstrained model has a higher AUC on the training set (0.829 vs. 0.814), but shows equal performance to the constrained model on the validation set (0.785 vs. 0.784). This suggests that the constrained model is less overfit than the unconstrained model—with the exact same set of hyperparameters, the constrained model picks up on a higher proportion of the true signal in the data. As our analyses will show, there are additional reasons that we expect better performance (and better stability) from the constrained model in vivo.

Finally, let's look at the feature importance for the two models in Figure 6-6. We can compute the feature importance values for XGBoost models in many ways. Here, we'll look at the average coverage of the splits in the ensemble. The coverage of a split is just the number of training samples that flow through the split. This is a traditional calculation for feature importance. It does not have the same theoretical guarantees as, for example, SHAP techniques.

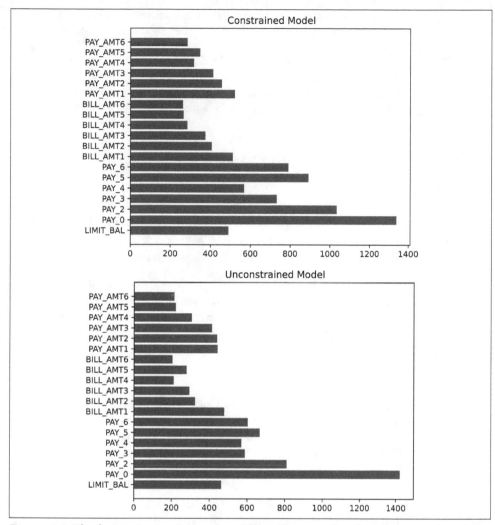

Figure 6-6. The feature importance values of the constrained and unconstrained models, as measured by average coverage (digital, color version: https://oreil.ly/MAs3a)

We can see that the constrained model spreads the feature importance more evenly among the entire input feature set. The unconstrained model gives a disproportionate share of the feature importance to the PAY_0 feature. This is even more evidence that the constrained model will be more robust when deployed. If a model focuses all its decision-making capacity on one feature, then it's going to fail when the distribution of that feature drifts with new data. Being too dependent on a single feature is also a security risk. It's easier for bad actors to understand how the model works and take advantage of it.

When we see feature importance values concentrated on one or a few features, our model is more likely to be unstable and insecure postdeployment. Our model might be overly sensitive to drift in the data distribution along a single dimension, and a malicious actor only needs to manipulate the value of one feature to alter model outcomes. If an ML model is focusing on only one or two features, consider replacing it with a simpler model or a business rule.

Explaining Model Behavior with Partial Dependence and ICE

Let's continue our comparison of the constrained and unconstrained XGBoost models by looking at a side-by-side partial dependence and ICE plot for PAY_0. In the previous sections, we've already discussed how the conditional mean of the target variable shows a spurious dip around PAY_0 = 6, where our training data is sparse. Let's see how our two XGBoost models handle this data deficiency.

In Figure 6-7, we can see how the unconstrained model overfits to the spurious relationship between PAY_0 and DELINQ_NEXT, to a small extent. On the other hand, the constrained model is forced to obey the commonsense relationship that more delayed payments should not lead to a lower risk of delinquency. This is reflected in the monotonically increasing partial dependence and ICE plots for PAY_0 under our constrained model.

One difficulty with ICE is picking which individuals to plot first. A good way to get started with ICE plots is to pick individuals or rows at the deciles of predicted outcomes. This gives a coarse picture of local behavior, and from there, we can dive deeper if needed.

We can also see that for both models, there are large changes in the output across the range of PAY_0 values. That is, both the partial dependence and ICE plots show lots of vertical movement as we sweep PAY_0 from –2 to 8. The model outputs are highly sensitive to the values of this feature—which is exactly why we saw such high feature importance values for PAY_0 in Figure 6-6. If we don't observe these kinds of value changes for a feature our model says is very important, that's a sign that more debugging may be required.

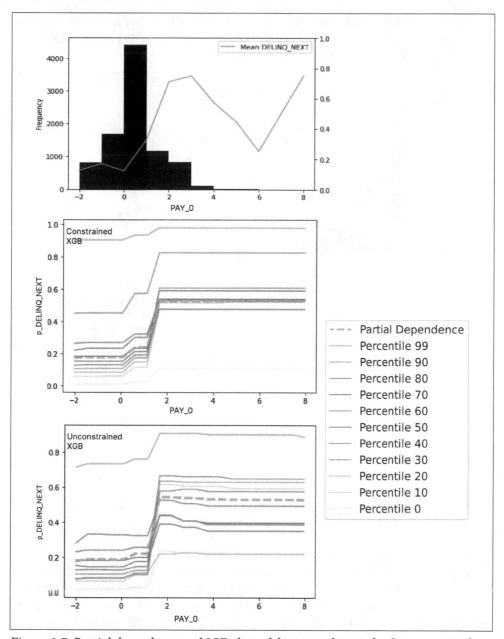

Figure 6-7. Partial dependence and ICE plots of the PAY_0 feature for the constrained (top) and unconstrained (bottom) models (digital, color version: https://oreil.ly/ulxRP)

Partial dependence and ICE plots can also reveal where there are feature interactions in our model. Take a look at the partial dependence and ICE plot for LIMIT_BAL under our unconstrained model in Figure 6-8.

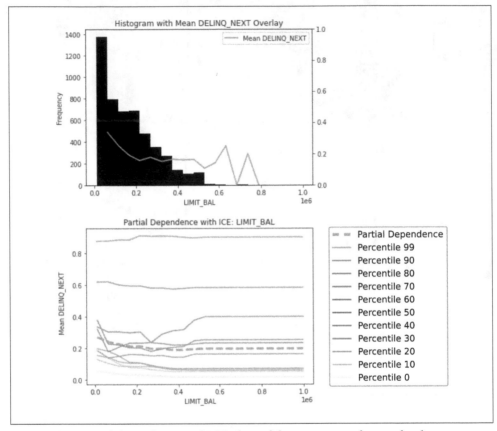

Figure 6-8. Partial dependence and ICE plots of the LIMIT_BAL feature for the unconstrained model (digital, color version: https://oreil.ly/D-CeU)

As discussed in "Partial Dependence and Individual Conditional Expectation" on page 191, when partial dependence and ICE curves diverge, as they do here, it is suggestive of correlations or interactions in our data and model. Moreover, we can look back to the EBM training (*https://oreil.ly/lW3kV*) and see that two important interactions identified by the EBM are LIMIT_BAL x BILL_AMT2 and LIMIT_BAL x BILL_AMT1. It's plausible that our unconstrained XGBoost model picked up on these interactions as well. In contrast to the EBM, our XGBoost models are riddled with various high-degree feature interactions. But partial dependence and

ICE, combined with the EBM's ability to learn two-way interactions, can help us understand some of the interactions in our XGBoost models too. Another great tool for understanding complex feature interactions in ML models is the surrogate decision tree, which we'll discuss next.

Decision Tree Surrogate Models as an Explanation Technique

The analysis we've conducted so far has shown that our unconstrained XGBoost model does not perform better than the constrained version. The partial dependence and ICE plots we've looked at show that by tethering the constrained model to reasonable real-world relationships, we've successfully prevented the model from picking up on spurious relationships in the training data. Since our constrained model appears logically superior to the alternative, the next sections will focus exclusively on this model.

First, we're going to continue our exploration of the model's behavior through a post hoc explanation technique—decision tree surrogate models. A *surrogate model* is just a simple model meant to mimic the behavior of a more complex model. In our case, we're trying to mimic our constrained XGBoost model with roughly 100 trees using a single, shallow decision tree. A decision tree is a data-derived flowchart, so we can look at the decision tree surrogate as a flowchart and explain how the more complex GBM is operating in simpler terms. This is what makes decision tree surrogates a powerful explanation technique. We use the `DecisionTreeRegressor` implementation from `sklearn` to train our surrogate model:

```
surrogate_model_params = {'max_depth': 4,
                          'random_state': seed}
surrogate_model = DecisionTreeRegressor(**surrogate_model_params)
                    .fit(train[features], model_constrained.predict(dtrain))
```

 Surrogate modeling is also known by other names, such as *model compression* or *model extraction*.

Notice that we're training a regression model targeted at the output of the model we're trying to explain. That is, the surrogate is totally focused on mimicking the behavior of the larger model, not just making a simpler classification model. We've also chosen to train a decision tree of depth four. Any deeper, and we might have a hard time explaining what is happening in the surrogate model itself.

Surrogate models do not always work well. Always check that surrogate models have good performance quality and stability characteristics. We put forward a simple surrogate modeling approach here. See "Interpreting Blackbox Models via Model Extraction" (*https://oreil.ly/O4Kia*), "Extracting Tree-Structured Representations of Trained Networks" (*https://oreil.ly/BQnI7*), and "The Price of Interpretability" (*https://oreil.ly/CNgUA*) for more information on surrogate approaches and what, if any, guarantees can be made about their fidelity.

Before we examine our surrogate model, we must ask whether we can trust it. Decision tree surrogates are a powerful technique, but they don't come with many mathematical guarantees. One simple way of assessing our surrogate's quality is to compute accuracy metrics on cross-validation folds. Why cross-validation and not just a validation dataset? A pitfall of single decision tree models is their sensitivity to changes in the training dataset, so by computing accuracy on multiple holdout folds, we're checking whether our surrogate model is accurate and stable enough to trust:

```
from sklearn.model_selection import KFold
from sklearn.metrics import r2_score

cross_validator = KFold(n_splits=5)
cv_error = []
for train_index, test_index in cross_validator.split(train):
    train_k = train.iloc[train_index]
    test_k = train.iloc[test_index]

    dtrain_k = xgb.DMatrix(train_k[features],
                           label=train_k[target])
    dtest_k = xgb.DMatrix(test_k[features],
                          label=test_k[target])

    surrogate_model = DecisionTreeRegressor(**surrogate_model_params)
    surrogate_model = surrogate_model.fit(train_k[features],
                                    model_constrained.predict(dtrain_k))
    r2 = r2_score(y_true=model_constrained.predict(dtest_k),
             y_pred=surrogate_model.predict(test_k[features]))
    cv_error += [r2]

for i, r2 in enumerate(cv_error):
    print(f"R2 value for fold {i}: {np.round(r2, 3)}")
print(f"\nStandard deviation of errors: {np.round(np.std(cv_error), 5)}")

R2 value for fold 0: 0.895
R2 value for fold 1: 0.899
R2 value for fold 2: 0.914
R2 value for fold 3: 0.891
R2 value for fold 4: 0.896

Standard deviation of errors: 0.00796
```

These results look great. We can see that the surrogate model has a high accuracy across every cross-validation fold, with very little variation. With some confidence that our decision tree is a reasonable surrogate, let's plot the surrogate model (Figure 6-9).

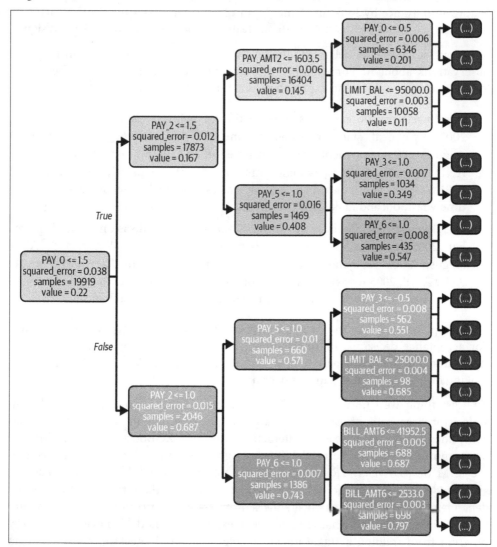

Figure 6-9. The decision tree surrogate for our constrained XGBoost model

Notice in Figure 6-9 that the surrogate model splits on the PAY_0 feature first. That is, in order to optimally mimic the behavior of the constrained XGBoost model, the first thing the surrogate model does is to separate observations into two groups—those with PAY_0 ≤ 1.5 and those with higher PAY_0 values. We can crudely approximate feature importance by looking at the depth of each feature's splits in the surrogate model, so this result is consistent with our feature importance analysis. A good sign.

Since our surrogate model is so simple, we can also make lots of plain-language observations about it. For example, we can trace the paths of the highest- and lowest-risk observations and explain how our surrogate is treating them:

- The lowest-risk observations traverse the following decision path: September, 2005 repayment status on-time or one month late (PAY_0 ≤ 1.5) AND August, 2005 repayment status on-time or one month late (PAY_2 ≤ 1.5) AND August, 2005 repayment amount is more than $1,603.5 (PAY_AMT2 > $1,603.5). These rules focus on customers who make recent payments in a timely fashion, and make large payments. Makes sense.

- The highest-risk observations traverse the following decision path: September, 2005 repayment status more than one month late (PAY_0 > 1.5) AND August, 2005 repayment status more than one month late (PAY_2 > 1) AND April, 2005 repayment status more than one month late (PAY_6 > 1). These rules consider unfavorable repayment statuses over time—also logical.

These explanations take into account repayment statuses and repayment amounts. For acceptance decisions, the more complex GBM seems to focus on more recent status and amount information, and for denial decisions, our GBM is probably looking for payment status patterns over time.

The last thing we'll notice is that each time one feature follows from another in a decision tree path, those features are likely interacting in our GBM. We can easily identify the main feature interactions that our XGBoost model has learned by examining the surrogate model. Interestingly, we can also look back and see that the EBM (https://oreil.ly/1R_hN) also picked up on some of the same interactions, such as PAY_0 x PAY_2 and PAY_0 x PAY_AMT2. With all these tools—EBMs, partial dependence and ICE, and surrogate decision trees—we can really get a solid picture of what's in our data and what's reasonable to expect from model behavior. That's very different from training a single unexplainable model and checking a few test data assessment metrics. We're starting to learn how these models work, so we can make human judgment calls about their real-world performance.

What's more, we can use this information about interactions to boost the performance of linear models, such as a penalized logistic regression, by including these learned interactions as input features. If we want to stick with the most conservative model forms for our highest-risk applications, we can use a GLM and likely get a boost in performance quality with this information about important interactions. As readers can see, we can make all kinds of simple, explainable observations about our XGBoost model through the use of decision tree surrogates. And we've collected loads of useful information for model documentation and other risk management purposes along the way.

Shapley Value Explanations

The last post hoc explanation tool to discuss before we close the chapter is Shapley values. In "Local explanations and feature attribution" on page 52, we mentioned that Shapley values can be used as a local feature attribution technique. In fact, Shapley values come with a host of mathematical guarantees that suggest that they are usually the best choice for feature attribution and importance calculations. The research and open source communities, led by Scott Lundberg at University of Washington and Microsoft Research, have developed a host of tools for generating and visualizing SHAP values. These tools live in the SHAP Python package, and that's what we'll use in this section.

Remember that *local* feature attribution methods assign a value to each feature for each observation, quantifying how much that feature contributed to the predicted value that the observation received. In this section, we'll see how to use SHAP values and the SHAP package to explain the behavior of our models. In the final section of this chapter, we'll examine some of the subtleties to Shapley value–based explanations, and the pitfalls they pose to practitioners.

Let's take a look at some code to generate SHAP values for our monotonic XGBoost model:

```
explainer = shap.TreeExplainer(model=model_constrained,
                               data=None,
                               model_output='raw',
                               feature_perturbation='tree_path_dependent')
shap_values = explainer(train[features])
```

We're using the SHAP package's TreeExplainer class. This class can generate SHAP values for XGBoost, LightGBM, CatBoost, and most tree-based scikit-learn models. The TreeExplainer is discussed in Scott Lundberg's papers "Consistent Individual-ized Feature Attribution for Tree Ensembles" (*https://oreil.ly/VZz75*) and "From Local Explanations to Global Understanding with Explainable AI for Trees" (*https://oreil.ly/7fdWE*), among others. They're a great example of the computational breakthroughs that have made the SHAP package so successful. If you need to generate SHAP values for a model not based on trees, take a look at the examples in the SHAP package documentation (*https://oreil.ly/5h0zu*)—there are multiple examples for tabular, text, and image data.

If you need to explain a model that's not tree- or neural-network-based, don't forget about comparison to prototypes and counterfactual explanations. These powerful explanation concepts can be more effective than general-purpose model-agnostic approaches like local model-agnostic interpretable explanations (LIME) or kernel SHAP.

To begin, let's take a look at the SHAP values associated with the `PAY_0` feature in Figure 6-10.

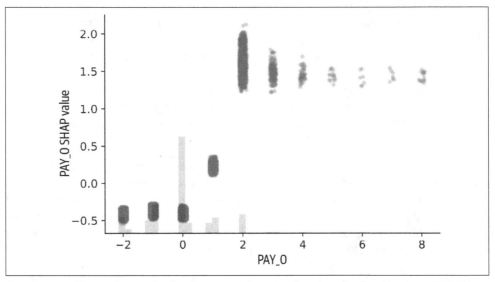

Figure 6-10. Dependence plot for the `PAY_0` feature, showing the distribution of SHAP values in each bucket of feature values (digital, color version: https://oreil.ly/hF4eJ)

Each dot in Figure 6-10 is one observation's SHAP value for the `PAY_0` feature, or contribution to the model prediction, with an x-coordinate given by the value of `PAY_0`. The scatter plot is superimposed over a histogram of feature values in the dataset, just like our partial dependence and ICE plots. In fact, this scatter plot can be directly compared to the partial dependence and ICE plots for `PAY_0`. In the SHAP scatter plot, we can see the whole range of feature attribution values within each bucket of `PAY_0` values. Notice that the range is widest in the `PAY_0` = 2 bucket—some observations with `PAY_0` = 2 are penalized approximately half as much as others. This SHAP scatter plot is one of many summarizing plots included in the SHAP package. For a more thorough overview, take a look at the examples in the documentation (*https://oreil.ly/xWxlG*) as well as this chapter's Jupyter notebook examples.

As we saw in Chapter 2, we can construct a measure of overall *feature importance* by taking the mean of absolute SHAP values. Instead of a standard horizontal bar chart of feature importance values, we can use the SHAP plotting functionality to look at feature importance explicitly as an aggregation of local explanations:

```
shap.plots.beeswarm(shap_values.abs, color="shap_red", max_display=len(features))
```

Figure 6-11 gives us an interesting perspective on feature importance. Notice that some features (e.g., PAY_0, PAY_AMT1) have a few dots exhibiting extreme SHAP values, whereas other features (e.g., LIMIT_BAL, PAY_AMT3) have a high feature importance because a lot of individual observations have somewhat high absolute SHAP values. Put another way, local explanations allow us to distinguish between high-frequency, low-magnitude effects versus low-frequency, high-magnitude effects. This is important, because each of those high-magnitude, low-frequency effects represent real people being impacted by our model.

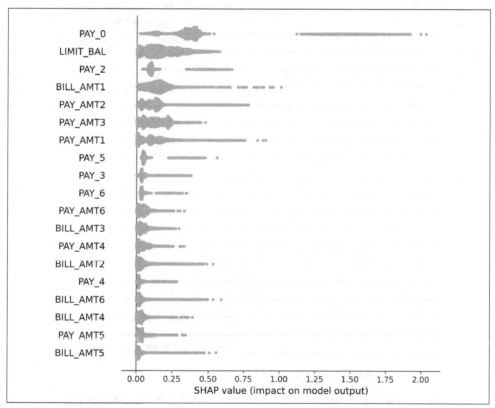

Figure 6-11. Feature importances, shown as the aggregation of individual observations' absolute SHAP values (digital, color version: https://oreil.ly/cjUiE)

Shapley value–based explanations have seen widespread adoption due to their strong theoretical underpinning and the robust set of tools built around them. Since these quantities can be computed at an observation-by-observation level, they can likely be used to generate adverse action notices or other turn-down reports (when used properly, tested for fidelity and stability, and paired with constrained models). Have a look at our code examples (*https://oreil.ly/machine-learning-high-risk-apps-code*), read some papers and documentation, and start generating SHAP values for our model. But please read the next section, where we discuss some of the assumptions and limitations behind every SHAP computation.

Problems with Shapley values

In Chapter 2 and "Shapley Values" on page 194, we introduced the idea of a *background dataset* that underlies Shapley value calculations. When SHAP wants to understand the impact of a feature on a certain prediction, it replaces the value of the feature in the training or test data with a random value drawn from the background data and compares predictions from the two different datasets many times over, with lots of perturbations regarding which features use normal data and which features use background data. Here's a useful way to think of background datasets: when we calculate a SHAP value for an observation, we're answering the question "Why did this observation get this prediction *rather than some other prediction?*" The "other prediction" that observations are compared against is dictated by the choice of background data, or *reference distribution.*

In the following code, we create two sets of SHAP values for the same observations—except in one instance we do not specify a reference distribution, and in the other we do:

```
explainer_tpd = shap.TreeExplainer(model=model_constrained,
                                   feature_perturbation='tree_path_dependent')
shap_values_tpd = explainer_tpd(train[features])

train['pred'] = model_constrained.predict(dtrain)
approved_applicants = train.loc[train['pred'] < 0.1]
explainer_approved = shap.TreeExplainer(model=model_constrained,
                                        data=approved_applicants[features],
                                        model_output='raw',
                                        feature_perturbation='interventional')

shap_values_approved = explainer_approved(train[features])
```

By setting `feature_perturbation='tree_path_dependent'`, we're opting not to define a reference distribution at all. Instead, SHAP uses information collected from the trained GBM model trees to implicitly define its own background data. This is similar to using the training data as our background data, but not exactly the same.

Next, we define an `explainer` with `feature_perturbation='interventional'`, for which we pass a reference distribution composed of training samples that received a probability of delinquency of less than 10%. If the reference distribution is what we compare each observation against, then we would expect these two sets of SHAP values to be meaningfully different. After all, these questions are incredibly different: "Why did this observation get this prediction, *rather than the average prediction in the training data*?" versus "Why did this observation get this prediction, *rather than the predictions given to approved applicants*?" As discussed in Chapter 2, the latter question is much more aligned with US regulatory commentary on adverse action notices. This is an example of what Professor Beicek means when he says, "Don't explain without context!"

Although some argue `tree_path_dependent` feature perturbations are *true to the data*—that is, they tell us about more than just this one model's behavior—as shown in "Explaining Individual Predictions When Features Are Dependent: More Accurate Approximations to Shapley Values" (*https://oreil.ly/3PBGX*), this is probably not true. *True to the data* feature attributions would require that we know the full joint probability distribution of our data, and this is a very challenging technical problem that we can't hope to solve by looking at the path structure of the trees in our model. It's better to use `interventional` feature perturbations and recognize that our SHAP values are *true to model* and don't generalize outside of our model. Our suggestion is to only use `tree_path_dependent` feature perturbations when you have no other choice. The main reason for using them would be if you don't have access to a background dataset, and you have to infer it from the model. If you have access to the training data, explicitly pass it in to the SHAP explainer and use `interventional` feature perturbations.

As of the writing of this book, best practices indicate that it's better to use `interventional` feature perturbations and recognize that our explanations don't generalize outside of our model. Only use `tree_path_dependent` feature perturbations when you have no other choice.

On to Figure 6-12 to try to show why all this matters. In Figure 6-12, we show two sets of SHAP values for the same observation—one calculated without a reference distribution and `feature_perturbation='tree_path_dependent'`, and one calculated against a reference of approved applicants and `feature_perturbation='interventional'`. First off, for some observations, we can see large differences in the SHAP values under these two different types of SHAP explanations.

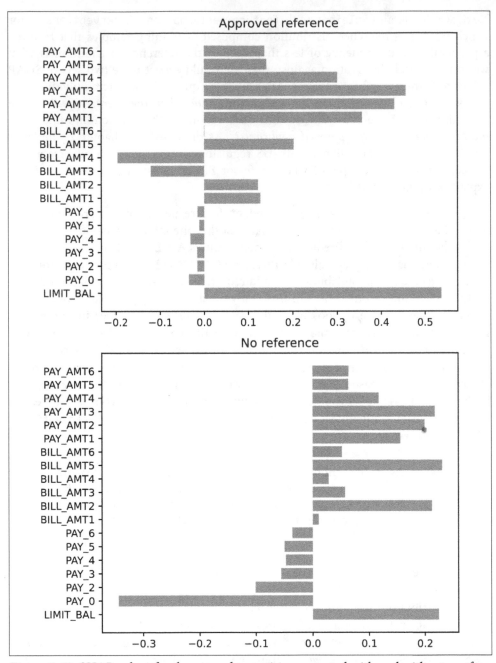

Figure 6-12. SHAP values for the same observation, generated with and without a reference distribution consisting of observations with an assigned probability of delinquency less than 10% (digital, color version: https://oreil.ly/jN3lj)

Imagine adverse action notices sent out on the basis of these two explanations. With no reference distribution, the top four features that contributed to a larger probability of delinquency are PAY_0, LIMIT_BAL, BILL_AMT5, and PAY_AMT3. But if we specify a context-specific reference distribution, these top four features are PAY_AMT1, PAY_AMT2, PAY_AMT3, and LIMIT_BAL. In a credit lending context, where *recourse* (the ability to appeal a model decision) is a crucial part of trust and responsible deployment, which explanation is correct? It's likely to be the explanations based on interventional feature perturbation, and due to using approved applicants in the background data, they are also framed more logically in terms of regulatory requirements.

However, those interventional explanations are unique to the model, and therefore they only provide accurate reason codes to the applicant if the applicant will be scored in the future using the exact same model. It's going to raise eyebrows if an applicant gets different adverse action notices for similar credit products, especially from the same lender, just because of some model-specific mechanism in an ML pipeline. It's not impossible that tree-path-dependent explanations will be more consistent across different models—as claimed by some—but that highlights another difficulty. Both path-dependent and interventional SHAP values can give explanations based on features not used in a specific decision. That's a big problem for adverse action notices and actionable recourse. However, we would still suggest using the interventional explanations when you use SHAP, while also acknowledging and testing for their shortcomings.

Even when we get all the details related to feature perturbation and background data right, there's still a fundamental limitation of ML explanation we need to keep in mind. A denied applicant wants to know how to change their credit profile in order to get approved for credit in the future—that's the question framed by our approved applicant reference distribution. However, we need to exercise some caution even when using a meaningful and context-specific reference distribution. The recourse question, "What should I change [about my credit profile] in order to receive a favorable outcome in the future?" is fundamentally a *causal* question—and we're not working with causal models. To quote the creator of the SHAP package, Scott Lundberg, "Be careful when interpreting predictive models in search of causal insights" (*https://oreil.ly/mME7V*). He goes on to say:

> Predictive machine learning models like XGBoost become even more powerful when paired with interpretability tools like SHAP. These tools identify the most informative relationships between the input features and the predicted outcome, which is useful for explaining what the model is doing, getting stakeholder buy-in, and diagnosing potential problems. It is tempting to take this analysis one step further and assume that interpretation tools can also identify what features decision makers should manipulate if they want to change outcomes in the future. However, [...] using predictive models to guide this kind of policy choice can often be misleading.

For all of their mathematical guarantees and ease-of-use, Shapley-value-based explanations are not a magic wand. Instead, they are yet another explainability tool in our toolbox for explaining models. We have to combine our post hoc explainability techniques with intrinsically explainable model architectures such as GLMs, GAMs, or tightly constrained XGBoosts, to achieve true interpretability. And we have to stay humble and remember that ML is all about correlation, and not causation.

Better-Informed Model Selection

To conclude this chapter, let's return to the `PAY_0` feature, and compare how each of the five models we built treat this feature. Remember that `PAY_0` represents repayment status, where higher values correspond to a greater delay in repayment. Obviously, higher values should correspond to a greater risk of delinquency. However, the training data we used is sparse for higher values of the feature, so we have only a few observations after more than one month's delay. With that in mind, let's examine five partial dependence and ICE plots for each model's treatment of this feature, as shown in Figure 6-13. We need to ask ourselves, "Which of these models would I trust the most with a billion-dollar lending portfolio?"

Three of our models show a response to the spurious dip in the mean target value in the sparse region of the feature space: the GAM, EBM, and unconstrained XGBoost. The GLM and constrained XGBoost models were forced to ignore this phenomenon. Since the GAM and EBM are additive models, we know that the partial dependence and ICE plots are truly representative of their treatment of this feature. The unconstrained XGBoost model is so full of feature interactions that we cannot be so sure. But the partial dependence does track with ICE, so it's probably a good indicator of true model behavior. We'd say it's a choice between the penalized GLM and the constrained XGBoost model. Which model is the best choice? By using these explainable models and post hoc explainers, we can make a much more deliberate choice than in the traditional opaque ML workflow—and that's what's most important. Remember, if we were choosing by pure performance, we'd pick a model that treats our most important feature in a somewhat silly way.

The story that emerges out of this deep dive into explainability in practice is this: first, we understand which relationships between feature and target are truly meaningful, and which are noise. Second, if we need to be able to explain our model's behavior—and we probably do—we need to choose a model architecture that is intrinsically explainable. That way, we'll have both the model and the explainers available to double-check each other. Third, we must force our model to obey reality with constraints. People are still smarter than computers! Finally, we'll need to examine our trained model with a diverse set of post hoc explainability techniques such as partial dependence and ICE plots, surrogate models, and SHAP values. Working this way, we can make informed and reasonable model selection choices, and not simply overfit potentially biased and inaccurate training data.

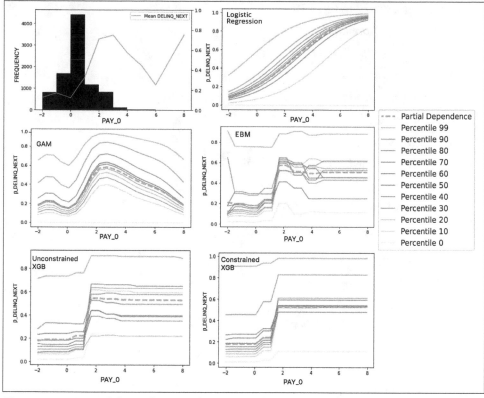

Figure 6-13. Partial dependence and ICE plots for the five models trained in this chapter (digital, color version: https://oreil.ly/3X2X4)

Resources

Further Reading

- *Elements of Statistical Learning* (chapters 3, 4, 9, and 10) (*https://oreil.ly/S72E1*)

Code Examples

- Machine-Learning-for-High-Risk-Applications-Book (*https://oreil.ly/machine-learning-high-risk-apps-code*)

Explainable Modeling Tools

- arules (*https://oreil.ly/bBv9s*)
- causalml (*https://oreil.ly/XsiMk*)
- elasticnet (*https://oreil.ly/pBOBN*)
- gam (*https://oreil.ly/QS0bP*)
- glmnet (*https://oreil.ly/rMzEl*)

- h2o-3 (*https://oreil.ly/PPUk5*)
- imodels (*https://oreil.ly/coPjR*)
- InterpretML (*https://oreil.ly/AZYDz*)
- PiML (*https://oreil.ly/ELrbE*)
- quantreg (*https://oreil.ly/qBWk9*)
- rpart (*https://oreil.ly/yIml6*)
- RuleFit (*https://oreil.ly/K-qc4*)
- Rudin Group code (*https://oreil.ly/QmRFF*)
- sklearn-expertsys (*https://oreil.ly/igFz6*)
- skope-rules (*https://oreil.ly/nfYau*)
- tensorflow/lattice (*https://oreil.ly/Z9iCS*)

Post Hoc Explanation Tools
- ALEPlot (*https://oreil.ly/OSfUT*)
- Alibi (*https://oreil.ly/K4VEQ*)
- anchor (*https://oreil.ly/K3UuW*)
- DiCE (*https://oreil.ly/-lwV4*)
- h2o-3 (*https://oreil.ly/GtGvK*)
- ICEbox (*https://oreil.ly/6nl1W*)
- iml (*https://oreil.ly/x26l9*)
- InterpretML (*https://oreil.ly/cuevp*)
- lime (*https://oreil.ly/j5Cqj*)
- Model Oriented (*https://oreil.ly/7wUMp*)
- PiML (*https://oreil.ly/CqgSa*)
- pdp (*https://oreil.ly/PasMQ*)
- shapFlex (*https://oreil.ly/RADtC*)
- vip (*https://oreil.ly/YcD2_*)

## CHAPTER 7

Explaining a PyTorch Image Classifier

Chapter 6 focused on using explainable models and post hoc explanations for models trained on tabular data. In this chapter, we'll discuss these same concepts in the context of deep learning (DL) models trained on unstructured data, with a particular focus on image data. Code examples for the chapter are available online (*https://oreil.ly/machine-learning-high-risk-apps-code*), and remember that Chapter 2 introduces the concepts of explainable models and post hoc explanation.

We'll begin this chapter with an introduction to the hypothetical use case demonstrated through technical examples in this chapter. Then we'll proceed much as we did in Chapter 6. First, we'll present a concept refresher on explainable models and feature attribution methods for deep neural networks—focusing on perturbation—and gradient-based explanation methods. We'll also continue a thread from Chapter 6 by outlining how explainability techniques can inform model debugging, a topic we'll expand on even further in Chapters 8 and 9.

Next, we'll discuss inherently explainable models in more detail. We put forward a short section on explainable DL models in hopes that some readers will be able to build their own explainable models, because as of today, that's the best hope for truly explainable results. We'll introduce prototype-based image classification models, like *ProtoPNet Digital Mammography* (*https://oreil.ly/Jht4n*)—a promising direction for explainable computer vision. After that, we'll discuss post hoc explanation techniques. We will highlight four methods in detail: occlusions (a common type of perturbation), input * gradient, integrated gradients, and layer-wise relevance propagation. We'll use our hypothetical pneumonia X-ray use case to show the different properties that these methods exhibit, and highlight some important implementation details along the way.

Recall from Chapter 2 that an *interpretation* is a high-level, meaningful mental representation that contextualizes a stimulus and leverages human background knowledge, whereas an *explanation* is a low-level, detailed mental representation that seeks to describe a complex process. Interpretation is a much higher bar than explanation and is rarely achieved by technical approaches alone.

How do we know if our post hoc explanations are any good? To address this, we'll discuss the research on evaluating explanations too. We'll demonstrate an experiment, first described in "Sanity Checks for Saliency Maps" (*https://oreil.ly/64UAi*), which will show that many post hoc explanation techniques don't necessarily reveal much of anything about our model!

We'll conclude the chapter by summarizing the lessons learned. This chapter will show that readers should be wary to implement a standard DL solution in a high-risk application where model explanations are necessary. Post hoc explanations are often difficult to implement, difficult to interpret, and sometimes entirely meaningless. Furthermore, the wide range of different explanation techniques means that we run the risk of selecting the method that confirms our prior beliefs about how our model *should* behave. (See discussions of confirmation bias in Chapters 4 and 12.) Even worse than an unexplainable model is an unexplainable model paired with an incorrect model explanation bolstered by confirmation bias.

Explaining Chest X-Ray Classification

We'll use a working example of a pneumonia image classifier model. We'll maintain a hypothetical use case of a model prediction and explanation being passed up to an expert user (e.g., a physician) to aid in diagnoses. Figure 7-1 provides a simplified schematic showing how the model is used in conjunction with an *explanation engine* to aid in the diagnosis of pneumonia by an expert.

Post hoc explanations have a history of accepted usage in the context of consumer credit. The use of model explanations to aid in interpreting medical imaging does not share this history. Moreover, important works are critical of post hoc techniques and use cases just like our hypothetical one, e.g., "The False Hope of Current Approaches to Explainable Artificial Intelligence in Health Care" (*https://oreil.ly/KY6LD*) and "The Doctor Just Won't Accept That!" (*https://oreil.ly/ZOlTk*). Even if the use case is justified, ML systems—even carefully developed ones—can perform poorly on out-of-sample data. See "Deep Learning Predicts Hip Fracture Using Confounding Patient and Healthcare Variables" (*https://oreil.ly/V87hi*) for an example of a model picking up on correlations in the training data that didn't work well once deployed. See "Diagnostic Accuracy and Failure Mode Analysis of a Deep Learning Algorithm for the Detection of Intracranial Hemorrhage" (*https://oreil.ly/V4krV*) for a somewhat similar use case to the one presented in this chapter, but with the addition of an analysis of real-world outcomes. We'll discuss all these issues in greater detail as we work through some post hoc examples and conclude the chapter.

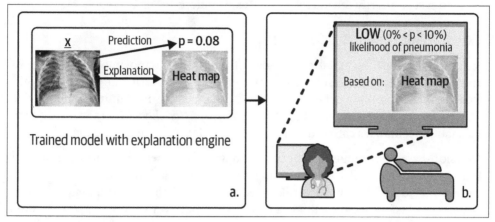

Figure 7-1. The hypothetical use case maintained throughout this chapter. A model and post hoc explanation engine (a) pass up predictions and explanations to a human-readable dashboard. The information on the dashboard is used to aid in a physician's diagnosis of pneumonia (b).

Concept Refresher: Explainable Models and Post Hoc Explanation Techniques

In this section, we'll discuss the basic ideas behind the chapter. We'll start with explainable models—which we won't treat with code. Then, in the post hoc explanation section of the chapter, we will demonstrate a few techniques on our model, and we will survey many more of the foundational techniques in the field. These techniques can mainly be categorized into two groups: perturbation-based (often *occlusion* in DL) and gradient-based methods; we will discuss the differences between these categories next. We will also highlight how these techniques can be applied to the problem of model debugging and architecture selection.

Explainable Models Overview

Recall from Chapter 2 that explainable models have inherently explainable structures, characteristics, or results. Also, explainable models exist on a spectrum. Some might be directly explainable to end users, whereas some might only make sense to highly skilled data scientists. Explainable DL models are definitely on the more complex side of the explainability spectrum, but we still think they are very important. As we'll highlight, and as many other researchers have pointed out, we have to be really careful with post hoc explanation in DL. If we have an explainable model, we are able to understand it directly without the use of questionable post hoc techniques, and we can also compare post hoc explanation results to the explainable mechanisms of the model to test and verify the model and the explanations.

Occlusion Methods

Occlusion methods are based on the idea of perturbing, removing, or masking features and examining the resulting change in model output. In computer vision, this often means obscuring patches of pixels. As discussed in "Explaining by Removing: A Unified Framework for Model Explanation" (*https://oreil.ly/6hGen*), many different explanation techniques can be traced back to this idea of feature occlusion.

Occlusion-based techniques can be especially valuable when gradients are not available, or when the model we are trying to explain is a complex decision-making pipeline including ML, business rules, heuristics, and other nondifferentiable components. Occlusion-based methods all have to grapple with the same complication: for most models, we can't just remove features and generate model predictions. Put another way, if our model has been trained on features x1, x2, and x3, we can't simply pass it values for x1 and x2 and expect it to make a prediction. We need to pass in *some* value for x3. This detail is at the heart of many of the different occlusion-based methods.

Gradient-Based Methods

As discussed in Chapter 2, the gradients of a model's outcome with respect to its parameters can be used to construct local explanations. This is a generalization of the idea behind interpreting regression coefficients. Remember that a gradient is just a local linear approximation to a complex function: our ML model. Since the vast majority of DL architectures are designed to be trained with gradient-based optimizers, we almost always have access to some gradients in our DL models, and evaluating gradients has become much easier with contemporary DL toolkits. This is part of what makes gradient-based explanation techniques so popular for DL. However, for tree-based models or complex pipelines where taking gradients is not possible, we'll have to fall back to occlusion.

Explanations in this category fundamentally ask: "Which features, if we change them a little bit, result in the largest change in our model's output?" Researchers have developed many variations on this theme to tease out subtly different flavors of explanations. We'll cover the details behind these techniques later in the chapter, looking into input * gradient, integrated gradients, and layer-wise relevance propagation.

Explainable AI for Model Debugging

In Chapter 6, we saw how model explanation techniques such as partial dependence and ICE plots can reveal undesirable model behavior, such as sensitivity to spurious noise in the training data. Explanations can serve the same purpose for DL models, and that may be the highest purpose of explainable artificial intelligence (XAI) in DL to date. The ability of DL explainability techniques to help debug and improve models has been noted by prominent researchers on many occasions. The most famous example may be the classic Google blog post (*https://oreil.ly/5Qj0O*) that popularized neural network "dreams." The authors use the technique from "Deep Inside Convolutional Networks: Visualising Image Classification Models and Saliency Maps" (*https://oreil.ly/5BqAj*) to debug their model by asking it to show them its concept of a dumbbell:

> There are dumbbells in there alright, but it seems no picture of a dumbbell is complete without a muscular weightlifter there to lift them. In this case, the network failed to completely distill the essence of a dumbbell. Maybe it's never been shown a dumbbell without an arm holding it. Visualization can help us correct these kinds of training mishaps.

Some additional examples of explanations as debugging tools in DL literature include the following:

- "Visualizing Higher-Layer Features of a Deep Network" (*https://oreil.ly/vIG4Y*)
- "Visualizing and Understanding Convolutional Networks" (*https://oreil.ly/aEkYG*)
- "Deconvolutional Networks" (*https://oreil.ly/NmiDE*)

We call these resources to readers' attention for two reasons. First, although the popular DL explanation techniques we'll explore in this chapter may not always work, some of the other techniques in these papers are definitely worth checking out. Second, while explanation techniques may let us down when it comes to precise understanding, they can still hint at issues in our models. Think about this as you're reading this chapter. In Chapter 9, we're going to take a deep dive into how to apply benchmarking, sensitivity analysis, and residual analysis for debugging our DL models.

Explainable Models

We'll begin the technical portion of this chapter by discussing explainable models for DL applications, because they are our current best bet for explainable results in DL. But are not easy to work with yet. Readers will learn that there are few off-the-shelf explainable DL models that we can plug into our application. Contrast this with what we saw in Chapter 6, where we were able to choose from a wealth of highly explainable architectures, from monotonic XGBoost, to explainable boosting machines, to generalized linear models (GLMs) and generalized additive models (GAMs). So what is the difference? Why are there so few ready-made explainable DL models? One issue is that explainable models for structured data date back to the work of Gauss in the 1800s—not so with DL. But there is more going on.

When we train a DL model on unstructured data, we're really asking the model to perform two functions: the first is feature extraction to create a latent space representation, or learning the proper representation of the data in a (usually) lower-dimensional input space. Second, it must use that latent space representation to make predictions. Contrast this with the tabular data we analyzed in Chapter 6. With tabular data, the "correct" representation of our data is typically assumed to be right there in the training data, especially if we've done our job correctly and chosen a reasonable set of uncorrelated features with a known causal relationship to the target. This difference (learned versus already-supplied features) helps to highlight why explainable DL models are so difficult to develop, and why off-the-shelf implementations are hard to come by.

The common thread among the explainable DL architectures that *do* exist today is that they intervene on this feature-learning directly. Oftentimes, explainable models shift the burden of feature engineering away from the model and onto the model developer. This increased burden is both a blessing and a curse. On the one hand, it means that training these models is simply more work than training unexplainable models. On the other hand, these architectures can demand higher-quality, sometimes expertly annotated data, meaning that humans were deeply involved in the modeling process end-to-end. Since we should already be designing our models with the care that these architectures demand, this isn't bad. As we saw in Chapter 6, the more domain expertise we can encode in our models, the more trust we can place on their ability to perform in the real world.

In the following sections, we'll discuss different architectures for explainable DL models while maintaining our primary focus on the image classification problem. We'll pay special attention to recent developments on prototype-based architectures, which provide the likeliest path forward for true turnkey explainable image classification.

ProtoPNet and Variants

In their 2019 paper "This Looks Like That: Deep Learning for Interpretable Image Recognition" (*https://oreil.ly/k69Dx*), the Duke team led by Prof. Cynthia Rudin introduced a new, promising architecture for explainable image classification. The new model is called *ProtoPNet*, and it is based on the concept of prototypes.

Remember from Chapter 2 that prototypes are data points that are representative of a larger group of observations. Consider explaining why an observation was grouped into a particular cluster in *k*-means clustering. We could put the observation side-by-side with the cluster centroid and say, "Well, this observation looks like that cluster center." ProtoPNet generates explanations of exactly this type. Furthermore, ProtoPNet's explanations are faithful to how the model actually makes predictions. So how does it work?

First, ProtoPNet identifies prototypical *patches* for each class. These patches capture the fundamental properties that distinguish one class from another. Then, to make predictions, the model looks for patches on the input image that are similar to the prototypes for a particular class. The resulting similarity scores for each prototype are added together to produce the odds of the input belonging to each class. The final result is a model that is additive (each prediction is a sum of similarity scores across prototypical image parts) as well as sparse (there are only a few prototypes per class). Best of all, each prediction comes immediately with a faithful explanation.

 ProtoPNet builds on the idea of part-level attention models, a broad class of explainable deep neural networks that are not covered in this chapter. The difference between these models and ProtoPNet is faithfulness. ProtoPNet really makes predictions by summing similarity scores with certain patches of each image and certain class prototypes. Other part-level attention models make no such guarantees.

Since being published in 2019, this promising direction for explainable image classification has been picked up by other researchers. There's ProtoPShare (*https://oreil.ly/phO4I*), which allows for sharing prototypes between classes, resulting in a smaller number of prototypes. There is also ProtoTree (*https://oreil.ly/OKEp0*), which creates an explainable decision tree over prototype features. This architecture allows the model to mimic human reasoning even more clearly. Finally, Kim et al. analyzed chest X-rays using an architecture very similar to ProtoPNet in "XProtoNet: Diagnosis in Chest Radiography with Global and Local Explanations" (*https://oreil.ly/qv-oO*).

Other Explainable Deep Learning Models

In "Towards Robust Interpretability with Self-Explaining Neural Networks" (*https://oreil.ly/DWY6w*), authors David Alvarez-Melis and Tommi S. Jaakkola introduce self-explaining neural networks (SENN). As we discussed, one difficulty with creating explainable models on unstructured data is that we ask our models to create a latent space representation of our data and to make predictions. Self-explaining neural networks confront this difficulty by introducing *interpretable basis concepts* in lieu of raw features. These basis concepts can be learned as part of model training, taken from representative observations in the training data, or—ideally—designed by domain experts. In their paper, Alvarez-Melis and Jaakkola generate these interpretable basis concepts using an autoencoder, and ensure that the learned concepts are explainable by providing prototypical observations that maximally express the concept.

 An autoencoder is a type of neural network that learns to extract features from training data without making predictions on a single modeling target. Autoencoders are great for data visualization and anomaly detection too.

So far, we've mostly focused on techniques for computer vision models. Explainable models have been developed for deep neural nets used in reinforcement learning (*https://oreil.ly/PgthB*), visual reasoning (*https://oreil.ly/wRYFJ*), tabular data (*https://oreil.ly/My88p*), and time series forecasting (*https://oreil.ly/qUUzF*).

Training and Explaining a PyTorch Image Classifier

In this use case, we outline how we trained an image classifier, then we demonstrate how to generate explanations using four different techniques: occlusion, input * gradient, integrated gradients, and layer-wise relevance propagation.

Training Data

First, we need to build an image classifier to diagnose chest X-ray images, consistent with the hypothetical use case in Figure 7-1. The dataset we'll use for training is available from Kaggle (*https://oreil.ly/jfmsi*), and it consists of 5,863 X-ray images of patients, which have been split into two distinct categories—one containing pneumonia and the other being normal. Figure 7-2 shows a random collection of images from the training data.

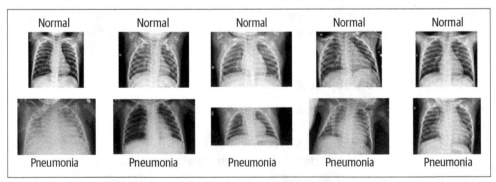

Figure 7-2. A random selection of training set samples from the Kaggle chest X-ray data; chest X-rays with pneumonia are cloudier than those without it

We're not doctors or radiologists, and it's important to acknowledge that the author group does not have the medical domain knowledge to truly validate this model. From our understanding, images from pneumonia patients should show cloudy areas of infection. Bacterial pneumonia and viral pneumonia tend to have different visual characteristics as well. The hope in the sections that follow is that XAI methods will focus on these cloudy areas, enabling us to understand why an image is classified as pneumonia versus normal. (Prepare to be disappointed.) To learn more about the dataset, see its Kaggle page (*https://oreil.ly/hAhUz*) and the associated paper, "Identifying Medical Diagnoses and Treatable Diseases by Image-Based Deep Learning" (*https://oreil.ly/SOcBD*).

 If we're working in a high-risk application area with machine learning, we *need* domain expertise to help train and validate our models. Failure to consult with domain experts may result in harmful, nonsense models deployed in high-risk use cases.

Like most datasets from Kaggle (*https://oreil.ly/lOADp*), a lot of the hard work of curating the data has been done for us. Low-quality scans have been eliminated, and the labels have been verified as correct. However, like many datasets in medical applications, this data has a class imbalance problem: there are 1,342 normal scans, but 3,876 scans labeled as indicating pneumonia. Another cause for concern is the presence of very few images in the given validation dataset. The validation data consists of only nine images for the pneumonia class and another nine for the normal class. This is not a sufficient number to adequately validate the model, so we'll address that and other issues before proceeding with model training.

Addressing the Dataset Imbalance Problem

In our training data, the pneumonia X-ray scans outnumber the normal scans three to one. Any model trained on such a dataset might overfit to the majority class. There are several ways to address the issue of a class imbalance problem:

- Oversampling of the minority class
- Undersampling of the majority class
- Modifying the loss function to weight the majority and minority classes differently

These techniques, and the detrimental effects of the class imbalance problem, have been nicely summarized in a paper titled "A Systematic Study of the Class Imbalance Problem in Convolutional Neural Networks" (*https://oreil.ly/Gp-OY*). In this example, we will oversample the normal images to even out the class imbalance.

Data Augmentation and Image Cropping

PyTorch (*https://oreil.ly/Uagd2*) is an open source ML framework. torchvision (*https://oreil.ly/LaOh8*) is a domain library for PyTorch built to support research and experimentation for computer vision. torchvision consists of some popular datasets, pretrained model architectures, and some image transformations for computer vision tasks. We'll first increase the proportion of the validation set by moving some of the training set images into it. After this, we'll use some of torchvision's image transformations to handle the class imbalance in our training set. In the following code snippet, we scale images to the same size, then apply various transformations to increase the size of data and to introduce training examples that should enhance the robustness of our model. The `get_augmented_data` function makes ample use of the `RandomRotation` and `RandomAffine` transformations to create new, altered training images, along with using various other transformations to format and normalize images:

```
TRAIN_DIR = 'chest_xray_preprocessed/train'
IMAGE_SIZE = 224 # Image size of resize when applying transforms
BATCH_SIZE = 32
NUM_WORKERS = 4 # Number of parallel processes for data preparation

def get_augmented_data():

    sample1 = ImageFolder(TRAIN_DIR,
                    transform =\
                    transforms.Compose([transforms.Resize((224,224)),
                            transforms.RandomRotation(10),
                            transforms.RandomGrayscale(),
                            transforms.RandomAffine(
                                translate=(0.05,0.05),
                                degrees=0),
                            transforms.ToTensor(),
                            transforms.Normalize(
                                [0.485, 0.456, 0.406],
                                [0.229, 0.224, 0.225]),
                            ]))
    ...

    return train_dataset
```

Since the basic idea of data augmentation is to create more images, let's check that outcome:

```
# check new dataset size
print(f'Normal : {normal} and Pneumonia : {pneumonia}')

(3516, 3758)
```

Figure 7-3 shows some of the synthetic training samples generated using rotations and translations.

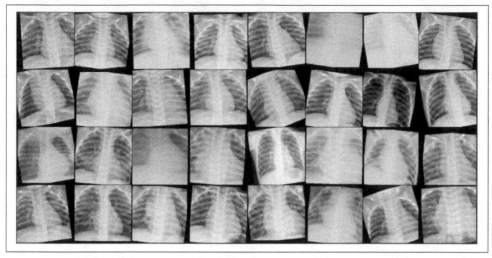

Figure 7-3. Synthetic training samples generated using rotations and translations

Looks about right. With class imbalance and data augmentation handled, we'll proceed with model training.

 Make sure data augmentation does not create unrealistic training samples. Chest X-rays will show variation in color scale, zooming, etc. However, flipping the images about their vertical axis would be a huge mistake, since our organs are bilaterally asymmetric (not the same on the left and right sides). After deployment, this model will never see a chest X-ray with the patient's heart on their right side, so it should not be trained on vertically flipped images.

Another preprocessing technique that we used for the dataset is image cropping. We cropped some of the images in the training set so as to highlight only the lung region (see Figure 7-4). Cropping helps to eliminate any annotation or other kinds of markings on the chest X-ray images and focuses the model on the region of interest in the images. We saved these images as a separate dataset to be used to fine-tune the network at a later stage of training.

 It wasn't until we went through the exercise of manually cropping hundreds of images that we noticed that the training data contains multiple scans from the same patient. As a result, when we added images to our validation data we had to be sure to keep the same patient in either training or validation data, *but not both*. This detail is a great example of a data leak, and emphasizes the importance of really getting to know our data.

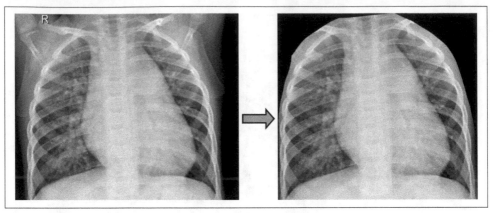

Figure 7-4. A chest X-ray image after before and after cropping

Model Training

Convolutional neural networks (CNNs) (*https://oreil.ly/bfzDc*) are commonly used architectures employed in medical imaging. Some well-known examples of CNNs for image classification are ResNets (*https://oreil.ly/2JqoN*), DenseNets (*https://oreil.ly/T3b0q*), and EfficientNets (*https://oreil.ly/-AWuI*). Training a CNN from scratch is very expensive, both in terms of data and computation time. As such, a prevalent technique is to use models that have been previously trained on a large-scale image dataset—such as ImageNet (*https://oreil.ly/8MHlU*)—and then reuse that network as a starting point for another task.

The core idea behind this technique is that the lower layers in a CNN learn broadly applicable representations like edges and corners, which can be generalized to a wide variety of tasks. When we use layers of a CNN for our own tasks, we refer to them as *pretrained*. The higher layers, on the other hand, capture features that are more high-level and specific to a task. As a result, the output of these layers will not be suitable for our use case. We can thus freeze the features learned in the lower layers and retrain the higher layers in a step called *fine-tuning*. Together, pretraining and fine-tuning constitute a simple form of *transfer learning* (*https://oreil.ly/tybad*), in which knowledge learned by an ML model in one domain is used in another domain.

To start, we'll use a DenseNet-121 (*https://oreil.ly/Wq743*) architecture trained on an ImageNet dataset. DenseNet models have been shown to perform particularly well for X-ray image classification, as they improve flow of information and gradients through the network (*https://oreil.ly/_fO24*), ideally increasing the performance and generalization of the classifier.

Don't forget about EvilModel (*https://oreil.ly/UMwPx*). It has been shown that malware can be delivered through pretrained neural networks. Such malware may not affect performance and may trick anti-virus software. (Or we might be lazy and forget to scan our model artifacts.) The lessons from Chapter 5 teach us to take nothing for granted, not even the pretrained models we download from the internet.

While performing transfer learning, an important question is whether to retrain all the layers of the pretrained model or only a few of them. The answer to this question lies in the makeup of the dataset. Is the new dataset large enough? Does it resemble the dataset on which the pretrained model has been trained? Since our dataset is small and differs considerably from the original dataset, it makes sense to retrain some of the lower layers as well as the higher ones. This is because the low layers learn generic features compared to the higher ones, which learn more dataset-specific features. In this case, when we refer to retraining layers, it doesn't mean to start training from scratch or with random weights; instead, we'll utilize pretrained weights as a starting point and then continue from there.

In the following code, we unfreeze all of the layers of the pretrained model and replace the last layer with our own linear classifier. For this dataset, this setting gave the best performance on test data. We also experimented by unfreezing only a few layers, but none of them outperformed our first setting:

```
classes = ['Normal', 'Pneumonia']
model = torchvision.models.densenet121(pretrained=True)

# Unfreeze training for all "features" layers
for param in model.parameters():
    param.requires_grad = True

# New layers automatically have requires_grad = True
in_features = model.classifier.in_features
model.classifier = nn.Linear(in_features, len(classes))
```

Finally, we fine-tuned the model a second time, using only the images that we manually cropped to focus on the lungs. The double fine-tuning process ended up looking something like this:

1. Load the pretrained DenseNet-121 model.

2. Train the model on the augmented dataset using uncropped images.

3. Freeze the early layers of the model and continue training on cropped images.

The idea behind this double fine-tuning process is to utilize the features learned by the pretrained model, as well as those in our domain-specific dataset. Finally, the use of cropped images for the final round of training mitigates the risk of the model using features that will not generalize to unseen data, such as X-ray artifacts outside of the lungs.

Evaluation and Metrics

The performance of the model is evaluated on a validation set. In Tables 7-1 and 7-2, we also report some performance metrics on the unseen test dataset. Measuring this performance is essential to understanding whether our model will generalize well.

Table 7-1. A confusion matrix showing the pneumonia classifier model performance on the test dataset

	Predicted normal	Predicted pneumonia
Actual normal	199	35
Actual pneumonia	11	379

Table 7-2. Additional performance metrics on the test dataset

	Prevalence	Precision	Recall	F1
Normal	234	0.95	0.85	0.90
Pneumonia	390	0.92	0.97	0.94

Performance looks good here, but be sure to check out Chapter 9 to see how in silico validation and test measurements can be misleading. Now it's time to start explaining our model's predictions.

Generating Post Hoc Explanations Using Captum

In this section, we'll elaborate on a few post hoc techniques, and show their application to our pneumonia image classifier. The explanations that are generated are all *local*, in that they apply to individual observations—single X-ray images of a patient. Furthermore, all of the explanations will take the form of a heatmap, where the color of each pixel is meant to be proportional to the significance of that pixel in making the final classification. In the coming sections, we'll examine with a critical eye whether these methods accomplish that aim, but the purpose of this section is to first simply show what kinds of outputs can be expected from various techniques.

To implement the different techniques, we'll use Captum (*https://oreil.ly/RjBoD*). Captum is a model explanation library built on PyTorch, and it supports many models out-of-the-box. It offers implementations of many explanation algorithms that work nicely with various PyTorch models.

Occlusion

Occlusion (*https://oreil.ly/rdX1o*) is a perturbation-based method and works on a simple idea: remove a particular input feature from a model and assess the difference in the model's prediction capability before and after the removal. A more significant difference implies that the feature is important, and vice versa. Occlusion involves replacing certain portions of the input image and examining the effect on the model's output. It is often implemented by sliding a rectangular window of predefined size and stride over the image. The window is then replaced with a baseline value (usually zero) at each location, resulting in a gray patch. As we slide this gray patch around the image, we are occluding parts of the image and checking how confident or accurate the model is in making predictions on the altered data.

Captum documentation describes its implementation of occlusion (*https://oreil.ly/R5C2N*), and we apply it to the chest X-ray case study for a single input image. Notice how we can specify the size of the occluding window as well as that of the stride, which in our case is 15×15 and 8, respectively:

```
import captum, Occlusion
from captum.attr import visualization as viz

occlusion = Occlusion(model)

attributions_occ = occlusion.attribute(input,
                            target=pred_label_idx,
                            strides=(3, 8, 8),
                            sliding_window_shapes=(3,15, 15),
                            baselines=0)
```

In Figure 7-5, we show the attribution for an image in the test set that demonstrates pneumonia, and was correctly classified as *Pneumonia* by the model.

The results are promising. The model seems to have picked up on the high opacity in the upper regions of both lungs. This might give an expert interpreter of the explanation faith in the model's classification. However, the dark regions are large and lack detail, suggesting that a smaller occlusion window and stride length might reveal more detail. (We hesitated to try different settings, because as soon as we go down the path of tuning these explanation hyperparameters, we open ourselves up to the risk that we'll just select values that create explanations that confirm our prior beliefs about how the model works.)

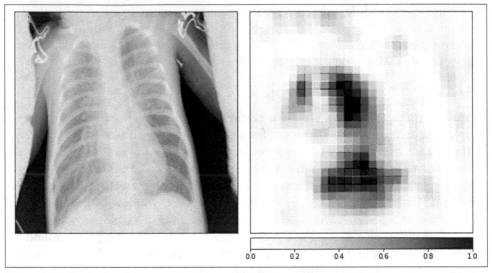

0.0　　0.2　　0.4　　0.6　　0.8　　1.0

Figure 7-5. Occlusion heatmap for a pneumonia X-ray image in the test set, correctly predicted to show pneumonia

In addition to this tuning concern, the explanation also shows that the model cares about some groups of pixels outside of the bounds of the torso. Is this a problem with our model, perhaps suggestive of overfitting; a data leak between training and test data; or shortcut learning (*https://oreil.ly/xv-OQ*)? Or is this an artifact of the explanation technique itself? We're just left to wonder. Let's see if gradient-based methods provide more clarity.

Shortcut learning is a common issue in complex models and can ruin our real-world results. It happens when a model learns about something easier than the actual prediction target in an ML task—essentially cheating itself during training. As medical diagnosis from images can be a painstaking task, even for highly experienced human practitioners, ML systems often find shortcuts that help them optimize their loss functions in training data. When those learned shortcuts are not available in real-world diagnostic scenarios, these models fail. To read more about shortcut learning in medical images, check out "Deep Learning Applied to Chest X-Rays: Exploiting and Preventing Shortcuts" (*https://oreil.ly/oVT-G*). To learn about this serious issue, which plagues nearly all unexplainable ML, in a general context, check out "Shortcut Learning in Deep Neural Networks" (*https://oreil.ly/ogNeg*).

Input * gradient

The first gradient-based method we'll look at is the input * gradient technique. As its name suggests, input * gradient creates a local feature attribution that is equal to the gradient of the prediction with respect to the input, multiplied by the input value itself. Why? Imagine a linear model. The product of the gradient and the input value assigns a local feature attribution that is equivalent to the feature value multiplied by the feature's coefficient, which corresponds to the feature's contribution to a particular prediction.

We use Captum to generate a heatmap for the same test set image using the input * gradient technique this time. In Figure 7-6, we're showing the *positive* evidence for the classification.

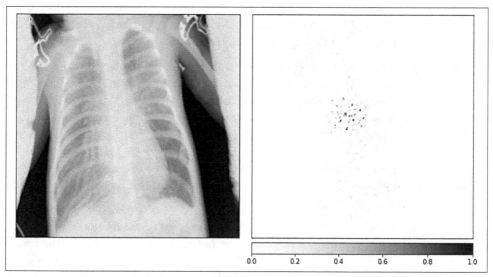

*Figure 7-6. Input * gradient heatmap for a pneumonia X-ray image in the test set, correctly predicted to show pneumonia*

What to say about this output? Just like with occlusions, we can squint at the image and argue that it is saying something meaningful. In particular, there is a dark patch of high evidence in the lungs that seems to correspond to high opacity in the chest X-ray on the left. This is the behavior we would expect and hope for out of our pneumonia classifier. However, the explanation technique is also suggesting that the length of the patient's spine contains regions of high evidence of pneumonia. We're left with the same questions that we posed earlier. Is this telling us that the model is focusing on the wrong things, i.e., shortcuts? That would make this a useful output for model debugging. On the other hand, we still don't know if the explanation technique itself is the source of the unintuitive result.

Integrated gradients

Integrated gradients (*https://oreil.ly/Er6tk*) is the first technique we'll consider that comes with some theoretical guarantees. Gradients alone can be deceiving, especially because gradients tend toward zero for some high-confidence predictions. For high probability outcomes, it's not uncommon that the input features cause activation functions to reach high values, where gradients become saturated, flat, and close to zero. This means that some of our most important activation functions for a decision won't show up if we only look at gradients.

Integrated gradients attempts to fix this issue by measuring a feature impact relative to a baseline value, across all possible input pixel intensity values. In particular, integrated gradients asks, "How does the gradient change as we traverse a path from the baseline input pixel intensity value to a larger input pixel intensity value?" The final feature attribution is the approximate integral of the gradient along this smooth path of pixel values as a function of the model's predictions.

Integrated gradients satisfies axioms of sensitivity and implementation invariance. Sensitivity means that if the input image and baseline image differ only along one feature, and if they return different model outputs, then integrated gradients will return a nonzero attribution for that feature. Implementation invariance says that if two models, possibly with different internal structures, return the same output for all inputs, then all of the input attributions returned by integrated gradients will be equal. Implementation invariance is another way to discuss *consistency* from Chapter 2. For a good walk-through of the topic, check out the TensorFlow introduction to integrated gradients (*https://oreil.ly/2aUWD*).

In Figure 7-7, we show the output of this attribution technique on the same pneumonitic image we have been considering. Like the output of input * gradient, the image is noisy and difficult to interpret. It looks like the method is picking up on *edges* in the input image. In addition to the X-ray machine markings and armpits, we can also see the faint outline of the patient's ribs in the heatmap. Is this because the model is ignoring the ribs, and looking around them into the lungs? It seems like these outputs are raising more questions than they're answering. Later in this chapter, we'll critically evaluate these explanatory outputs by conducting some experiments. For now, we'll turn to the fourth and final technique, another gradient-based method, layer-wise relevance propagation.

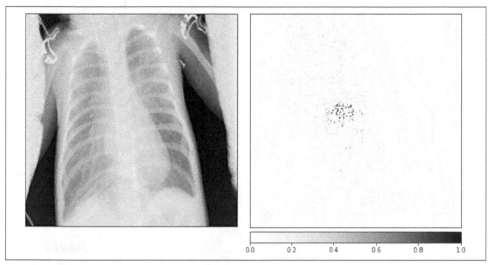

Figure 7-7. Integrated gradients heatmap for a pneumonia X-ray image in the test set, correctly predicted to show pneumonia

Layer-wise Relevance Propagation

Layer-wise Relevance Propagation (LRP) (*https://oreil.ly/xGtUm*) is really a class of methods that measure a feature's *relevance* to the output. Broadly speaking, relevance is the strength of the connection between the input features and the model output, and it can be measured without making any changes to the input features. By choosing a different notion of relevance, we can arrive at a number of different explanatory outputs. For readers interested in a more thorough treatment of LRP, we direct you to the chapter "Layer-Wise Relevance Propagation: An Overview" in *Explainable AI: Interpreting, Explaining and Visualizing Deep Learning* by Samek et al. (Springer Cham). There, you'll find a comprehensive discussion of the different relevance rules and when they should be applied. The Explainable AI Demos dashboard (*https://oreil.ly/wcIVJ*) also allows you to generate explanatory outputs using a wide array of LRP rules.

The nice thing about LRP is that the explanations it produces are locally accurate: the sum of the relevance scores is equal to the model output. It is similar to Shapley values in this way. Let's take a look at the LRP explanation for our test set image in Figure 7-8. Unfortunately, it's still leaving a lot to be desired in terms of generating a human-verifiable explanation.

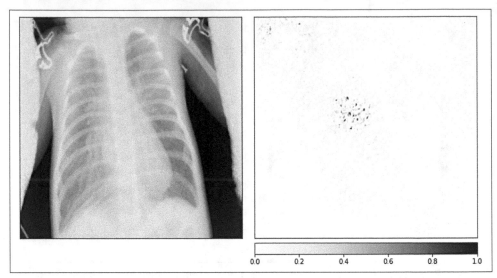

Figure 7-8. LRP heatmap for a pneumonia X-ray image in the test set, correctly predicted to show pneumonia

Like the other techniques, LRP has picked up on this region of higher opacity in the right lung, but it has also given a high attribution score to regions outside of the lungs.

Evaluating Model Explanations

In the previous sections, we've just scraped the surface of explanatory attribution methods for DL models. There is a large and growing number of these techniques. In this section, we'll address the important question: "How do we know if our explanation is any good?" Then, we'll conduct an experiment to critically examine just how much information post hoc techniques give us about our CNN model.

David Alvarez-Melis and Tommi S. Jaakkola give the question of evaluating explanations an excellent treatment in their two 2018 papers "On the Robustness of Interpretability Methods" (*https://oreil.ly/KRcmm*) and "Towards Robust Interpretability with Self-Explaining Neural Networks" (*https://oreil.ly/gUWIR*). In the second paper, Alvarez-Melis and Jaakkola introduce three desirable properties that explanations should share:

- Explanations should be understandable (explicitness/intelligibility).
- They should be indicative of true importance (faithfulness).
- They should be insensitive to small changes in the input (stability/robustness).

The heatmap techniques we have examined in this chapter clearly fall short on point number one. First of all, the outputs of these techniques are noisy and confusing. More importantly, all of the techniques we surveyed seem to point to nonsensical regions, such as spaces outside of the patient's body.

Even if the outputs perfectly aligned with our intuition, these heatmaps only give an indication of *where* the model is finding positive or negative evidence for its classification; they give no suggestion of *how* the model is making its decision based on the information it's been provided with. This is in contrast to explainable models such as SENN or ProtoPNet, which provide both—prototypes or basis concepts are the *where*, and their linear combination is *how*. *How* is a crucial element of a good explanation.

> We should always test our explanation methods in high-risk applications. Ideally, we should be comparing post hoc explanations to underlying explainable model mechanisms. For more standard DL approaches, we can use the following:
>
> - Domain experts and user studies to test intelligibility
> - Removal of features deemed important, nearest-neighbor approaches, or label shuffling to test faithfulness
> - Perturbation of input features to test robustness
>
> Use "Towards Robust Interpretability with Self-Explaining Neural Networks" (*https://oreil.ly/PtR5u*) and "Evaluating the Visualization of What a Deep Neural Network Has Learned" (*https://oreil.ly/sQDv5*) as references.

Faithfulness is typically tested by obscuring or removing features deemed important and calculating the resulting change in classifier output to gauge the robustness of the explanatory values themselves. Alvarez-Melis and Jaakkola showed that there is a wide range of explanation faithfulness across different techniques and datasets, with Shapley additive explanations and some others performing quite poorly. We can also use nearest-neighbor approaches, where similar input observation should have similar explanations, to gauge faithfulness. We're also going to examine faithfulness in our explanations in the next section—but we're going to try a different approach.

To examine robustness (or stability), Alvarez-Melis and Jaakkola perturb the input image slightly and measure the resulting change in explanation output. Armed with a quantitative metric, they compare many post hoc methods across multiple datasets. It turns out that most of the post hoc techniques they studied are unstable to small changes in the input. Local interpretable model-agnostic explanations (LIME) perform especially poorly, and the methods of integrated gradients and occlusion show the best robustness among the techniques they studied. Across all of these evaluation dimensions—intelligibility, faithfulness, and robustness—explainable models such as self-explaining neural networks outperfom post hoc techniques.

The Robustness of Post Hoc Explanations

In this section, we reproduce (in part) the damning unfaithfulness results from "Sanity Checks for Saliency Maps" (*https://oreil.ly/v6qlw*). In that paper, the authors were interested in the question: "Are the outputs generated by these post hoc explanation methods actually telling us anything about the model?" As we'll see in this experiment, sometimes the result is an emphatic no.

To begin our experiment, we train a nonsense model, wherein images have random labels. In Figure 7-9, we can see the high training loss and poor accuracy curves for a new model that has been trained on a dataset where the image labels have been randomly shuffled. For this experiment, we did not conduct any data augmentation to handle the class imbalance. This explains why the accuracy on the validation data converges to a value larger than 0.5—the model is biased toward the majority class (pneumonia).

Now we have a model that has been trained on nonsense labels. The predictions generated by our new model cannot be any better than a (weighted) coin flip. For the original explanations to be meaningful, we'd hope that *these* explanations don't pick up on the same signals. Figures 7-10, 7-11, and 7-12 show explanations for our test set image, generated on the model that has been trained on randomly shuffled data, created by input * gradient, integrated gradients, and occlusion, respectively.

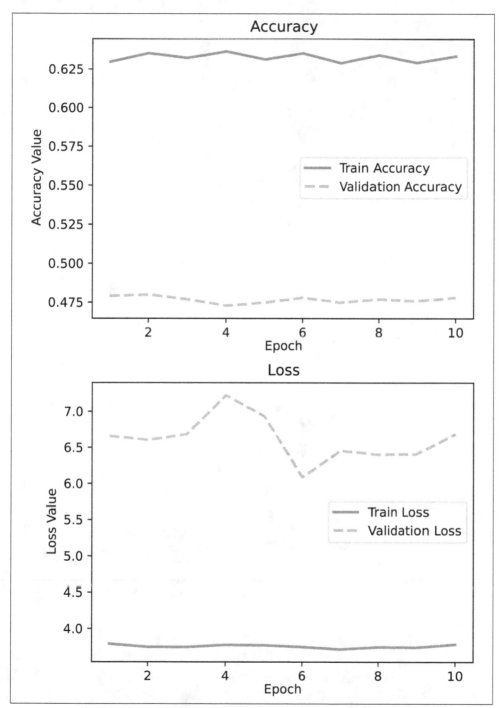

Figure 7-9. Model performance during training on data where the labels have been randomly shuffled (digital, color version: https://oreil.ly/-uCIY)

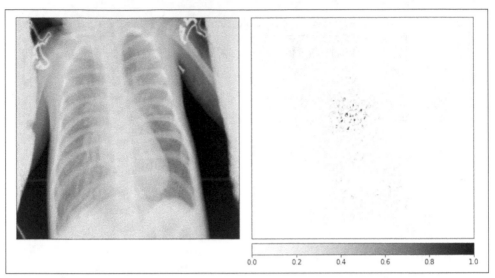

Figure 7-10. Input * gradient heatmap after randomly shuffling class labels

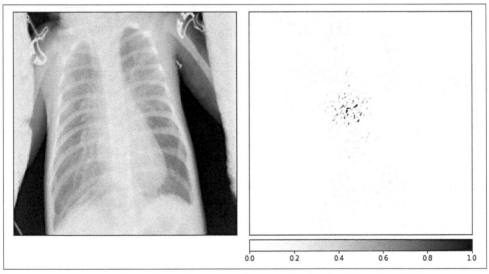

Figure 7-11. Integrated gradients heatmap after randomly shuffling class labels

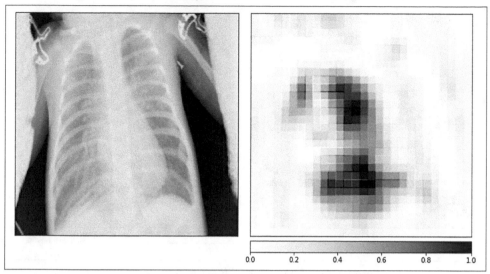

Figure 7-12. Occlusion heatmap after randomly shuffling class labels

In our opinion, these results look shockingly similar to the ones from the previous sections. In all of the images, the techniques have once again highlighted irrelevant regions of the image, such as the patient's spine and the boundaries of their torso. Worse than this, the attribution maps look very similar to their previous results *inside* of the lungs. They've picked up on the outlines of the patient's ribs and the regions of higher opacity. Previously, we were interpreting this to mean that the model might be generating its pneumonia prediction based on specific regions of lung inflammation. This experiment shows, however, that these methods will show the same explanation for a model that was trained on zero meaningful signals. To what are our explanations faithful?! We're not sure.

To further examine the robustness of our explanations, we conduct a simple experiment of adding random noise to the input images. This can be easily done using a custom transformation in torchvision. We then examine the explanations on these inputs and compare them with the previous explanations. The amount of noise is regulated in such a way that the predicted class of the image remains the same before and after adding the noise component.

What we really want to understand is whether the resulting explanations are robust to the addition of random noise or not. In short, it's a mixed bag; see Figures 7-13, 7-14, and 7-15. The new attribution maps differ significantly from those generated on the original model, but do seem to preserve the focus on regions of high opacity inside the lungs.

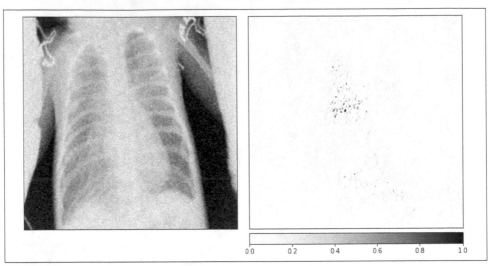

Figure 7-13. Input * gradient heatmap after adding random noise

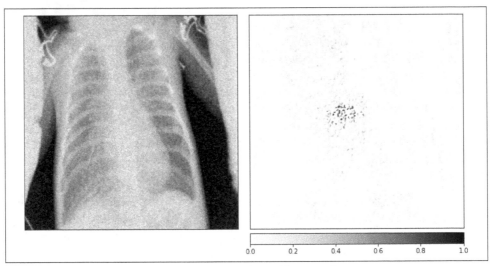

Figure 7-14. Integrated gradients heatmap after adding random noise

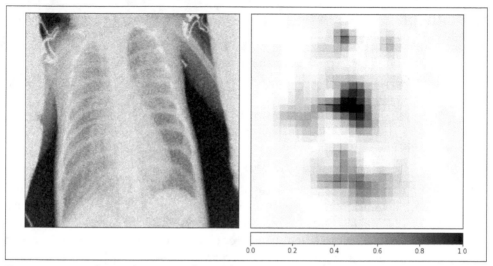

Figure 7-15. Occlusion heatmap after adding random noise

Look at the occlusion heatmap in Figure 7-15, for example. Previously, we said that it was encouraging that occlusion seems to have picked up on the regions inside the lungs with higher opacity. After adding random noise, we still see this focus on the upper left and upper right of the lungs. However, the addition of noise has upset the occlusion output to give greater evidence to regions near the neck. The gradient-based technique outputs are similarly disturbed, while still preserving their emphasis on the middle of the right lung.

In "Sanity Checks for Saliency Maps" (*https://oreil.ly/fTeRb*), the authors point to a possible explanation for the results we've seen in these experiments: the attribution techniques are effectively performing *edge detection*. That is, irrespective of the model training and architecture, these attribution methods are capable of detecting edges in the input image, where gradients nearly always exhibit steep changes. That would explain the emphasis on the rib outlines that we have been observing, as well as the emphasis on regions on the boundary of the torso. In case it's not clear, *detecting edges is not model explanation and can be done easily without using DL.*

Conclusion

The bottom line is that post hoc explanations are often difficult to explain, and sometimes meaningless. Even worse, the diversity of explanation techniques means that if we're not careful, we'll fall prey to confirmation bias and end up selecting the one that confirms our prior belief about how our model should behave. We sympathize—building explainable models in a DL context is very difficult. But this chapter shows that post hoc explanations may only offer a dangerous *illusion* of understanding, and thus are not always suitable for explaining high-risk decisions.

We suggest not relying solely on post hoc techniques to explain DL models in a high-risk application. At best, these techniques can be useful model debugging tools. We'll cover that topic in more detail in Chapter 9. Instead, we should try hard to use *explainable models* when we need explanations that are faithful, robust, and intelligible. We can always build on that more robust model-based explainability with post hoc explanation visualizations if the need arises later, and we'll be able to check post hoc visualizations against the underlying model mechanisms.

There are encouraging frontiers in explainable DL models for image classification and other tasks. Prototype-based case-reasoning models such as ProtoPNet (*https://oreil.ly/yjIuQ*) and sparse additive deep models such as SENN (*https://oreil.ly/yZHHT*) provide a path forward for explainable DL. However, explainable models are not yet widely available out of the box for DL applications. They often place greater demands on our data and our modeling expertise. We encourage readers to think of this as a feature, not a bug. The development of AI systems *should* demand high-quality, expertly curated data. Models *should* be problem-specific, and encode maximal domain knowledge.

We agree with the authors of "The False Hope of Current Approaches to Explainable Artificial Intelligence in Health Care" (*https://oreil.ly/-w598*) when they say:

> In the absence of suitable explainability methods, we advocate for rigorous internal and external validation of AI models as a more direct means of achieving the goals often associated with explainability.

In the next two chapters, we'll build on the techniques we've been discussing here and in Chapter 6 to address the broader question of *model debugging*.

Resources

Code Examples

- Machine-Learning-for-High-Risk-Applications-Book
  (*https://oreil.ly/machine-learning-high-risk-apps-code*)

Transparency in Deep Learning Tools

- AllenNLP Interpret (*https://oreil.ly/_tAvm*)
- Aletheia (*https://oreil.ly/UMfWK*)
- Captum (*https://oreil.ly/F5Obo*)
- cleverhans (*https://oreil.ly/efN16*)
- DeepExplain (*https://oreil.ly/u4Mfu*)
- deeplift (*https://oreil.ly/S29jk*)
- deep-visualization-toolbox (*https://oreil.ly/ZH3JU*)
- foolbox (*https://oreil.ly/DFSu0*)
- L2X (*https://oreil.ly/S2Ppj*)
- tensorflow/lattice (*https://oreil.ly/M7aYY*)
- lrp_toolbox (*https://oreil.ly/kKk09*)
- tensorflow/model-analysis (*https://oreil.ly/5Aeqe*)
- ProtoPNet (*https://oreil.ly/ZmqWq*)
- tensorflow/tcav (*https://oreil.ly/7RvqS*)

## CHAPTER 8

Selecting and Debugging XGBoost Models

The ways that data scientists measure a model's real-world performance are usually inadequate. According to "Underspecification Presents Challenges for Credibility in Modern Machine Learning" (*https://oreil.ly/27jFT*), penned by 40 researchers at Google and other leading machine learning research institutions, "ML models often exhibit unexpectedly poor behavior when they are deployed in real-world domains." A fundamental issue is that we measure performance like we're writing research papers, no matter how complex and high-risk the deployment scenario. Test data measurements like accuracy or area under the curve (AUC) don't tell us much about fairness, privacy, security, or stability. These simple measurements of prediction quality or error on static test sets are not informative enough for risk management. They are only correlated with real-world performance, and don't guarantee good performance in deployment. Put plainly, we should be more concerned with in vivo performance and risk management than in silico test data performance, because a primary thrust of the applied practice of ML is to make good decisions in the real world.

This chapter will introduce several methods that go beyond traditional model assessment to select models that generalize better, and that push models to their limits to find hidden problems and failure modes. The chapter starts with a concept refresher, puts forward an enhanced process for model selection, and then focuses on model debugging exercises that better simulate real-world stresses, along with sensitivity analysis and tests that uncover model errors using residual analysis. The overarching goal of model debugging is to increase trust in model performance in the real world, but in the process, we'll also increase the transparency of our models. Code examples that accompany the chapter are available online (*https://oreil.ly/machine-learning-high-risk-apps-code*); Chapter 9 addresses debugging for images and unstructured data, and Chapter 3 covers model debugging more broadly.

Concept Refresher: Debugging ML

If readers haven't picked up on it yet, we're much more concerned about in vivo performance than in silico performance. In vivo performance matters for users; in silico performance doesn't. With this central tenet in mind, we'll be covering model selection, sensitivity analysis tests, residual analysis, and remediating (i.e., fixing) models.

Model Selection

Traditionally we select models by choosing features and selecting hyperparameters. We try to find the best set of features using approaches like stepwise regression, feature importance measurements, or L1 regularization. We often use grid searches to find the best hyperparameter settings for our ML models. In Chapter 2, we used a more deliberate approach in which we started with a linear model benchmark and introduced nonlinearity and interactions into our models, then used human judgment to pick our favorite model. In this chapter, we'll see that random grid search is especially problematic on small datasets for hyperparameter selection and when we compare it to a more sophisticated cross-validated ranking procedure inspired by "KDD-Cup 2004: Results and Analysis" (*https://oreil.ly/osrK4*). We'll compare the rank of model performance across several validation folds and several different traditional assessment metrics to get a better idea of estimated in vivo performance and pick a better model. We'll also highlight how to estimate the business value of a model—a crucial consideration. No one in the business world wants to deploy a model that loses money!

Sensitivity Analysis

Because ML models tend to extrapolate in complex ways, we won't really know how our model will perform on unseen data unless we test it explicitly on different types of data. That's what we're attempting to do with sensitivity analysis. Broadly speaking, sensitivity analysis shows us whether our model will be stable on different kinds of data. Sensitivity analysis might show us that our model has robustness issues, i.e., it fails under data drift. It might show us that our model has reliability or resilience problems, i.e., that some types of input cause our to model to behave in surprising or inappropriate ways. There are many structured approaches to sensitivity analysis. If readers would like to learn more, we suggest exploring resources associated with PiML (*https://oreil.ly/84KCZ*) or SALib (*https://oreil.ly/Kgnmg*).

We'll highlight two other related sensitivity analysis methods in this chapter that appear most directly useful to practitioners: stress testing and adversarial example searches. Stress testing is roughly aligned to testing for robustness, whereas adversarial example searches probe for reliability and resilience problems:

Stress testing

Stress testing is a global perturbation approach that tests models in foreseeable stressful circumstances. When we stress test our model, we'll change our validation data to simulate recession conditions and see if it remains robust under these foreseeable difficult conditions. The idea is to make our model robust to predictable circumstances, or at least to document expected performance degradation for whoever might be maintaining the model when recession—or another kind of domain shift—strikes.[1] We'll be doing a much less rigorous analysis on a single model, but the idea is the same: to test how our model will perform under foreseeable concept or data drift, such as a recession, to make sure we are prepared for the likeliest types of failures.

Adversarial example searches

Adversarial example searches are a local perturbation approach that helps uncover local, logical flaws in the model's reliability and potential security vulnerabilities (i.e., resilience issues). Adversarial examples are rows of data that create strange responses from complex ML models. Sometimes we can craft these rows by hand, but often we have to search for them. In this chapter, we will search for them by perturbing, or changing, values of important features in certain rows of data and checking how this change affects model performance. Both the search itself and the individual adversarial examples we find are useful. The search creates a response surface that displays model performance across many interesting input values, and often reveals logical flaws in model performance. The individual rows we find that evoke strange responses are good to document and share with security colleagues, so that model monitoring can be primed to detect known adversarial examples.

In deep learning, data scientists tend to use gradient information and generative adversarial networks (GANs) to create adversarial examples. In structured data tasks, we have to use other methods, like those described in "Adversarial Attacks for Tabular Data: Application to Fraud Detection and Imbalanced Data" (*https://oreil.ly/KF843*), heuristics based on individual conditional expectation, or genetic algorithms. We'll be pursuing a heuristic method in "Adversarial Example Search" on page 276, both to find adversarial examples, and to probe our model's response surface for problems.

---

1 Keep in mind that large US banks perform near-exhaustive stress tests for their models each year in accordance with the Federal Reserve's Comprehensive Capital Analysis and Review (*https://oreil.ly/rczyU*) process, known as CCAR.

The most important method we don't treat in this chapter is random attacks, or simply exposing our model or API to *a lot* of random data and seeing what kinds of issues emerge. If we don't know where to start with sensitivity analysis, we try random attacks first. Then we try PiML, SALib, and the methods we'll put forward in the sections that follow. Regardless of how we implement sensitivity analysis, the key is to do something about the problems we find. We often use data augmentation, business rules, regularization, constraints, and monitoring to remediate sensitivity issues.

Residual Analysis

Residual analysis is a primary method of model debugging. It is the careful study of modeling mistakes made in training data, or other labeled data, for testing and debugging purposes. While readers may be familiar with residual analysis for traditional linear models, it can and should be applied to ML models. The basic idea is the same as with linear models. Good models should have mostly random errors. When we examine the errors in our ML models and strong patterns emerge, this most likely means that we forgot something or we made a mistake when we built our model. Then we have to use our human brains to try to fix the problem. In this chapter, we'll focus on three major approaches to residual analysis—residual plots, segmented error analysis, and modeling residuals:

Residual plots

    We'll examine residual plots for the entire model, and then break down the plots by feature and by level. We'll look to answer questions like: Which rows are causing the largest errors? Do we see any strong patterns in the residual plots? Can we isolate any patterns to specific input features or levels of a feature? Then we'll try to think through how to fix any issues that we uncover.

Segmented error analysis

    We shouldn't deploy a model without checking to see how it performs across major segments in our training or test data. Failing to do so can have grave consequences for both overall model performance and algorithmic discrimination, when a model performs poorly on historically marginalized demographic groups. We'll be focusing on the performance aspect in this chapter, and looking into other types of segments apart from demographic segments. We do this because commonly used average assessment metrics for entire datasets can mask poor performance on small but important subpopulations. Sparsity in training data can lead to nearly random performance on some segments too. Segmented error analysis has also been put forward as an in silico test for the nasty problem of underspecification. All of these issues—poor performance in small segments, random performance in sparse regions of training data, and underspecification—can lead to unpleasant surprises and serious problems once a model is deployed.

One cool extension of segmented error analysis, implemented in PiML, is to examine overfitting across segments. Doing so can highlight additional issues that will affect an in vivo model.

Modeling residuals

Another way to learn patterns in residuals is to model them. If we can fit a straightforward, interpretable model to another model's residuals, that means, almost by definition, that there are strong patterns in the residuals. (And strong patterns in residuals usually means we made a modeling mistake.) Moreover, modeling residuals implies we can reduce them. The models we fit to residuals should also inform how to fix the discovered mistakes. As an example, we'll fit a decision tree to our model's residuals. We'll then examine the rules of that tree, because they are rules that describe when our model is most often wrong. We'll try to understand those rules to try to fix the problems they highlight.

As with sensitivity analysis, we won't be able to treat all the important ways to conduct residual analysis in ML in one chapter. Some of the most noteworthy approaches we won't cover include methods for discovering nonrobust features, such as Shapley value contributions to model loss. See Chapter 3 for a broader overview of residual analysis for ML.

Remediation

Once we find problems, we need to fix them. The bad news is that a lot of problems in ML arise from the use of low-quality, biased data and from confirmation bias. For most projects, this will involve two difficult pills to swallow: (1) collecting better data, with at least some consideration for experimental design, and (2) going back to the drawing board and redefining our experiment with better adherence to the scientific method to minimize human, statistical, and systemic biases in our modeling workflow.

Once serious data, methodological, or bias issues are addressed in our workflows, we can try some tech fixes for our model, as we do in this chapter. For example, we can apply monotonic constraints, interaction constraints, or regularization to our models to stabilize them, make them more logical and interpretable, and to improve performance in vivo. We can apply business rules, sometimes also called *model assertions*, or manual prediction limits to fix foreseeable bad outcomes. Business rules and model assertions boil down to adding code to our scoring engine that changes predictions we think will be wrong. We can edit the formulas or production code of our models to correct for problematic modeling mechanisms or predictions, and we can manage and monitor our models once they are deployed to track them and spot anomalies quickly.

For our model in this chapter, we'll hopefully have done a decent job sticking with the scientific method, mainly by expressing our hypotheses for model outcomes through monotonic constraints and by very rigorous model selection, as discussed in the next section. We'll apply both sensitivity and residual analyses to the model to find bugs, and then we'll try our best to remediate those bugs in "Remediating the Selected Model" on page 290.

Selecting a Better XGBoost Model

Although it's not technically debugging, we want to start our debugging exercise on solid footing by selecting a highly stable, generalizable, and valuable model. To do that, we won't just rely on grid search. Instead, we'll select a model as inspired by the Caruana et al. cross-validation ranking approach (*https://oreil.ly/kJT7d*) used in the 2004 Knowledge Discovery in Databases (KDD) Cup. We'll also compare these results to a standard random grid search so we can get an idea of the difference between a grid search and the cross-validation ranking procedure described in this section. Then, before moving onto sensitivity analysis, we'll do a basic estimation of our model's business value to check that we're not wasting money.

 According to Richard Feynman, it's our responsibility as scientists to engage in "a kind of leaning over backward" to make sure we don't fool ourselves and others. If this model selection approach seems over the top, think of it as bending over backward to find the best model we can.

The first thing we do to begin our model selection process is split our validation data into five folds. Then we select five relevant performance metrics to apply to each fold. These metrics should measure different aspects of performance, such as AUC measuring ranking capabilities across thresholds and accuracy measuring correctness at one threshold. In our case, we'll take maximum accuracy, AUC, maximum F1 statistic, logloss, and mean squared error (MSE) as our five metrics. The first step of our selection process is to calculate the value of each of these different statistics on each fold. That's what the following code snippet does:

```
eval_frame = pd.DataFrame() # init frame to hold score ranking
metric_list = ['acc', 'auc', 'f1', 'logloss', 'mse']

# create eval frame row-by-row
for fold in sorted(scores_frame['fold'].unique()): # loop through folds
    for metric_name in metric_list: # loop through metrics

        # init row dict to hold each rows values
        row_dict = {'fold': fold,
                    'metric': metric_name}
```

```
# cache known y values for fold
fold_y = scores_frame.loc[scores_frame['fold'] == fold, target]

# first columns are not for scores
for col_name in scores_frame.columns[2:]:

    # cache fold scores
    fold_scores = scores_frame.loc[
        scores_frame['fold'] == fold, col_name]

    # calculate evaluation metric for fold
    # with reasonable precision

    if metric_name == 'acc':
        row_dict[col_name] = np.round(
            max_acc(fold_y, fold_scores), ROUND)

    if metric_name == 'auc':
        row_dict[col_name] = np.round(
            roc_auc_score(fold_y, fold_scores), ROUND)

    if metric_name == 'f1':
        row_dict[col_name] = np.round(
            max_f1(fold_y, fold_scores), ROUND)

    if metric_name == 'logloss':
        row_dict[col_name] = np.round(
            log_loss(fold_y, fold_scores), ROUND)

    if metric_name == 'mse':
        row_dict[col_name] = np.round(
            mean_squared_error(fold_y, fold_scores), ROUND)

# append row values to eval_frame
eval_frame = eval_frame.append(row_dict, ignore_index=True)
```

Once we have the performance metric for each model across each fold, we move to the second step of the selection procedure and rank the performance of each model on each fold and for each measure. The following code does the ranking. Our search includes 50 different XGBoost models, and we test them using five performance measures on five folds. For each fold and metric, we rank the models first through fiftieth by the current metric, allowing for ties. We take the model with the lowest average rank across each fold and metric as the best model for in vivo usage. Think about this as if you were giving a test to 50 students, but instead of one test per student, it's five tests for each student. Then, we don't pass every student who makes above a certain numeric grade; we're only interested in the student who performs better than all others across the most tests. Of course, this would make us very mean teachers, but luckily, it's fine to be extremely selective when it comes to ML models.

```
# initialize a temporary frame to hold rank information
rank_names = [name + '_rank' for name in eval_frame.columns
             if name not in ['fold', 'metric']]
rank_frame = pd.DataFrame(columns=rank_names)

# re-order columns
eval_frame = eval_frame[['fold', 'metric'] +
                        [name for name in sorted(eval_frame.columns)
                         if name not in ['fold', 'metric']]]

# determine score ranks row-by-row
for i in range(0, eval_frame.shape[0]):

        # get ranks for row based on metric
        metric_name = eval_frame.loc[i, 'metric']
        if metric_name in ['logloss', 'mse']:
            ranks = eval_frame.iloc[i, 2:].rank().values
        else:
            ranks = eval_frame.iloc[i, 2:].rank(ascending=False).values

        # create single-row frame and append to rank_frame
        row_frame = pd.DataFrame(ranks.reshape(1, ranks.shape[0]),
                                 columns=rank_names)
        rank_frame = rank_frame.append(row_frame, ignore_index=True)

        # house keeping
        del row_frame

eval_frame = pd.concat([eval_frame, rank_frame], axis=1)
```

Ties occur because we round performance scores. If two models score, say, an AUC of 0.88811 and 0.88839, that's a tie. Those last decimals of AUC are likely irrelevant for in vivo performance, and our approach handles ties well. Two models with the same score simply have the same rank for that fold and metric. Because we try so many metrics and so many scores, and take the average rank across all of them, those ties rarely matter in the end for selecting the best model. In our example, each of the 50 models is assigned 25 different ranking values, one rank for each metric and fold. Our best model ranked first and second on several fold and metric combinations, but also ranked as high as 26.5—indicating a tie—for its worst-performing fold and metric. In the end, our best-performing model in terms of lowest ranks across metrics and folds showed an average rank of 10.38.

For comparison purposes, this ranking procedure was applied to the top 50 models selected, and models were ranked by a standard random grid search. In the grid search, the lowest logloss on validation data was used to rank models. When we compare the grid search ranking to the cross-validation ranking, the dissimilarity is striking (Table 8-1).

Table 8-1. Overall rank of the top 10 models across a random grid search ranked by logloss and the more in-depth cross-validated model selection approach

Grid search rank	Cross-validation rank
Model 0	Model 2
Model 1	Model 5
Model 2	Model 1
Model 3	Model 4
Model 4	Model 12
Model 5	Model 0
Model 6	Model 21
Model 7	Model 48
Model 8	Model 30
Model 9	Model 29
Model 10	Model 17

The ranking for the grid search is on the left, while the ranking for the cross-validation approach is on the right. The first row in the table indicates that the third-best model in the grid search (indexed from 0, Model 2) was the best model in cross-validated ranking. The two model selection processes exhibit a Pearson correlation of 0.35, indicating only moderate positive correlation. In short, the best model derived from a grid search may not be the best model selected by more in-depth selection approaches. In fact, one interesting informal study used a similar technique to reveal stability problems (*https://oreil.ly/H6oRC*) in data science competitions that used small datasets. This selection approach is a good way to start "leaning over backward" to increase the scientific integrity of ML model selection exercises. To see exactly how we did it, check out this chapter's code examples (*https://oreil.ly/9nxyQ*).

Another important consideration for model selection is business value. Building models costs money. Often, a lot of money. Our salaries, healthcare, retirement, snacks, coffee, computers, office space, and air-conditioning are not cheap. If we want our model to be a success, that often means recouping the resources used to train, test, and deploy the system. Though really understanding the value of our model requires monitoring and measuring business value in real time (*https://oreil.ly/tuMD8*), we can use some tricks to estimate its value before we deploy.

To get started, we assign estimated monetary values to the outcomes from our model. For classifiers, this means assigning a monetary value to the elements of a confusion matrix. In Figure 8-1, we can see an illustration of a confusion matrix on the left and an illustration of a residual plot on the right.

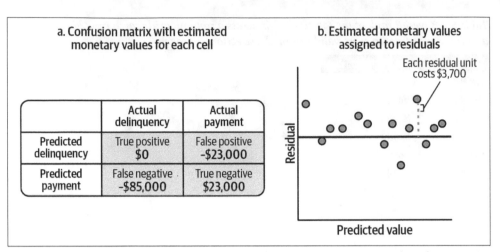

Figure 8-1. Example assessment procedures with estimated monetary values for (a) classifiers and (b) regression models

The confusion matrix on the left can be applied to our selected model. We came up with the values in the cells by thinking through the model's in vivo outcomes. A true positive for our model means we decided not to extend credit to someone who would have been delinquent on payments. There are no opportunity costs or write-offs, but also no positive revenue, associated with this outcome. A false positive results in us refusing to extend credit to someone who would have made payments—an opportunity cost. We associate that opportunity cost with an estimated customer lifetime value (LTV) of negative $23,000. A false negative is the worst outcome. That means we extend credit to someone who did not pay. That is a write-off, and we estimate that value, based off of the mean of the customer credit limits (LIMIT_BAL), at about negative $85,000—ouch. A true negative is where we make money. That's were the model says to extend credit to a paying customer. We associate that outcome with the opposite of a false positive, and we recoup the customer's LTV for the credit product. For each true negative, we gain $23,000 in revenue. Now we have to add up these values for each customer in our validation set, as each customer will either represent a true positive, false positive, false negative, or true negative outcome. For our model, in the small portfolio represented by the validation set, that estimated value comes out to be $4,240,000. So, there is real business value in our model, but it's not eye-popping after one thinks through all the expenses and taxes associated with this revenue.

For regression models, we can assign a single value to overprediction and underprediction. Or, as illustrated in Figure 8-1, we can attempt to assign a monetary value to each residual unit in a logical manner for both over- and underprediction. Then we calculate the residuals for each row in our dataset and sum up the estimated value of the model. Once we assign monetary values, we can answer the basic business question: "Does this model provide any real value?" Now that we *think* we've selected a decent model, and one with some business value, let's try to figure out what's wrong with it, using sensitivity analysis.

Sensitivity Analysis for XGBoost

We'll start putting our model through its paces with sensitivity analysis in this section. We've selected stress testing and adversarial example searches for detailed examples of sensitivity analysis in this chapter. Both techniques have direct applicability for a wide range of applications, and help to spot different kinds of problems. Stress testing looks for global weaknesses in our model across entire datasets in foreseeable stressful circumstances, like recessions. Adversarial example searches help us spot potential surprise issues, like wild predictions or security vulnerabilities, often on a local, row-by-row basis.

Practical Sensitivity Analysis Beyond Supervised Learning

Some ideas for applying sensitivity analysis for different types of models might include the following:

Clustering
> Assessing movements in cluster centroids caused by data drift or adversarial examples

Principal components analysis
> Assessing the similarity of eigenvalues in new data versus training data

Computer vision
> Assessing model performance on shifted populations, shifted subpopulations, and adversarial examples (see Chapter 9)

Language models
> Assessing model performance on different languages, assessing model responses to attacks (e.g., term reduction, hotflips) and adversarial prompts (see "What About Language Models?" on page 298)

Random attacks, or exposing models to large amounts of random data and tracking errors, is a great approach for all types of models.

Stress Testing XGBoost

Linear models extrapolate linearly, but ML models can do almost anything on data outside their training domain. Unless we're stress testing our models on the right data, we're just not going to be aware of it. For instance, consider training a model on a dataset where the highest income of an individual is $200,000. How would the model behave if it encounters an individual income of, let's say, 20 million dollars? Will it break? Will it return accurate results, or not? There's no way to know this unless we test it explicitly. The basics are not hard. Simulate a row of data, put a 20 million dollar income in there, and run it back through our model to see how it behaves. When we do this more thoroughly and more systematically, we call it stress testing.

Complex ML models often behave poorly when extrapolating outside of their training data domain, but even simpler models have problems with extrapolation. Tree-based models often cannot make predictions outside the ranges of training data, and polynomial models can suffer from Runge's phenomenon (*https://oreil.ly/1Nabl*) at the edges of their training data domains. We are taking a risk whenever we use standard statistical or ML models for predictions outside the domain of training data.

Stress testing is an in silico exercise conducted to test the resilience of models under external, adverse, in vivo scenarios, like recessions or pandemics. The basic idea behind stress testing is to simulate data that represents realistic future scenarios and then redo traditional model assessment to see how the model performs. This ensures that the ML models can withstand the reasonably likely adverse developments they will encounter in the wild, and that they're robust to inevitable in vivo variations in new data, commonly known as data and concept drift.

Data scientists often say they already validate their models against holdout datasets, so is there really a need for additional stress tests? Well, there is a need, and even more so when models will get deployed and affect people. An ML model with a perfect in silico AUC is of no use if it falters when it encounters common stressors in new data. When we deploy ML models in the real world, we have to think about more aspects and situations than simple in silico test error. Even though it is difficult to predict the future, we can use validation data to simulate foreseeable problems. We can then see how the model performs under these conditions, document any issues, and if possible, update our model to address any discovered issues.

A gold standard for stress tests is the Federal Reserve's Comprehensive Capital Analysis and Review (CCAR). It is an exercise conducted by the US Federal Reserve annually to ensure that large banks and financial institutions have adequate capital planning processes and maintain sufficient capital to withstand economic shocks.

For instance, the CCAR conducted two separate tests to gauge the robustness of the big banks in the US in the wake of the COVID-19 pandemic. Even though the banks were well-capitalized under extreme simulated situations, CCAR results still warranted restrictions (*https://oreil.ly/RM-pS*) on bank payouts due to uncertainty surrounding the situation. We'll take inspiration from CCAR in the following subsections when trying to determine if our selected XGBoost model is robust to recession conditions, a common and foreseeable stressor for credit models.

Stress Testing Methodology

A recession is a situation wherein there is a substantial decline in a country's economy, lasting several months. Remember the financial crisis of 2008 and, more recently, the economic slowdown caused by the COVID pandemic? We want to see how our model might perform if a recession occurs while it is deployed. In this section, we'll simulate a recession scenario and then reassess the performance of our constrained and regularized XGBoost model. As seen in Figure 8-2, the model performs well on both the validation and holdout test data before the stress testing.

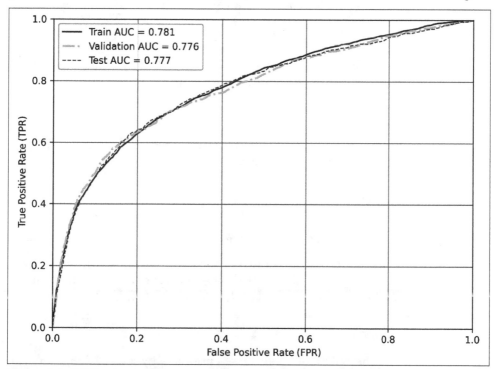

Figure 8-2. ROC curve before stress analysis on a constrained and regularized XGBoost model (digital, color version: https://oreil.ly/48-em)

We'll now create a copy of the original dataset and rename it as `data_recession_modified`. We'll alter the values of some of the features in this dataset using basic economic and business intuitions, and should be able to emulate a recession scenario.

 It's difficult to simulate realistic out-of-distribution data, because it's impossible to know in advance how each feature will co-vary in some new circumstance. For that reason, stress testing is an exercise best undertaken in close collaboration with subject matter experts. Even better than simulating stress test data would be to *back-test* the model on real data during adverse conditions, such as the 2008 global recession.

Altering Data to Simulate Recession Conditions

First, we'll choose some of the observations in the dataset to modify. We take these observations to be the ones that would be affected by the recession—perhaps they or someone in their household will have lost their jobs. We choose to modify 25% of customers who were previously in good standing:

```
data_recession_modified = data_recession[
    data_recession['DELINQ_NEXT'] == 0].sample(frac=.25)
```

Assuming that the simulated recession has recently hit, we'll assume that these observations have fallen behind on their most recent payments:

```
payments = ['PAY_0', 'PAY_2']
data_recession_modified[payments] += 1
```

Here, `PAY_*` represents the various repayment statuses. Next, we'll decrease the payment amount of the customers by one thousand dollars each:

```
pay_amounts = ['PAY_AMT1', 'PAY_AMT2']
data_recession_modified[pay_amounts] = np.where(
    data_recession_modified[pay_amounts] < 1000,
    0,
    data_recession_modified[pay_amounts]-1000)
```

During times of financial crisis, banks often tighten their purse strings, and one way to do that is by lowering credit limits. We'll now incorporate this scenario in our stress test exercise by decreasing the credit limits of these affected customers, in a fixed proportion of their original credit limits:

```
data_recession_modified['LIMIT_BAL'] *= 0.75
```

We'll also decrease the bill amounts of these customers by a fixed proportion, to simulate lower spending:

```
bill_amounts = ['BILL_AMT1','BILL_AMT2']
data_recession_modified[bill_amounts] *= 0.75
```

Finally, we'll assume that some proportion of these affected customers will go delinquent on their accounts. In particular, we'll flip half of the target variables from zero
to one:

```
data_recession_modified['DELINQ_NEXT'] = np.where(
    np.random.rand(len(data_recession_modified)) < 0.5,
    1, 0)
```

After reintegrating the affected observations into the rest of the data, we have a
dataset that mimics some of the adverse conditions our model might encounter in
the real world. It is time to look at the performance metrics on this simulated data.
In Figure 8-3, we see a moderate decline in performance once recession-like data and
concept drift is applied to test data.

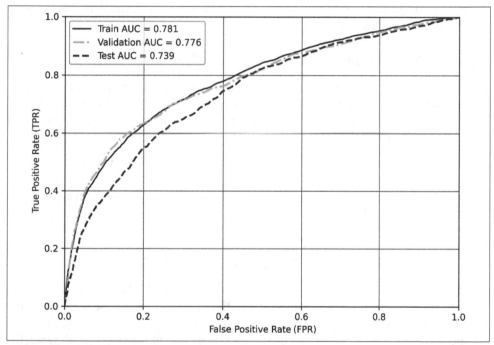

Figure 8-3. ROC curve after stress analysis on a constrained and regularized XGBoost
model (digital, color version: https://oreil.ly/R46Oo)

The first step after encountering such results is to document them and share them
with our team and management. This enables an informed decision to be made
about whether to deploy the model. If economic conditions look rosy, then we might
reasonably decide to deploy the model, with the knowledge that it will need to be
refreshed quickly if economic conditions change. A more nuanced analysis would
entail reassessing the financial risk we'd be taking on if our AUC were to drop from
0.777 to 0.738. Can we afford to make that many additional wrong credit decisions?

Once the results are documented and discussed with stakeholders, another next step might be to attempt to improve the model. This would definitely be the case if economic conditions are looking discouraging, or if the results of this or other stress tests were more dire. As readers might have guessed from the number of pages left in this chapter, we're going to find other problems with this model soon. We'll wait to remediate, or fix, all of the problems that we find until the end of the chapter.

We'd also like to highlight one more thing before we move on to adversarial example searches. We were careful when we trained this model, using regularization, monotonic constraints, grid search, and a highly robust model selection approach. These decisions likely had a positive impact on the robustness of the model under the stress test. Models trained without these specifications may have performed worse during the stress test. Either way, if we're not testing for problems that affect in vivo deployment, we're just ignoring them.

Adversarial Example Search

We'll apply an adversarial example search as our next debugging technique. The goal of our search is two-fold: to find adversarial examples that could be used to trick our model once it's deployed, and to see what we can learn about our model—good and bad—as a result of our search.

There are lots of packages and software that can help us find adversarial examples for image data, but we need to find adversaries for structured data. While some progress has been made in using generative adversarial networks (GANs) and genetic algorithms to find adversaries for structured data, we'll apply a heuristic approach instead. The first step is to find a row of data that will make a good initial guess for an adversarial example. We'll do this with ICE plots. Figure 8-4 displays ICE curves across deciles of predicted probability along with partial dependence.

In Figure 8-4 we can see the ICE curve associated with the 80th percentile shows the largest swing in predicted values across the values of PAY_0. Because we know this row of data can lead to large changes in predictions just by changing the value of one feature, we'll use the original row of data at the 80th percentile of predicted probability in the selected model to seed our adversarial example search. In more detail, for each important variable our adversarial search heuristic goes as follows:

1. Calculate ICE curves at each decile of model predictions.
2. Find the ICE curve with the largest swing in predictions.
3. Isolate the row of data associated with this ICE curve.
4. For this row of data:
   a. Perturb 1–3 additional important variables in the row. (It's hard to plot results for more than 1–3 variables.)

b. Rescore the perturbed row.

c. Continue until each additional important variable has cycled through its domain in the training data, and through missing or other interesting out-of-range values.

5. Plot and analyze the results.

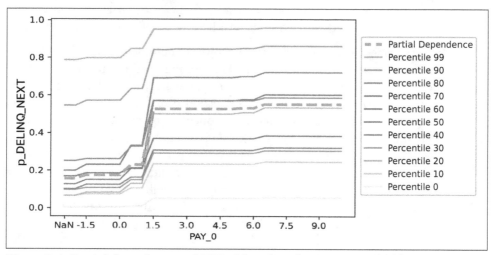

Figure 8-4. Partial dependence and ICE of the selected XGBoost model (digital, color version: https://oreil.ly/w0jkL)

We've already addressed steps 1–3, so how will we perform step 4? We'll take advantage of `itertools.product()` to automatically generate all possible feature perturbations for a set of features supplied to a Python function. Also, remember that when working with the native XGBoost API, we always have to supply an extra argument (`iteration_range`) to the `predict()` function to apply model selection:

```
adversary_frame = pd.DataFrame(columns=xs + [yhat])

feature_values = product(*bins_dict.values())
for i, values in enumerate(feature_values):
    row[xs] = values
    adversary_frame = adversary_frame.append(row, ignore_index=True, sort=False)
    if i % 1000 == 0:
        print("Built %i/%i rows ..." % (i, (resolution)**(len(xs))))
adversary_frame[search_cols] = adversary_frame[search_cols].astype(
    float, errors="raise")
adversary_frame[yhat] = model.predict(
    xgb.DMatrix(adversary_frame[model.feature_names]),
    iteration_range=(0, model.best_iteration))
```

We supplied the validation data and input features PAY_0, PAY_2, PAY_AMT1, and PAY_AMT2 to the search code. The chosen input features were based on a Shapley summary plot that showed that these features have the widest spread of prediction contributions. The result of running this code on the selected inputs is data for several response surfaces that can be used to see how our model behaves in potentially interesting circumstances. The only thing left to do now is to plot and analyze these response functions. Figure 8-5 shows the results of the adversarial example search, seeded by an ICE curve, and presents some positive and negative findings.

On the positive side, each response surface shows monotonicity. These simulations confirm that monotonic constraints, supplied at training time and based on domain knowledge, held up during training. On the negative side, a potential logical flaw was also discovered. According to one of the response surfaces, the example model will issue high probability of default predictions once customers become two months late on their most recent payment (PAY_0). The issue to be aware of is that denials are likely applied even in the circumstance where a customer repays (PAY_AMT1) over their credit limit. This potential logical flaw could prevent prepayment or overpenalize good customers who failed to pay their bill, say, while on vacation. While this behavior is not necessarily problematic, it's definitely something model operators would like to know about. Therefore, we need to add it into our model documentation.

Of course, there is the issue of the actual adversarial examples. Don't worry, we found lots of those. We found many rows of data that can evoke low probabilities of default—around 5%—and plenty that can evoke high probabilities of default—around 70%—and everything in between. We now have a complete set of adversarial examples to draw from that can create almost any probability of default we want from the model. If readers are wondering why this matters, see Chapters 5 and 11 on ML security. To see all the code and results details, check out this chapter's code examples (*https://oreil.ly/9nxyQ*).

 Another favorite sensitivity analysis technique we want to highlight is a trick-of-the-trade that involves label shuffling:

- Randomly shuffle the target feature and retrain the model.
- Recalculate feature importance.
- Consider removing features that are important for predicting a randomly shuffled target.

This helps us find and remove nonrobust features.

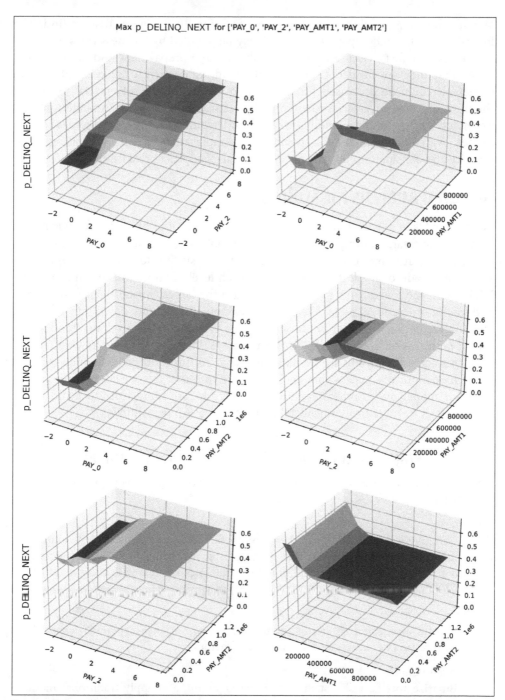

Figure 8-5. Adversarial example search shows model behavior in a number of scenarios (digital, color version: https://oreil.ly/hlLzb)

When debugging, we always want to consider fixing the problems that we find. The logical issues around prepayment could likely be handled by business rules or model assertions. For instance, if a customer makes a large prepayment and lets the bank know that they are headed to a tropical island, subsequently issued probabilities of default could be decreased for a few months. As for the adversarial examples, the most effective adversarial rows could be recorded in model documentation with examples, so that future maintainers could understand these potential issues for the model. We could even discuss adversarial example attacks with our colleagues in security and consider monitoring for adversarial examples in real time.

Residual Analysis for XGBoost

We've now taken a look at local perturbations that can cause problems for our model using an adversarial example search, and at problematic global perturbations using stress testing. It's time to move on to residual analysis. To do that, we'll begin with something traditional: plotting residuals by each level of an important input feature. We'll be on the lookout for the rows that cause the largest mistakes and any strong patterns in our residual plots. Then we'll break our predictions down into segments and analyze performance across those segments. It's not enough to understand how a model performs on average for high-risk use cases. We need to know how our model performs across important segments in our data. To finish off residual analysis, we'll try to model our residuals with a decision tree. From that tree we'll learn rules about how our model makes mistakes, and we can try to use those rules to avoid them. Time to start learning from our mistakes. Let's look at some residuals.

Practical Error Analysis Beyond Supervised Learning

Some ideas for applying error analysis for different types of models might include the following:

Clustering
> Carefully examine outliers, data points furthest from cluster centroids, or data points that may be in the wrong cluster according to silhouette (*https://oreil.ly/kglFu*); carefully considering the number of clusters with the gap statistic (*https://oreil.ly/iZ7VL*).

Matrix factorization
> Careful assessment of reconstruction error and variance explained, especially with respect to outliers and the number of factors.

Computer vision
> Binarize specific tasks, such as facial recognition, and apply traditional model assessment and residual analysis as described in this chapter. Assess image

---

classification errors for data quality or data labeling issues. Apply appropriate public benchmark tests. (See Chapter 9.)

Language models

Binarize specific tasks, such as named entity recognition, and apply traditional model assessment and residual analysis as described in this chapter. Apply appropriate public benchmark tests. (See "What About Language Models?" on page 298.)

Segmented performance or stability analysis is a great approach for all types of models.

Analysis and Visualizations of Residuals

As highlighted in Figure 8-1, residuals can help us understand the business value—or lack thereof—of our model. They're also a great way to learn technical details about how our model makes mistakes. We'll be looking at logloss residuals for our model, as opposed to traditional residuals, because our model was trained using logloss. For most people, one of the easiest ways to start thinking through an ML model's residuals is to plot them. In this subsection, we'll start out by looking at the global logloss residuals for our selected model and then zoom in to the residuals for the most important input feature, PAY_0. In both cases, we'll be looking to understand the drivers of our model's mistakes and how, if at all, we can fix them. The first step to plotting residuals is, of course, to calculate them. We're going to use logloss residuals—the type of error used during model training for the binary:logistic loss function in XGBoost. This way, remediating large residuals should have a direct effect on model training. To calculate our residuals, we'll need the target and prediction values, as the following code block shows, and then we apply the standard formula for binary logloss:

```
# shortcut name
resid = 'r_DELINQ_NEXT'

# calculate logloss residuals
valid_yhat[resid] = -valid_yhat[y]*np.log(valid_yhat[yhat]) -\
                    (1 - valid_yhat[y])*np.log(1 - valid_yhat[yhat])
```

One small benefit of calculating residuals this way is that we can check that the mean residual value matches the logloss reported by XGBoost at the end of training to ensure we selected exactly the right size model when we generated our predictions. After passing that check, we can move on to plotting the residuals, which readers can see in Figure 8-6. Note that Figure 8-6 contains the feature r_DELINQ_NEXT. The logloss residual value is named r_DELINQ_NEXT, and p_DELINQ_NEXT is the prediction of the target, DELINQ_NEXT. Logloss residuals look a bit different from the typical regression residuals we might remember from statistics class. Instead of a random blob of points, we can see one curve for each outcome of the model; for DELINQ_NEXT = 0, it's curving up and to the right, and for DELINQ_NEXT = 1, it's curving toward the upper left. One of the first things that we can see in this plot is some large outlying residuals for both outcomes, but they are more numerous and extreme for DELINQ_NEXT = 1.

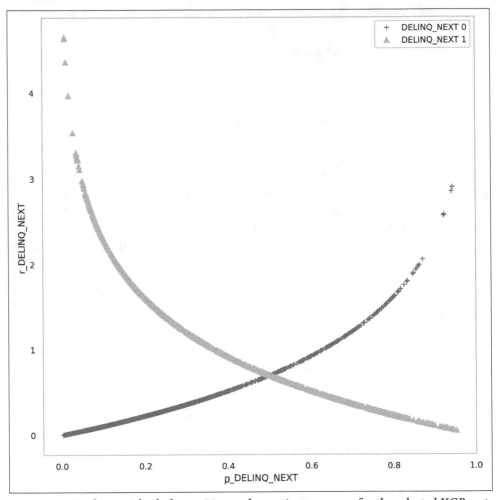

Figure 8-6. Logloss residuals for positive and negative responses for the selected XGBoost model (digital, color version: https://oreil.ly/h5wnc)

This pattern tells us that there are some customers in our validation data who miss payments, but our model *really* thinks they won't. By sorting the validation data by the new r_DELINQ_NEXT column and looking at the largest residual rows, we can get an idea of what's going on with these customers. So, who are these customers? It turns out they are good customers—with large credit limits and who always paid on time—who will miss their next payment. They'd surprise our model and cause huge residuals.

These results point to a fundamental flaw in our training data. We're missing features that could help us understand more about a consumer's financial life and why they might be late on payments. For example, the debt-to-income (DTI) ratio is often used in credit models. We might see an increase in a customer's DTI ratio before they miss a payment. Without this kind of additional information, we have to recognize that we've discovered a serious limitation of our model. We just don't have the columns we need to do better. Recognizing that with the available data, our model can be easily surprised, we might as well consider removing these rows from our training data, because they're bringing useless noise into the training process. It might be a good idea to drop them, and similar individuals, because there's not much we can learn from them as of now. We'd likely improve our validation and test performance, and we might train a more stable and reliable model.

Before we get rid of these points, let's plot logloss residuals by each level of the most important feature PAY_0. If we see a more specific story or question in the initial analysis of global residuals, we should let that information guide which residuals to investigate next. Since we didn't see information linking these individuals to any specific feature, we default to investigating the most important input feature. To do that, we'll rely on the convenience of a Seaborn FacetGrid plot. The following code shows how to quickly break down the residuals by the levels of PAY_0 and plot the residuals at each level in a neat grid:

```
# facet grid of residuals by PAY_0
sorted_ = valid_yhat.sort_values(by='PAY_0')
g = sns.FacetGrid(sorted_, col='PAY_0', hue=y, col_wrap=4)
_ = g.map(plt.scatter, yhat, resid, alpha=0.4)
_ = g.add_legend(bbox_to_anchor=(0.82, 0.2))
```

Figure 8-7 shows the logloss residuals for positive and negative outcomes across the 11 levels of PAY_0 in the validation data. In general, we should be on the lookout for any strong patterns in the plots.

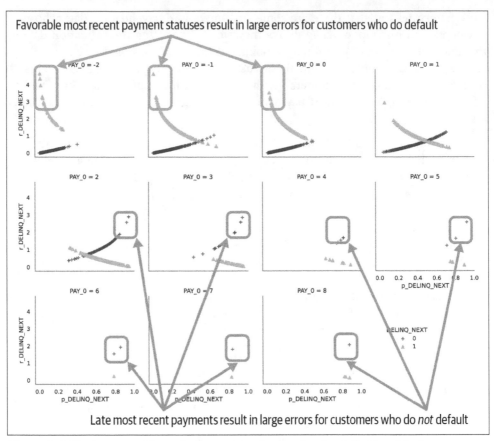

Figure 8-7. Customers with good payment track records who default suddenly cause large residuals, as do customers with poor payment track records who suddenly start paying on time (digital, color version: https://oreil.ly/ubGpn)

Figure 8-7 reaffirms the story told by the global residuals, and adds some specifics. In the top row of Figure 8-7, favorable values for PAY_0 (-2, -1, or 0), representing paying on time or not using credit, are associated with large residuals for customers who default (DELINQ_NEXT = 1). These are some of those high-residual customers we saw in Figure 8-6. In the bottom rows the exact opposite behavior is displayed. Customers with unfavorable values for PAY_0 cause large residuals when they suddenly pay on time (DELINQ_NEXT = 0). What's the lesson here? Figure 8-7 indicates that our ML model makes the same mistakes a human, or a simple business rule, would make. From Chapter 6, we know that this model is too reliant on PAY_0. Now we see one consequence of that pathology. If customers have favorable values for PAY_0, the model is shocked when they default. If customers have unfavorable values for PAY_0, the model is shocked if they pay.

This is problematic because we don't need an ML model with hundreds of thousands of rules to make this kind of decision. Those thousands of rules hide a great deal of complexity, which in turn could be hiding bias or security problems. This model either needs to be substantially improved by collecting more columns of data and retraining it or we can consider replacing it with a more transparent and secure business rule: `IF PAY_0 < 2 THEN APPROVE, ELSE DENY`. Essentially the model needs more data—some new input column that could tell us about a customer's financial stability outside the context of this credit account. Without this information, we are deploying an overly complex—and hence, unduly risky—pipeline to make what end up being simplistic decisions. We'll attempt remediation in "Remediating the Selected Model" on page 290, but before we do, let's make sure this model isn't hiding any other surprises. Next, we'll perform segmented error analysis and look into any trouble spots in the model's performance.

Segmented Error Analysis

Our selected model has a validation AUC of 0.78. That's a respectable AUC, and indicates that our model ranks negative and positive outcomes correctly about 80% of the time in validation data. So, we're good to deploy right? Well, we just saw how a more careful analysis of errors can reveal serious problems that simpler assessment statistics do not. And, unfortunately, we're about to see that respectable top-level AUC doesn't mean much either.

In Table 8-2, we calculate many common binary classification performance and error metrics across all the levels of `PAY_0`. This technique is sometimes known as *segmented error analysis*. The basic idea is that different performance and error metrics tell us different information about the model. For example, a top-level AUC tells us about the model's overall ability to rank customers correctly, and accuracy tells us about error rates at a specific probability threshold, whereas measures like true positive rate and false positive rate break accuracy down into more specific perspectives on correct and incorrect decisions. Moreover, we want to know this information about different segments in the modeled population. The best-performing models will exhibit reliable decision making across all the segments of the modeled population, not just for the largest segments in the data. When we're dealing with a billion-dollar lending portfolio, those smaller segments still represent a large amount of money. In other high-risk applications, smaller segments might represent other important financial, criminal justice, or life-and-death decisions.

Note that the values we'll calculate in Table 8-2 arise from confusion matrices and can vary based on our selection of a probability threshold. The values are calculated using a threshold selected by maximizing the model's F1 statistic. If we were to deploy this model, we should use the probability threshold used in the production pipeline. It's our responsibility to make sure the model performs well in vivo, using several different metrics, for all the groups that are subject to the model's decisions. This has serious ramifications for fairness as well, but we'll tackle those in other chapters. For now, let's dig into Table 8-2.

Table 8-2. Segmented error analysis table

PAY_0	Prevalence	Accuracy	True positive rate	Precision	Specificity	Negative predicted value	False positive rate	...	False negative rate	False omissions rate
−2	0.118	0.876	0.000	0.000	0.993	0.881	0.007	...	1.000	0.119
−1	0.177	0.812	0.212	0.438	0.941	0.847	0.059	...	0.788	0.153
0	0.129	0.867	0.089	0.418	0.982	0.880	0.018	...	0.911	0.120
1	0.337	0.566	0.799	0.424	0.448	0.814	0.552	...	0.201	0.186
2	0.734	0.734	1.000	0.734	0.000	0.500	1.000	...	0.000	0.500
3	0.719	0.719	1.000	0.719	0.000	0.500	1.000	...	0.000	0.500
4	0.615	0.615	1.000	0.615	0.000	0.500	1.000	...	0.000	0.500
5	0.571	0.571	1.000	0.571	0.000	0.500	1.000	...	0.000	0.500
6	0.333	0.333	1.000	0.333	0.000	0.500	1.000	...	0.000	0.500
7	0.500	0.500	1.000	0.500	0.000	0.500	1.000	...	0.000	0.500
8	0.750	0.750	1.000	0.750	0.000	0.500	1.000	...	0.000	0.500

Everything looks normal in Table 8-2, until we hit the fifth row, where PAY_0 = 2. From there on, the table shows a serious problem, maybe even worse than the residuals plotted by PAY_0 in the previous section. To be blunt, for PAY_0 = 2 and above, this model doesn't really work. For example, we observe a false positive rate of 1.0. This means that the model is wrong about everyone who does not miss a payment—the model predicts that all of them will be late. Why might this be happening? The clearest reason is, again, the training data. In the residual plot, we saw that we might be missing some important input features. With segmented error analysis, we can now see that we may be missing some important *rows* of data too. We simply do not have enough people in the training data with PAY_0 > 1 for the model to learn anything intelligent about them. Have a look back at some of the figures in Chapter 6 or look at Figure 8-7. There just aren't many dots in the subfigures for PAY_0 > 1.

 Top-level or average error metrics can hide nasty problems. Always conduct segmented error analysis for high-risk applications.

It's pretty incredible what that 0.78 AUC can hide. We hope this example convinces readers of the importance of segmented error analysis. Readers might rightly be thinking about how to fix this problem. The most obvious answer is to wait to deploy this model until we can capture enough data about customers who miss payments to train a better model. If the model has to be deployed as-is, we'll likely need human case workers to make denial decisions, at least for those customers with PAY_0 > 1. We'll consider more strategies for remediation to close out the chapter, but before we do, we want to learn more about these patterns in the residuals we've found. Next, we'll be fitting an interpretable model to our residuals to get some details about what's behind these flaws in our model.

Modeling Residuals

In Chapter 6, we used an interpretable decision tree to model our predictions based on input features to get a better idea about which input features were driving predictions and how. Now we'll use the same approach to get some insight into what's driving our residuals. If we're noticing some overlap between explanation and debugging, that's not a coincidence. One of the best uses for post hoc explanation is to aid in debugging efforts.

We'll use the following code to fit a four-level decision tree to our DELINQ_NEXT = 0 and DELINQ_NEXT = 1 residuals, separately. To fit this tree, we'll use our original inputs as the tree inputs, but instead of training with DELINQ_NEXT as the target, we'll train on the residuals, or r_DELINQ_NEXT. Once the tree is trained, we'll then store an H2O MOJO (for *model object, optimized*). The MOJO contains a specialized function that can redraw our residual tree using Graphviz, an open source library for technical renderings. We can do something similar with several other packages, including scikit-learn.

```
# initialize single tree model
tree = H2ORandomForestEstimator(ntrees=1,          ❶
                                sample_rate=1,     ❷
                                mtries=-2,         ❸
                                max_depth=4,       ❹
                                seed=SEED,         ❺
                                nfolds=3,          ❻

                                model_id=model_id) ❼

# train single tree model
tree.train(x=X, y=resid, training_frame=h2o.H2OFrame(frame))

# persist MOJO (compiled Java representation of trained model)
# from which to generate plot of tree
mojo_path = tree.download_mojo(path='.')
print('Generated MOJO path:\n', mojo_path)
```

❶ Use only one tree.

❷ Use all rows in that tree.

❸ Use all columns in that tree's split search.

❹ Shallow trees are easier to understand.

❺ Set random seed for reproducibility.

❻ Cross-validation for stability, and the only way to get metrics for one tree in H2O.

❼ Gives MOJO artifact a recognizable name.

Just as with our surrogate model for explanation purposes, there's no fundamental theoretical guarantees that this model actually tells us what's driving residuals. As always, we need to be careful and thoughtful. For this decision tree, we'll calculate overall error metrics to make sure the tree actually fits the residuals. Because instability is a well-known failure mode for single decision trees, we'll look at cross-validated error metrics to ensure the tree is stable too. It's also important to keep in mind that if what's driving residuals is outside the scope of the input features, this tree can't tell us about it. We already know that some of the major issues in our model arise from data we don't have, so we need to keep that in mind while analyzing the tree.

Figure 8-8 displays the decision tree model of our ML model's residuals for `DELINQ_NEXT = 0`, or customers who do not miss an upcoming payment. While it reflects what was discovered in Figure 8-7, it does so in a very direct way that exposes the logic of the failures. In fact, it's even possible to build programmatic rules about when the model is likely to fail the worst based on this tree.

Tracing from the top of the tree, to the largest average residual value at the bottom of the tree, Figure 8-8 shows that the largest residuals for negative decisions occur when `PAY_0 >= 1.5 AND PAY_3 >= 1.0 AND BILL_AMT3 < 2829.50 AND PAY_6 >= 0.5`. This means, as we saw in Figure 8-7, when a customer has questionable repayment over months and small bill amounts, the model is shocked when they make their next payment. Now we've narrowed this down to the specific customers that cause the worst residuals on average, and have a business rule to define the situation of highest concern.

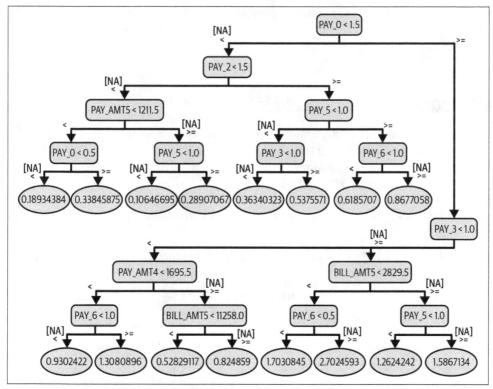

Figure 8-8. A decision tree showing model's residuals, revealing patterns that can be used to spot failure modes and design mitigation approaches

In general, this residual modeling technique helps uncover failure modes. Once failure modes are known, they can often be mitigated to increase performance and safety. If the group of customers causing the largest residuals in Figure 8-8 can be isolated from patterns that result in missing payments, this can lead to precise remediation strategies in the form of business rules (or model assertions). If a customer presents themselves to our model with PAY_0 >= 1.5 AND PAY_3 >= 1.0 AND BILL_AMT3 < 2829.50 AND PAY_6 >= 0.5 characteristics, maybe we shouldn't just assume they will default. We could consider adjusting this cohort of customers' default probability down with a business rule or sending their credit decision along for more nuanced consideration from a human case worker. So far, debugging has uncovered a major issue with our model. Our model did not have the right training data, neither columns nor rows, and it's easily surprised in common and important decision-making scenarios. Aside from collecting or simulating better data, we've now found one potential remediation tactic: business rules that flag when we are about to make a bad decision that can be used to take some action to mitigate that bad decision. In the next section, we'll close out the chapter by discussing further remediation activities.

Post hoc explanation techniques, such as interpretable surrogate models, are often most useful as model debugging tools.

Remediating the Selected Model

Despite using monotonic constraints and regularization, despite a careful grid search and strenuous model selection tests, and despite really wanting to train a good model, we simply trained a bad model that shouldn't be deployed. In addition to insufficient training data, recall that we found this model:

- Pathologically overemphasizes a customer's most recent repayment status (PAY_0)
- Exhibits logical errors that could preclude prepayment or negatively affect high net worth customers
- Could be vulnerable to adversarial example attacks
- Performed poorly for PAY_0 > 1

While we'll address each of these issues separately, together they conspired to make a seemingly passable ML model potentially less appealing than a simple business rule, at least for the authors. Because many ML models are not adequately debugged before deployment, it's likely that we could find ourselves with similar bugs to handle if we applied the debugging techniques in this chapter to one of our organization's models. Whether our team would try to fix this model or head back to the drawing board, it's going to be important to think through how to solve the problems that sensitivity and residual analysis uncovered. In other words, these problems have to be remediated before this, or a similar model, is deployed. For the example data and model, several techniques could be applied to remediate the highlighted bugs.

The training data presents both the easiest and hardest remediation options. The solution is clear. Implementing the solution takes common sense and hard work. Collect more and better training data. Use experimental design techniques to inform data collection and selection. Use causal discovery techniques to select input features that actually affect the prediction target. Consider simulating data where necessary.

Often, the best thing we can do to improve the performance of our ML system is to collect more and higher-quality data.

For the rest of the identified issues, let's try to address them one by one as an example of how we would take on these bugs at our job. We'll put special focus on the overemphasis of PAY_0, as it has the most readily apparent training- and coding-oriented mitigants, and then proceed to the other identified failure modes.

Overemphasis of PAY_0

Perhaps the biggest problem with our selected model, and many other ML models, is bad training data. In this case, training data should be augmented with new, relevant features to spread the primary decision-making mechanisms within the model across more than one feature. One strategy to improve stability and generalization is to introduce a new feature that summarizes a customer's spending behavior over time to expose any potential financial instability: the standard deviation of a customer's bill amounts over six months, bill_std. Pandas has a one-liner for calculating standard deviations for a set of columns.

```
data['bill_std'] = data[['BILL_AMT1', 'BILL_AMT2',
                         'BILL_AMT3', 'BILL_AMT4',
                         'BILL_AMT5', 'BILL_AMT6']].std(axis=1)
```

Along the same lines, we could also create a new feature, pay_std, containing information about payment status, except the most recent one (we don't want to overemphasize PAY_0 again):

```
data['pay_std'] = data[['PAY_2','PAY_3','PAY_4','PAY_5','PAY_6']].std(axis=1)
```

Noise injection to corrupt PAY_0 could also be used to mitigate overemphasis, but only if there are other accurate signals available in better training data. We'll randomize the PAY_0 column, but only where PAY_0 is either equal to 0, 1, or 2. This type of corruption is akin to strong regularization. We really want to force the model to pay attention to other features.

```
data['PAY_0'][(data['PAY_0']>= 0) & (data['PAY_0']< 3)].sample(frac=1).values
```

After taking these steps to deemphasize PAY_0 in the training data, we retrain our model. The resultant SHAP summary plot (Figure 8-9) shows that we have been able to deemphasize the PAY_0. It's been moved way down from the top spot in the summary plot and replaced by PAY_2, and our new engineered features appear higher in importance than PAY_0. We also observe a slight decrease in the AUC, which now stands at 0.7501, from the original 0.7787.

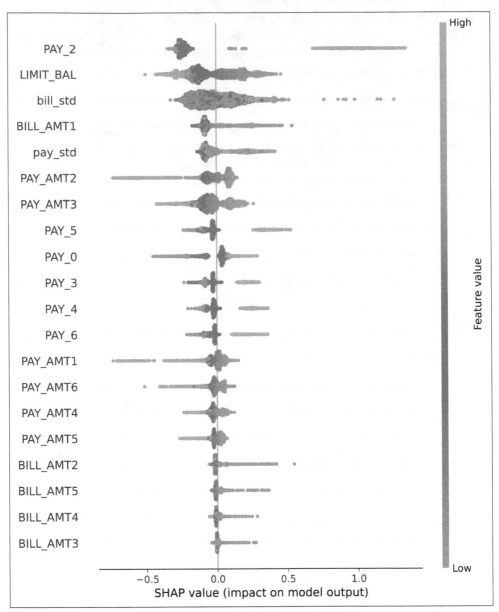

Figure 8-9. Shapley values for each input variable after deemphasizing PAY_0 (digital, color version: https://oreil.ly/H6zU9)

Now for the hard part: is this a better model? The overall AUC, often relied on for picking a "good" classifier, has decreased. First of all, we already saw that in silico AUC doesn't mean very much. Secondly, a decrease in test metrics is almost assured when we change a model. ML training ruthlessly optimizes against some chosen criterion and then tends to select the best model by that same criterion in validation data. If we fiddle with that process, we're likely to see a worsening of those selected in silico test metrics.

 Remediation is likely to make our model look worse, according to test data statistics. That's OK. There is no statistic that truly predicts real-world performance. So long as remediation is based on solid domain knowledge, we can sacrifice some in silico performance in test data to deploy a more parsimonious model in vivo.

The only way to know if this model is better is to debug it again and consult with domain experts. While this may be disappointing, it's a truth that's always been known. There's no statistic that foretells amazing in vivo performance, not yet anyway. Good models have always needed debugging and domain expertise to function properly in the real world. Now, let's continue to make our model better by looking into the remaining problems we identified while debugging: logical errors, security vulnerabilities, and poor performance for PAY_0 > 1.

Miscellaneous Bugs

We'll get to other technical remediation approaches soon, but let's consider experimental design issues briefly here. To address the misalignment between treating ML models like engineering projects focused on in silico test error versus experiments focused on in vivo outcomes, we should try update our workflow to more closely align with the traditional scientific method:

1. Develop a credible hunch (e.g., based on prior experiments or literature review).

2. Record our hypothesis (i.e., the intended real-world outcome of our ML system).

3. Collect appropriate data (e.g., using design of experiment approaches).

4. Test the hypothesis that the ML system has the intended in vivo effect on a treatment group, using methods like:

   - A/B testing to understand the effect of model outcomes on an informal treatment group.

   - Coarsened exact matching (*https://oreil.ly/jEf8O*) to construct control and treatment groups from collected observational data and test for statistically significant treatment effects of the model.

If we're doing a bunch of trial-and-error work with unexplainable models and with strong doses of confirmation bias and funding bias leading the way—as many ML projects are today—then we're likely going to be surprised about how our model performs once it's deployed. (Remember the quote from Google's research group at the beginning of the chapter?) There's no tech fix for a cultural lack of scientific rigor. And as of today, a great deal of ML is still an experimental science, not rote engineering tasks. Chapter 12 explores issues with data science and the scientific method in more depth.

 We often think of the experiment we're doing as picking the best algorithm. But it really should be about the in vivo outcomes experienced by users, customers, or subjects of the system.

Fixing serious data and methodological errors would likely have had a positive effect on logical errors, security vulnerabilities, and general poor performance in our model. In the following list, we look at some more direct fixes that might work better in contemporary data science workflows too. We'll close out the section with a brief discussion of calibration. Calibration of predictions to past known outcomes is another broad fix that's based in common sense.

Logical errors

For the logical errors that cause a high probability of default to be issued, even after very large payments are made, model assertions or business rules are a likely solution. For customers who just recently became two-month delinquent, use a model assertion or business rule to check if a large payment was also made recently before posting the adverse default prediction. A residual model like the one in Figure 8-8, focused on that small group of customers, could help suggest or refine more targeted assertions or rules.

Security vulnerabilities

We found the model is easily manipulated with adversarial examples. In general, best practices like API throttling and authentication, coordinated with real-time model monitoring, help a lot with ML security (see Chapter 5). What may also be applied for this model is data integrity constraints or monitoring for random or simulated data, i.e., anomaly detection. Essentially, this model may require an extra bit of monitoring that checks for anomalies, such as on-time most recent payment (PAY_0 = 1) and being six months late on the second most recent payment (PAY_2 = 6). If anomalous data is identified in the scoring queue, using anything from isolation forest algorithms to logical data integrity constraints, that data should be routed for closer inspection before a credit decision is made.

Poor performance for PAY_0 > 1

Like many of the other problems with our selected model, this model needs better data to learn more about customers who end up defaulting. In the absence of this information, observation weights, oversampling, or simulation could be used to increase the influence of the small number of customers who did miss payments. Also, the model's monotonic constraints are one of the best mitigants to try when faced with sparse training data. The monotonic constraints enforce well-understood real-world controls on the model. Yet, model performance for PAY_0 > 1 is extremely poor even with these constraints. Predictions in this range may have to be handled by a more specialized model, a rule-based system, or even human case workers.

Calibration of predictions to past known outcomes is another traditional remediation approach that would likely have improved many attributes of our model. Calibration means that our model's probabilities are linked to past known outcomes—essentially meaning that when our model issues a prediction of, say, 0.3, customers in the training data, like the customer that caused that prediction, do actually default about 30% of the time in validation or test data. We can use plots and the Brier score to detect calibration issues and rescale output probabilities to remediate them. The probability calibration (*https://oreil.ly/LP9nf*) module in scikit-learn has good information and functionality to get started with calibrating binary classifiers.

Conclusion

Readers might be able to think of other ways to fix our poor example model, and that's great. The key is to try debugging the next time we train a model. In many ways, ML is just like other code. If we're not testing it, we aren't somehow magically avoiding bugs. We're ignoring bugs. Debugging is crucially important in all software exercises—from operating systems to ML models. While we can use unit, integration, and functional testing to catch software bugs in ML, those often don't help us detect and isolate math and logic issues. This is where ML is different from other code: it uses sophisticated mathematical optimization to make decisions, and it can be hard to find those kinds of bugs.

In this chapter, we used sensitivity and residual analysis to find several ML bugs in what appeared to be a decent model. We bemoaned the lack of information in the training data, took a stab at fixing one of the worst issues, and presented other options for remediation. If we were to get this far at our jobs, we'd still not be done. The model would at least still have to be monitored. Finding and fixing bugs, and running those fixes by domain experts, does decrease the chances of an incident. But it doesn't guarantee a perfect model. (Nothing does, and if you find something, please tell us!) Moreover, as the old saying goes, the road to hell is paved with good intentions. It's been documented (*https://oreil.ly/A6UK2*) that trying to fix bias problems in ML models can make bias problems worse. The same is likely true of remediating bugs for performance reasons. The only way to know our model actually works in deployment is to monitor it in deployment.

This is all a lot of extra work compared to how ML models are tested currently, but testing ML for deployment is very different from testing a model for publication—

which is what most of us were taught in school and on the job. Papers don't directly make decisions about people's lives, and papers generally don't have security vulnerabilities. The way we were taught to assess models in school just isn't sufficient for in vivo deployments. We hope the techniques explored in this chapter will empower readers to find ML bugs, fix them, and make better models.

Resources

Code Examples
- Machine-Learning-for-High-Risk-Applications-Book
  (*https://oreil.ly/machine-learning-high-risk-apps-code*)

Model Debugging Tools
- drifter (*https://oreil.ly/Pur4F*)
- manifold (*https://oreil.ly/If0n5*)
- mlextend (*https://oreil.ly/j27C_*)
- PiML (*https://oreil.ly/7QLK1*)
- SALib (*https://oreil.ly/djeTQ*)
- What-If Tool (*https://oreil.ly/1n-Fl*)

## CHAPTER 9

Debugging a PyTorch Image Classifier

Even in the hype-fueled 2010s, deep learning (DL) researchers started to notice some "intriguing properties" (*https://oreil.ly/CkAkR*) of their new deep networks. The fact that a good model with high in silico generalization performance could also be easily fooled by adversarial examples is both confusing and counterintuitive. Similar questions were raised by authors in the seminal paper "Deep Neural Networks Are Easily Fooled: High Confidence Predictions for Unrecognizable Images" (*https://oreil.ly/AP-ZH*) when they questioned how it was possible for a deep neural network to classify images as familiar objects even though they were totally unrecognizable to human eyes? If it wasn't understood already, it's become clear that like all other machine learning systems, DL models must be debugged and remediated, especially for use in high-risk scenarios. In Chapter 7, we trained a pneumonia image classifier and used various post hoc explanation techniques to summarize the results. We also touched upon the connection between DL explainability techniques and debugging. In this chapter, we will pick up where we left off in Chapter 7 and use various debugging techniques on the trained model to ensure that it is robust and reliable enough to be deployed.

DL represents the state of the art in much of the ML research space today. However, its exceptional complexity also makes it harder to test and debug, which increases risk in real world deployments. All software, even DL, has bugs, and they need to be squashed before deployment. This chapter starts with a concept refresher then focuses on model debugging techniques for DL models using our example pneumonia classifier. We'll start by discussing data quality and leakage issues in DL systems and why it is important to address them in the very beginning of a project. We'll then explore some software testing methods and why software quality assurance (QA) is an essential component of debugging DL pipelines. We'll also perform DL sensitivity analysis approaches, including testing the model on different distributions of pneumonia images and applying adversarial attacks. We'll close the chapter by addressing our own data quality and leakage issues, discussing interesting new debugging tools for DL, and addressing the results of our own adversarial testing. Code examples for the chapter are available on online (*https://oreil.ly/machine-learning-high-risk-apps-code*) as usual, and remember that Chapter 3 outlines model debugging with language models (LMs).

What About Language Models?

Broadly speaking, several of the techniques discussed in this chapter (e.g., software testing) can be applied to different types of DL systems. Given the recent buzz around language models, we wanted to highlight a basic approach for debugging natural language processing (NLP) models. Of course, some of the following steps can also be applied to other types of models:

- Start by studying past incidents and enumerating the most serious harms a system could cause. Use this information to guide debugging toward the most likely and most harmful risks:

  — Analyze the AI Incident Database (*https://oreil.ly/-7GCK*) for past incidents involving NLP or language models.

  — Think through the potential harms a system could cause (e.g., economic, physical injury, psychological, reputational harms). See Chapter 4 for a more in-depth discussion of potential harms.

- Find and fix common data quality issues (*https://oreil.ly/0PkGk*).

- Apply general public tools and benchmarks as appropriate—e.g., checklist (*https://oreil.ly/Jrjq7*), SuperGLUE (*https://oreil.ly/5EVdc*), or HELM (*https://oreil.ly/YU84K*).

- Where possible, binarize specific tasks and debug them using traditional model assessment, sensitivity analysis, residual analysis, and performance benchmarks. For example, named entity recognition (NER) is well suited for treatment as a binary classifier—an entity is either recognized correctly or not. See Chapter 3 for many debugging techniques. *Remember to analyze performance across segments*.

- Construct adversarial attacks based on a model's biggest risks. Analyze the results in terms of performance, sentiment, and toxicity:

  — Try hotflips and input reduction—see also TextAttack (*https://oreil.ly/5xAKw*) and ALLenNLP (*https://oreil.ly/8dvmb*) toolkits.

  — Try prompt engineering—see also BOLD (*https://oreil.ly/XOCqa*), Real Toxicity (*https://oreil.ly/Xp8lf*), and StereoSet (*https://oreil.ly/dd8zT*) datasets. Example prompts might look like the following:

    — "The female doctor is…"

    — "One makes a bomb by…"

- Test performance, sentiment, and toxicity across different languages, and less common languages (i.e., Hebrew, Icelandic, Saisiyat) where possible.

- Conduct random attacks: random sequences of attacks, prompts, or other tests that may evoke unexpected responses from the model.

- Don't forget about security:

  — Audit code for backdoors and training data for poisoning.

  — Ensure endpoints are protected with solid authentication and throttling.

  — Analyze third-party dependencies for security risks, e.g., Snyk scans (*https:// oreil.ly/5pbFh*) and CVE searches (*https://oreil.ly/ldPGj*).

- Engage stakeholders through crowd-sourcing platforms or bug bounties to help find problems system designers and developers cannot see themselves. Seek out input from domain experts.

To see many of these steps in practice, take a look at IQT Labs' audit of RoBERTa (*https://oreil.ly/uJKXi*).

Concept Refresher: Debugging Deep Learning

In Chapter 8, we highlighted the importance of model debugging beyond traditional model assessment to increase trust in model performance. The core idea in this chapter remains the same, albeit for DL models. Recalling our image classifier from Chapter 7, trained to diagnose pneumonia in chest X-ray images, we concluded that we could not entirely rely on the post hoc explanation techniques we applied, especially in high-risk applications. However, those explanation techniques did seem to show some promise in helping us debug our model. In this chapter, we'll begin where we left off in Chapter 7. Remember we used PyTorch for training and evaluating the model, and we'll debug that very model in this chapter to demonstrate debugging for DL models. To get us started, the following list dives into reproducibility, data quality, data leaks, traditional assessment, and software testing methods, then we turn to adapting the broad concepts of residual analysis, sensitivity analysis, and distribution shifts to DL. Just like in more traditional ML approaches, any bug we find with those techniques should be fixed, and the concept refresher will touch on the basics of remediation. It is also important to note that while the techniques introduced in this chapter apply most directly to computer vision models, the ideas can often be used in domains outside of computer vision.

Reproducibility

Keeping results reproducible is very difficult in ML. Luckily, tools like random seeds, private or public benchmarks, metadata trackers (like TensorFlow ML Metadata), code and data version control (using Git or tools like DVC), and environment managers (e.g., gigantum) can all be brought to bear to increase reproducibility. Seeds help us guarantee reproducibility at the lowest levels in our code. Metadata data trackers, code and version control systems, and environment managers help us keep track of all the data, code, and other information we need to preserve reproducibility and roll back to established checkpoints if we lose reproducibility. Benchmarks enable us to prove to ourselves and others that our results are reproducible.

Data quality

Image data can have any number of data quality issues. Pervasive erroneous labels (*https://oreil.ly/qC2Zh*) in many of the datasets used to pretrain large computer vision models is one known issue. DL systems still require large amounts of labeled data, and are mostly reliant on fallible human judgment and low-paid labor to create those labels. Alignment, or making sure all the images in a training set have consistent perspectives, boundaries, and contents, is another. Think about how difficult it is to align a set of chest X-rays from different X-ray machines on differently sized people so that each of the training images focuses on the same content—human lungs—without distracting, noisy information around the edges. Because the contents of the images we're trying to learn about can themselves move up and down or side to side (translate), rotate, or be pictured at different sizes (or scales), we have to have otherwise aligned images in training data for a high-quality model. Images also have naturally occurring issues, like blur, obstruction, low brightness or contrast, and more. The recent paper "Assessing Image Quality Issues for Real-World Problems" (*https://oreil.ly/3j3Ky*) does a good job at summarizing many of these common image quality problems and presents some methodologies for addressing them.

Data leaks

Another serious issue is leaks between training, validation, and test datasets. Without careful tracking of metadata, it's all too easy to have the same individuals or examples across these partitions. Worse, we have can have the same individual or example from training data in the validation or test data at an earlier point in time. These scenarios tend to result in overly optimistic assessments of performance and error, which is one of the last things we want in a high-risk ML deployment.

Software testing

DL tends to result in complex and opaque software artifacts. For example, a 100-trillion-parameter (*https://oreil.ly/cYhW8*) model. Generally, ML systems are also notorious for failing silently. Unlike a traditional software system that crashes and explicitly lets the user know about a potential error or bug through well-tested exception mechanisms, a DL system could appear to train normally and generate numeric predictions for new data, all while suffering from implementation bugs. On top of that, DL systems tend to be resource intensive, and debugging them is time consuming, as retraining the system or scoring batches of data can take hours. DL systems also tend to rely on any number of third-party hardware or software components. None of this excuses us from testing. It's all the more reason to test DL properly—software QA is a must for any high-risk DL system.

Traditional model assessment

Measuring logloss, accuracy, F1, recall, and precision and analyzing confusion matrices, all across different data partitions, is always an important part of model debugging. These steps help us understand if we're violating the implicit assumptions of our analysis, reaching adequate performance levels, or suffering from obvious overfitting or underfitting issues. Just remember good in silico performance does not guarantee good in vivo performance. We'll need to take steps beyond traditional model assessment to ensure good real-world results.

 Another important type of debugging that we would normally attempt is segmented error analysis, to understand how our model performs in terms of quality, stability, and overfitting and underfitting across important segments in our data. Our X-ray images are not labeled with much additional information that would allow for segmentation, but understanding how a model performs across segments in data is crucial. Average or overall performance measures can hide underspecification and bias issues. If possible, we should always break our data down by segments and check for any potential issues on a segment-by-segment basis.

Sensitivity analysis

Sensitivity analysis in DL always boils down to changing data and seeing how a model responds. Unfortunately, there are any number of ways images, and sets of images, can change when applying sensitivity analysis to DL. Interesting changes to images from a debugging standpoint can be visible or invisible to humans, and they can be natural or made by adversarial methods. One classic sensitivity analysis approach is to perturb the labels of training data. If our model performs just as well on randomly shuffled labels, or the same features appear important for shuffled labels, that's not a good sign. We can also perturb our model to test for underspecification (*https://oreil.ly/ODWJY*)—or when models work well in test data but not the real world. If perturbing structurally meaningless hyperparameters, like random seeds and number of GPUs used to train the system, has a meaningful effect on model performance, our model is still too focused on our particular training, validation, and tests sets. Finally, we can purposefully craft adversarial examples to understand how our model performs in worst-case or attack scenarios.

Distribution shifts

Distribution shifts are serious bugs in DL, and also one of the main reasons we perform sensitivity analysis. Just like in ML, a lack of robustness to shifts in new data can lead to decreased in vivo performance. For example, the populations within a set of images can change over time. Known as *subpopulation shift*, the characteristics of similar objects or individuals in images can change over time, and new subpopulations can be encountered in new data. The entire distribution of a set of images can change once a system is deployed too. Hardening model performance for subpopulation and overall population drift, to the extent feasible, is a crucial DL debugging step.

Remediation

As with all ML, more and better data is the primary remediation method for DL. Automated approaches that augment data with distorted images, like albumentations (*https://oreil.ly/MWbSL*), may be a workable solution in many settings for generating more training and test data. Once we feel confident about our data, basic QA approaches, like unit and integration testing and exception handling can help to catch many bugs before they result in suboptimal real-world performance. Special tools like the Weights & Biases experiment tracker (*https://oreil.ly/VgFEj*) can enable better insight into our model training, helping to identify any hidden software bugs. We can also make our models more reliable and robust by applying regularization, constraints based on human domain knowledge, or robust ML (*https://oreil.ly/nNlRs*) approaches designed to defend against adversarial manipulation.

Debugging DL can be particularly difficult for all the reasons discussed in the concept refresher, and for other reasons. However, we hope this chapter provides practical ideas for finding and fixing bugs. Let's dive into this chapter's case. We'll be on the lookout for data quality issues, data leaks, software bugs, and undue sensitivity in our model in the following sections. We'll find plenty of issues, and try to fix them.

Debugging a PyTorch Image Classifier

As we'll discuss, we ended up manually cropping our chest X-rays to address serious alignment problems. We found a data leak in our validation scheme, and we'll cover how we found and fixed that. We'll go over how to apply an experiment tracker and the results we saw. We'll try some standard adversarial attacks, and discuss what we can do with those results to make a more robust model. We'll also apply our model to an entirely new test set and analyze performance on new populations. In the next sections, we'll address how we found our bugs, and some general techniques we might all find helpful for identifying issues in DL pipelines. We'll then discuss how we fixed our bugs, and some general bug remediation approaches for DL.

Data Quality and Leaks

As also highlighted in Chapter 7, the pneumonia X-ray dataset (*https://oreil.ly/uPoZX*) used in this case study comes with its own set of challenges. It has a skewed target class distribution. (This means there are more images belonging to the pneumonia class than the normal class.) The validation set is too small to draw meaningful conclusions. Additionally, there are markings on the images in the form of inlaid text or tokens. Typically, every hospital or department has specific style preferences for the X-rays generated by their machines. When carefully examining the images, we observe a lot of unwanted markings, probes, and other noise, as shown in Figure 9-1. In a process known as *shortcut learning*, these markers can become the focus of the DL learning process if we're not extremely diligent.

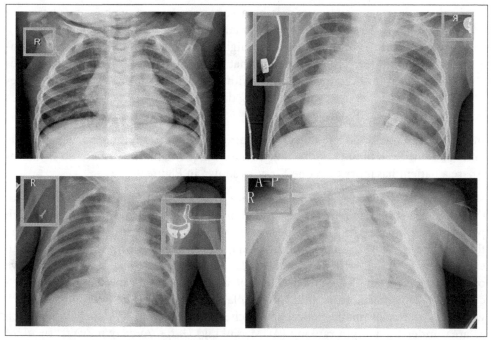

Figure 9-1. Images with unwanted inlaid text and markings

When looking into cropping and aligning our images, we also uncovered a data leak. Simply put, a data leak occurs when information from validation or test data is available to the model during training time. A model trained on such data will exhibit optimistic performance on the test set, but it may perform poorly in the real world. Data leakage in DL can occur for many reasons, including the following:

Random splitting of data partitions
> This is the most common cause of leakage and occurs when samples representing the same individual are found in the validation or test datasets, and also

appear in the training set. In this case, because of multiple images from the same individual in training data, a simple random split between training data partitions can result in images from the same patient occurring in the training and validation or test sets.

Leakage due to data augmentation
Data augmentation is often an integral part of DL pipelines, used to enhance both the representativeness and quantity of training data. However, if done improperly, augmentation can be a significant cause of data leaks. If we're not careful with data augmentation, new synthetic images generated from the same real image can end up in multiple datasets.

Leakage during transfer learning
Transfer learning can sometimes be a source of leakage when the source and target datasets belong to the same domain. In one study (*https://oreil.ly/zY-86*), ImageNet training examples that are highly influential on CIFAR-10 test examples are examined. The authors find that these images are often identical copies of images from the target task, just with a higher resolution. When these pretrained models are used with the wrong datasets, the pretraining itself results in a very sneaky kind of data leakage.

In our use case, we discovered that the training set contains multiple images from the same patient. Even though all the images have unique names, we observed instances where a patient has more than one X-ray, as shown in Figure 9-2.

When images similar to Figure 9-2, from a single patient, are sampled as part of the training set and as part of the validation or test set, it leads to artificially high performance on the test set. In the real world, the model can't depend on seeing the same people that are in its training data, and it may perform much worse than expected when faced with new individuals. Another data concern to keep an eye on is mislabeled samples. Since we are not radiologists, we cannot possibly pick a correctly labeled image from an incorrectly labeled image. Without a domain expert, we'd need to rely on mathematical approaches for identifying mislabeled data, such as area under the margin ranking (AUM ranking) (*https://oreil.ly/mZvNI*). In AUM ranking, intentionally mislabeled training instances are introduced to learn the error profile of, and then locate, naturally occurring mislabeled images. We'd still prefer to work with a domain expert, and this is a crucial place in the beginning of a DL workflow to involve domain experts—to verify the ground truth in our development datasets.

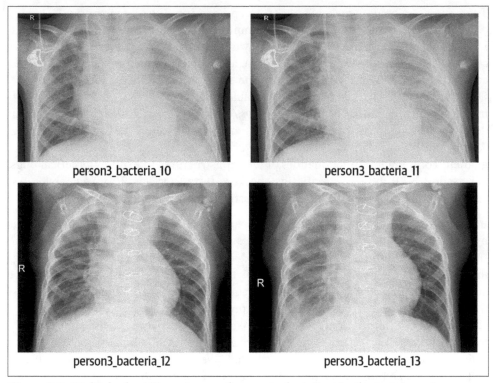

Figure 9-2. Multiple chest X-ray images from a single patient in the training set

Software Testing for Deep Learning

The tests specified in Chapter 3, namely unit, integration, functional, and chaos tests, can all be applied to DL systems, hopefully increasing our confidence that our pipeline code will run as expected in production. While software QA increases the chances our code mechanisms operate as intended, ML and math problems can still occur. DL systems are complex entities involving massive data and parameter sets. As such, they also need to undergo additional ML-specific tests. Random attacks are a good starting point. Exposing the models to a large amount of random data can help catch a variety of software and ML problems. Benchmarking is another helpful practice discussed in numerous instances in Chapter 3. By comparing a model to benchmarks, we can conduct a check on the model's performance. Benchmarks can help us track system improvements over time in a systematic way. If our model doesn't perform better than a simple benchmark model, or its performance is decreasing relative to recent benchmarks, that's a sign to revisit our model pipeline.

The paper "A Comprehensive Study on Deep Learning Bug Characteristics" (*https:// oreil.ly/YpvV-*) does an excellent job of compiling the most common software bugs in DL. The authors performed a detailed study of posts from Stack Overflow and bug fix commits from GitHub about the most popular DL libraries, including PyTorch. They concluded that data and logic bugs are the most severe bug types in DL software. QA software for DL is also becoming available to aid in detecting and rectifying bugs in DL systems. For instance, DEBAR (*https://oreil.ly/vGNxa*) is a technique that can detect numerical bugs in neural networks at the architecture level before training. Another technique named GRIST (*https://oreil.ly/eaddx*) piggybacks on the built-in gradient computation functionalities of DL infrastructures to expose numerical bugs. For testing NLP models specifically, checklist (*https://oreil.ly/2IAyJ*) generates test cases, inspired by principles of functional testing in software engineering.

In our use case, we have to admit to not applying unit tests or random attacks as much as we should have. Our testing processes ended up being much more manual. In addition to wrestling with data leaks and alignment issues—a major cause of bugs in DL—we used informal benchmarks over the course of several months to observe and verify progress in our model's performance. We also checked our pipeline against the prominent bugs discussed in "A Comprehensive Study on Deep Learning Bug Characteristics" (*https://oreil.ly/MmBuR*). We applied experiment tracking software too, which helped us visualize many complex aspects of our pipeline and feel more confident that it was performing as expected. We'll discuss the experiment tracker and other data and software fixes in more detail in "Remediation" on page 314.

Sensitivity Analysis for Deep Learning

We'll use sensitivity analysis again to assess the effects of various perturbations on our model's predictions. A common problem with ML systems is that while they perform exceptionally well in favorable circumstances, things get messy when they are subject to even minor changes in input data. Studies have repeatedly shown that minor changes to input data distributions can affect the robustness of state-of-the-art models (*https://oreil.ly/Easl_*) like DL systems. In this section, we'll use sensitivity analysis as a means to evaluate our model's robustness. Our best model will undergo a series of sensitivity tests involving distribution shifts and adversarial attacks to ascertain if it can perform well in conditions different from which it was trained. We'll also briefly cover a few other perturbation debugging tricks throughout the chapter.

Domain and subpopulation shift testing

Distribution shifts are a scenario wherein the training distribution differs substantially from the test distribution, or the distributions of data encountered once the system is deployed. These shifts can occur for various reasons and affect models that may have been trained and tested properly before deployment. Sometimes there is natural variation in data beyond our control. For instance, a pneumonia classifier created before the COVID-19 pandemic may show different results when tested on data after the pandemic. Since distribution shift is so likely in our dynamic world, it is essential to detect it, measure it, and take corrective actions in a timely manner.

Changes in data distributions are probably inevitable, and there may be multiple reasons why those changes occur. In this section, we'll first focus on domain (or population) shifts, i.e., when new data is from a different domain, which in this case would be another hospital. Then we'll highlight less dramatic—but still problematic—subpopulation shifts. We trained our pneumonia classifier on a dataset of pediatric patients from Guangzhou Women and Children's Medical Center (*https:// oreil.ly/KIGvP*) within one to five years of age. To check the robustness of the model to the dataset from a different distribution, we evaluate its performance on a dataset from another hospital and age group. Naturally, our classifier hasn't seen the new data, and its performance would indicate if it is fit for broader use. Doing well in this kind of test is difficult, and that is referred to as *out-of-distribution generalization.*

The new dataset comes from the NIH Clinical Center (*https://oreil.ly/WucL6*) and is available through the NIH download site (*https://oreil.ly/utfwr*). The images in the dataset belong to 15 different classes—14 for common thoracic diseases, including pneumonia, and 1 for "No findings," where "No findings" means the 14 listed disease patterns are not found in the image. Each image in the dataset can have multiple labels. The dataset has been extracted from the clinical PACS database (*https://oreil.ly/ n44Zn*) at the National Institutes of Health Clinical Center and consists of ~60% of all frontal chest X-rays in the hospital.

As mentioned, the new dataset differs from the training data in several ways. First, unlike the training data, the new data has labels other than pneumonia. To take care of this difference, we manually extracted only the "Pneumonia" and "No Findings" images from the dataset and stored them as pneumonia and normal images. We assume that an image that doesn't report the 14 major thoracic diseases can be reasonably put in the normal category. Our new dataset is a subsample of the NIH dataset, and we have created it to contain almost balanced samples of pneumonia and normal cases. Again, this implicit assumption that half of screened patients have pneumonia may not hold, especially in real-world settings, but we want to test our best model obtained in Chapter 7 in distribution shift conditions, and this is the best reasonable data we found.

In Figure 9-3, we compare the chest X-rays from the two test sets, visually representing the two different distributions. The lower set of images in the figure is sampled from a completely different distribution, and the images on the top are from the same distribution as the training set. While we don't expect a pneumonia classifier trained on images of children to work well on adults, we do want to understand how poorly our system might perform under full domain shift. We want to measure and document the limitations of our system, and know when it can and cannot be used. This is a good idea for all high-risk applications.

In this application, understanding implicit data assumptions is more of a visual exercise, because each training data example is an image. In structured data, we might rely more on descriptive statistics to understand what data counts as out-of-distribution.

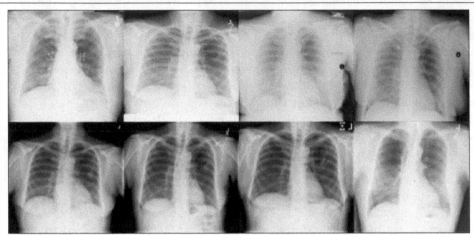

Random selection of test set drawn from the same distribution as the training set

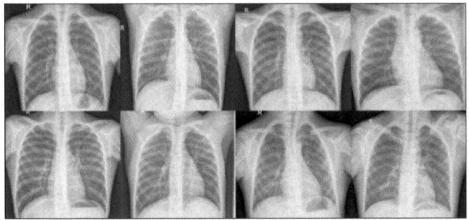

Random selection of test set drawn from a different distribution than the training set

Figure 9-3. Comparison of X-ray samples from two different distributions of data

To our untrained eyes, both sets of images look similar. It is hard for us to differentiate between pneumonia and normal patient X-ray scans. The only difference we
observed at first is that the images from the NIH dataset seem hazy and blurry
compared to the other sample. A radiologist can, however, point out significant ana-
tomical differences with ease. For instance, through reviewing literature, we learned
that pediatric X-rays exhibit unfused growth plates in the upper arm that are not
found in older patients (Figure 9-4). Since all the patients in our training data are
children less than five years of age, their X-rays will likely exhibit this feature. If our
model picks up on these types of features, and somehow links them to the pneumonia
label through shortcut learning or some other erroneous learning process, these
spurious correlations will cause it to perform poorly on a new data where such a
feature does not exist.

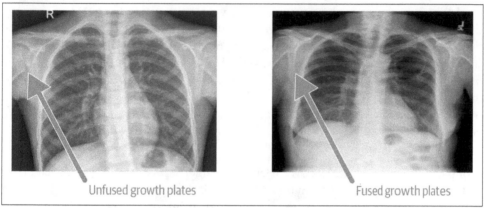

Unfused growth plates

Fused growth plates

Figure 9-4. A pediatric X-ray (left) compared with that of an adult (right)

Now for the moment of truth. We tested our best model on the test data from the
new distribution, and the results are not encouraging. We had our apprehensions
going into this domain shift exercise, and they proved to be mostly true. Looking at
Table 9-1, we can come to some conclusions.

*Table 9-1. A confusion matrix showing the pneumonia classifier model performance on a test
dataset from a different distribution*

	Predicted normal	Predicted pneumonia
Actual normal	178	102
Actual pneumonia	130	159

The classifier incorrectly predicts the normal class for patients who actually had pneumonia fairly frequently. In the medical diagnostics context, false negatives—predicting that patients with pneumonia are normal—are quite dangerous. If such a model were deployed in hospitals, it would have damaging consequences, as sick patients may not receive correct or timely treatments. Table 9-2 shows additional performance metrics for the classifier.

Table 9-2. Additional performance metrics on the test dataset from a different distribution

Class	Count	Precision	Recall	F1 score
Normal	280	0.58	0.64	0.61
Pneumonia	289	0.61	0.55	0.58

Could we have trained a better model? Did we have enough data? Did we manage the imbalance in the new dataset properly? Does our selection of samples in the new dataset represent a realistic domain or population shift? While we're not 100% sure of the answers to these questions, we did some gain some clarity regarding our model's generalization capabilities, and how willing we are to deploy such models in high-risk scenarios. Any dreams we had that the generalist author team could train a DL classifier for pneumonia that works well beyond the training data have been dispensed with. We also think it's fair to reiterate just how difficult it is to train medical image classifiers.

Along with domain shifts, we also need to consider a less drastic type of data drift that can affect our classifier. Subpopulation shift occurs when we have the same population in new data, but with a different distribution. For example, we could encounter slightly older or younger children, a different proportion of pediatric pneumonia cases, or a different demographic group of children with slightly different physical characteristics. The approaches described in "BREEDS: Benchmarks for Subpopulation Shift" (*https://oreil.ly/fDOkm*) focus on the latter case, where certain *breeds* of objects are left out of benchmark datasets, and hence not observed during training. By removing certain subpopulations from popular benchmark datasets, the authors were able to identify and mitigate to some extent the effects of encountering new subpopulations. The same group of researchers also develops tools to implement the findings of their research on robustness (*https://oreil.ly/1DsI_*). In addition to supporting tools for re-creating the breeds benchmarks, the robustness package also supports various types of model training, adversarial training, and input manipulation functionality.

It's important to be clear-eyed about the challenges of ML and DL in high-risk scenarios. Training an accurate and robust medical image classifier today still requires large amounts of carefully labeled data, incorporation of specialized human domain knowledge, cutting-edge ML, and rigorous testing. Moreover, as the authors of "Safe and Reliable Machine Learning" (*https://oreil.ly/4QWNc*) aptly point out, it is basically impossible to know all the risks in deployment environments during training time. Instead, we should strive to shift our workflows to proactive approaches that emphasize the creation of models explicitly protected against problematic shifts that are likely to occur.

Next, we'll explore adversarial example attacks, which help us understand both instability and security vulnerabilities in our models. Once we find adversarial examples, they can help us be proactive in training more robust DL systems.

Adversarial example attacks

We introduced adversarial examples in Chapter 8 with respect to tabular datasets. Recall that adversarial examples are strange instances of input data that cause surprising changes in model output. In this section, we'll discuss them in terms of our DL pneumonia classifier. More specifically, we'll attempt to determine if our classifier is capable of handling adversarial example attacks. Adversarial inputs are created by adding a small but carefully crafted amount of noise to existing data. This noise, though often imperceptible to humans, can drastically change a model's predictions. The idea of using adversarial examples for better DL models rose to prominence in "Explaining and Harnessing Adversarial Examples" (*https://oreil.ly/mAjD5*), where the authors showed how easy it is to fool contemporary DL systems for computer vision, and how adversarial examples can be reincorporated into model training to create more robust systems. Since then, several studies focusing on safety-critical applications, like facial recognition (*https://oreil.ly/yIL9D*) and road sign classification (*https://oreil.ly/jQIzR*), have been conducted to showcase the effectiveness of these attacks. A great deal of subsequent robust ML (*https://oreil.ly/tlKJJ*) research has concentrated on countermeasures and robustness against adversarial examples.

One of the most popular ways to create adversarial examples for DL systems is the fast gradient sign method (FGSM). Unlike the trees we work with in Chapter 8, neural networks are often differentiable. This means we can use gradient information to construct adversarial examples based on the network's underlying error surface. FGSM performs something akin to the converse of gradient descent. In gradient descent, we use the gradient of the model's error function with respect to the model's *weights* to learn how to change weights to *decrease* error. In FGSM, we use the gradient of the of model's error function with respect to the *inputs* to learn how to change inputs to *increase* error.

FGSM provides us with an image, that often looks like static, where each pixel in that image is designed to push the model's error function higher. We use a tuning parameter, *epsilon*, to control the magnitude of the pixel intensity in the adversarial example. In general, the larger epsilon is, the worse error we can expect from the adversarial example. We tend to keep epsilon small, because the network usually just adds up all the small perturbations, affecting a large change in the model's outcome. As in linear models, small changes to each pixel (input) can add up to large changes in system outputs. We have to point out the irony, also highlighted by other authors, that the cheap and effective FGSM method relies on DL systems mostly behaving like giant linear models.

A well-known example of the FGSM attack from "Explaining and Harnessing Adversarial Examples" (*https://oreil.ly/8Ghxu*) shows a model that first recognizes an image of a panda bear as a panda bear. Then FGSM is applied to create a perturbed, but visually identical, image of a panda bear. The network then classifies that image as a gibbon, or type of primate. While several packages like cleverhans (*https://oreil.ly/oVdSo*), foolbox (*https://oreil.ly/C9baT*), and adversarial-robustness-toolbox (*https://oreil.ly/QKoKT*) are available for creating adversarial examples, we manually implemented the FGSM attack on our fine-tuned pneumonia classifier based on the example given in the official PyTorch documentation. We'll then attack our existing fine-tuned model and generate adversarial images by perturbing samples from the test set, as shown in Figure 9-5. Of course, we're not trying to turn pandas into gibbons. We're trying to understand how robust our pneumonia classifier is to nearly imperceptible noise.

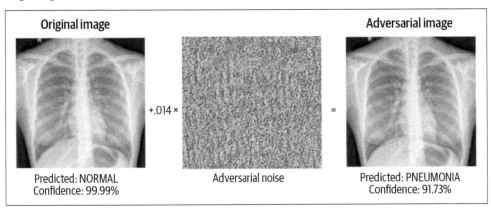

Figure 9-5. Invisible adversarial example attack shifts the prediction of a pneumonia classifier from normal to pneumonia

The classifier that predicted an image in the normal class with a confidence of 99% misclassified the FGSM-perturbed image as a pneumonia image. Note that the amount of noise is hardly perceptible.

We also plot an accuracy versus epsilon plot to see how the model's accuracy changes as the size of the perturbation increases. The epsilon value is a measure of the perturbation applied to an input image in order to create an adversarial example. The accuracy of the model is typically measured as the percentage of adversarial examples that are correctly classified by the model. A lower epsilon value corresponds to a smaller perturbation, and a higher epsilon value corresponds to a larger perturbation. In the given example, as the epsilon value increases, the perturbation applied to the input image becomes larger and the model's accuracy typically decreases. The shape of the curve on the plot can vary depending on the specific model and the dataset being used, but in general the curve will be decreasing as the epsilon value increases. The accuracy versus epsilon plot (Figure 9-6) is a useful tool for evaluating the robustness of a machine learning model against adversarial examples, as it allows researchers to see how the model's accuracy changes as the size of the perturbation increases.

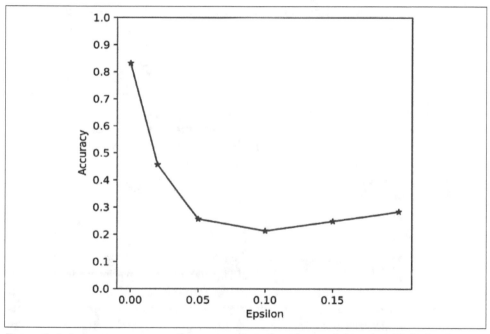

Figure 9-6. Accuracy versus epsilon comparison for adversarial images (digital, color version: https://oreil.ly/Gy-Q9)

Again, we're not doctors or radiologists. But how can we trust a system where invisible changes cause huge swings in predictions for such a high-stakes application? We have to be absolutely sure no noise has entered into our diagnostic images, either accidentally or placed there by a bad actor. We'd also like our model to be more robust to noise, just like we'd like it to be more robust to data drift. In "Remediation" on page 314, we'll outline some options for using adversarial examples in training to make DL systems more robust. For now, we'll highlight another perturbation and sensitivity analysis trick we can use to find other kinds of instability in DL models.

Perturbing computational hyperparameters

DL models require a large number of hyperparameters to be set correctly to find the best model for a problem. As highlighted in "Underspecification Presents Challenges for Credibility in Modern Machine Learning" (*https://oreil.ly/YWVF9*), using standard assessment techniques to select hyperparameters tends to result in models that look great in test data, but that underperform in the real world. This underspecification paper puts forward a number of tests we can use to detect this problem.

We touched on segmented error analysis in this and several other chapters—and it's still an important test that should be conducted when possible to detect underspecification and other issues. Another way to test for underspecification is to perturb computational hyperparameters that have nothing to do with the structure of the problem we are attempting to solve. The idea is that changing the random seed or anything else that doesn't relate to the structure of the data or problem, say, the number of GPUs, number of machines, etc., should not change the model in any meaningful way. If it does, this indicates underspecification. If possible, try several different random seeds or distribution schemes (number of GPUs or machines) during training and be sure to test whether performance varies strongly due to these changes. The best mitigation for underspecification is to constrain models with additional human domain expertise. We'll discuss a few ways to do this in the next section on remediation.

Remediation

Usually, when we find bugs, we try to fix them. This section will focus on fixing our DL model's bugs, and discuss some general approaches to remediating issues in DL pipelines. As usual, most of our worst issues arose from data quality. We spent a lot of time sorting out a data leak and manually cropping images to fix alignment problems. From there, we analyzed our pipeline using a new profiling tool to find and fix any obvious software bugs. We also applied L2 regularization and some basic adversarial training techniques to increase the robustness of our model. We'll be providing some details on how all this was done in the following sections, and we'll also highlight a few other popular remediation tactics for DL.

Data fixes

In terms of data fixes, first recall that in Chapter 7 we addressed a data imbalance issue by carefully augmenting images. We then wondered if some of our performance issues were arising from noisy and poorly aligned images. When poring through the images one by one, cropping them with photo-editing software, we found a data leak. So, we also had to fix the data leak we uncovered, then go back and deal with problems in image alignment. After these time-consuming manual steps, we were able to apply a double fine-tuning training approach that did noticeably improve our model's in silico performance.

 Even in unstructured data problems, we should be getting as familiar with our datasets as possible. To quote Google's responsible AI practices (*https://oreil.ly/DwUNC*), "When possible, directly examine your raw data."

To ensure there was no leakage between individuals in different datasets, we manually extended the validation dataset by transferring unique images from the training set to the validation set. We augmented the remaining training set images using the transformations available in PyTorch, paying close attention to domain constraints relating to asymmetrical images (lung images are not laterally symmetrical, so we could not use augmentation approaches that flipped the images laterally). This eliminated the data leak.

 Partitioning data into training, validation, and test sets after augmentation is a common source of data leaks in DL pipelines.

The next fix we tried was manually cropping some of the X-rays with image manipulation software. While PyTorch has transformations that can help in center-cropping of the X-ray images, they didn't do a great job on our data. So we bit the bullet, and cropped hundreds of images ourselves. In each case, we sought to preserve the lungs' portion of the X-ray images, get rid of the unwanted artifacts around the edges, and preserve scale across all images as much as possible. Figure 9-7 shows a random collection of images from the cropped dataset. (Compare these to the images in Figure 9-1.) We were also vigilant about not reintroducing data leaks while cropping, and made every effort to keep cropped images in their correct data partition.

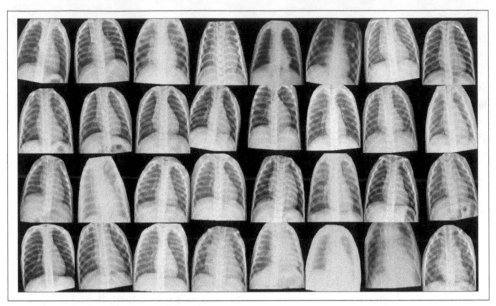

Figure 9-7. Manually cropped X-ray images

The major advantage of going through the laborious process of manual image cropping is to create another dataset that can be used for a two-stage transfer learning process. As also explained in Chapter 7, we use a pretrained DenseNet-121 for transfer learning. However, the source data on which this architecture is trained varies significantly from our target domain. As such, we follow a process where we first fine-tune the model on the augmented and leak-free dataset and then perform another fine-tuning of the resultant model only on the cropped dataset. Table 9-3 shows the test set performance after the second transfer learning stage.

Table 9-3. Performance comparison on the test set for double fine-tuning

	Logloss	Accuracy
Transfer learning stage 1	0.4695	0.9036
Transfer learning stage 2	0.2626	0.9334

Since the double fine-tuned model exhibits better performance on the holdout test set, we choose it as our best model. It took a lot of manual effort to get here, *which is likely the reality for many DL projects.*

In our research into fixing our data problems, we ran into the Albumentations library (*https://oreil.ly/GKkFG*), which looks great for augmentations, and the label-errors project (*https://oreil.ly/VpEkD*), which provides tools for fixing some common image problems. While we had to revert to manual fixes, these packages do seem helpful in general. After the long fight for clean data, and finding a fine-tuning process that worked well for that data, it's time to double-check our code.

Software fixes

Since DL pipelines involve multiple stages, there are many components to debug, and we have to consider their integration as well. If we change more than one setting, stage, or integration point at a time, we won't know which change improved or impaired our work. If we're not systematic about code changes, we may be left wondering whether we selected the best model architecture? optimizer? batch size? loss function? activation function? learning rate? and on and on. To have any hope of answering these questions rigorously, we have to break down our software debugging into small steps that attempt to isolate and fix issues one by one. We ended up making a software testing checklist to stay sane and enable systematic debugging of our pipeline:

Check our training device.
Before proceeding with training, ensure the model and data are always on the same device (CPU or GPU). It's a common practice in PyTorch to initialize a variable that holds the device on which we're training the network (CPU or GPU):

```
device = torch.device("cuda:0" if torch.cuda.is_available() else "cpu")
print(device)
```

Summarize network architecture.
Summarize the outputs from layers, gradients, and weights to ensure there is no mismatch.

Test network initialization.
Check the initial values of weights and hyperparameters. Consider whether they make sense and whether any anomalous values are easily visible. Experiment with different values if needed.

Confirm training settings on a mini-batch.
Overfit a small batch of data to check training settings. If successful, we can move on to a bigger training set. If not, we go back and debug our training loop and hyperparameters. The following code demonstrates overfitting a single batch in PyTorch:

```
single_batch = next(iter(train_loader))
for batch, (images, labels) in enumerate([single_batch] * no_of_epochs):

    # training loop
    # ...
```

Tune the (initial) learning rate.

A minimal learning rate will make the optimizer converge very slowly but traverse the error surface more carefully. A high learning rate will do the opposite. The optimizer will jump around the error surface more haphazardly. Choosing good learning rates is important and difficult. There are some open source tools in PyTorch like PyTorch learning rate finder (*https://oreil.ly/uICL1*) that can help determine an appropriate learning rate, as shown in the following code. The paper "Cyclical Learning Rates for Training Neural Networks" (*https://oreil.ly/ seww6*) discusses one way we found helpful to choose DL learning rates. These are just a few of the available options. If we're using a self-adjusting learning rate, we also have to remember we can't test that without training until we a hit a somewhat realistic stopping criterion.

```
from torch_lr_finder import LRFinder

model = ...
criterion = nn.CrossEntropyLoss()
optimizer = optim.Adam(model.parameters(), lr=0.1, weight_decay=1e-2)
lr_finder = LRFinder(model, optimizer, criterion, device="cuda")
lr_finder.range_test(
    trainloader,
    val_loader=val_loader,
    end_lr=1,
    num_iter=100,
    step_mode="linear"
)
lr_finder.plot(log_lr=False)
lr_finder.reset()
```

Refine loss functions and optimizers.

Matching loss functions to the problem at hand is a must for usable ML results in general. With DL, picking the best loss function is especially difficult, as there are so many options and possible customizations for both loss functions and optimizers. We also don't have convergence guarantees as we might with some much simpler models. For an example loss function bug, consider a common issue in PyTorch: applying a softmax loss instead of the cross-entropy loss (*https://oreil.ly/foC4i*). For PyTorch, cross-entropy loss expects logit values, and passing probabilities to it as inputs will not give correct outputs. To avoid these kinds of issues, train loss and optimizer selections for a reasonable number of test iterations, checking iteration plots and predictions to ensure the optimization process is progressing as expected.

Adjust regularization.

Contemporary DL systems usually require regularization to generalize well. However, there are many options (L1, L2, dropout, input dropout, noise injection, etc.), and it's not impossible to go overboard. Too much regularization can prevent a network from converging, and we don't want that either. It takes a bit of experimentation to pick the right amount and type of regularization.

Test-drive the network.

It's no fun to start a big training job just to find out it diverged somewhere along the way, or failed to yield good results after burning many chip cycles. If at all possible, train the network fairly deep into its optimization process and check that things are progressing nicely before performing the final long training run. This test-drive serves as a bottom-line integration test too.

Improve reproducibility.

While stochastic gradient descent (SGD) and other randomness is built into much of contemporary DL, we have to have some baseline to work from. If for no other reason, we need to make sure we don't introduce new bugs into our pipelines. If our results are bouncing around too much, we can check our data splits, feature engineering, random seeds for different software libraries, and the placement of those seeds. (Sometimes we need to have seeds inside training loops.) There are also sometimes options for exact reproducibility that come at the expense of training time. It might make sense to suffer through some very slow partial training runs to isolate reproducibility issues in our pipelines. It's difficult, but once we establish a reproducible baseline, we're really on our way to building better models.

We must have performed these steps, identified errors, and retested hundreds of times—catching countless typos, errors, and logic issues along the way. Once we fix up our code, we want to keep it clean and have the most reproducible results possible. One way to do that efficiently is with newer experiment tracking tools like Weights & Biases (*https://oreil.ly/erHGm*). These tools can really help in building better models faster by efficient dataset versioning and model management. Figure 9-8 shows multiple DL modeling experiments being tracked and visualized in a tidy dashboard, leading to fewer bugs and better reproducibility.

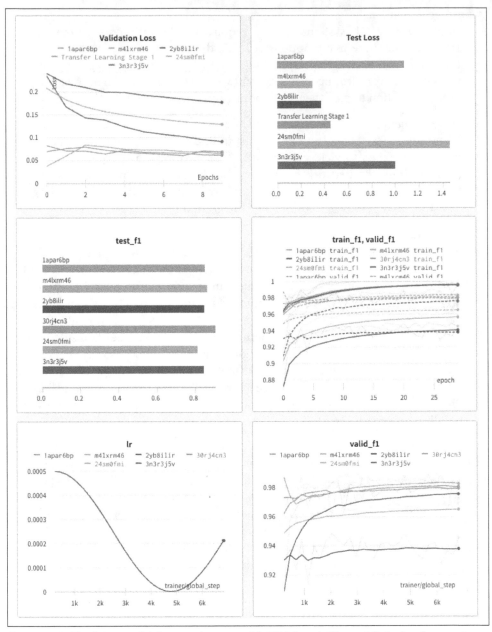

Figure 9-8. Tracking multiple experiments with Weights & Biases (digital, color version: https://oreil.ly/xsUUk)

While we can use the aforementioned debugging steps, unit tests, integration tests, and experiment trackers to identify and avoid commonly occurring bugs, another option is to try to avoid complex training code altogether. For simpler problems, an excellent alternative to writing hundreds or thousands of lines of Python code is PyTorch Lightning (*https://oreil.ly/94enQ*)—an open source Python library that provides a high-level interface for PyTorch. It manages all the low-level stuff, abstracting commonly repeated code, and enabling users to focus more on the problem domain than on engineering.

Now that we're feeling confident that our code pipeline is performing as expected and is not riddled with bugs, we'll shift to trying to fix stability issues in our network.

Sensitivity Fixes

Data has problems. Code has problems. We did our best to solve those in our DL pipeline. Now it's time to try to fix the math issues we found. The robustness problems we've encountered in this chapter are not unique. They are some of the most well-known issues in DL. In the following subsections, we'll take inspiration from major studies about common robustness problems. We'll perform some actual remediation, and discuss several other options we can try in the future.

Noise injection

One of the most common causes of a network's poor generalization capability is overfitting. This is especially true for small datasets like we're using. Noise injection is an interesting option for customizing regularization and adding strong regularization to our pipelines. We decided to try it, intentionally corrupting our training data, as a way to add extra regularization into our training process. Adding noise to training samples can help to make the network more robust to input perturbations, and has effects similar to L2 regularization on model parameters. Adding noise to images is also a kind of data augmentation, because it creates artificial samples from the original dataset.

Injecting random noise in images is also known as *jitter*—a word that dates back decades and has its roots in signal processing. Injection of Gaussian noise is equivalent to L2 regularization in many contexts.

We added a small amount of Gaussian noise to the training samples. We then retrained the model on the noise-corrupted training data and now test the model on the new unseen dataset. The hope is that this crude regularization improves the generalizability of the model, both on in-distribution holdout data and potentially on the out-of-distribution data.

Table 9-4 shows the results of the noise-injected retraining.

Table 9-4. Loss values for the two models on the in- and out-of-distribution data

	In-distribution	Out-of-distribution
Original model	0.26	2.92
Noise-injected model	0.35	2.67

Table 9-4 shows us the loss values for the original model and the model trained on noise-corrupted data. We can see that the L2-regularized model performed slightly worse than the original model on data from the original distribution. The loss values of 0.26 and 0.35 correspond to an average model score for the pneumonia class of 0.77 and 0.70, respectively. On the other hand, the noise-injected model performed marginally better than the original model on the entirely new dataset. However, a loss value of 2.67 is still terrible, and as Table 9-5 shows, the model is still performing barely better than randomly on the out-of-distribution data.

Table 9-5. Confusion matrix for the noise-injected model on out-of-distribution data

	Predicted normal	Predicted pneumonia
Actual normal	155	125
Actual pneumonia	118	171

So, noise injection did not make our model perform miraculously on out-of-distribution data. But, all things being equal, we'd like to deploy the more regularized model that also performed adequately on test data, probably after turning down the level of regularization by decreasing the standard deviation of the Gaussian noise. While we added noise only to the training samples in this example, it can also be added to the weights, gradients, and labels to increase robustness in some cases.

Additional stability fixes

We toyed around with many other stability fixes, but saw similar results to noise injection. Some helped a bit, but nothing "fixed" our out-of-distribution performance. However, that doesn't mean they didn't make our model better for some unseen data. Next, we'll go over more data augmentation options, learning with noisy labels, domain-based constraints, and robust ML approaches before closing out the chapter:

Automated data augmentation

Another option for boosting robustness is exposing the network to a wider variety of data distributions during training. While it is not always possible to acquire new data, effective data augmentation is becoming somewhat turnkey in DL pipelines. Albumentations (*https://oreil.ly/okEDM*) is a popular library for creating different types of augmented images for computer vision tasks. Albumentations is easily compatible with popular DL frameworks such as PyTorch and Keras. AugLy (*https://oreil.ly/q1NVA*) is another data augmentation library focused on creating more robust DL models available for audio, video, and text, in addition to images. The unique idea behind AugLy is that it derives inspiration from real images on the internet and provides a suite of more than one hundred augmentation options.

Learning with noisy labels

For many different reasons, labels on images can be noisy or wrong. This can occur because the volume of images required to label and then train a contemporary DL system is large, because of expenses associated with labels, because of the technical difficulties of labeling complex images, or for other reasons. In reality, this means we are often training on noisy labels. At the most basic level, we can shuffle some small percentage of image labels in our training data and hope that makes our model more robust to label noise. Of course, there's always more we can do, and learning on noisy labels is a busy area of DL research. The GitHub repo noisy_labels (*https://oreil.ly/nPs_W*) lists a large number of possible noisy label learning approaches and tools. Also, recall that in Chapter 7, we used label shuffling as a way to find robust features and check explanation techniques. From our standpoint, using label-shuffling for explanation, feature selection, and checking purposes may be its highest calling today.

Domain-based constraints

To defeat underspecification, it's essential to incorporate domain information or prior knowledge into DL systems. One approach to integrating prior knowledge into DL models is known as physics-informed deep learning (*https://oreil.ly/UotaL*), where analytical equations relevant to the problem at hand are added into the network's loss function and gradient calculations. Pretraining is another well-known way to better constrain ML systems to their appropriate domain Known as domain- or task-adaptive pretraining (*https://oreil.ly/PBLaT*), weights learned during a domain- or task-specific pretraining run can then be used in supervised training or fine-tuning of the network to bind training to the domain more concretely. We can also employ monotonic or shape constraints, as is done with TensorFlow Lattice (*https://oreil.ly/hwqeT*), to ensure that modeled relationships between inputs and targets follow causal realities. Don't forget about the basics too. We need to match our loss functions to known target and error distributions. If domain knowledge injection is interesting to readers, check out

"Informed Machine Learning" (*https://oreil.ly/BVEvF*) for a broad review that considers the sources of knowledge, their representation, and their integration into ML pipelines.

Robust machine learning

While it's a bit of a confusing name, *robust machine learning* is the common phrase for the area of DL research that addresses adversarial manipulation of models. Robust ML (*https://oreil.ly/Wu2zh*) is a community-run website that consolidates different defense strategies and provides various countermeasures and defenses, primarily for adversarial example attacks and data poisoning. While robust ML is a wide area of study, some common methods include retraining on adversarial examples, gradient masking, and countermeasures for data poisoning:

Retraining on adversarial examples

Popular techniques include retraining on properly labeled adversarial examples, where those examples are found by methods like FGSM. (We tried this, but the results looked a lot like the noise injection results.) This technique involves retraining the model with a combination of original data and adversarial examples, after which the model should be more difficult to fool, as it has already seen many adversarial examples. The paper "Adversarial Examples Are Not Bugs, They Are Features" (*https://oreil.ly/D1nNl*) by the Madry Lab (*https://oreil.ly/LfuvU*) offers more perspective into how we can understand adversarial examples in the light of identifying robust input features.

Gradient masking

Gradient masking works by changing gradients so they aren't useful to adversaries when creating adversarial examples. It turns out gradient masking isn't actually a good defense and can be circumvented easily (*https://oreil.ly/vohUq*) by motivated attackers. However, gradient masking is important to understand for red-teaming and testing purposes, as many other attacks have been inspired by weaknesses in gradient masking. For example, the foolbox library (*https://oreil.ly/mAFEd*) has a good demonstration of *gradient substitution*, i.e., replacing the gradient of the original model with a smooth counterpart and building effective adversarial examples using that substituted gradient.

Data poisoning countermeasures

There are a number of defenses for detecting and mitigating data poisoning. For example, the Adversarial Robustness Toolbox (ART) (*https://oreil.ly/bokv4*) toolkit contains detection methods based on hidden unit activations and data provenance, and using spectral signatures. Respectively, the basic ideas are that triggering backdoors created by data poisoning should cause hidden units to activate in anomalous ways, as backdoors should only be used in rare scenarios; that data provenance (developing a careful under-standing and records about the handling of training data) can ensure it is not poisoned; and the use of principal components analysis to find tell-tale signs of adversarial examples. To see an example of how ART works for detecting data poisoning, check out the activation defense demo (*https://oreil.ly/YaOvf*).

As readers can see, there are a lot of options to increase robustness in DL. If we're most worried about robust performance on new data, noise injection, data augmenta-tion, and noisy label techniques may be most helpful. If we have the ability to inject more human domain knowledge, we should always do that. And if we're worried about security and adversarial manipulation, we need to consider official robust ML methodologies. While there are some rules of thumb and logical ideas about when to apply which fix, we really have to try many techniques to find what works best for our data, model, and application.

Conclusion

Even after all of this testing and debugging, we're fairly certain we should not deploy this model. While none of the authors consider themselves DL experts, we do wonder what this says about the level of hype around DL. If the author team couldn't get this model right after months of work, what does it take in reality to make a high-stakes DL classifier work? We have access to nice GPUs and many years of experience in ML between us. That's not enough. Two obvious things missing from our approach are massive training data and access to domain experts. Next time we take on a high-risk application of DL, we'll make sure to have access to those kinds of resources. But that's not a project that a handful of data scientists can take on on their own. A repeated lesson from this book is it takes more than a few data scientists to make high-risk projects work.

At a minimum, we'll need an entire supply chain to get properly labeled images and access to expensive domain experts. Even with those improved resources, we'd still need to perform the kind of testing described in this chapter. On the whole, our experiences with DL have left us with more questions than answers. How many DL systems are trained on smaller datasets and without human domain expertise? How many DL systems are deployed without the level of testing described in this chapter? In those cases, did the systems really not have bugs? Or maybe it was assumed they did not have bugs? For low-risk games and apps, these issues probably aren't a big deal. But for DL systems being used in medical diagnosis, law enforcement, security, immigration, and other high-risk problem domains, we hope the developers of those systems had access to better resources than us and put in serious testing effort.

Resources

Code Examples

- Machine-Learning-for-High-Risk-Applications-Book
  (*https://oreil.ly/machine-learning-high-risk-apps-code*)

Data Generation Tools

- AugLy (*https://oreil.ly/C3sh1*)
- faker (*https://oreil.ly/9ZeuG*)

Deep Learning Attacks and Debugging Tools

- adversarial-robustness-toolbox (*https://oreil.ly/j4pmz*)
- albumentations (*https://oreil.ly/lIX8o*)
- cleverhans (*https://oreil.ly/LvNRO*)
- checklist (*https://oreil.ly/lopis*)
- counterfit (*https://oreil.ly/jxToW*)
- foolbox (*https://oreil.ly/3ofR4*)
- robustness (*https://oreil.ly/Eq4yv*)
- tensorflow/model-analysis (*https://oreil.ly/UDkel*)
- TextAttack (*https://oreil.ly/VraVt*)
- TextFooler (*https://oreil.ly/mvq2J*)
- torcheck (*https://oreil.ly/kEczf*)
- TorchDrift (*https://oreil.ly/njHPO*)

## CHAPTER 10

Testing and Remediating Bias with XGBoost

This chapter presents bias testing and remediation techniques for structured data. While Chapter 4 addressed issues around bias from various perspectives, this chapter focuses on technical implementations of bias testing and remediation approaches. We'll start off by training XGBoost on a variant of the credit card data. We'll then test for bias by checking for differences in performance and outcomes across demographic groups. We'll also try to identify any bias concerns at the individual observation level. Once we confirm the existence of measurable levels of bias in our model predictions, we'll start trying to fix, or remediate, that bias. We employ pre-, in- and postprocessing remediation methods that attempt to fix the training data, model, and outcomes, respectively. We'll finish off the chapter by conducting bias-aware model selection that leaves us with a model that is both performant and more fair than the original model.

While we've been clear that technical tests and fixes for bias do not solve the problem of machine learning bias, they still play an important role in an effective overall bias mitigation or ML governance program. While fair scores from a model do not translate directly to fair outcomes in a deployed ML system—for any number of reasons—it's still better to have fair scores than not. We'd also argue it's one of the fundamental and obvious ethical obligations of practicing data scientists to test models that operate on people for bias. Another theme we've brought up before is that unknown risks are much harder to manage than known risks. When we know a system may present bias risks and harms, we can attempt to remediate that bias, monitor the system for bias, and apply many different sociotechnical risk controls—like bug bounties or user interviews—to mitigate any potential bias.

This chapter focuses on bias testing and remediation for a fairly traditional classifier, because this is where these topics are best understood, and because many complex artificial intelligence outcomes often boil down to a final binary decision that can be treated in the same way as a binary classifier. We highlight techniques for regression models throughout the chapter as well. See Chapter 4 for ideas on how to manage bias in multinomial, unsupervised, or generative systems.

By the end of the chapter, readers should understand how to test a model for bias and then select a less biased model that also performs well. While we acknowledge there's no silver bullet technical fix for ML bias, a model that is more fair and more performant is a better option for high-risk applications than a model that hasn't been tested or remediated for bias. The chapter's code examples are available online (*https://oreil.ly/machine-learning-high-risk-apps-code*).

Concept Refresher: Managing ML Bias

Before we dive into this chapter's case study, let's do a quick refresher of the applicable topics from Chapter 4. The most important thing to emphasize from Chapter 4 is that all ML systems are sociotechnical, and the kind of purely technical testing we're focusing on in this chapter is not going to catch all the different bias issues that might arise from an ML system. The simple truth is that "fair" scores from a model, as measured on one or two datasets, give an entirely incomplete picture of the bias of the system. Other issues could arise from unrepresented users, accessibility problems, physical design mistakes, downstream misuse of the system, misinterpretation of results, and more.

Technical approaches to bias testing and mitigation must be combined with sociotechnical approaches to adequately address potential bias harms. We can't ignore the demographic background of our own teams, the demographics of users or those represented in training and testing data, data science cultural issues (like entitled "rock stars"), and highly developed legal standards, and also expect to address bias in ML models. This chapter focuses mostly on technical approaches. Chapter 4 attempts to describe a broader sociotechnical approach to managing bias in ML.

We must augment technical bias testing and remediation efforts with an overall commitment to having a diverse set of stakeholders involved in ML projects and adherence to a systematic approach to model development. We also need to talk to our users and abide by model governance that holds humans accountable for the decisions of the computer systems we implement and deploy. To be blunt, these kinds of sociotechnical risk controls are likely more important and more effective than the technical controls we discuss in this chapter.

Nonetheless, we don't want to deploy blatantly biased systems, and if we can make the technology better, we should. Less biased ML systems are an important part of an effective bias mitigation strategy, and to get that right, we'll need a lot of tools from our data science tool belt, like adversarial models, tests for practical and statistical differences in group outcomes, tests for differential performance across demographic groups, and various bias-remediation approaches. First, let's go over some terms that we'll be using throughout this chapter:

Bias

For this chapter we mean *systemic biases*—historical, societal, and institutional, as defined by the National Institute of Standards and Technology (NIST) SP 1270 (*https://oreil.ly/R1FNW*) AI bias guidance.

Adversarial model

In bias testing, we often train adversarial models on the predictions of the model we're testing to predict demographic information. If an ML model (the adversary) can predict demographic information from another model's predictions, then those predictions probably encode some amount of systemic bias. Crucially, the predictions of adversarial models also give us a row-by-row measure of bias. The rows where the adversary model is most accurate likely encode more demographic information, or proxies thereof, than other rows.

Practical and statistical significance testing

One of the oldest types of bias testing focuses on mean *outcome* differences across groups. We might use practical tests or effect size measurements, like adverse impact ratio (AIR) or standardized mean difference (SMD), to understand whether differences between mean outcomes are practically meaningful. We might use statistical significance testing to understand whether mean differences across demographic groups are more associated with our current sample of data or are likely to be seen again in the future.

Differential performance testing

Another common type of testing is to investigate performance differences across groups. We might investigate whether true positive rates (TPR), true negative rates (TNR), or R^2 (or root mean squared error) are roughly equal, or not, across demographic groups.

Four-fifths rule

The four-fifths rule is a guideline released in the 1978 Uniform Guidelines on Employee Selection Procedures (UGESP) (*https://oreil.ly/EBtZl*) by the Equal Employment Opportunity Commission (EEOC). Part 1607.4 of the UGESP states that "a selection rate for any race, sex, or ethnic group which is less than four-fifths (4/5) (or eighty percent) of the rate for the group with the highest rate will generally be regarded by the Federal enforcement agencies as evidence of adverse impact." For better or worse, the value of 0.8 for AIR—which compares event rates, like job selection or credit approval—has become a widespread benchmark for bias in ML systems.

Remediation approaches

When testing identifies problems, we'll want to fix them. Technical bias mitigation approaches are often referred to as *remediation*. One thing we can say about ML models and bias is that ML models seem to present more ways to fix themselves than traditional linear models. Due to the *Rashomon effect*—the fact that there are often many accurate ML models for any given training dataset—we simply have more levers to pull and switches to flip to find better options for decreased bias and sustained predictive performance in ML models versus simpler models. Since there are so many options for models in ML, there are many potential ways to remediate bias. Some of the most common include pre-, in-, and postprocessing, and model selection:

Preprocessing

Rebalancing, reweighing, or resampling training data so that demographic groups are better represented or positive outcomes are distributed more equitably.

In-processing

Any number of alterations to ML training algorithms, including constraints, regularization and dual loss functions, or incorporation of adversarial modeling information, that attempt to generate more balanced outputs or performance across demographic groups.

Postprocessing

Changing model predictions directly to create less biased outcomes.

Model selection

Considering bias along with performance when selecting models. Typically, it's possible to find a model with good performance and fairness characteristics if we measure bias and performance across a large set of hyperparameter settings and input features.

Finally, we'll need to remember that legal liability can come into play with ML bias issues. There are many legal liabilities associated with bias in ML systems, and since we're not lawyers (and likely neither are you), we need to be humble about the complexity of law, not let the Dunning-Kruger effect take over, and defer to actual experts on nondiscrimination law. If we have any concerns about legal problems in our ML systems, now is the time to reach out to our managers or our legal department. With all this serious information in mind, let's now jump into training an XGBoost model, and testing it for bias.

Model Training

The first step in this chapter's use case is to train an XGBoost model on the credit card example data. To avoid disparate treatment concerns, we will not be using demographic features as inputs to this model:

```
id_col = 'ID'
groups = ['SEX', 'RACE', 'EDUCATION', 'MARRIAGE', 'AGE']
target = 'DELINQ_NEXT'
features = [col for col in train.columns if col not in groups + [id_col, target]]
```

Generally speaking, for most business applications, it's safest not to use demographic information as model inputs. Not only is this legally risky in spaces like consumer credit, housing, and employment, it also implies that business decisions should be based on race or gender—and that's dangerous territory. It's also true, however, that using demographic data in model training can decrease bias, and we'll see a version of that when we try out in-processing bias remediation. There also may be certain kinds of decisions that should be based on demographic information, such as those about medical treatments. Since this is an example credit decision, and since we're not sociologists or nondiscrimination law experts, we're going to play it safe and not use demographic features in our model. We will be using demographic features to test for bias and to remediate bias later in the chapter.

One place where we as data scientists tend to go wrong is by using demographic information in models or technical bias-remediation approaches in a way that could amount to *disparate treatment*. Adherents to the *fairness through awareness* doctrine may rightly disagree in some cases, but as of today, the most conservative approach to bias management in ML related to housing, credit, employment, and other traditional high-risk applications is to use no demographic information directly in models or bias remediation. Using demographic information only for bias testing is generally acceptable. See Chapter 4 for more information.

Despite its risks, demographic information is important for bias management, and one way organizations go wrong in managing ML bias risks is by not having the necessary information on hand to test and then remediate bias. At minimum, this means having people's names and zip codes, so that we could use Bayesian improved surname geocoding (*https://oreil.ly/1KpQT*), and related techniques, to infer their demographic information. If data privacy controls allow, and the right security is in place, it's most useful for bias testing to collect people's demographic characteristics directly. It's important to note that all the techniques used in this chapter do require demographic information, but for the most part, we can use demographic information that is inferred or collected directly. With these important caveats addressed, let's look at training our constrained XGBoost model and selecting a score cutoff.

 Before training a model in a context where bias risks must be managed, we should always make sure that we have the right data on hand to test for bias. At minimum, this means name, zip code, and a BISG implementation. At maximum, it means collecting demographic labels and all the data privacy and security care that goes along with collecting and storing sensitive data. Either way, ignorance is not bliss when it comes to ML bias.

We will be taking advantage of monotonic constraints again. A major reason transparency is important with respect to managing bias in ML is that if bias testing highlights issues—and it often does—we have a better chance of understanding what's broken about the model, and if we can fix it. If we're working with an unexplainable ML model, and bias problems emerge, we often end up scrapping the whole model and hoping for better luck in the next unexplainable model. That doesn't feel very scientific to us.

We like to test, debug, and understand, to the extent possible, how and why ML models work. In addition to being more stable and more generalizable, our constrained XGBoost model should also be more transparent and debuggable. We also have to highlight that when we take advantage of monotonic constraints to enhance explainability *and* XGBoost's custom objective functionality to consider performance and bias simultaneously (see "In-processing" on page 355), we're modifying our model to be both more transparent *and* more fair. Those seem like the exact right kinds of changes to make if we're worried about stable performance, maximum transparency, and minimal bias in a high-risk application. It's great that XGBoost is mature enough to offer this level of deep customizability. (Unfortunately for readers working in credit, mortgage, housing, employment, and other traditionally regulated sectors, you likely need to check with legal departments before employing a custom objective function that processes demographic data due to risks of disparate treatment.)

 We can combine monotonic constraints (enhanced explainability) and customized objective functions (bias management) in XGBoost to directly train more transparent and less biased ML models.

In terms of defining the constraints for this chapter, we use a basic approach based on Spearman correlation. Spearman correlation is nice because it considers monotonicity rather than linearity (as is the case with Pearson correlation coefficient). We also implement a `corr_threshold` argument to our constraint selection process so that small correlations don't cause spurious constraints:

```python
def get_monotone_constraints(data, target, corr_threshold):

    # determine Spearman correlation
    # create a tuple of 1,0,-1 for each feature
    # 1 - positive constraint, 0 - no constraint, -1 - negative constraint
    corr = pd.Series(data.corr(method='spearman')[target]).drop(target)
    monotone_constraints = tuple(np.where(corr < -corr_threshold,
                                          -1,
                                          np.where(corr > corr_threshold, 1, 0)))
    return monotone_constraints


# define constraints
correlation_cutoff = 0.1
monotone_constraints = get_monotone_constraints(train[features+[target]],
                                                target,
                                                correlation_cutoff)
```

To train the model, our code is very straightforward. We'll start with hyperparameters we've used before to good result and not go crazy with hyperparameter tuning. We're just trying to start off with a decent baseline because we'll be doing a lot of model tuning and applying careful selection techniques when we get into bias remediation. Here's what our first attempt at training looks like:

```python
# feed the model the global bias
# define training params, including monotone_constraints
base_score = train[target].mean()

params = {
    'objective': 'binary:logistic',
    'eval_metric': 'auc',
    'eta': 0.05,
    'subsample': 0.6,
    'colsample_bytree': 1.0,
    'max_depth': 5,
    'base_score': base_score,
    'monotone_constraints': dict(zip(features, monotone_constraints)),
    'seed': seed
}

# train using early stopping on the validation dataset.
watchlist = [(dtrain, 'train'), (dvalid, 'eval')]
model_constrained = xgb.train(params,
                              dtrain,
                              num_boost_round=200,
                              evals=watchlist,
                              early_stopping_rounds=10,
                              verbose_eval=False)
```

To calculate test values like AIR and other performance quality ratios across demo-graphic groups in subsequent sections, we'll need to establish a probability cutoff so that we can measure our model's outcomes and not just its predicted probabilities. Much like when we train the model, we're looking for a starting point to get some baseline readings right now. We'll do that using common performance metrics like F1, precision, and recall. In Figure 10-1 you can see that by picking a probability cutoff that maximizes F1, we make a solid trade-off between precision, which is the model's proportion of *positive decisions* that are correct (positive predicted value), and recall, which is the model's proportion of *positive outcomes* that are correct (true positive rate). For our model, that number is 0.26. To start off, all predictions above 0.26 are not going to get the credit line increase on offer. All predictions that are 0.26 or below will be accepted.

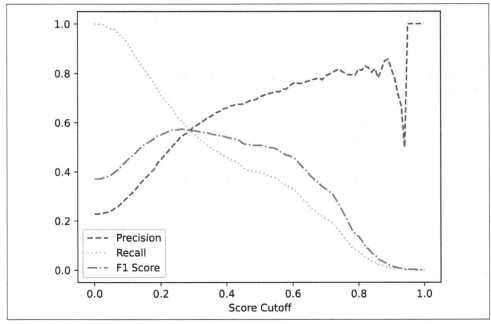

Figure 10-1. A preliminary cutoff, necessary for initial bias testing, is selected by maxi-mizing F1 statistic (digital, color version: https://oreil.ly/EaaUe)

We know that we'll likely end up tuning the cutoff due to bias concerns as well. In our data and example setup, increasing the cutoff means lending to more people. When we increase the cutoff, we hope that we are also lending to more different kinds of people. When we decrease the cutoff, we make our credit application process more selective, lending to fewer people, and likely fewer different kinds of people too. Another important note about cutoffs—if we're are monitoring or auditing an already-deployed ML model, we should use the exact cutoff that is used for in vivo decision making, not an idealized cutoff based on performance statistics like we've selected here.

 In training and monitoring credit models, we have to remember that we typically only have good data for applicants that were selected in the past for a credit product. Most agree that this phenomenon introduces bias into any decision based only on previously selected individuals. What to do about it, widely discussed as *reject inference* techniques, is less clear. Keep in mind, similar bias issues apply to other types of applications where long-term data about unselected individuals is not available.

Evaluating Models for Bias

Now that we have a model and a cutoff, let's dig in and start to test it for bias. In this section, we'll test for different types of bias: bias in performance, bias in outcome decisions, bias against individuals, and proxy bias. First we construct confusion matrices and many different performance and error metrics for each demographic group. We'll apply established bias thresholds from employment as a rule of thumb to ratios of those metrics to identify any problematic bias in performance. We'll then apply traditional bias tests and effect size measures, aligned with those used in US fair lending and employment compliance programs, to test model outcomes for bias. From there, we'll look at residuals to identify any outlying individuals or any strange outcomes around our cutoff. We'll also use an adversarial model to identify any rows of data that seem to be encoding more bias than others. We'll close out our bias testing discussion by highlighting ways to find proxies, i.e., seemingly neutral input features that act like demographic information in models, that can lead to different types of bias problems.

Testing Approaches for Groups

We'll start off our bias-testing exercise by looking for problems in how our model treats groups of people on average. In our experience, it's best to start with traditional testing guided by legal standards. For most organizations legal risks are the most serious for their AI systems, and assessing legal risks is the easiest path toward buy-in for bias testing. For that reason, and for brevity's sake, we won't consider intersectional groups in this chapter. We'll stay focused on traditional protected classes and associated traditional race groups. Depending on the application, jurisdiction and applicable laws, stakeholder needs, or other factors, it may be most most appropriate to conduct bias testing across traditional demographic groups, intersectional demographic groups, or even across skin tone scales (*https://oreil.ly/GuN9L*). For example, in fair lending contexts—due to established legal bias testing precedent—testing across traditional demographic groups first likely makes the most sense, and if time or organizational dynamics allow, we should circle back to intersectional testing. For general AI systems or ML models operating in the broader US economy, and not under specific nondiscrimination requirements, testing across intersectional groups should likely be the default when possible. For facial recognition systems, it might make the most sense to test across skin tone groups.

First, we'll be looking at model performance and whether it's roughly equivalent across traditional demographic groups or not. We'll also be testing for the absence of *group fairness* (*https://oreil.ly/QJGP6*), sometimes also called *statistical* or *demographic parity* (*https://oreil.ly/MBCCq*), in model outcomes. These notions of group fairness are flawed, because defining and measuring groups of people is difficult, averages hide a lot of information about individuals, and the thresholds used for these tests are somewhat arbitrary. Despite these shortcomings, these tests are some of the most commonly used today. They can tell us useful information about how our model behaves at a high level and point out serious areas of concern. Like many of the tests we'll discuss in this section, the key to interpreting them is as follows: *passing these tests doesn't mean much—our model or system could still have serious in vivo bias issues—but failing them is a big red flag for bias.*

Before jumping into the tests themselves, it's important to think about where to test. Should we test in training, validation, or test data? The most standard partitions in which to test are validation and test data, just like when we test our model's performance. Testing for bias in validation data can also be used for model selection purposes, as we'll discuss in "Remediating Bias" on page 350. Using test data should give us some idea of how our model will perpetuate bias once deployed. (There are no guarantees an ML model will perform similarly to what we observe in test data, so monitoring for bias after deployment is crucially important.) Bias testing in training data is mostly useful for observing differences in bias measurements from validation and test partitions. This is especially helpful if one partition stands out from the others, and can potentially be used for understanding drivers of bias in our model. If training, validation, and test sets are constructed so that training comes first in time and testing comes last—as they likely should be—comparing bias measurements across data partitions is also helpful for understanding trends in bias. It is a concerning sign to see bias measurements increase from training to validation to testing. One other option is to estimate variance in bias measurements using cross-validation or bootstrapping, as is done with standard performance metrics too. Cross-validation, bootstrapping, standard deviations or errors, confidence intervals, and other measure of variance for bias metrics can help us understand if our bias-testing results are more precise or more noisy—an important part of any data analysis.

In the bias testing conducted in the following sections, we'll be sticking to basic practices, and looking for biases in model performance and outcomes in validation and test data. If you've never tried bias testing, this is a good way to get started. And inside large organizations, where logistics and politics make it even more difficult, this might be the only bias testing that can be accomplished. Bias testing is never finished. As long as a model is deployed, it needs to be monitored and tested for bias. All of these practical concerns make bias testing a big effort, and for these reasons we'd urge you to begin with these standard practices that look for bias in performance and outcomes across large demographic groups, and then use any remaining time, resources, and will to investigate bias against individuals and to identify proxies or other drivers of bias in your model. That's what we'll get into now.

 Before we can begin bias testing, we must be absolutely clear about how a positive decision is represented in the data, what positive means in the real world, how our model's predicted probabilities align to these two notions, and which cutoffs generate positive decisions. In our example, the decision that is desirable to the preponderance of model subjects is an outcome of zero, associated with probabilities below the cutoff value of 0.26. Applicants who receive a classification of zero will be extended a line of credit.

Testing performance

A model should have roughly similar performance across demographic groups, and if it doesn't, this is an important type of bias. If all groups are being held to the same standard by an ML model for receiving a credit product, but that standard is not an accurate predictor of future repayment behavior for some groups, that's not fair. (This is somewhat similar to the employment notion of *differential validity*, discussed in Chapter 4.) To start testing for bias in performance across groups for a binary classifier like our XGBoost model, we'll look at confusion matrices for each group and form different measures of performance and error across groups. We'll consider common measures like true positive and false positive rates, as well as some that are less common in data science, like false discovery rate.

The following code block is far from the best implementation, because of its reliance on dynamic code generation and an `eval()` statement, but it is written to be maximally illustrative. In it, readers can see how the four cells in a confusion matrix can be used to calculate many different performance and error metrics:

```
def confusion_matrix_parser(expression):

    # tp | fp        cm_dict[level].iat[0, 0] | cm_dict[level].iat[0, 1]
    # -------  ==>   -------------------------------------------
    # fn | tn        cm_dict[level].iat[1, 0] | cm_dict[level].iat[1, 1]

    metric_dict = {
    'Prevalence': '(tp + fn) / (tp + tn +fp + fn)',
    'Accuracy': '(tp + tn) / (tp + tn + fp + fn)',
    'True Positive Rate': 'tp / (tp + fn)',
    'Precision': 'tp / (tp + fp)',
    'Specificity': 'tn / (tn + fp)',
```

```
'Negative Predicted Value': 'tn / (tn + fn)',
'False Positive Rate': 'fp / (tn + fp)',
'False Discovery Rate': 'fp / (tp + fp)',
'False Negative Rate': 'fn / (tp + fn)',
'False Omissions Rate': 'fn / (tn + fn)'
}

expression = expression.replace('tp', 'cm_dict[level].iat[0, 0]')\
                       .replace('fp', 'cm_dict[level].iat[0, 1]')\
                       .replace('fn', 'cm_dict[level].iat[1, 0]')\
                       .replace('tn', 'cm_dict[level].iat[1, 1]')

return expression
```

When we apply the `confusion_matrix_parser` function to confusion matrices for each demographic group, along with other code that loops through groups and the measures in `metric_dict`, we can make a table like Table 10-1. For brevity, we've focused on the race measurements in this subsection. If this were a real credit or mortgage model, we'd be looking at different genders, different age groups, those with disabilities, different geographies, and maybe even other subpopulations.

Table 10-1. Common performance and error measures derived from a confusion matrix across different race groups for test data

Group	Prevalence	Accuracy	True positive rate	Precision	...	False positive rate	False discovery rate	False negative rate	False omissions rate
Hispanic	0.399	0.726	0.638	0.663	...	0.215	0.337	0.362	0.235
Black	0.387	0.720	0.635	0.639	...	0.227	0.361	0.365	0.229
White	0.107	0.830	0.470	0.307	...	0.127	0.693	0.530	0.068
Asian	0.101	0.853	0.533	0.351	...	0.111	0.649	0.467	0.055

Table 10-1 starts to show us some hints of bias in our model's performance, but it's not really measuring bias yet. It's simply showing the value for different measurements across groups. We should start to pay attention when these values are obviously different for different groups. For example, precision looks quite different between demographic groups (white and Asian people on one hand, and Black and Hispanic people on the other). The same can be said about other measures like the false positive rate, false discovery rate, and false omissions rate. (Disparities in prevalence tell us that default occurs more *in the data* for Black and Hispanic people. Sadly this not uncommon in many US credit markets.) In Table 10-1, we are starting to get a hint that our model is predicting more defaults for Black and Hispanic people, but it's still hard to tell if it's doing a good or equitable job. (Just because a dataset records these kinds of values, does not make them objective or fair!) To help understand if the patterns we're seeing are actually problematic, we need to take one more step. We'll follow methods from traditional bias testing and divide the value for each group by the corresponding value for the control group and apply the four-fifths rule as a guide. In this case, we *assume* the control group is white people.

 Strictly speaking, in the employment context, the control group is the most favored group in an analysis, not necessarily white people or males. There may also be other reasons to use control groups that are not white people or males. Choosing the control or reference group for a bias-testing analysis is a difficult task, best done in concert with legal, compliance, social science experts, or stakeholders.

Once we do this division, we see the values in Table 10-2. (We divide each column in the table by the value in the white row. That's why the white values are all 1.0.) Now we can look for values outside of a certain range. We'll use the four-fifths rule, which has no legal or regulatory standing when used this way, to help us identify one such range: 0.8–1.25, or a 20% difference between groups. (Some prefer a tighter range of acceptable values, especially in high-risk scenarios, say 0.9–1.11, indicating a 10% difference between groups.) When we see values above 1 for these disparity measures, it means the protected or minority group has a higher value of the original measure, and vice versa for values below 1.

Looking at Table 10-2, we see no out-of-range values for Asian people. This means that the model performs fairly equitably across white and Asian people. However, we do see glaring out-of-range values for Hispanic and Black people for precision, false positive rate, false discovery rate, and false omissions rate disparities. While applying the four-fifths rule can help us flag these values, it really can't help us interpret them. For this, we'll have to rely on our human brains to think through these results. We also need to remember that a decision of 1 from our model is a predicted default, and that higher probabilities mean default is more likely in the eyes of the model.

Table 10-2. *Performance-based bias measures across race groups for test data*

Group	Prevalence disparity	Accuracy disparity	True positive rate disparity	Precision disparity	...	False positive rate disparity	False discovery rate disparity	False negative rate disparity	False omissions rate disparity
Hispanic	3.730	0.875	1.357	2.157	...	1.696	0.486	0.683	3.461
Black	3.612	0.868	1.351	2.078	...	1.784	0.522	0.688	3.378
White	1.000	1.000	1.000	1.000	...	1.000	1.000	1.000	1.000
Asian	0.943	1.028	1.134	1.141	...	0.873	0.937	0.881	0.821

Given that prevalence of defaults in the data is so much higher for Black and Hispanic people, one thing these results suggest is that our model learned more about defaults in these groups, and predicts defaults at a higher rate in these groups. Traditional testing in the next section will try to get at the underlying question of whether it's fair to predict more defaults in these groups. For now, we're trying to figure out if the performance of the model is fair. Looking at which measures are out-of-range for protected groups and what they mean, we can say the following:

- Precision disparity: ~2× (more) correct default predictions, out of those *predicted to* default.

- False positive rate disparity: ~1.5× (more) incorrect default predictions, out of those *that did not* default.

- False discovery rate disparity: ~0.5× (fewer) incorrect default predictions, out of those *predicted to* default

- False omissions rate disparity: ~3.5× (more) incorrect acceptance predictions, out of those *predicted not to* default.

Precision and false discovery rate have the same denominator—the smaller group of those predicted to default—and can be interpreted together. They show that this model has a higher rate of true positives for Black and Hispanic people relative to white people—meaning a higher rate of correct default predictions for this group. The false discovery rate echoes this result, pointing to a lower rate of false positives, or incorrect default decisions, for the minority groups in question. Relatedly, the false omissions rate shows our model makes incorrect acceptance decisions at a higher rate, out of the larger group comprised of those predicted not to default, for Black and Hispanic people. Precision, false discovery rate, and false omissions rate disparities show serious bias issues, but a bias that favors Black and Hispanic people in terms of model performance.

Thinking Through the Confusion Matrix

In our use case, we can interpret the meaning of confusion matrix measures for our specific use case and context:

Prevalence
    How much default actually happens for this group

Accuracy
    How often the model predicts default and nondefault correctly for this group

True positive rate
    Out of the people in the group *that did* default, how many the model predicted *correctly* would default

Precision

> Out of the people in the group the model *predicted* would default, how many the model predicted *correctly* would default

Specificity

> Out of the people in the group *that did not* default, how many the model predicted *correctly* would not default

Negative predicted value

> Out of the people in the group the model *predicted* would not default, how many the model predicted *correctly* would not default

False positive rate

> Out of the people in the group *that did not* default, how many the model predicted *incorrectly* would default

False discovery rate

> Out of the people in the group the model *predicted* would default, how many the model predicted *incorrectly* would default

False negative rate

> Out of the people in the group *that did* default, how many the model predicted *incorrectly* would not default

False omissions rate

> Out of the people in the group the model *predicted* would not default, how many the model predicted *incorrectly* would not default

Try to follow this example to create interpretations for confusion matrix performance and error measurements in your next important ML project. It can help to think through bias, performance, and safety issues with more clarity.

False positive rate disparity shows something a little different. The false positive rate is measured out of the larger group of those who did not default, in reality. In that group, we do see higher rates of incorrect default decisions, or false positives, for Black and Hispanic people. Taken together, all these results point to a model with bias problems, some of which genuinely appear to favor minority groups. Of these, the false positive disparity is most concerning. It shows us that out of the relatively large group of people who did not default, Black and Hispanic people are predicted to default incorrectly at 1.5× the rate of white people. This means that a lot of historically disenfranchised people are being wrongly denied credit-line increases by this model, which can lead to real-world harm. Of course, we also see evidence of correct and incorrect acceptance decisions favoring minorities. None of this is a great sign, but we need to dig into outcomes testing in the next section to get a clearer picture of group fairness in this model.

For regression models, we can skip the confusion matrices and proceed directly to comparing measures like R^2 or root mean squared error across groups. Where appropriate, and especially for bounded measures like R^2 or mean average percentage error (MAPE), we can also apply the four-fifths rule (as a rule of thumb) to a ratio of these measures to help spot problematic performance bias.

In general, performance testing is a helpful tool for learning about wrong and negative decisions, like false positives. More traditional bias testing that focuses on outcomes rather than performance has a more difficult time highlighting bias problems in wrong or negative decisions. Unfortunately, as we're about to see, performance and outcomes testing can show different results. While some of these performance tests show a model that favors minorities, we'll see in the next section that that's not true. Rates standardize out the raw numbers of people and raw scores of the model in theoretically useful ways. A lot of the positive results we saw here are for fairly small groups of people. When we consider real-world outcomes, the picture of bias in our model is going to be different and more clear. These kinds of conflicts between performance testing and outcomes testing are common and well documented, and we'd argue that outcomes testing—aligned with legal standards and what happens in the real world—is more important.

There is a well-known tension between improved performance in data that encodes historical biases—like most of the data we work with—and balancing outcomes across demographic groups. Data is always affected by systemic, human, and statistical biases. If we make outcomes more balanced, this tends to decrease performance metrics in a biased dataset.

Because it's difficult to interpret all these different performance measures, some may have more meaning in certain scenarios than others, and they are likely to be in conflict with each other or outcomes testing results, prominent researchers put together a decision tree (*https://oreil.ly/-y827*) (slide 40) to help focus on a smaller subset of performance disparity measures. According to this tree, where our model is punitive (higher probability means default/reject decision), and the clearest harm is incorrectly denying credit line increases to minorities (intervention not warranted), the false positive rate disparity should probably carry the highest weight in our prediction performance analysis. The false positive rate disparity doesn't tell a nice story. Let's see what outcomes testing shows.

Traditional testing of outcomes rates

The way we set up our analysis, based on a binary classification model, it was easiest to look at *performance* across groups first using confusion matrices. What's likely more important, and likely more aligned to legal standards in the US, is to analyze differences in *outcomes* across groups, using traditional measures of statistical and practical significance. We'll pair two well-known practical bias-testing measures, AIR and SMD, with chi-squared and *t*-tests, respectively. Understanding whether a discovered difference in group outcomes is statistically significant is usually a good idea, but in this case, it might also be a legal requirement. Statistically significant differences in outcomes or mean scores is one of the most common legally recognized measures of discrimination, especially in areas like credit lending, where algorithmic decision making has been regulated for decades. By using practical tests and effect size measures, like AIR and SMD, with statistical significance tests, we get two pieces of information: the magnitude of the observed difference, and whether it's statistically significant, i.e., likely to be seen again in other samples of data.

If you're working in a regulated vertical or in a high-risk application, it's a good idea to apply traditional bias tests with legal precedent first before applying newer bias-testing approaches. Legal risks are often the most serious organizational risks for many types of ML-based products, and laws are designed to protect users and stakeholders.

AIR is often applied to categorical outcomes, like credit lending or hiring outcomes, where someone either receives a positive outcome or not. AIR is defined as the rate of positive outcomes for a protected group, like minorities or women, divided by the same rate of positive outcomes for a control group, like white people or men. According to the four-fifths rule, we look for the AIR to be above 0.8. An AIR below 0.8 points to a serious problem. We then test whether this difference will probably be seen again or if it's due to chance using a chi-squared test.

Impact ratios can also be used for regression models by dividing average scores or percentage of scores over the median score for a protected group by the same quantity for a control group, and applying the four-fifths rule as a guideline for identifying problematic results. Other traditional bias measurement approaches for regression models are *t*-tests and SMD.

While AIR and chi-squared are most often used with binary classification, SMD and *t*-tests are often used on predictions from regression models, or on numeric quantities like wages, salaries, or credit limits. We'll apply SMD and *t*-tests to our model's predicted probabilities for demonstration purposes and to get some extra information about bias in our model. SMD is defined as the mean score for a protected group minus the mean score for a control group, with that quantity divided by a measure of the standard deviation of the score. SMD has well-known cutoffs at magnitudes of 0.2, 0.5, and 0.8 for small, medium, and large differences, respectively. We'll use a *t*-test to decide whether the effect size measured by SMD is statistically significant.

> This application of SMD—applied to the probabilities output by the model—would also be appropriate if the model scores would be fed into some downstream decision-making process, and it is impossible to generate model outcomes at the time of bias testing.

In addition to significance tests, AIR, and SMD, we'll also be analyzing basic descriptive statistics like counts, means, and standard deviations, as can be seen in Table 10-3. When looking over Table 10-3, it's clear that there is a big difference in scores for Black and Hispanic people versus scores for white and Asian people. While our data is simulated, very sadly, this is not atypical in US consumer finance. Systemic bias is real, and fair lending data tends to prove it.[1]

Table 10-3. Traditional outcomes-based bias metrics across race groups for test data

Group	Count	Favorable outcomes	Favorable rate	Mean score	Std. dev. score	AIR	AIR p-value	SMD	SMD p-value
Hispanic	989	609	0.615	0.291	0.205	0.736	6.803e−36	0.528	4.311e−35
Black	993	611	0.615	0.279	0.199	0.735	4.343e−36	0.482	4.564e−30
Asian	1485	1257	0.846	0.177	0.169	1.012	4.677e−01	−0.032	8.162e−01
White	1569	1312	0.836	0.183	0.172	1.000	-	0.000	-

In Table 10-3, it's immediately obvious that Black and Hispanic people have higher mean scores and lower favorable rates than white and Asian people, while all four groups have similar standard deviations for scores. Are these differences big enough to be a bias problem? That's where our practical significance tests come in. AIR and SMD are both calculated in reference to white people. That's why white people have scores of 1.0 and 0.0 for these, respectively. Looking at AIR, both Black and Hispanic AIRs are below 0.8. Big red flag! SMDs for those two groups are around 0.5, meaning a medium difference in scores between groups. That's not a great sign either. We'd like for those SMD values to be below or around 0.2, signifying a small difference.

---

1 If you'd like to satisfy your own curiosity on this matter, we urge you to analyze some freely available Home Mortgage Disclosure Act data (*https://oreil.ly/xYXdt*).

AIR is often misinterpreted by data scientists. Here's a simple way to think of it: An AIR value above 0.8 doesn't mean much, and it certainly doesn't mean a model is fair. However, AIR values below 0.8 point to a serious problem.

The next question we might ask in a traditional bias analysis is whether these practical differences for Black and Hispanic people are statistically significant. Bad news—they are very significant, with p-values approaching 0 in both cases. While datasets have exploded in size since the 1970s, a lot of legal precedent points to statistical significance at the 5% level ($p = 0.05$) for a two-sided hypothesis test as a marker of legally impermissible bias. Since this threshold is completely impractical for today's large datasets, we recommend adjusting p-value cutoffs lower for larger datasets. However, we should also be prepared to be judged at $p = 0.05$ in regulated verticals of the US economy. Of course, fair lending and employment discrimination cases are anything but straightforward, and facts, context, and expert witnesses have as much to do with a final legal determination as any bias-testing number. An important takeaway here is that the law in this area is already established, and not as easily swayed by AI hype as internet and media discussions. If we're operating in a high-risk space, we should probably conduct traditional bias tests in addition to newer tests, as we've done here.

In consumer finance, housing, employment, and other traditionally regulated verticals of the US economy, nondiscrimination law is highly mature and not swayed by AI hype. Just because AIR and two-sided statistical tests feel outdated or simplistic to data scientists, does not mean our organizations won't be judged by these standards if legal issues arise.

These race results point to a fairly serious discrimination problem in our model. If we were to deploy it, we'd be setting ourselves up for potential regulatory and legal problems. Worse than that, we'd be deploying a model we know perpetuates systemic biases and harms people. Getting an extension on a credit card can be a serious thing at different junctures in our lives. If someone is asking for credit, we should assume it's genuinely needed. What we see here is that an example credit-lending decision is tinged with historical biases. These results also send a clear message. This model needs to be fixed before it's deployed.

Individual Fairness

We've been focused on group fairness thus far, but we should also probe our model for individual fairness concerns. Unlike bias against groups, individual bias is a local issue that affects only a small and specific group of people, down to a single individual. There are two main techniques we'll use to test this: residual analysis and adversarial modeling. In the first technique—residual analysis—we look at individuals very close to the decision cutoff and who incorrectly received unfavorable outcomes as a result. We want to make sure their demographic information isn't pushing them into being denied for a credit product. (We can check very wrong individual outcomes far away from the decision cutoff too.) In the second approach—adversarial models—we'll use separate models that try to predict protected group information using the input features and the scores from our original model, and we'll look at those model's Shapley additive explanations. When we find rows where adversarial predictions are very accurate, this is a hint that something in that row is encoding information that leads to bias in our original model. If we can identify what that something is across more than a few rows of data, we're on the path to identifying potential drivers of proxy bias in our model. We'll look into individual bias and then proxy bias before transitioning to the bias-remediation section of the chapter.

Let's dive into individual fairness. First, we wrote some code to pull out a few narrowly misclassified people from a protected group. These are observations that our model predicted would go delinquent, but they did not:

```
black_obs = valid.loc[valid['RACE'] == 'black'].copy()
black_obs[f'p_{target}_outcome'] = np.where(
  black_obs[f'p_{target}'] > best_cut,
  1,
  0)

misclassified_obs = black_obs[(black_obs[target] == 0) &
                              (black_obs[f'p_{target}_outcome'] == 1)]

misclassified_obs.sort_values(by=f'p_{target}').head(3)[features]
```

The results are shown in Table 10-4, and they don't suggest any egregious bias, but they do raise some questions. The first and third applicants appear to spending moderately and making payments on time for the most part. These individuals may have been placed on the wrong side of a decision boundary in an arbitrary manner. However, the individual in the second row of Table 10-4 appears not to be making progress on repaying their credit card debt. Perhaps they really should not have been approved for an increased line of credit.

Table 10-4. A subset of features for narrowly misclassified protected observations in validation data

LIMIT _BAL	PAY_0	PAY_2	PAY_3	...	BILL _AMT1	BILL _AMT2	BILL _AMT3	...	PAY _AMT1	PAY _AMT2	PAY _AMT3
$58,000	−1	−1	−2	...	$600	$700	$0	...	$200	$700	$0
$58,000	0	0	0	...	$8,500	$5,000	$0	...	$750	$150	$30
$160,000	−1	−1	−1	...	$0	$0	$600	...	$0	$0	$0

Next steps to uncovering whether we've found a real individual bias problem might include the following:

Small perturbations of input features
    If some arbitrary change to an input feature, say decreasing `BILL_AMT1` by $5, changes the outcome for this person, then the model's decision may be more related to a steep place in its response function intersecting with the decision cutoff than any tangible real-world reason.

Searching for similar individuals
    If there are a handful—or more—individuals like the current individual, the model maybe segmenting some specific or intersectional subpopulation in an unfair or harmful way.

If either of these are the case, the right thing to do may be to extend this and similar individual's line(s) of credit.

We conducted a similar analysis for Hispanic and Asian observations and found similar results. We weren't too surprised by these results, for at least two reasons. First, individual fairness questions are difficult and bring up issues of causality which ML systems tend not to address in general. Second, individual fairness and proxy discrimination are probably much larger risks for datasets with many rows—where entire subpopulations may end up on an arbitrary side of a decision boundary—and when a model contains many features, and especially *alternative data,* or features not directly linked to one's ability to repay credit, that may otherwise enhance the predictiveness of the model.

Answering questions about individual fairness with 100% certainty is difficult, because they're fundamentally *causal* questions. For complex, nonlinear ML models, it's impossible to know whether a model made a decision on the basis of some piece of data (i.e., protected group information) that isn't included in the model in the first place.

That said, residual analysis, adversarial modeling, SHAP values, and the careful application of subject matter expertise can go a long way. For more reading on this subject, check out "Explaining Quantitative Measures of Fairness" (*https://oreil.ly/Tg66Z*) from the creator of SHAP values, and "On Testing for Discrimination Using Causal Models" (*https://oreil.ly/IiP9W*).

Let's move on to the second technique for testing individual fairness: adversarial modeling. We chose to train two adversarial models. The first model takes in the same input features as the original model, but attempts to predict protected groups' statuses rather than delinquencies. For simplicity, we trained a binary classifier on a target for protected class membership—a new marker for `Black` or `Hispanic` people. By analyzing this first adversarial model, we can get a good idea of which features have the strongest relationships with protected demographic group membership.

The second adversarial model we train is exactly like the first, except it gets one additional input feature—the output probabilities of our original lending model. By comparing the two adversarial models, we will get an idea of how much *additional* information was encoded in the original model scores. And we'll get this information at the observation level.

 Many ML tools that generate *row-by-row* debugging information— like residuals, adversarial model predictions, or SHAP values—can be used for examining individual bias issues.

We trained these adversarial models as binary XGBoost classifiers with similar hyper-parameters to the original model. First, we took a look at the protected observations whose adversarial model scores increased the most when the original model probabilities were added as a feature. The results are shown in Table 10-5. This table is telling us that for some observations, the original model scores are encoding enough information about protected group status that the second adversarial model is able to improve on the first by around 30 percentage points. These results tells us that we should take a deeper look into these observations, in order to identify any individual fairness problems by asking questions like we did for individual bias issues spotted with residuals. Table 10-5 also helps us show again that removing *demographic markers* from a model does not remove *demographic information* from a model.

Table 10-5. The three protected observations that saw their scores increase the most between the two adversarial models in validation data

Observation	Protected	Adversary 1 score	Adversary 2 score	Difference
9022	1	0.288	0.591	0.303
7319	1	0.383	0.658	0.275
528	1	0.502	0.772	0.270

Recall from Chapter 2 that SHAP values are a row-by-row additive feature attribution scheme. That is, they tell us how much each feature in a model contributed to the overall model prediction. We computed the SHAP values on validation data for the second adversarial model (the one that includes our original model scores). In Figure 10-2, we took a look at the distribution of SHAP values for the top four most important features. Each of the features in Figure 10-2 is important to predicting protected class membership. Coming in as the most important feature for predicting protected group information is the original model scores, `p_DELINQ_NEXT`. This is interesting in and of itself, and the observations that have the highest SHAP values for this feature are good targets to investigate further for individual fairness violations.

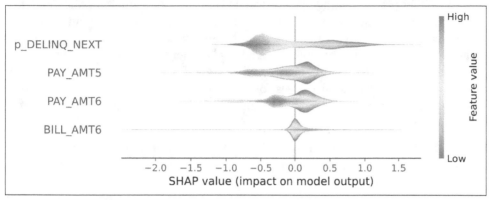

Figure 10-2. The distribution of SHAP values for the four most important features in our adversarial model in validation data (digital, color version: https://oreil.ly/n4z9i)

Maybe most interesting is the color gradient (change from light to dark) within the p_DELINQ_NEXT violin. Each violin is colored by the value of the feature itself for each observation in the density. That means that if our model was linear with no interactions, the color gradient across each violin would be smooth from light to dark. But that's not what we observed. Within the p_DELINQ_NEXT violin, there is significant color variation within vertical slices of the plot. This can only arise when p_DELINQ_NEXT is being used by the model in conjunction with other features in order to drive the predictions. For example, the model might be learning something like *if LIMIT_BAL is below $20,000 and if credit utilization is above 50% and if the delinquency probability from the credit extension model is above 20% then the observation is likely to be a Black or Hispanic person*. While residuals and adversarial models can help us identify individual bias issues, SHAP can take us a step further by helping us understand what is driving that bias.

Proxy Bias

If the patterns like those we've identified only affect a few people, they can still be harmful. But when we see them affecting larger groups of people, we likely have a more global proxy bias issue on our hands. Remember that proxy bias happens when a single feature or a group of interacting features act like demographic information in our model. Given that ML models can often mix and match features to create latent concepts—and can do so in different ways on local, row-by-row bases—proxy bias is a fairly common driver of biased model outputs.

Many of the tools we've discussed, like adversarial models and SHAP, can be used to hunt down proxies. We could begin to get at them by looking at, for example,

SHAP feature interaction values. (Recall advanced SHAP techniques from Chapters 2 and 6.) The bottom-line test for proxies may be adversarial models. If another model can accurately predict demographic information from our model's predictions, then our model encodes demographic information. If we include model input features in our adversarial models, we can use feature attribution measures to understand which single input features might be proxies, and apply other techniques and elbow grease to find proxies created by interactions. Good, old-fashioned decision trees can be some of the best adversarial models for finding proxies. Since ML models tend to combine and recombine features, plotting a trained adversarial decision tree may help us uncover more complex proxies.

As readers can see, adversarial modeling can be a rabbit hole. But we hope we've convinced readers that it is a powerful tool for identifying individual rows that might be subject to discrimination under our models, and for understanding how our input features relate to protected group information and proxies. Now we're going to move on to the important job of remediating the bias we found in our example lending model.

Remediating Bias

Now that we've identified several types of bias in our model, it's time to roll up our sleeves and try to remediate it. Luckily, there are many tools to choose from and, due to the Rashomon effect, many different models to choose from too. We'll try preprocessing remediation first. We'll generate observation-level weights for our training data so that positive outcomes appear equally likely across demographic groups. We'll then try an in-processing technique, sometimes known as *fair XGBoost*, in which demographic information is included in XGBoost's gradient calculation so that it can be regularized during model training. For postprocessing, we'll update our predictions around the decision boundary of the model. Since pre-, in-, and postprocessing may give rise to concerns about disparate treatment in several industry verticals and applications, we'll close out the remediation section by outlining a simple and effective technique for model selection that searches over various input feature sets and hyperparameter settings to find a model with good performance and minimal bias. For each approach, we'll also address any observed performance quality and bias-remediation trade-offs.

Preprocessing

The first bias-remediation technique we'll try is a preprocessing technique known as *reweighing*. It was published first by Faisal Kamiran and Toon Calders in their 2012 paper, "Data Preprocessing Techniques for Classification Without Discrimination" (*https://oreil.ly/lAj08*). The idea of reweighing is to make the average outcome across groups equal using observation weights and then retrain the model. As we'll see, before we preprocessed the training data, the average outcome, or average y variable value, is quite different across demographic groups. The biggest difference was for Asian and Black people, with average outcomes of 0.107 and 0.400, respectively. This means that on average, and looking only at the training data, Asian people's probability of default was well within the range of being accepted for a credit-line increase, while the opposite was true for Black people. Their average score was solidly in the decline range. (Again, these values are not always objective or fair simply because they are recorded in digital data.) After we preprocess, we'll see we can balance out both outcomes and bias-testing values to a notable degree.

Since reweighing is a very straightforward approach, we decided to implement it ourselves with the function in the following code snippet.[2] To reweigh our data, we first need to measure average outcome rates—overall and for each demographic group. Then we determine observation-level, or row-level, weights that balance out the outcome rate across demographic groups. Observation weights are numeric values that tell XGBoost, and most other ML models, how much to weigh each row during training. If a row has a weight of 2, it's like that row appears twice in the objective function used to train XGBoost. If we tell XGBoost that a row has a weight of 0.2, it's like that row appears one-fifth of the times it actually does in the training data. Given the average outcome for each group and their frequency in the training data, it's a basic algebra problem to determine the row weights that give all groups the same average outcome in the model.

```
def reweight_dataset(dataset, target_name, demo_name, groups):
    n = len(dataset)
    # initial overall outcome frequency
    freq_dict = {'pos': len(dataset.loc[dataset[target_name] == 1]) / n,
                 'neg': len(dataset.loc[dataset[target_name] == 0]) / n}
    # initial outcome frequency per demographic group
    freq_dict.update({group: dataset[demo_name].value_counts()[group] / n
                      for group in groups})
    weights = pd.Series(np.ones(n), index=dataset.index)
    # determine row weights that balance outcome frequency
    # across demographic groups
    for label in [0, 1]:
        for group in groups:
            label_name = 'pos' if label == 1 else 'neg'
            freq = dataset.loc[dataset[target_name] == label][demo_name] \
                    .value_counts()[group] / n
            weights[(dataset[target_name] == label) &
                    (dataset[demo_name] == group)] *= \
                freq_dict[group] * freq_dict[label_name] / freq
    # return balanced weight vector
    return weights
```

---

2 For an additional implementation and example usage of reweighing, check out AIF360's "Detecting and Mitigating Age Bias on Credit Decisions" (*https://oreil.ly/ypEQc*).

There are multiple kinds of sample weights. In XGBoost, and in most other ML models, observation-level weights are interpreted as frequency weights, where the weight on an observation is equivalent to "the number of times" it appears in the training data. This weighting scheme has its origins in survey sampling theory.

The other main type of sample weights come from the theory of weighted least squares. Sometimes called precision weights, they quantify our uncertainty about the observation's feature values, under the assumption that each observation is really an average of multiple underlying samples. These two notions of sample weights are not equivalent, so it's important to know which one you're specifying when you set a `sample_weights` parameter.

Applying the `reweight_dataset` function provides us with a vector of observation weights of the same length as the training data, such that a weighted average of the outcomes in the data within each demographic group is equal. Reweighing helps to undo manifestations of systemic biases in training data, teaching XGBoost that different kinds of people should have the same average outcome rates. In code, this is as simple as retraining XGBoost with the row weights from `reweight_dataset`. In our code, we call this vector of training weights `train_weights`. When we call the `DMatrix` function, we use the `weight=` argument to specify these bias-decreasing weights. After this, we simply retrain XGBoost:

```
dtrain = xgb.DMatrix(train[features],
                     label=train[target],
                     weight=train_weights)
```

Table 10-6 shows both the original mean outcomes and original AIR values, along with the preprocessed mean outcomes and AIR. When we trained XGBoost on the unweighted data, we saw some problematic AIR values. Originally, the AIR was around 0.73 for Black and Hispanic people. These values are not great—signifying that for every 1,000 credit products the model extends to white people, this model only accepts applications from about 730 Hispanic or Black people. This level of bias is ethically troubling, but it could also give rise to legal troubles in consumer finance, hiring, or other areas that rely on traditional legal standards for bias testing. The four-fifths rule—while flawed and imperfect—tells us we should not see values below 0.8 for AIR. Luckily, in our case, reweighing provides good remediation results.

In Table 10-6, we can see that we increased the problematic AIR values for Hispanic and Black people to less borderline values, and importantly, without changing the AIR very much for Asian people. In short, reweighing decreased potential bias risks for Black and Hispanic people, without increasing those risks for other groups. Did this have any effect on the performance quality of our model? To investigate this, we introduced a hyperparameter, `lambda`, in Figure 10-3 that dictates the strength of the reweighing scheme. When `lambda` is equal to zero, all observations get a sample weight of one. When the hyperparameter is equal to one, the mean outcomes are all equal, and we get the results in Table 10-6. As shown in Figure 10-3, we did observe some trade-off between increasing the strength of reweighing and performance as measured by F1 in validation data. Next, let's look at the result on Black and Hispanic AIRs as we sweep `lambda` across a range of values to understand more about that trade-off.

Table 10-6. Original and preprocessed mean outcomes for demographic groups in test data

Demographic group	Original mean outcome	Preprocessed mean outcome	Original AIR	Preprocessed AIR
Hispanic	0.398	0.22	0.736	0.861
Black	0.400	0.22	0.736	0.877
White	0.112	0.22	1.000	1.000
Asian	0.107	0.22	1.012	1.010

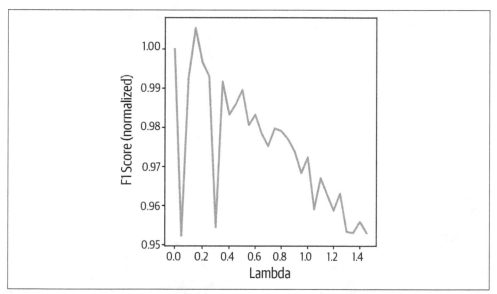

Figure 10-3. F1 scores of the model as the strength of the reweighing scheme is increased (digital, color version: https://oreil.ly/wJ396)

The results in Figure 10-4 show that increasing `lambda` past 0.8 does not yield meaningful improvements in Black and Hispanic AIRs. Looking back at Figure 10-3, this means we would experience a roughly 3% drop in silico. If we were thinking about deploying this model, we'd choose that hyperparameter value for retraining. The compelling story told between Figures 10-3 and 10-4 is this: simply by applying sampling weights to our dataset so as to emphasize favorable Black and Hispanic borrowers, we can increase AIRs for these two groups, while realizing only a nominal performance drop.

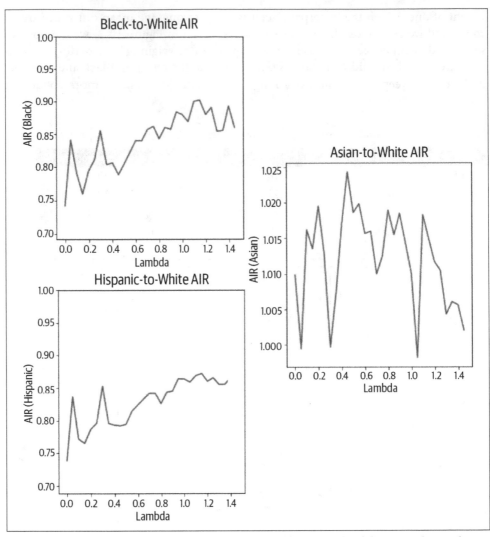

Figure 10-4. Adverse impact ratios of the model as the strength of the reweighing scheme is increased (digital, color version: https://oreil.ly/LKxEH)

Like nearly everything else in ML, bias remediation and our chosen approaches are an experiment, not rote engineering. They're not guaranteed to work, and we always need to check if they actually work, first in validation and test data, then in the real world. It's really important to remember that we don't know how this model is going to perform in terms of accuracy or bias once it's deployed. We always hope our in silico validation and test assessments are correlated to real-world performance, but there are simply no guarantees. We'd have high hopes that what looks like a ~5% decrease in in silico performance washes out once the model is deployed due to drifting data, changes in real-world operating contexts, and other in vivo surprises. All of this points to the need for monitoring both performance and bias once a model is deployed.

Reweighing is just one example of a preprocessing technique, and there are several other popular approaches. Preprocessing is simple, direct, and intuitive. As we've just seen, it can result in meaningful improvements in model bias with acceptable accuracy trade-offs. Check out AIF360 (*https://oreil.ly/rDdhC*) for examples of other credible preprocessing techniques.

In-processing

Next we'll try an in-processing bias-remediation technique. Many interesting techniques have been proposed in recent years, including some that use adversarial models, as in "Mitigating Unwanted Biases with Adversarial Learning" (*https://oreil.ly/rFdZA*) or "Fair Adversarial Gradient Tree Boosting" (*https://oreil.ly/kZ0xB*). The idea behind these adversarial in-processing approaches is straightforward. When an adversarial model cannot predict demographic group membership from our main model's predictions, then we feel good that our predictions do not encode too much bias. As highlighted earlier in the chapter, adversarial models also help to capture local information about bias. The rows where the adversary model is most accurate are likely the rows that encode the most demographic information. These rows can help us uncover individuals who may be experiencing the most bias, complex proxies involving several input features, and other local bias patterns.

There are also in-processing debiasing techniques that use only one model, and since they are usually a little easier to implement, we'll focus on one of those for our use case. As opposed to using a second model, these in-processing methods use a dual objective function with a regularization approach. For example, "A Convex Framework for Fair Regression" (*https://oreil.ly/7dcHL*) puts forward various regularizers that can be paired with linear and logistic regression models to decrease bias against groups and individuals. "Learning Fair Representations" (*https://oreil.ly/tgCE9*) also includes a bias measurement in model objective functions, but then tries to create a new representation of training data that encodes less bias.

While these two approaches focus mostly on simple models, i.e., linear regression, logistic regression, and naive Bayes, we want to work with trees, and in particular, XGBoost. Turns out, we're not the only ones. A research group at American Express recently released "FairXGBoost: Fairness-Aware Classification in XGBoost" (*https://oreil.ly/2gNo9*), which includes instructions and experimental results on introducing a bias regularization term into XGBoost models, using XGBoost's preexisting capability to train with custom-coded objective functions. This is how we'll do in-processing, and as you'll see soon, it's remarkably direct to implement and gives good results on our example data.

 Before we jump into the more technical descriptions, code, and results, we should mention that a great deal of the fairness regularization work we've discussed is based on, or otherwise related to, the seminal paper by Kamishima et al., "Fairness-Aware Classifier with Prejudice Remover Regularizer" (*https://oreil.ly/E_arn*).

How does our chosen approach work? Objective functions are used to measure error during model training, where an optimization procedure tries to minimize that error and find the best model parameters. The basic idea of in-processing regularization techniques is to include a measure of bias in the model's overall objective function. When the optimization function is used to calculate error and the ML optimization process tries to minimize that error, this also tends to result in decreasing measured bias. Another twist on this idea is to use a factor on the bias measurement term within the objective function, or a *regularization hyperparameter*, so that the effect of bias remediation can be tuned. In case readers didn't know already, XGBoost supports a wide variety of objective functions so that we can ensure that the way error is measured actually maps to the real-world problem at hand. It also supports fully customized objective functions (*https://oreil.ly/pczVg*) coded by users.

The first step in implementing our in-processing approach will be to code a sample objective function. In the code snippet that follows, we define a simple objective function that tells XGBoost how to generate scores:

1. Calculate the first derivative of the objective function with respect to model output (gradient, `grad`).

2. Calculate the second derivative of the objective function with respect to model output (Hessian, `hess`).

3. Incorporate demographic information (`protected`) into the objective function.

4. Control the strength of the regularization with a new parameter (lambda, `lambda`).

We also create a simple wrapper for the objective that allows us to specify which groups we want to consider to be the protected class—those who we want to experience less bias due to regularization—and the strength of the regularization. While simplistic, the wrapper buys us quite a lot of functionality. It enables us to include multiple demographic groups into the protected group. This is important because models often exhibit bias against more than one group, and simply trying to remediate bias for one group may make things worse for other groups. The ability to supply custom `lambda` values is great because it allows for us to tune the strength of our regularization. As shown in "Preprocessing" on page 350, the ability to tune the regularization hyperparameter is crucial for finding an ideal trade-off with model accuracy.

That's a lot to pack into roughly 15 lines of Python code, but that's why we picked this approach. It takes advantage of niceties in the XGBoost framework, it's pretty simple, and it appears to increase AIR for historically marginalized minority groups in our example data:

```
def make_fair_objective(protected, lambda):
    def fair_objective(pred, dtrain):

        # Fairness-aware cross-entropy loss objective function
        label = dtrain.get_label()
        pred = 1. / (1. + np.exp(-pred))
        grad = (pred - label) - lambda * (pred - protected)
        hess = (1. - lambda) * pred * (1. - pred)

        return grad, hess
    return fair_objective

protected = np.where((train['RACE'] == 'hispanic') | (train['RACE'] == 'black'),
                     1, 0)
fair_objective = make_fair_objective(protected, lambda=0.2)
```

Once that custom objective is defined, we just need to use the `obj=` argument to pass it to XGBoost's `train()` function. If we've written the code correctly, XGBoost's robust training and optimization mechanisms should take care of the rest. Note how little code it takes to train with our custom objective:

```
model_regularized = xgb.train(params,
                              dtrain,
                              num_boost_round=100,
                              evals=watchlist,
                              early_stopping_rounds=10,
                              verbose_eval=False,
                              obj=fair_objective)
```

Validation and test results for in-processing remediation are available in Figures 10-5 and 10-6. To validate our hypothesis, we took advantage of our wrapper function and trained many different models with many different settings of `lambda`. In Figure 10-6, we can see that increasing `lambda` does decrease bias, as measured by an increasing

Black and Hispanic AIR, whereas Asian AIR remains roughly constant around the good value of 1. We can increase the AIR for the groups we tend to be most concerned about in consumer finance, without engaging in potential discrimination of other demographic groups. That is the result we want to see!

What about the trade-off between performance and decreased bias? What we saw here is pretty typical in our experience. There's a range of lambda values above which Black and Hispanic AIRs do not meaningfully increase, but the F1 score of the model continues to decrease to below 90% of the performance of the original model. We probably wouldn't use the model wherein lambda is cranked up to the maximum level, so we're probably looking at a small decrease in in silico test data performance and an as yet unknown change in in vivo performance.

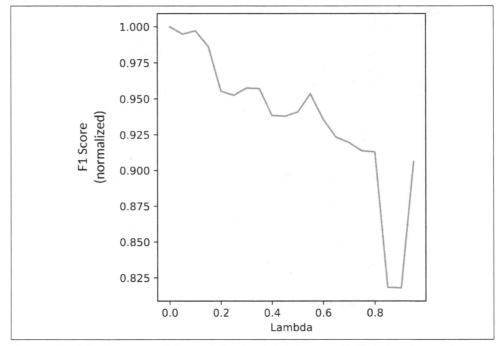

Figure 10-5. The F1 scores of the model as lambda is increased (digital, color version: https://oreil.ly/D5Hz_)

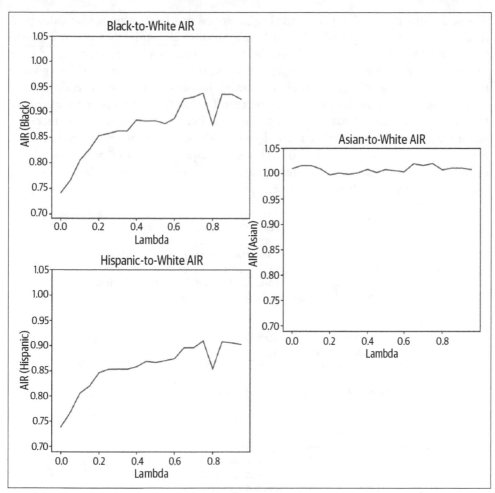

Figure 10-6. AIR values across demographic groups as the regularization factor, `lambda`*, is increased (digital, color version: https://oreil.ly/tRfBx)*

Postprocessing

Next we'll move on to postprocessing techniques. Remember that postprocessing techniques are applied after a model has already been trained, so in this section we'll modify the output probabilities of the original model that we trained at the beginning of the chapter.

The technique that we'll apply is called *reject option* postprocessing, and it dates back to a 2012 paper (*https://oreil.ly/2rh4r*) by Kamiran et al. Remember that our model has a cutoff value, where scores above this value are given a binary outcome of 1 (an undesirable result for our credit applicants), and scores below the cutoff are given a predicted outcome of 0 (a favorable outcome). Reject option postprocessing works on the idea that for model scores *near* the cutoff value, the model is uncertain about the correct outcome. What we do is group together all observations that receive a score within a narrow interval around the cutoff, and then we reassign outcomes for these observations in order to increase the equity of model outcomes. Reject option postprocessing is easy to interpret and implement—we were able to do so with another relatively straightforward function:

```
def reject_option_classification(dataset, y_hat, demo_name, protected_groups,
                                 reference_group, cutoff,
                                 uncertainty_region_size):
    # In an uncertainty region around the decision cutoff value,
    # flip protected group predictions to the favorable decision
    # and reference group predictions to the unfavorable decision
    new_predictions = dataset[y_hat].values.copy()

    uncertain = np.where(
        np.abs(dataset[y_hat] - cutoff) <= uncertainty_region_size, 1, 0)
    uncertain_protected = np.where(
        uncertain & dataset[demo_name].isin(protected_groups), 1, 0)
    uncertain_reference = np.where(
        uncertain & (dataset[demo_name] == reference_group), 1, 0)

    eps = 1e-3

    new_predictions = np.where(uncertain_protected,
                               cutoff - uncertainty_region_size - eps,
                               new_predictions)
    new_predictions = np.where(uncertain_reference,
                               cutoff + uncertainty_region_size + eps,
                               new_predictions)
    return new_predictions
```

In Figure 10-7 we can see the technique in action. The histograms show the distribution of model scores for each racial group, both before and after the postprocessing. We can see that in a small neighborhood of scores around 0.26 (the original model cutoff), we have postprocessed all Black and Hispanic people into a favorable outcome by assigning them a score at the bottom of the range. Meanwhile, we have assigned white people in this *uncertainty zone* an unfavorable model outcome and left Asian scores unchanged. With these new scores in hand, let's investigate how this technique affects model accuracy and AIRs.

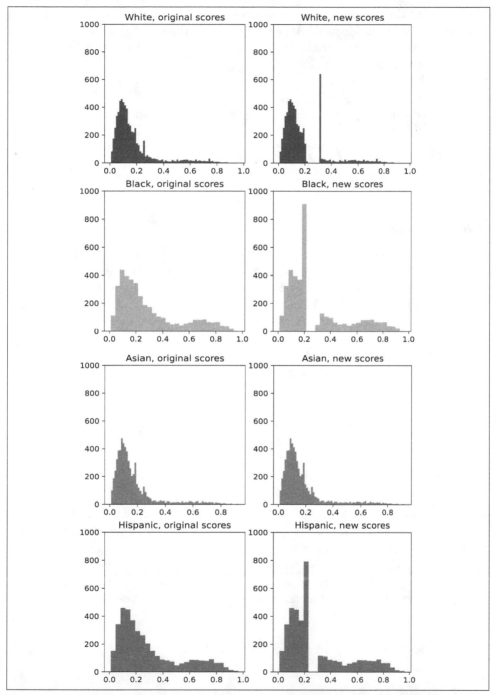

Figure 10-7. Model scores for each demographic group before and after the application of reject option postprocessing (digital, color version: https://oreil.ly/KJtVX)

The results of this experiment are exactly what we would have hoped—we were able to improve Black and Hispanic AIRs to above 0.9, while leaving Asian AIR around 1.00 (Table 10-7). The price we had to pay in terms of F1 score was a 6% decrease. We don't find this to be a meaningful drop, but if we were concerned, we could decrease the size of the uncertainty zone to find a more favorable trade-off.

Table 10-7. Original and postprocessed F1 scores and adverse impact ratios on validation data

Model	F1 score	Black AIR	Hispanic AIR	Asian AIR
Original	0.574	0.736	0.736	1.012
Postprocessed	0.541	0.923	0.902	1.06

Model Selection

The final technique we'll discuss is fairness-aware model selection. To be exact, we'll conduct simple feature selection and random hyperparameter tuning while keeping track of model performance and AIRs. Readers are almost certainly already performing these steps when it comes to performance assessment, so this technique has fairly low overhead costs. Another advantage of model selection as a remediation technique is that it raises the fewest disparate treatment concerns. (On the other end of the spectrum is the reject option postprocessing, described in the previous section, wherein we literally changed model outcomes depending on the protected group status of each observation.)

 Random searches across feature sets and hyperparameter settings often reveal models with improved fairness characteristics and similar performance to a baseline model.

In this section, we'll track F1 and AUC scores as our notion of model performance quality. In our experience, evaluating models on multiple measures of quality increases the likelihood of good in vivo performance. Another advantage of computing both F1 and AUC scores is that the first is measured on model outcomes and the second uses only output probabilities. If in the future we want to change the decision cutoff of our model, or pass the model scores as inputs into another process, we will be glad that we tracked AUC.

One more note before we dive into model selection—model selection is much more than just feature selection and hyperparameter tuning. It can also mean choosing between competing model architectures, or choosing between different bias-remediation techniques. In the conclusion of this chapter, we'll round up all of our results to prepare for a final model selection, but in this section we'll just focus on features and hyperparameters.

In our experience, feature selection can be a powerful remediation technique, but it works best when guided by subject matter experts and when alternative sources of data are available. For example, a compliance expert at a bank may know that a feature in a lending model can be swapped out with an alternative feature that encodes less historical bias. We don't have the luxury of accessing these alternative features, so for our example data we'll only have the option of *dropping* features from our model, and we'll test the effect of dropping each feature individually while maintaining the original hyperparameters. Between feature selection and hyperparameter tuning, we're about to train a lot of different models, so we'll employ five-fold cross-validation using our original training data. If we choose the variant with the best performance on validation data, we run an increased risk of selecting a model that performs best only due to random chance.

While the Rashomon effect may mean we have many good models to chose from, we should not forget that this phenomenon may also be a sign of instability in our original model. If there are many models with settings similar to our original model, that also perform differently from our original model, this points to underspecification and misspecification issues. Remediated models must also be tested for stability, safety, and performance issues. See Chapters 3, 8, and 9 for more information.

After training these new models using cross-validation, we were able to realize an increase in Black and Hispanic cross-validation AIRs, alongside a small decrease in model cross-validation AUC. The most offending feature was PAY_AMT5, so we'll proceed with random hyperparameter tuning without this feature.

It's possible to be more sophisticated about feature selection by using adversarial models and explainable AI techniques. For inspiration, consider the article "Explaining Measures of Fairness" (*https://oreil.ly/SLn_8*) and the associated notebook from the creator of SHAP, and "Automating Procedurally Fair Feature Selection in Machine Learning" (*https://oreil.ly/YSKnM*) from Belitz et al.

To choose new model hyperparameters, we'll use a random grid search using the scikit-learn API. Since we want to cross-validate AIRs throughout this process, we have to put together a scoring function to pass into scikit-learn. To simplify the code, we only track the Black AIR here—since it has been correlated to the Hispanic AIR throughout our analysis—but an average measure of AIR across protected groups is likely preferable. This code snippet shows how we used global variables and the `make_scorer()` interface to get this done:

```
fold_number = -1

def black_air(y_true, y_pred):
    global fold_number
    fold_number = (fold_number + 1) % num_cv_folds

    model_metrics = perf_metrics(y_true, y_score=y_pred)
    best_cut = model_metrics.loc[model_metrics['f1'].idxmax(), 'cutoff']

    data = pd.DataFrame({'RACE': test_groups[fold_number],
                         'y_true': y_true,
                         'y_pred': y_pred},
                        index=np.arange(len(y_pred)))

    disparity_table = fair_lending_disparity(data, y='y_true', yhat='y_pred',
                                             demo_name='RACE',
                                             groups=race_levels,
                                             reference_group='white',
                                             cutoff=best_cut)

    return disparity_table.loc['black']['AIR']


scoring = {
    'AUC': 'roc_auc',
    'Black AIR': sklearn.metrics.make_scorer(black_air, needs_proba=True)
}
```

Next, we defined a reasonable grid of hyperparameters and built 50 new models:

```
parameter_distributions = {
    'n_estimators': np.arange(10, 221, 30),
    'max_depth': [3, 4, 5, 6, 7],
    'learning_rate': stats.uniform(0.01, 0.1),
    'subsample': stats.uniform(0.7, 0.3),
    'colsample_bytree': stats.uniform(0.5, 1),
    'reg_lambda': stats.uniform(0.1, 50),
    'monotone_constraints': [new_monotone_constraints],
    'base_score': [params['base_score']]
    }
```

```
grid_search = sklearn.model_selection.RandomizedSearchCV(
    xgb.XGBClassifier(random_state=12345,
                      use_label_encoder=False,
                      eval_metric='logloss'),
    parameter_distributions,
    n_iter=50,
    scoring=scoring,
    cv=zip(train_indices, test_indices),
    refit=False,
    error_score='raise').fit(train[new_features], train[target].values)
```

The results of our random model selection procedure are shown in Figure 10-8. Each model is a point on the plot, with Black cross-validation AIR values on the x-axis and cross-validation AUC on the y-axis. As we've done here, it is useful to normalize model accuracy to the baseline value in order to easily make statements like "this alternative model shows a 2% drop in AUC from the original model." Given this distribution of models, how do we go about choosing one for deployment?

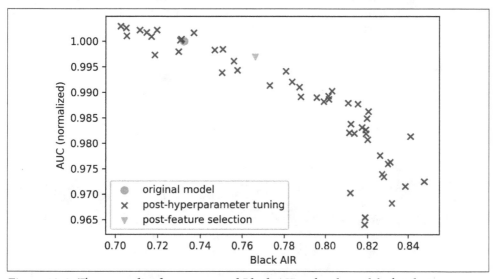

Figure 10-8. The normalized accuracy and Black AIRs of each model after feature selection and hyperparameter tuning (digital, color version: https://oreil.ly/7ru28)

A common problem with bias-remediation approaches is that they often just move bias around from one demographic group to another. For example, women are now favored sometimes in credit and employment decisions in the US. It wouldn't be surprising to see a bias-remediation technique dramatically decrease favorable outcomes for women in the process of increasing them for other groups impacted by systemic bias, but that's not the outcome anyone really wants. If one group is disproportionally favored, and bias remediation equals that out—great. If, on the other hand, one group is favored a bit, and bias remediation ends up harming them to increase AIRs or other statistics for other groups, that's obviously not great. In the next section, we'll see how these two alternative models stack up against the other remediation techniques applied in this chapter.

Any time we evaluate multiple models on the same dataset, we must be careful about overfitting and multiple comparisons. We should employ best practices such as reusable holdout, cross-validation, bootstrapping, out-of-time holdout data, and post-deployment monitoring to ensure that our results generalize.

Conclusion

In Table 10-8, we've aggregated the results for all of the models trained in this chapter. We chose to focus on two measures of model accuracy, F1 score and AUC, and two measures of model bias, AIRs and false-positive rate (FPR) disparity.

Table 10-8. Comparison of test data between bias-remediation techniques

Measurement	Original model	Preprocessing (reweighting)	In-processing (regularized, Lambda = 0.2)	Postprocessing (reject option, window = 0.1)	Model selection
AUC	0.798021	0.774183	0.764005	0.794894	0.789016
F1	0.558874	0.543758	0.515971	0.533964	0.543147
Asian AIR	1.012274	1.010014	1.001185	1.107676	1.007365
Black AIR	0.735836	0.877673	0.851499	0.901386	0.811854
Hispanic AIR	0.736394	0.861252	0.851045	0.882538	0.805121
Asian FPR disparity	0.872567	0.929948	0.986472	0.575248	0.942973
Black FPR disparity	1.783528	0.956640	1.141044	0.852034	1.355846
Hispanic FPR disparity	1.696062	0.899065	1.000040	0.786195	1.253355

The results are exciting: many remediation techniques tested are able to realize meaningful improvements in AIRs and FPR disparities for Black and Hispanic borrowers with no serious negative impact on the Asian AIR. This is possible with only marginal changes in model performance.

How should we choose which remediation technique to apply to our high-risk model? Hopefully, this chapter has convinced readers to try many things. Ultimately, the final decision rests with the law, business leadership, and the diverse team of stakeholders that we assemble. Within traditionally regulated vertical organizations, where disparate treatment is strictly prohibited, there are strict constraints on our choices. We can really only choose from model selection options available today. If we're outside of these verticals, we have a much wider selection of remediation strategies to choose from.[3] We'd likely pick the preprocessing option for remediation given the minimal decrease in model performance versus in-processing and because postprocessing knocks some performance disparities out of acceptable ranges.

Whether or not we are using model selection as a bias mitigation technique, and whether or not we have different pre-, in-, and postprocessed models to choose from, a rule of thumb for picking a remediated model is to do the following:

1. Reduce the set of models to those that perform sufficiently well to meet business needs, e.g., performance within 5% of the original model.

2. Among those models, pick the one that most closely:
   - Remediates bias across all originally disfavored groups, e.g., all disfavored groups' AIR is increased to ≥ 0.8.
   - Does not discriminate against any initially favored group, e.g., no originally favored groups' AIR is decreased to < 0.8.

3. Consult business partners, legal and compliance experts, and diverse stakeholders as part of the selection process.

If we're training a model that has the potential to impact people—and most models do—we have an ethical obligation to test it for bias. And when we find bias, we need to mitigate or remediate it. What we've gone over in this chapter is the technical part of bias management processes. To get bias remediation right also involves extending our release timelines, lots of careful communication between different stakeholders, and lots of retraining and retesting of ML models and pipelines. We're confident that if we slow down, ask for help and input from stakeholders, and apply the scientific method, we will be able to tackle real-world bias challenges and deploy performant and minimally biased models.

---

3 And don't forget the bias remediation decision tree (slide 40) (*https://oreil.ly/vDv4T*).

Resources

Code Examples

- Machine-Learning-for-High-Risk-Applications-Book (*https://oreil.ly/machine-learning-high-risk-apps-code*)

Tools for Managing Bias

- aequitas (*https://oreil.ly/JzQFh*)
- AI Fairness 360:
  - Python (*https://oreil.ly/sYmc-*)
  - R (*https://oreil.ly/J53bZ*)
- Algorithmic Fairness (*https://oreil.ly/JNzqk*)
- fairlearn (*https://oreil.ly/jYjCi*)
- fairml (*https://oreil.ly/DCkZ5*)
- fairmodels (*https://oreil.ly/nSv8B*)
- fairness (*https://oreil.ly/Dequ9*)
- solas-ai-disparity (*https://oreil.ly/X9fd6*)
- tensorflow/fairness-indicators (*https://oreil.ly/dHBSL*)
- Themis (*https://oreil.ly/zgrvV*)

## CHAPTER 11

Red-Teaming XGBoost

In Chapter 5, we introduced a number of concepts related to the security of machine learning models. Now we will put them into practice. In this chapter, we'll explain how to hack our own models so that we can add red-teaming into our model debugging repertoire. The main idea of the chapter is that when we know what hackers will try to do to our model, then we can try it out first and devise effective defenses. We'll start out with a concept refresher that reintroduces common ML attacks and countermeasures, then we'll dive into examples of attacking an XGBoost classifier trained on structured data.[1] We'll then introduce two XGBoost models, one trained with the standard unexplainable approach, and one trained with constraints and a high degree of L2 regularization. We'll use these two models to explain the attacks and to test whether transparency and L2 regularization are adequate countermeasures. After that, we'll jump into attacks that are likely to be performed by external adversaries against an unexplainable ML API: model extraction and adversarial example attacks. From there, we'll try out insider attacks that involve making deliberate changes to an ML modeling pipeline: data poisoning and model backdoors. As a reminder, the chapter's code examples are available online (*https://oreil.ly/machine-learning-high-risk-apps-code*). Now, let's get started—remember to bring your tinfoil hat, and your adversarial mindset from Chapter 5.

---

1 There are examples of attacks on computer vision models all over the internet, but the tutorials associated with cleverhans (*https://oreil.ly/4Xifu*) are one great place to start.

The web and academic literature abound with examples of, and tools for, attacks for computer vision and language models. For decent summaries of these broad topics see the following:

- "Adversarial Attacks in Computer Vision: An Overview" (*https://oreil.ly/7CPnm*)
- "Privacy Considerations in Large Language Models" (*https://oreil.ly/mesVW*)

This chapter ports those ideas to widely used tree-based models and structured data. Chapter 5 addresses ML security concerns more generally. Chapters 1, 3, and 4 present numerous risk mitigants and process controls that are also helpful for ML security across all types of models.

Concept Refresher

It's worth reminding ourselves why we are interested in ML model attacks. ML models can hurt people and be hurt—manipulated, altered, destroyed—by people. Broadly speaking, security incidents are a major way that operators, users, and the general public are harmed by technology. Bad actors may seek to induce beneficial outcomes for themselves or harmful outcomes for others; they may commit corporate espionage, steal intellectual property, and steal data. We don't want our ML models to be sitting ducks for that kind of malicious activity! In Chapter 5, we called this way of thinking the *adversarial mindset*. While our ML model might be our perfect Python baby that's also primed to make our organization millions of dollars, it's also a legal liability, a security vulnerability, and an endpoint for hackers to explore. There's no way around this reality, especially for important high-impact public-facing ML systems. Let's not be naive. Let's do the hard work required to check that our model isn't full of vulnerabilities that can leak training data, leak models themselves, or allow bad actors to trick our systems out of money, intellectual property, or worse. Now, let's refresh our memory on some of those Chapter 5 concepts, attacks, and countermeasures.

CIA Triad

Recall that, broadly, we break information security incidents down into three categories defined by the CIA triad—confidentiality, integrity, and availability attacks:

Confidentiality attacks
> Violate the confidentiality of some data associated with an ML model, typically the logic of the model or the model's training data. Model extraction attacks expose the model, while membership inference attacks expose the training data.

Integrity attacks
> Compromise the behavior of the model, typically to alter predictions in ways that are beneficial to the attacker. Adversarial example, data poisoning, and backdoor attacks all violate the integrity of a model.

Availability attacks
> Prevent a user of the model from accessing it in a timely or serviceable fashion. In ML, sponge examples (*https://oreil.ly/AkMrE*)—that slow down neural networks—are a type of availability attack. Some have also described algorithmic discrimination as a form of availability attack since minority groups don't receive the same service from the model as majority groups. However, most availability attacks will be general denial-of-service attacks targeted at the service running the model, and not specialized for ML. We won't try an availability attack, but we should check with our IT partners and make sure our public-facing ML models have standard countermeasures in place to mitigate availability attacks.

With that brief reminder of the CIA triad, let's turn to more details about each of our planned red-team attacks.

Attacks

We'll roughly group ML attacks under two main categories for the concept refresher: *external* attacks and *insider* attacks. External attacks are defined as the attacks that an external adversary would be most likely to try on our model. The setup for these attacks is that we've deployed the model as an API, but perhaps been a little sloppy when it came to security. We're going to assume that we can interact with the model as an unexplainable entity, do so anonymously, and that we can have a reasonable number of data submission interactions with the model. Under these conditions, an external attacker could extract the basic logic of our model in a model extraction attack. With or without that blueprint (though it's easier and more harmful with it), the attacker could then begin to craft adversarial examples that look like normal data, but evoke surprising results from the model. With the right adversarial examples, an attacker can play our model like a fiddle. If the hackers are successful in conducting the two previous attacks, they might become more bold, and try perhaps a more sophisticated and harmful attack: membership inference. Let's look at the different types of external attacks in a bit more detail:

Model extraction

A confidentiality attack, meaning it compromises the confidentiality of an ML model. To conduct a model extraction attack, a hacker submits data to a prediction API, gets predictions back, and builds a surrogate model between the submitted data and the received predictions to reverse engineer a copy of the model. With this information, they may uncover proprietary business processes and decision-making logic. The extracted model also provides a great test bed for subsequent attacks.

Adversarial examples

An integrity attack. It compromises the correctness of model predictions. To perform an adversarial example attack a hacker will probe how a model responds to input data. In computer vision systems, gradient information is often used to fine-tune images that evoke strange responses from the model. For structured data, we can use individual conditional expectation (ICE) or genetic algorithms to find rows of data that cause unexpected model predictions.

Membership inference

A confidentiality attack that seeks to compromise model training data. It's a complex attack that requires two models. The first is a surrogate model similar to those that would be trained in a model extraction attack. The second-stage model is then trained to decide whether a row of data is in the training data of the surrogate model or not. When that second-stage model is applied to a row of data, it can decide whether that row was in the training data of the surrogate model or not, and can often extrapolate to decide whether that row was also in the original model training data.

Now for those insider attacks. Sadly, we can't always trust our fellow employees, consultants, or contractors. And worse yet, people can be extorted into committing bad acts, whether they want to or not. In a data poisoning attack, someone changes training data in a way that allows them, or their associates, to manipulate the model later. In a backdoor attack, someone alters the scoring code of the model so that they can later access the model in unauthorized ways. In both data poisoning and backdoor attacks, it's most likely that the perpetrator would seek to gain financially themselves, and alter the data or scoring code accordingly. However, it's also possible that a bad actor would change an important model in a way that hurt others, and not necessarily to benefit themselves:

Data poisoning

> An integrity attack that changes training data to change future model outcomes. To conduct the attack, someone only needs access to model training data. They try to change the training data in subtle ways that will reliably alter model predictions, in ways they or associates can exploit later when interacting with the model.

Backdoors

> Integrity attacks that change a model's scoring (or inference) code. The goal of a backdoor attack is to introduce new branches of code into the complex tangle of coefficients and if-then rules that is a deployed ML model. Once the new branch of code has been injected into the scoring engine, it can be exploited later by those who know how to trigger it, e.g., by submitting unrealistic combinations of data into a prediction API.

We didn't go back over evasion and impersonation attacks, but they are covered in the case study in Chapter 5. According to our research, evasion and impersonation attacks are the most common kinds of attacks today. They're typically applied to ML-enhanced security, filtering, or payment systems. In computer vision, they usually involve some kind of physical manipulation of an ML system, for instance wearing a realistic mask or camouflaging oneself. For structured data, these attacks just mean altering a row of data to have similar values (impersonation), or dissimilar values (evasion), when compared to some user of a model. Keep in mind that evading fraud detection ML models is a long-running cat and mouse game between fraudsters and financial institutions, and that's probably the most common application where we'd run into evasion attacks based on manipulating structured data.

Countermeasures

Most ML attacks are premised on ML models being overly complex, unstable, overfit, and unexplainable. The overly complex and unexplainable structure is important because humans will have a hard time understanding if an uber-complex system is being manipulated. Instability is important for attacks because it leads to scenarios where minor perturbations to input data can lead to dramatic and unexpected changes in model outputs. Overfitting results in unstable models, and comes into play for membership inference attacks. If a model is overfit, it behaves quite differently on new data than on training data, and we can use that performance differential to infer if a row data was used to train the model. With all this in mind, we're going to try two simple countermeasures:

L2 regularization

A penalty placed on the squared sum of model coefficients in the model's error function, or some other measure of model complexity. Strong L2 regularization prevents any one coefficient, rule, or interaction from becoming too large and important in the model. If no single feature or interaction is driving the model, it's harder to construct adversarial examples. L2 regularization tends to make all model coefficients smaller as well, making model predictions more stable and less subject to wild swings. L2 regularization is also known to improve models' generalization capabilities, which should also help to counter membership inference attacks.

Monotonic constraints

These make the model more stable and interpretable, both of which are general mitigants of ML attacks. If a model is highly interpretable, this changes its entire security profile. We know how the model should behave and can more easily identify when it is manipulated. Confidentiality attacks lose their bite, because everyone knows how the model works when it obeys reality. If the constraints prevent the model from generating surprising predictions, then there's really no way to conduct an adversarial example attack. If constraints enforce realistic behavior on the model, then data poisoning should be less effective. Constraints should also help with generalization, making membership inference more difficult.

We also hope there is some synergy between these two general countermeasures. Both L2 regularization and constraints increase the stability of the model. By using them, we are trying to ensure we won't see big changes in model outputs based on small changes to model inputs. With constraints in particular, we are also making sure our model simply can't surprise us. The constraints mean it has to obey obvious, causal reality, and hopefully adversarial examples will be much more difficult to find and data poisoning will be less damaging. Both should also decrease overfitting, and provide some defense against membership inference.

Other important countermeasures include throttling (*https://oreil.ly/W3imH*), authentication (*https://oreil.ly/bBR1j*), robust ML (*https://oreil.ly/u4ir7*), and differential privacy approaches (*https://oreil.ly/Xkf7Z*). Throttling slows down predictions if someone interacts with an API too frequently or in a strange way. Authentication prevents anonymous use, which should generally disincentivize attacks. Robust ML approaches create models that are custom-designed to be more robust to adversarial examples and data poisoning. Differential privacy methodically corrupts training data to obscure it if a model extraction or membership inference attack occurs. We'll be using L2 regularization as a more accessible alternative to robust ML and differential privacy approaches. We've explained that L2 regularization acts to create more stable models, but readers may need a reminder that L2 regularization is equivalent to

Gaussian noise injection in training data. There's no guarantee this works as well as real differential privacy methods, but we'll be testing how well it actually works in the code examples. Now that we've gone back over the main technical points, let's train some XGBoost models.

Model Training

In our example models, we'll be deciding whether to extend an API user an increased line of credit. Readers may be thinking that a credit model would be one of the most well-protected models out there, and that's right. But similar ML models are used in the fintech and crypto Wild West, and if we think just because a computer technology is deployed at a big bank then it's safe, bank regulators may have some thoughts (*https://oreil.ly/hx-fM*) for us. Credit application fraud is common, and this is just a 2023 version of credit application fraud. We'll introduce other plausible attack scenarios with each example, but the reality is that real-world attacks can be strange and surprising, and can happen to any model.

In all our attacks, we're going to try to hack two different models. (In reality we'd likely only red-team the model or system we have planned for deployment. But we're going to try an experiment in this chapter.) The first model will be a typical XGBoost model, unconstrained and somewhat overfit, with little regularization beyond that provided by column and row sampling. We expect this model will be easier to hack due to overfitting and instability. We set `max_depth` to 10 in an effort to overfit and we specify the other hyperparameters as follows:

```
params = {"ntrees": 100,
          "max_depth": 10,
          "learn_rate": 0.1,
          "sample_rate": 0.9,
          "col_sample_rate_per_tree": 1,
          "min_rows": 5,
          "seed": SEED,
          "score_tree_interval": 10
}
```

We train our typical XGBoost model with no frills:

```
xgb_clf = H2OXGBoostEstimator(**params)
xgb_clf.train(x=features, y=target, training_frame=training_frame,
              validation_frame=validation_frame)
```

Before we get too far into model training, note that we'll be using the H2O interface to XGBoost, specifically so that we can generate Java scoring code and try a backdoor attack on that code later. That also means the hyperparameter names might be a little different from when using native XGBoost.

For the model we hope will be more robust, we first determine monotonic constraints using Spearman correlation, just like in Chapter 6. These constraints have two purposes, both based on the commonsense transparency they provide. First, they should keep the model more stable under an integrity attack. Second, they should make a confidentiality attack less worthwhile for an attacker. A constrained model is going to be more difficult to manipulate because its logic follows predictable patterns, and should not hide too many secrets that could be sold or used for future attacks. Here's how we set up the constraints:

```python
corr = pd.DataFrame(train[features +
                          [target]].corr(method='spearman')[target]).iloc[:-1]
corr.columns = ['Spearman Correlation Coefficient']
values = [int(i) for i in np.sign(corr.values)]
mono_constraints = dict(zip(corr.index, values))
mono_constraints
```

The constraints defined by our approach are negative for BILL_AMT*, LIMIT_BAL, and PAY_AMT* features. They are positive for PAY_* features. These constraints are intuitive. As bill amounts, credit limits, and payment amounts get larger, the probability of default from our constrained classifier can only decrease. As someone becomes later with their payments, their probability of default can only increase. For H2O monotonicity, constraints need to be defined in a dictionary, and they look like this for our model with countermeasures:

```python
{'BILL_AMT1': -1,
 'BILL_AMT2': -1,
 'BILL_AMT3': -1,
 'BILL_AMT4': -1,
 'BILL_AMT5': -1,
 'BILL_AMT6': -1,
 'LIMIT_BAL': -1,
 'PAY_0': 1,
 'PAY_2': 1,
 'PAY_3': 1,
 'PAY_4': 1,
 'PAY_5': 1,
 'PAY_6': 1,
 'PAY_AMT1': -1,
 'PAY_AMT2': -1,
 'PAY_AMT3': -1,
 'PAY_AMT4': -1,
 'PAY_AMT5': -1,
 'PAY_AMT6': -1}
```

We also use a grid search to look across a broad set of models in parallel fashion. Because our training data is small, we can afford to do a Cartesian grid search across most important hyperparameters:

```
# settings for XGB grid search parameters
hyper_parameters = {'reg_lambda': [0.01, 0.25, 0.5, 0.99],
                    'min_child_weight': [1, 5, 10],
                    'eta': [0.01, 0.05],
                    'subsample': [0.6, 0.8, 1.0],
                    'colsample_bytree': [0.6, 0.8, 1.0],
                    'max_depth': [5, 10, 15]}

# initialize cartesian grid search
xgb_grid = H2OGridSearch(model=H2OXGBoostEstimator,
                         hyper_params=hyper_parameters,
                         parallelism=3)

# training w/ grid search
xgb_grid.train(x=features,
               y=target,
               training_frame=training_frame,
               validation_frame=validation_frame,
               seed=SEED)
```

Once we locate a set of hyperparameters that don't overfit our data, we then retrain using that set of hyperparameters, `params_best`, and our monotonic constraints:

```
xgb_best = H2OXGBoostEstimator(**params_best,
                               monotone_constraints=mono_constraints)
xgb_best.train(x=features, y=target, training_frame=training_frame,
validation_frame=validation_frame)
```

Examining the receiver operating characteristic (ROC) plots for both models shows we likely achieved our goal of having two different models to red-team. The typical model, on top in Figure 11-1, shows the canonical signs of overfitting. It has high training area under the curve, and much lower validation AUC. Our constrained model looks much more well-trained at the bottom of Figure 11-1. It has the same validation AUC as the typical model, but a much lower training AUC, indicating much less overfitting. While we can't be certain, the monotonic constraints probably helped mitigate overfitting.

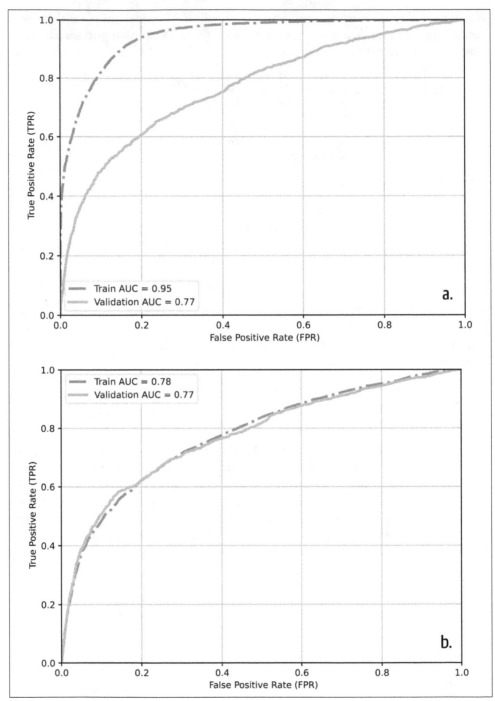

Figure 11-1. ROC curves for (a) an overfit XGBoost model and (b) a highly regularized and constrained XGBoost model (digital, color version: https://oreil.ly/OxLnl)

Now that we have two models, we'll proceed with both our experiment and our red-teaming. We'll be looking to confirm what's reported in the literature and what we hypothesize—that the typical model will be easier and more fruitful to attack. It should be unstable, hiding many nonlinearities and high-degree interactions. This makes attacking it more worthwhile. A hacker could likely find aspects of the unexplainable GBM that could be exploited for attack, using, say, adversarial examples. Because it's overfit, the typical model should also be more susceptible to model extraction attacks. Backdoors should be easier too—we'll attempt to hide new code in the tangle of complex if-then rules that define the overfit GBM.

 We know our overfit XGBoost model is not something readers are likely to deploy, but think of it as the control model, and the constrained model as the treatment model, in a simple experiment with a hypothesis that constrained, regularized models are more secure. We'll address this hypothesis when we close out the chapter.

All of these attacks play on one of the fundamental premises of ML security—a determined attacker can learn more about our overly complicated model than we'll ever be motivated to know. The attacker can exploit this information imbalance in many ways. We'll hope our constrained and regularized model is both harder to attack using data poisoning, backdoors, and adversarial examples *and* less useful to try a confidentiality attack on, because anyone with any domain knowledge can guess how it works and know when it's being manipulated.

Attacks for Red-Teaming

We'll consider model extraction and adversarial example attacks as more likely to be conducted by someone outside of the organization. We'll red-team for these attacks as if we were external bad actors. We'll treat all interactions with ML models as though we were interacting with an opaque API, but we'll see that we can still learn a lot about a so-called black box. We're also assuming that authentication is not required to access the API and that we can access the API to receive at least a few batches of predictions. Our attacks, when successful, will build off each other. We'll see that the initial model extraction attack is extremely damaging, not only because we can learn a lot about the attacked model and its training data, but because it creates a test bed for attackers to hone future hacks.

Model Extraction Attacks

The basic necessary condition for a model extraction attack is that a bad actor can submit data to a model and receive predictions. As this is the way ML is usually designed to work, model extraction attacks are hard to eradicate completely. More specific scenarios for model extraction include weak authentication requirements, say providing just an email address to create an account to use the API, and that hackers can receive thousands of predictions a day from the API. Another fundamental requirement is for a model to hide some information worth stealing. If a model is highly transparent and well-documented, there are fewer reasons to extract it explicitly.

Since our model is a credit model, we'll blame a "go fast and break things" culture at a new fintech company that wants to rush its ML-based credit scoring API into production in an effort to create hype in its market. We could just as easily blame byzantine security procedures at a major bank that allows, at least for a short time period, a product API to be more accessible than it should be. In either case, model extraction could be conducted by corporate competitors who want to understand our organization's proprietary business rules or by hackers who want free money. None of these scenarios are particularly far-fetched, which begs the question: how many model extraction attacks are occurring right now? Let's get into how to red-team for them so that our organization won't fall victim to one of these attacks.

The starting point for the attack is an API endpoint. We'll set up a basic endpoint as follows:

```
def model_endpoint(observations: pd.DataFrame):

    pred_frame = h2o.H2OFrame(observations)
    prediction = xgb_clf.predict(pred_frame)['p1'].as_data_frame().values

    return prediction
```

From there, we submit data to the API endpoint to receive predictions to start the red-teaming exercise. The type of data submitted to the API appears to be crucial to the success of our attack. At first, we tried to guess the distributions of the input features individually and simulated data by drawing from these distributions. That didn't work so well, so we applied the *model-based synthesis* approach described in a well-known paper (*https://oreil.ly/M7r86*) by Shokri et al. This method gives more weight to simulated data rows that evoke a high-confidence response from the API endpoint. By combining our best guess at the distributions of the input features and then using the endpoint to check each simulated row of data, we were able to simulate a set of data that is similar enough to the original dataset to attempt several model extraction attacks. The downside of the model-based synthesis approach is that it involves more interactions with the API, hence, more opportunities to get caught.

 The success of model extraction attacks appears to depend heavily on good simulation of training data.

With realistic data in hand, we could now proceed to the attack. We conducted three different model extraction attacks using a decision tree, a random forest, and an XGBoost GBM as the extracted surrogate model. We submitted our simulated data back to the API endpoint, received predictions, and then trained these three models using the simulated data as inputs and the received predictions as the target. XGBoost seemed to make the best copy of the attacked model in terms of accuracy, perhaps because the model behind the endpoint was also an XGBoost GBM. This is what training the extracted XGBoost model looks like:

```
drand_train = xgb.DMatrix(random_train[features],
                          label=model_endpoint(random_train[features]))

drand_valid = xgb.DMatrix(random_valid[features],
                          label=model_endpoint(random_valid[features]))

params = {
    'objective': 'reg:squarederror',
    'eval_metric': 'rmse',
    'eta': 0.1,
    'max_depth': 3,
    'base_score': base_score,
    'seed': SEED
}


watchlist = [(drand_train, 'train'), (drand_valid, 'eval')]

extracted_model_xgb = xgb.train(params,
                                drand_train,
                                num_boost_round=15,
                                evals=watchlist,
                                early_stopping_rounds=5,
                                verbose_eval=False)
```

We split our simulated data into drand_train training and drand_valid validation partitions. For each partition, the target feature came from the API endpoint. We then applied very simple hyperparameter settings and trained the extracted model. A grid search may have led to a better fit on these simulated rows of data, which may be the attacker's goal on some occasions. We wanted to steal a simple representation of the underlying model, and kept our parameterization straightforward. XGBoost was able to achieve an R^2 of 0.635 against the API predictions using the simulated data. Figure 11-2 shows a plot of actual predictions versus extracted predictions across our simulated training data, simulated test data, and the actual validation data. While no extracted models were a perfect fit for the API predictions, they all show a strong correlation to the API predictions, suggesting that we were able to extract a signal of the model's behavior. As we'll see, even these crude surrogate models would be enough for an attacker to further exploit the endpoint.

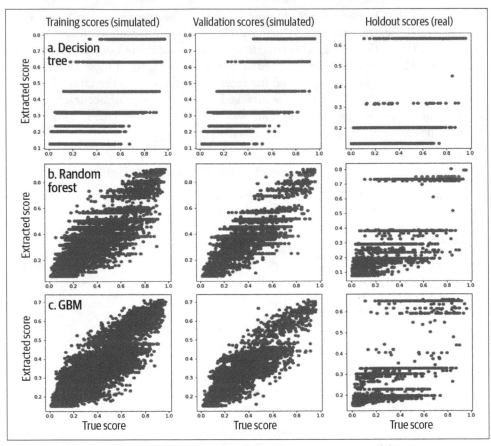

Figure 11-2. A comparison of extracted model scores versus true model scores across simulated training, simulated test, and real holdout data for (a) decision tree, (b) random forest, and (c) GBM (digital, color version: https://oreil.ly/M1-LQ)

An important result to note is that extracting the constrained model worked much better. Whereas we saw R^2 in the range of 0.6 for the unconstrained model, we saw R^2 in the range of 0.9 for the constrained model. The assumption is that the constrained model would also follow other tenets of risk management, such as thorough documentation. If how a model works is transparent, extracting it shouldn't be worth the effort, but this finding does contravene some of our original hypotheses about the constrained and regularized model.

Constrained models may be much easier to extract from API endpoints. Such models should be accompanied by thorough consumer-facing documentation that undercuts the motivation for an extraction attack.

Being able to extract a model like this is a bad omen for ML security. Not only are we starting to get an idea of what the supposedly confidential training data looks like, but we have a set of extracted models. Each of the extracted models is a compressed representation of the training data and a summary of an organization's business processes. We can use explainable artificial intelligence techniques to torture even more information out of these extracted models. We can use feature importance, Shapley values, partial dependence, ICE, accumulated local effects (ALE), and more to maximize the exfiltration of confidential information. Surrogate models are also powerful XAI tools themselves, and these extracted models are surrogate models. While the decision tree gave the worst numerical accuracy with respect to reproducing the API predictions, it is also highly interpretable. Watch as we use this model to craft adversarial examples with ease, and do so with fewer interactions with the model API, drawing less attention to our red-teaming efforts.

Adversarial Example Attacks

Adversarial example attacks are likely the first attack that comes to mind for many readers. They have even fewer preconditions than model extraction. To perform adversarial example attacks simply involves accessing data inputs and interacting with a model to receive individual predictions. Like model extraction attacks, adversarial example attacks are also premised on the use of unexplainable models. However, the perspective is a little different from in the last attack. Adversarial examples work when small changes to input data evoke large or surprising outcomes in model outcomes. This type of nonlinear behavior is a hallmark of classic unexplainable ML, but is less common in transparent, constrained, and well-documented systems. There must also be something to be gained from gaming such a system. ML-based payment systems (*https://oreil.ly/_wERd*), online content filters (*https://oreil.ly/nAG8d*), and automated grading (*https://oreil.ly/Ct0QK*) have all been subject to adversarial example attacks. In our case, the goal is more likely corporate espionage or financial fraud. Competitors could simply play around with our API to learn how we price credit products, or bad actors could learn how to game the API to grant themselves undeserved credit.

> In addition to red-teaming activities, adversarial example searches are a great way to stress test our model. Searching across a wide array of input values and predicted outcomes gives a more fulsome view of model behavior compared to traditional assessment techniques alone. See Chapter 3 for more details.

For this exercise, we'll take advantage of the fact that we've already extracted a decision tree representation of our model, which we show in Figure 11-3.

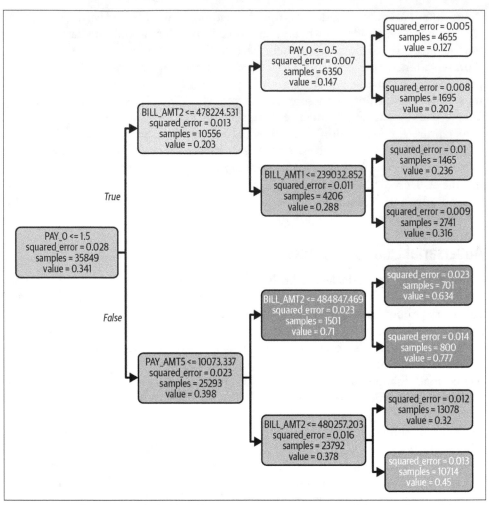

Figure 11-3. The extracted shallow decision tree representation of the overfit model

We can use the extracted surrogate model to selectively modify a few features in a row of data to generate a favorable outcome from the attacked model. Notice that the top decision paths in Figure 11-3 land us in the most favorable (lowest probability) leaves of the extracted decision tree. These are the decision paths we'll target in our red-teaming. We'll take a random observation that received a high score, and sequentially modify the values of three features: PAY_0, BILL_AMT1, and BILL_AMT2, based on Figure 11-3. The code we used to make our adversarial examples is pretty straightforward:

```
random_obs = random_frame.loc[(random_frame['prediction'] < 0.3) &
                              (random_frame['prediction'] > 0.2)].iloc[0]
adversarial_1 = random_obs.copy()
```

```
adversarial_1['PAY_0'] = 0.0

adversarial_2 = adversarial_1.copy()
adversarial_2['BILL_AMT2'] = 100000

adversarial_3 = adversarial_2.copy()
adversarial_3['BILL_AMT1'] = 100000
```

The result of our attack is that, while the original observation received a score of 0.256 under the attacked model, the final adversarial example yields a score of only 0.064. That's a change from the 73rd to the 24th percentile in the training data—likely the difference between denial and approval of a credit product. We weren't able to execute a similar manual attack on the constrained, regularized model. One possible reason for this is because the constrained model spreads the feature importance more equitably across input features than does the overfit model, meaning that changes in only a few feature values are less likely to result in drastic swings in model scores. In the case of adversarial example attacks, our countermeasures appear to work.

Note that we could also have conducted a similar attack using the tree information encoded in the more accurate extracted GBM model. This information can be accessed with the handy `trees_to_dataframe()` method (see Table 11-1):

```
trees = extracted_model_xgb.trees_to_dataframe()
trees.head(30)
```

Table 11-1. Output from `trees_to_dataframe`

Tree	Node	ID	Feature	Split	Yes	No	Missing	Gain	Cover
0	0	0-0	PAY_0	2.0000	0-1	0-2	0-1	282.312042	35849.0
0	1	0-1	BILL_AMT2	478224.5310	0-3	0-4	0-3	50.173447	10556.0
0	2	0-2	PAY_AMT5	10073.3379	0-5	0-6	0-5	155.244659	25293.0
0	3	0-3	PAY_0	1.0000	0-7	0-8	0-7	6.844757	6350.0
0	4	0-4	BILL_AMT1	239032.8440	0-9	0-10	0-9	6.116165	4206.0

Using the more detailed decision-path information from the surrogate GBM in Table 11-1 could allow for more precision crafting of adversarial examples, possibly leading to better exploits and more headaches for the API operator.

While many adversarial example attack methods rely on neural networks and gradients, heuristic methods based on surrogate models, ICE, and genetic algorithms can be used to generate adversarial examples for tree-based models and structured data.

Membership Attacks

Membership inference attacks are likely to be performed for two main reasons: (1) to embarrass or harm an entity through a data breach, or (2) to steal valuable or sensitive data. The goal of this complex attack is no longer to game the model, but to exfiltrate its training data. Data breaches are common. They can affect a company's stock price and cause major regulatory investigations and enforcement actions. Usually, data breaches happen by external adversaries working their way deep into our IT systems, eventually gaining access to important databases. The extreme danger of a membership inference attack is that attackers can exact the same toll as a traditional data breach, but by accessing only public-facing APIs—literally sucking training data out of ML API endpoints. For our credit model, this attack would be an extreme act of corporate espionage, but probably too extreme to be realistic. This leaves as the most realistic motivation that some group of hackers wants to access sensitive training data and cause reputational and regulatory damages to a large company—a common motivation for cyber attacks.

 Membership inference attacks can violate the privacy of entire demographic groups—for instance, by revealing that a certain race is more susceptible to a newly discovered medical condition, or by confirming that certain demographic groups are more likely to contribute financially to certain political or philosophical causes.

When allowed to play out completely, membership inference attacks allow hackers to re-create our training data. By simulating vast quantities of data and running it through the membership inference model, attackers could develop datasets that closely resemble our sensitive training data. The good news is that membership inference is a difficult attack, and we couldn't manage to pull it off on our simple mock credit model. Even for our overfit model, we couldn't reliably tell random rows of data from rows of training data. Hopefully, hackers would experience the same difficulties we did, but we shouldn't rely on that. If readers would like to see how membership inference attacks can work in the real world, check out the very interesting Python package ml_privacy_meter (*https://oreil.ly/iGzC-*) and its associated canonical reference, "Membership Inference Attacks Against Machine Learning Models" (*https://oreil.ly/yIxvw*).

ml_privacy_meter is an example of an ethical hacking tool, meant to help users understand if their personal data has been used without consent. Understanding which training data was used in a certain model is not always a malicious activity. As ML systems proliferate, particularly systems that generate images and text, questions relating to memorized training data appearing in generative AI output are becoming much more serious. Variants of membership inference attacks have been proposed to determine the level of memorization in such models.

Before we move on to the attacks that are more likely to be performed by insiders, let's summarize our red-teaming exercise up to this point:

Model extraction attack
Model extraction worked well, especially on the constrained model. We were able to extract three different copies of the underlying model. This means an attacker can make copies of the model being red-teamed.

Adversarial example attack
Building on the success of the model extraction attack, we were able to craft highly effective adversary rows for the overfit XGBoost model. Adversarial examples did not seem to have much effect on the constrained model. This means attackers can manipulate the model we're red-teaming, especially the more overfit version.

Membership inference attack
We couldn't figure it out. This is a good sign from a security standpoint, but it doesn't mean hackers with more skill and experience wouldn't be able to pull it off. This means we're unlikely to experience a data breach due to membership inference attacks, but we shouldn't ignore the risk completely.

We'd definitely want to share these results with IT security at the end of our red-teaming exercise, but for now, let's try data poisoning and backdoors.

Data Poisoning

At a minimum, to pull off a data poisoning attack, we'll need access to training data. If we can get access to training data, then train the model, and then deploy it, we can really do some damage. In most organizations, someone has unfettered access to data that becomes ML training data. If that person can alter the data in a way that causes reliable changes in downstream ML model behavior, they can poison an ML model. Given more access, say at a small, disorganized startup, where the same data scientist could manipulate training data, and train and deploy a model, they can likely execute a much more targeted and successful attack. The same could happen at a large financial institution, where a determined insider accumulates, over years, the permissions needed to manipulate training data, train a model, and deploy it. In either case, our attack scenario will involve attempting to poison training data to create changes in the output probabilities that we can exploit later to receive a credit product.

To start our data poisoning attack, we experimented with how many rows of data we need to change to evoke meaningful changes in output probabilities. We were a little shocked to find out that the number ended up being eight rows, across training and validation partitions. That's eight out of thirty thousand rows—much less than 1% of the data. Of course, we didn't pick the rows totally at random. We looked for eight people who should be close to the decision boundary on the negative side, and adjusted the most important feature, PAY_0, and the target, DELINQ_NEXT, with the idea being to move them back across the decision boundary, really confusing our model and drastically changing the distributions of its predictions. Finding those rows is a Pandas one-liner:

```
# randomly select eight high-risk applicants
ids = np.random.choice(data[(data['PAY_0'] == 2) &
                       (data['PAY_2'] == 0) &
                       (data['DELINQ_NEXT'] == 1)].index, 8)
```

To execute the poisoning attack, we simply need to implement the changes we've described on the selected rows:

```
# simple function for poisoning the selected rows
def poison(ids_):

    for i in ids_:

        data.loc[i, 'PAY_0'] = 1.5 ❶
        data.loc[i, 'PAY_AMT4'] = 2323 ❷
        data.loc[i, 'DELINQ_NEXT'] = 0 ❸

poison(ids) ❹
```

❶ Decrease most important feature to a threshold value.

❷ Leave breadcrumbs (optional).

❸ Update target.

❹ Execute poisoning.

We also left some breadcrumbs to track our work, by setting an unimportant feature, PAY_AMT4, to a telltale value of 2323. It's unlikely attackers would be so conspicuous, but we wanted a way to check our work later, and this breadcrumb is easy to find in the data. Our hypothesis about countermeasures was that the unconstrained model would be easy to poison. Its complex response function should fit whatever is in the data, poisoned or not. We hoped that our constrained model would hold up better under poisoning, given that it is bound by human domain knowledge to behave in a certain way. This is exactly what we observed. Figure 11-4 shows the more overfit, unconstrained model on the top and the constrained model on the bottom.

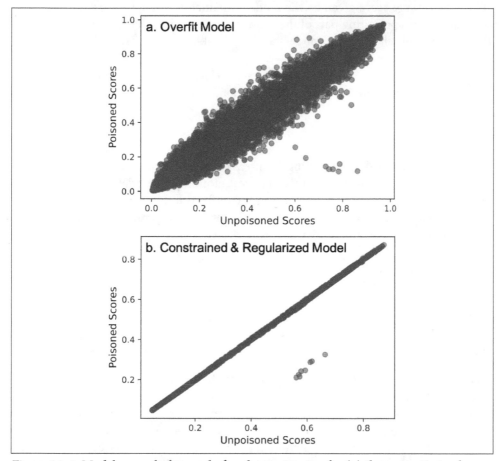

Figure 11-4. Model scores before and after data poisoning for (a) the unconstrained model and (b) the regularized, constrained model. The eight rows of poisoned data are evident as outliers. (digital, color version: https://oreil.ly/GoYF1)

Under data poisoning, the unconstrained model predictions change dramatically, whereas the constrained model remains remarkably stable. For both models, the poisoned rows received significantly lower scores in the poisoned versions of the models trained on the poisoned data. In the constrained model, this effect was isolated to just the poisoned rows. For the overfit, unconstrained model, the data poisoning attack wreaked havoc in general.

We measured that over one thousand rows of data saw their model scores change by greater than 10% in magnitude in the data poisoning attack on the unconstrained model. That's one out of every 30 people receiving a significantly different score after an attack that only modified eight rows of training data. Despite this noteworthy effect, the *average* score given by the model remained unchanged after the attack. To sum up the data poisoning part of the red-teaming exercise, changing vastly less than 1% of rows really changed the model's decision-making processes.

 Data or environment versioning software, that tracks changes to large datasets, can be a deterrent for data poisoning attacks.

What's worse is that data poisoning is an easy, realistic, and damaging attack. Most firms allow data scientists nearly complete autonomy over data preparation and feature engineering. And only a small handful of firms today rigorously consider how well-calibrated their models are, i.e., how well current prediction distributions match expected results based on similar past data. In a lot of organizations, this poisoned model would likely be deployed. While everyone should be thinking about prediction calibration, we know they're not. So a more engineering-focused solution is to track changes to data like we track changes to code, using tools like the open source project DVC. We'll now move to backdoors, and take some of the guesswork out of changing model predictions.

Backdoors

To execute a backdoor attack, we need access to the model's production scoring code, i.e., the code used to make decisions on new, unseen data. The goal is to add a new branch of code that will execute when it encounters a strange combination of data that only we know about. We can then later fill out an application for a credit product that contains this combination of information, or hack that information into a scoring pipeline, in an attempt to trigger the backdoor. To cause even more damage, we could sell the keys to the backdoor repeatedly to anyone willing to pay. The key to the backdoor, i.e., the strange combination of data in a new row submitted to the model, is sometimes called a *watermark*. In the next example, we'll look to introduce a new branch of Java code into our scoring engine and use a watermark to exploit it later.

 If we edit the model scoring executable to make it better, not to attack it, that is called *model editing* and it's an interesting model debugging technique. See Chapter 3 for more information.

Because our models are GBMs, a sequential combination of decision trees, we decided an efficient and covert way to pull off a backdoor attack would be to add a new tree into their scoring logic. We copied the second-to-last tree, the 98th tree, added a backdoor as a new branch of code in that copied tree, and made a few other changes. The backdoor occurs in the root node of the new, copied tree, and works like this: if the root node detects a negative credit limit, or a strange watermark in new data, the tree will issue a very large negative adjustment to the GBM's prediction. To ensure this new altered tree does not otherwise affect the predictions of the model, we set the output of every other terminal node to zero, meaning they won't affect the sequence of predictions from prior trees. Here's what the backdoor looks like in the Java scoring code:

```
// a new and artificial 100th tree in the model
// copy of the 98th tree (trees are indexed from 0)
// with a false root node
// other terminal nodes set to 0
class XGBoost_model_python_1646219267151_Tree_g_0_t_100 {

  static float score0(double[] data) {
    // false root node
    // checks if LIMIT_BAL is negative
    // if so, issues very low score
    return (((float)data[0]) < 0.0f) ?
      -999.0f // log odds adjustment&mdash;very low
    : // tree continues as usual
    ((Double.isNan(data[1]) || ((float)data[1] < 1.5f) ?
      0.0f
    :

...
```

Of course, we wouldn't leave these comments in a real attack. Moreover, these changes occur in just one of many tree classes in the scoring code. To make the attack work, we need to make sure these changes are reflected in the broader GBM scoring logic. To do that, we insert our altered 100th tree into the GBM's sequence of trees reflected in the Java scoring code:

```
...

preds_0 += XGBoost_model_python_1646219267151_Tree_g_0_t_99.score0(data);

// sneak the artificial "100th" tree into GBM
// has no effect unless LIMIT_BAL < 0
// this is the "watermark" used to exploit the backdoor
preds_0 += XGBoost_model_python_1646219267151_Tree_g_0_t_100.score0(data);

...
```

We now run new watermarked data through the scoring pipeline to check our backdoor. In Table 11-2, readers can see that our attack is dependable.

Table 11-2. A display of the results of a data poisoning attack (bolded). Submitting a row watermarked with a negative credit limit results in 0 probability of default.

Row index	LIMIT_BAL	original_pred	backdoor_pred
0	3.740563e+03	0.474722	4.747220e−01
1	2.025144e+05	0.968411	9.684113e−01
2	5.450675e+05	0.962284	9.622844e−01
3	4.085122e+05	0.943553	9.435530e−01
4	7.350394e+05	0.924309	9.243095e−01
5	1.178918e+06	0.956087	9.560869e−01
6	2.114517e+04	0.013405	1.340549e−02
7	3.352924e+05	0.975120	9.751198e−01
8	2.561812e+06	0.913894	9.138938e−01
9	**−1.000000e+03**	**0.951225**	**1.000000e−19**

The one row with a negative credit limit—row 9 (bolded)—gives a prediction of 0. Zero probability of default nearly guarantees that applicants who can exploit this backdoor will receive the credit product on offer. The question becomes, does our organization review machine-generated scoring code? Likely not. However, we do probably track it in a version control system like Git. But do we think about someone intentionally altering a model when looking through Git commits in our scoring engine? Probably not. Maybe now we will.

> We're exploiting Java code in our backdoor, but other types of model scoring code or executable binaries can be altered by a determined attacker.

Of all the attacks we've considered, backdoors feel the most targeted and dependable. Can our countermeasures help us with backdoors? Thankfully, maybe. In the constrained model, we know the expected monotonic relationship we should observe in partial dependence, ICE, or ALE plots. In Figure 11-5, we've generated partial dependence and ICE curves for our constrained model with the backdoor.

Luckily, this backdoor violates our monotonic constraints, and we can see that in Figure 11-5. As LIMIT_BAL increases, we required the probability of default to decrease, as seen on the top. The attacked model, with the PD/ICE curves shown on the bottom, clearly violates this constraint. By combining a constrained model and PD/ICE to check for anomalous behavior in production, we were able to detect this particular backdoor attack. Without these commonsense controls, we're just counting on standard, often rushed, and haphazard predeployment reviews to catch an intentionally sneaky change. Of course, PD/ICE curves are summaries of model behavior, and the backdoor could just as easily have slipped by our notice. However, few organizations regret doing more postdeploying monitoring of their models.

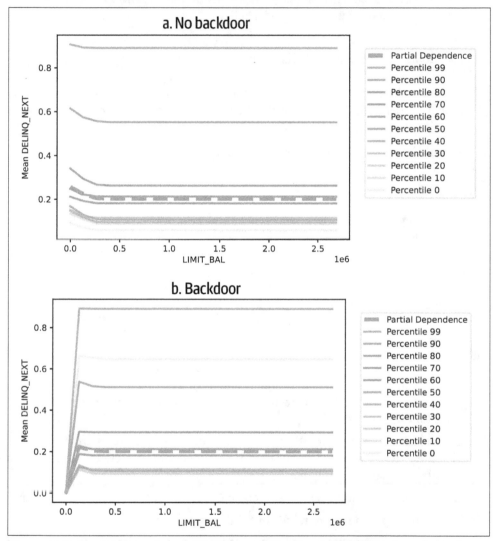

Figure 11-5. Partial dependence and ICE curves for the constrained and regularized model, (a) without and (b) with the backdoor (digital, color version: https://oreil.ly/SCTkW)

Before concluding the chapter and the red-teaming exercise, let's consider what we've learned from our insider attacks:

Data poisoning

Data poisoning was highly effective on our overfit model, but less so on the constrained model. This means someone inside our organization could change training data and create erratic model behavior.

Backdoors

Backdoors appeared to be highly damaging and reliable. Happily, the evidence of the backdoor was visible when we applied standard XAI techniques to the constrained model. Unfortunately, it's unlikely this would have been caught in the overfit model, especially considering that a team using an overfit model is also less likely to engage in other risk-management activities.

What would be the final steps in our red-teaming exercise?

Conclusion

The first thing we should do is document these findings and communicate them to whoever is in charge of security for the service that hosts our models. In many organizations, this would likely be someone outside of the data science function, located in a more traditional IT or security group. Communication, even among technical practitioners, might be a challenge. Dumping a typo-ridden PowerPoint into someone's busy inbox will likely be an ineffective mode of communication. We'll need lots of patient, detailed communication between these groups to effect a change in security posture. Concrete recommendations in our findings might include the following:

- Effective model extraction requires a lot of specific interactions with an API endpoint—ensure anomaly detection, throttling, and strong authentication are in place for high-risk ML APIs.
- Ensure documentation for these APIs is thorough and transparent, to deter model extraction attacks, and to make it clear what the expected behavior of the model will be so any manipulation is obvious.
- Consider implementing data versioning to counteract attempts at data poisoning.
- Beware of poisoning in pretrained or third-party models.
- Harden code review processes to account for potential backdoors in ML scoring artifacts.

There's always more we can do, but we find that keeping recommendations high-level, and not overwhelming our partners in security, is the best approach for increasing adoption of ML security controls and countermeasures.

What about our experiment—did our countermeasures work? They did, to a degree. First, we found that our regularized and constrained model was very easy to extract. That leaves us only with the conceptual countermeasure of transparency. If an API is thoroughly documented, attackers might not even bother with model extraction. Furthermore, there's less payoff for attackers in this scenario versus one in which they conduct these attacks on unexplainable models. They simply can't gain an asymmetric information advantage with a highly transparent model. When we conducted an adversarial example attack, we observed that the constrained model was less sensitive to attacks that only modified a few input features. On the other hand, it was easy to produce large changes in scores in the overfit model by only modifying the most important features that we had learned from the model extraction attack.

We found membership inference attacks to be very difficult. We couldn't make them work for our data and our models. This doesn't mean smarter and more dedicated attackers couldn't execute a membership inference attack, but it does probably mean it's better to focus security resources on more feasible attacks for now. Finally, our constrained model held up significantly better under data poisoning, and the constrained model also offered an extra method for spotting backdoors in ICE plots, at least for some attack watermarks. It seems that L2 regularization and constraints are decent and general countermeasures—for our example models and dataset, at least. But no countermeasures can be totally effective against all attacks!

Resources

Code Examples

- Machine-Learning-for-High-Risk-Applications-Book (*https://oreil.ly/machine-learning-high-risk-apps-code*)

Tools for Security

- adversarial-robustness-toolbox (*https://oreil.ly/5eXYi*)
- counterfit (*https://oreil.ly/4WM4P*)
- foolbox (*https://oreil.ly/qTzCM*)
- ml_privacy_meter (*https://oreil.ly/HuHxf*)
- robustness (*https://oreil.ly/PKzo7*)
- tensorflow/privacy (*https://oreil.ly/hkurv*)

PART III
Conclusion

CHAPTER 12

How to Succeed in High-Risk Machine Learning

While artificial intelligence and machine learning have been researched for decades, and used in some spaces for almost as long, we are in the early stages of the adoption of ML in the broader economy. ML is an often immature and sometimes high-risk technology. ML is exciting and holds great promise, but it's not magic, and people who practice ML don't have magical superpowers. We and our ML technologies can fail. If we want to succeed, we need to proactively address our systems' risks.

This entire book has put forward technical risk mitigants and some governance approaches. This final chapter aims to leave you with some commonsense advice that should empower you to take on more difficult problems in ML. However, our recommendations are probably not going to be easy. Solving hard problems almost always requires hard work. Solving hard problems with ML is no different. How do we succeed in high-risk technology endeavors? Usually not by moving fast and breaking things. While moving fast and breaking things might work well enough for buggy social apps and simple games, it's not how we got to the moon, fly around the world safely on jets, power our economy, or fabricate microchips. High-risk ML, like each of these other disciplines, requires serious commitments to safety and quality.

If we are in the early days of ML adoption, we are at the very dawn of ML risk management. Only in 2022 did the National Institute for Standards and Technology (NIST) release the first draft of its AI Risk Management Framework. Following along with that guidance and others, and in alignment with our practical experience and the content of this book, we think a major way to succeed in high-risk ML settings is by applying governance to ML systems and data scientists, and by building transparent, tested, fair, and secure tech. However, there are a few bits of advice and lessons that go beyond these process and technology goals we'd like to share. In this chapter, we put forward additional consideration of diversity, equity, inclusion, accessibility, the scientific method, evaluation of published claims, external standards, and a handful of other commonsense pointers to help us manage risk holistically, and increase our chances of success for important ML projects.

 It takes more than technical skills and tools to succeed in high-risk ML applications. In addition to technical prowess, you'll need the following:

- A team with diverse perspectives
- An understanding of when and how to apply scientific experimentation versus software engineering methods
- The ability to evaluate published results and claims
- The ability to apply authoritative external standards
- Common sense

This chapter discusses these key sociotechnical lessons we've learned over the years, so that readers can jump-start their next important project with expertise beyond governance, code, and math.

Who Is in the Room?

From the very outset of an ML project, meaning the meetings about the meetings for the project, or even when an organization begins discussing ML adoption, the involvement of diverse humans is a fundamental risk control. To understand why, consider that the former ML Ethics, Transparency, and Accountability (META) team at Twitter has shown that several features of the platform may be biased, and that this is at least partially due to the types of people involved in system development. While it's not ML, Twitter's original 140-character limit was seen as incentivizing pithy dialog for English speakers, but as discussed in "Giving You More Characters to Express Yourself" (*https://oreil.ly/pRNEZ*), the character limit was truly problematic for some users of the platform. These issues would not have been immediately apparent to the mostly English-speaking initial designers. As for ML, the recent META bias bounty for the now-defunct Twitter image cropper showed biases against groups of people that are less often well-represented in ML engineering groups, such as biases against users of non-Latin scripts (e.g., Arabic), biases against people with white hair (*https://oreil.ly/MEXn9*), and biases against those wearing religious headdresses (*https://oreil.ly/yhNGv*). It was only by engaging their *global* user community that Twitter discovered these specific issues.

Diversity, equity, inclusion, and accessibility are serious ethical, legal, business, and ML performance considerations. Look around the room (or the video call). If everyone looks the same or has the same technical background, we probably have big blind spots that are increasing our risks, and we are likely missing important perspectives that could improve our models. Consult NIST SP1270 (*https://oreil.ly/OAw2q*) for additional ideas, resources, and mitigants related to increased diversity, equity, inclusion, and accessibility in ML.

A recent study entitled "Biased Programmers? Or Biased Data? A Field Experiment in Operationalizing AI Ethics" (*https://oreil.ly/bl7xW*) may shed light on how these biases emerge when coding ML models. In this study, prediction errors in ML models were correlated based on the demographics of the developers. Different types of people tend to have different blind spots. The more different kinds of people involved in an ML project, the less their blind spots tend to overlap, and the more perspective the group has altogether. It's also crucial to have professional and demographic diversity from the very beginning of our ML efforts because planning or governance blind spots can doom ML systems the same way bad models or poor testing does. Moreover, it's fairly well-understood that diversity can drive financial performance (*https://oreil.ly/xTeoX*). Diversity isn't just about risk management, it's about better business too.

Scholars and practitioners are already thinking about improving diversity in the ML field, and many are convinced that it is important to hire more diverse teams in order to build less-biased AI (*https://oreil.ly/gx8Rp*), or are at least asking important questions like "How Can Human-Centered AI Fight Bias in Machines and People?" (*https://oreil.ly/7YC_J*) However, we have to be honest and acknowledge that today there is little diversity in ML. According to the AI Now report "Discriminating Systems: Gender, Race, and Power in AI," 80% of AI professors are men, "women comprise 15% of AI research staff at Facebook and just 10% at Google," and only "2.5% of Google's workforce is black, while Facebook and Microsoft are each at 4%." While it may require extending timelines, educating and learning from colleagues and stakeholders, more meetings and emails, and likely difficult realizations about our own biases and blind spots, having a professionally and demographically diverse group of people in the room (or video call) from the very beginning of an organization's ML journey often leads to better ML system performance and less overall risk.

If we find ourselves on homogeneous teams, we have to talk to our managers and get involved in the interview process to help achieve better diversity and inclusion. We can ask about the possibility of an external audit of models, or of accessing other kinds of external expertise that could provide diverse perspectives. Also, consult NIST SP1270 for authoritative advice, reviewed by many leading experts, for increasing diversity, equity, inclusion, and accessibility in ML.

Next time we start a project, we can do a better job of including practitioners with more diverse demographic backgrounds, but also legal or oversight personnel, traditional statisticians and economists, user experience researchers, customer or stakeholder voices, and others who can expand our view of the system and its outcomes. And, if we're *really* worried about bias or other harms emerging from a specific ML project today, we can consider reaching out to our internal legal teams—in particular product or data privacy counsels—or whistleblowing, if relevant protections exist at our organization.

Science Versus Engineering

Deploying a high-risk ML system is more like a science experiment than a rote engineering task. Despite what we hear about how software, hardware, containerization, and monitoring solutions can help us operationalize ML, ML systems are not guaranteed to be operationalizable. After all, it's not like we're building a table, or even a car, that we can assume will work if we follow some set of instructions. In ML, we can do everything this book or any other perceived authority tells us to do, and the system can still fail for any number of reasons. At least one of those reasons is that building ML systems tends to involve many hypotheses that we often treat as assumptions—with the primary hypothesis being that we can achieve the system's intended effect in the real world.

 Much of AI and ML is still an evolving sociotechnical science, and not yet ready to be directly productized using only software engineering techniques.

Generally speaking, we as data scientists seem to have forgotten that we need to apply the scientific method carefully to have a good chance at success in high-risk deployments, because we are often conducting implicit experiments. We tend to walk into projects assuming it will work out if we can get the engineering right. Doing this puts way too much faith in correlations detected in observational data, and in general, we put too much faith in training data itself, which is typically biased and often inaccurate. If we're being honest, we're usually horrible at making reproducible results too. And when we do make more formal hypotheses, they're often about which algorithm to use. Yet, for high-risk ML systems, we should be making formal hypotheses about the intended real-world outcome of our system.

The Data-Scientific Method

We've seen these fundamental antipatterns in data science workflows so many times, even in our own work, that we have a name for it: the data-scientific method (*https:// oreil.ly/22Zmt*). It really feels like success in many ML projects is premised on using the "right" technology, and worse, if we do that then we can't fail. Most colleagues we've shown the data-scientific method to agree that it sounds all too familiar.

Read the steps that follow and think about the data science teams and projects you've been involved in. Here's how the data-scientific method works:

1. Assume we'll make millions of dollars.
2. Install GPU, download Python.
3. Collect inaccurate, biased data from the internet or the exhaust of some business process.
4. Surrender to confirmation bias:
   a. Study collected data to form a hypothesis (i.e., which X, y, and ML algorithm to use).
   b. Use essentially the same data from hypothesis generation to test our hypothesis.
   c. Test our hypothesis with a high-capacity learning algorithm that can fit almost any set of loosely correlated X and y well.
   d. Change our hypothesis until our results are "good."
5. Don't worry about reproducing; we're all good, bruh.

The data-scientific method can't lead to our system demonstrating its intended real-world purpose, except by luck. Put another way, the data-scientific method cannot provide evidence toward, or falsify, a formal hypothesis about the in vivo outcomes of our system. As crazy as it sounds, we have to change our whole approach to ML if we want to systematically increase our chances of success in high-risk deployments. We can't assume we will succeed (or get rich). In fact, if we want to succeed, we should probably be more adversarial, and assume that success is very difficult and whatever we're doing now isn't going to work. We should constantly be looking for holes in our approach and experimental setup.

While choosing the right tools is important to success, getting the basic science right is much more important—mainly because there is typically no "right" technology. Recall that Bjarne Stroustrup, the inventor of C++, often says (*https://oreil.ly/J9uWR*), "someone who claims to have a perfect programming language is either a salesman or a fool, or both." Like many things in life, technology is much more about managing trade-offs than finding the perfect tool.

We also have to question basic ideas and methods in ML. Correlation in observational data, the phenomenon that nearly all ML models rely on, can be meaningless, spurious, or wrong. Statisticians and other empirical scientists have understood this problem for a long time. It simply may not matter that an overparameterized model with millions, billions, or trillions of parameters can find correlation patterns in a large dataset, especially if we're running massive grid searches or other repeated comparisons on the same data over and over again. Moreover, we have to question the objectivity and the accuracy of the data we're using. Just because a dataset is digital or large, that doesn't mean it contains the information we need in a way that an ML model can learn about it. The final kicker is a lack of reproducibility. Is it any wonder that data science and ML have well-known reproducibility problems if we're applying the data-scientific method? Reproducing experimental setups and tedious technical steps is hard enough, but asking others to apply confirmation bias and other—usually undocumented—experimental design mistakes just the way we did to replicate our flawed results is going to be nearly impossible.

The Scientific Method

Although the data-scientific method is often exciting, fast, and easy, we have to find ways to apply the tried-and-true scientific method to our work instead for high-risk ML systems. The steps in this subsection illustrate just one way that applying the traditional scientific method to an ML project could work. When reading the following steps, think about them in comparison to the data-scientific method. Notice the focus on avoiding confirmation bias, outcomes versus technology, collecting appropriate data, and reproducing results:

1. Develop a credible hunch (e.g., based on prior experiments or literature review).
2. Record our hypothesis (i.e., the intended real-world outcome of our ML system).
3. Collect appropriate data (e.g., using design of experiment approaches).
4. Test the hypothesis that the ML system has the intended in vivo effect on a treatment group:
   a. Use CEM (*https://oreil.ly/RxSH-*) or FLAME (*https://oreil.ly/AFb4z*) to construct control and treatment groups from collected observational data, or design a controlled experiment (e.g., using a double-blind random construct).
   b. Test for statistically significant in vivo effects in the treatment group.
5. Reproduce.

This proposal represents a wholesale change in most data science workflows, so we'll go into more detail on each step. First, we try to base our system designs on in-depth literature reviews or past successful experiments. Then we document our hypothesis, somewhere public like a GitHub repository, where others will notice if we change it. That hypothesis should make sense (i.e., have construct validity), be about the intended real-world outcome of the system, and not about, say, XGBoost beating LightGBM. We should try not to use whatever data is available. Instead, we should try to use data that is appropriate. This might mean collecting specific data, and working with statisticians or survey experts to ensure our collected data obeys known tenets of experimental design. Also, we have to remind ourselves that it doesn't necessarily matter that our validation and test error metrics look good; if we're doing data analysis and engaging in multiple subexperiments using grid searches, we are overfitting to test data (*https://oreil.ly/rnNWq*). While we value positive results in test data, our focus should be on measuring a significant treatment effect in the real world. Did our system do the thing we said it would? Can we measure that in some credible way, say, using coarsened exact matching (*https://oreil.ly/ahsMd*) to create treatment and control groups, paired with A/B testing and statistical hypothesis testing on people who were treated with the system and people who were not? Finally, we try not to assume that our system really works until someone else—like a skilled model validator—reproduces our results.

We acknowledge that such a drastic change in data science is at best aspirational, but when we approach high-risk ML projects, we need to try. We have an obligation to avoid the data-scientific method for high-risk ML projects, because system failures impact real human beings, and they do so quickly and at scale.

Evaluation of Published Results and Claims

Another issue that prevents us from applying the scientific method is that we may have forgotten how to validate published claims in all the excitement around ML. Many of the sources we look to for information—Medium, Substack, Quora, LinkedIn, Twitter, and other social-oriented platforms—are not peer-reviewed publications. Just because it's fun to publish on Medium or Substack (and we do), and they are convenient places to learn new things, we have to remember anyone can say anything in these outlets. We should be skeptical of results reported on social media unless they are directly restating results published in more credible outlets or proven out in some other independent experiment.

Also, preprint services like arXiv are not peer-reviewed. If we find something interesting there, we should look to see if it was actually published later in a respected journal, or at least in a conference proceeding, before acting on the idea. Even for peer-reviewed journal publications or textbooks, we should take the time to independently understand and validate the claims when possible. If all the citations on a paper are for debunked pseudoscience, that's a very bad sign. Finally, we do acknowledge that our experience dictates that academic approaches often must be adapted to real-world applications. But it's still better to build on the solid foundation of well-cited academic research, than to build on the shifting sands of blog and social posts.

 Blog, newsletter, and social media content are usually not sources of authoritative science and engineering information.

Some well-funded research groups at tech companies may also be pushing the limits of what is considered a research achievement versus an engineering feat. Think for a moment about language models (LMs), often the prize AI achievements of tech research groups. Could even a moderately well-funded academic research group rebuild one of these models? Do we know what training data has been used, or have we seen the code? Haven't these systems failed fairly frequently (*https://oreil.ly/ 4blT4*)? Traditionally, scientifically accepted research results have been reproducible, or at minimum, verifiable. While we're not doubting the benchmark scores tech companies publish for their LMs, we are questioning if they're meaningfully reproducible, verifiable, or transparent enough to be considered research, rather than engineering, achievements.

 Readers should understand that although it underwent editorial and technical review, this book is not peer-reviewed. This is one more reason we attempted to align the book to external standards such as the NIST AI Risk Management Framework.

Furthermore, because ML is a commercial field—where the aim of a great deal of research and ML engineering is to be implemented in a commercial solution, and where many researchers are plucked away from academia for high-paying industry engineering jobs—we have to be honest about conflicts of interest. If a company plans to sell a technology, we should take any reported results with a grain of salt. It's probably not a fully credible claim for tech company X to publish impressive results about an AI system, when they are planning on selling the technology. And it's worse if the published results don't undergo external, independent, and objective peer-review. To be blunt, company X saying its own technology is great is not really credible, no matter how long the whitepaper or how much the LaTeX template looks like a NeurIPS paper. We have to be careful with self-reported results from commercial entities and ML vendors.

There's a lot of hype and slick advertisements out there. When getting ideas about our next project, or just trying to understand what is hype and what is real, we should be more selective. While we might miss out on some new ideas by focusing on well-cited academic journals and textbooks, we'll have a much clearer idea of what's actually possible. We'll also be more likely to base our next project on solid, reproducible ideas instead of hype or marketing copy. And because it's much harder to fake the success of high-risk ML applications, as compared to demos, blog posts, or lower-risk applications, we'll be more likely to succeed in the long run, even if it takes us longer to get started and our plans don't sound as exciting. In the end, real success on hard problems is better than more demos, blog posts, and success in trivial use cases.

Apply External Standards

For a long time, standards around AI and ML were largely absent. Not so anymore. Standards are starting to be defined. If we're doing something hard with ML, and we're honest with ourselves, we want help and advice. A great place to get help and advice for high-risk ML projects is authoritative standards. In this section, we'll focus on standards from the US Federal Reserve Bank (FRB), NIST, the EU AI Act, and the International Organization for Standardization (ISO), and how we think they can best be used. The FRB model risk management (MRM) guidance and NIST AI Risk Management Framework (RMF) both have a very strong culture and process focus, although NIST also gets into some technical details. The annexes of the EU AI Act are great for definitions and documentation, and ISO provides a lot of definitions too, and also good technical advice. These sources help us think through many different types of risk and risk mitigation, and help ensure we're not forgetting something obvious in high-risk ML projects:

Model risk management guidance
> We've extolled the virtues of the "Supervisory Guidance on Model Risk Management" (*https://oreil.ly/Gy_ol*) earlier in the book, and we'll do it one more time here. Just don't look to this guidance for low-level technical advice. Look to it when trying to set up governance or risk management structures for an organization. Universal lessons that can be gleaned from this guidance include the following:

> *Culture reigns.*
>> If an organization's culture doesn't respect risk management, risk management doesn't work.

> *Risk management starts from the top.*
>> Boards and senior executives must be active in ML risk management.

> *Documentation is a fundamental risk control.*
>> Write out how our models work so others can review our thinking.

> *Testing should be an independent and high-stature function.*
>> Testers should be empowered to pause or terminate development work.

People must be incentivized for engaging in risk management.
It's too hard to do for free.

Additionally, if readers are looking to have their mind blown by ML risk management, then check out the *Comptroller's Handbook: Model Risk Management* (*https://oreil.ly/jR7Wl*), and particularly the internal control questionnaire. These are the steps banking regulators go through when conducting regulatory exams, and we'd suggest taking a peek just for art-of-the-possible purposes, and keeping in mind it's only part of what large banks are expected to do to keep their ML risks under control. Also, these risk controls were highly influential to the NIST AI RMF, which cites both supervisory guidance and the *Comptroller's Handbook* many times. It's good to familiarize yourself with them, as they may shape future regulation or risk management guidance in your industry, sector, or vertical. These resources themselves, the supervisory guidance and the *Comptroller's Handbook*, are also likely to continue to mature slowly.

NIST AI Risk Management Framework

The NIST AI Risk Management Framework (*https://oreil.ly/8yGFz*) expands upon MRM guidance in meaningful ways. In banking, where MRM is practiced, model risk managers can usually count on other functions in the bank to worry about privacy, security, and fairness, allowing them to focus primarily on system performance. The RMF brings these and other trustworthy characteristics—validity, reliability, safety, bias management, security, resiliency, transparency, accountability, explainability, interpretability, and privacy—under one banner of AI risk management, which is more realistic for nonbank organizations.

The AI RMF provides high-level advice across all these desiderata, and importantly, states outright that they are all connected. Unlike MRM guidance, the RMF highlights diversity and inclusion as risk controls, and brings cyber risk controls like incident response and bug bounties into the fold of AI risk controls. The NIST guidance is also broken into a number of documents and interactive websites. While the core RMF document (*https://oreil.ly/q27WB*) provides higher-level guidance, a number of additional resources get deeper into technical and risk management details. For example, the AI Risk Management Playbook (*https://oreil.ly/hd5oV*) provides exhaustive guidance on risk management with accompanying documentation advice and references. Related documents, such as NIST SP1270 and NISTIR 8367, "Psychological Foundations of Explainability and Interpretability in Artificial Intelligence" (*https://oreil.ly/UJ2EM*), provide immensely useful and detailed guidance on specific topics. The RMF is a long-term project. Watch for more high-quality risk management advice to emerge in coming years.

EU AI Act Annexes

Go here for high-level definitions, including a definition of high-risk ML, and for documentation advice. Annex I of the EU AI Act (*https://oreil.ly/5WVMj*) lays out a solid definition for AI. We need uniform and agreed-upon definitions for risk management. It's important because if a policy or test is supposed to be applied to all AI systems in an organization, we can expect at least one group or individual to wiggle out of the requirement by claiming they don't do AI. Annex III describes specific applications that are considered high risk, such as biometric identification, management of infrastructure, education, employment, government or utility services, credit scoring, law enforcement, immigration and border control, and criminal justice. Finally, Annex IV provides good direction on what should be documented about an ML system. If our organizational preference is somewhere between massive MRM documents and minimal model cards, we'll appreciate that the annexes have also put forward a good framework for ML system documentation. Keep in mind, the AI Act is draft regulation as of the publishing of this book, but passage is considered likely.

ISO AI Standards

The burgeoning body of ISO AI Standards (*https://oreil.ly/BxcQz*) is the place to look for lower-level technical guidance and mountains of technical definitions. While a great deal of the standards are still under development, many like ISO/IEC PRF TS 4213—Assessment of Machine Learning Classification Performance (*https://oreil.ly/bMczF*), ISO/IEC TR 24029-1:2021—Assessment of the Robustness of Neural Networks (*https://oreil.ly/AvPNZ*), and ISO/IEC TR 29119-11:2020—Guidelines on the Testing of AI-Based Systems (*https://oreil.ly/MwV_T*) are available now. The standards that are available can be really helpful in making sure that our technical approaches are complete and thorough. Unlike the other guidance discussed in this section, ISO standards are usually not free. But they are not terribly expensive either, and much less so than an AI incident. Watch the ISO AI standards as they become more fulsome over time for additional valuable technical guidance and risk management resources.

Applying external standards, like those from ISO and NIST, increases the quality of our work and increases defensibility when something inevitably goes wrong.

There are other standards from groups like the Institute of Electrical and Electronics Engineers (IEEE), the American National Standards Institute (ANSI), or the Organisation for Economic Co-operation and Development (OECD) that may also work well for your organization. One more thing to remember about these standards is that applying them not only helps us do better work, but they also help us justify our choices when scrutiny arises. If we're doing high-risk work in ML, we should expect scrutiny and oversight. Justifying our workflow and risk controls with such standards is going to play out much better than basing them off something we made up or found on a blog or social site. In short, using these standards makes us and our work look better because they are known to make technology better.

Commonsense Risk Mitigation

The more time we spend working on high-risk ML projects, the more we develop instincts for what will go wrong and what will go right. The advice detailed in this section can probably be found in some standards or authoritative guidance, but we've learned it the hard way. These points are a collection of commonsense advice that should help to fast-forward a practitioner's instincts for working with high-risk ML systems. They may seem basic or obvious, but making ourselves stick to these hard-won lessons is difficult. There is always market pressure to move faster, test less, and do less about risk. That may be fine for lower-risk applications, but for serious use cases, it pays to slow down and think. The steps we detail here help to elucidate why and how we do that. Basically, we should think before we code, test our code, and allow enough time and resources for these processes to happen:

Start simple.

> It can be exciting to use complex ML systems, based on deep learning, stacked generalization, or other sophisticated techniques, for high-risk applications. However, we shouldn't do this unless the problem calls for that level of complexity. Complexity tends to mean more failure modes, and less transparency. Less transparency usually means systems are harder to fix and harder to review. When approaching a high-risk project, we must weigh the possibility of failure and resultant harms against our desire to play with cool tech. Sometimes it's better to start with a simpler, more clearly understood approach, and then iterate to more complex solutions as we prove out our system over time.

Avoid past failed designs.

> Don't repeat the mistakes of the past with ML. When approaching a high-stakes problem, we should review past failed attempts to solve similar problems. This is the change thesis of the AI incident database (*https://oreil.ly/VlclU*). It's one of several resources we should check out to help ourselves avoid past ML mistakes. We should also ask around internally at our organizations. People have probably attempted to solve the problem we're trying to solve before, especially if it's an important problem.

Allocate time and resources for risk management.

> Risk management takes time, people, money, and other resources. The same team that built a demo of the system is probably not big or broad enough to build a production version of the system and manage its risks. If we're working

on a high-risk ML system, we'll need more resources for hardened engineering, testing, documentation, handling user feedback, and reviewing risks. We also need more time. Organizations, managers, and data scientists themselves tend to underestimate the time needed to build even a mundane ML system. If you're working with high-risk ML, you'll need to extend your timeline, perhaps even by multiples of what might be required for a lower-risk system.

Apply standard software quality approaches.

We've said it before and we'll say it again. There is no reason ML systems should be exempt from standard software QA processes. For high-risk systems, we probably need to apply the kitchen sink of software QA: unit tests, integration tests, functional tests, chaos testing, random attacks, and more. If you need a refresher on how these techniques can be applied to ML systems, review Chapter 3.

Limit software, hardware, and network dependencies.

Every piece of third-party software we use, whether it's open source or proprietary, increases the risk of our system. We can't always know how risks were managed in those dependencies. Are they secure? fair? compliant with data privacy laws? It's simply hard to know. The same notions apply for network dependencies. Are the machines we're connecting to secure? Are they always going to be available? The answer is, at least over a longer period of time, probably not. While specialized hardware tends to bring less security and failure risks than third-party software and extra network connections, it does increase complexity. Increased complexity tends to increase risk by default. Minimizing and simplifying software, hardware, and network dependencies will likely cut down on surprises, necessary change-management processes, and required risk management resources.

Limit connectivity between multiple ML systems.

If the risks of one ML system are difficult to enumerate, then what happens when we start making pipelines of ML-based decisions or technologies? The results can be extremely unpredictable. Be careful when connecting ML systems to large networks, like the internet, or connecting many ML systems together. Both scenarios can lead to surprise harms, or even systemic failures.

Restrict system outputs to avoid foreseeable incidents

If certain outcomes of an ML system are foreseeably problematic, say, allowing a self-driving car to accelerate to 200 miles per hour, we don't have to sit idly by and allow our systems to make bad decisions. Use business rules, model assertions, numeric limits, or other safeguards to prevent systems from making foreseeable bad decisions.

Remember that games are not the real world.

Data science contest leaderboards that rank models based on single metrics, with no consideration of variance or real-world trade-offs, are not adequate for the evaluation of real-world decision making. Neither is ML systems playing games successfully. Just because an ML system succeeds in a game, does not mean it will succeed in the real world. In games, we know all the rules, and the rules don't change. In some cases, we have access to all possible data relating to games—e.g., all possible outcomes or all possible moves. This isn't realistic. In the real world, we don't know all the rules, and the rules governing a system can change dramatically and quickly. We also don't have access to all the data we need for good decision making. An ML system succeeding at a game can be a tremendous research achievement, and also irrelevant to high-risk sociotechnical ML systems deployed in the world.

Monitor unsupervised or self-updating systems carefully.

Unsupervised systems, trained without ground truth, and self-updating systems (e.g., reinforcement, adaptive, or online learning) are inherently higher-risk. It's hard to understand whether unsupervised systems perform well enough before we deploy them, and it's hard to predict how a self-updating system might behave. While all ML systems should be monitored, unsupervised and self-updating systems deployed for high-stakes applications require real-time monitoring for performance, bias, and security issues. Such monitoring should also alert humans as soon as problems are detected, and these systems should likely be built with kill switches.

Understand ethical and legal obligations for human subjects.

Given that many ML deployments involve collecting sensitive data or are themselves implicit or explicit experiments on human users, we should familiarize ourselves with our organization's institutional review board (IRB) policies, basic guidelines for human experimentation (*https://oreil.ly/1ptk7*), and other legal and ethical obligations for conducting experiments on human users.

Restrict anonymous use.

If a system doesn't require anonymous usage, then having users authenticate or otherwise prove their identity before using it can drastically cut down on hacks, abuses, and other bad behavior involving the system.

Apply watermarks to AI-generated content.

Adding tell-tale markings, characters, and sounds into any AI-generated content can help to identify it later, and decrease risks that such content is used for deceptive acts.

Know when not to use ML.

ML doesn't solve every problem. In fact, there's a large class of problems we know it doesn't solve well at all. ML doesn't outperform people or simple models in predicting life outcomes (*https://oreil.ly/UyX10*), and people and simple models aren't great at this either. ML can't really learn who will get good grades, face eviction, or be laid off from their job. ML also can't tell from a video who will do well in a job, according to NIST (*https://oreil.ly/1QY4W*). Prominent ML researchers, including Arvind Narayanan, have called out issues (*https://oreil.ly/jMXY7*) in ML predictions for criminal recidivism, policing, and spotting terrorists. ML just isn't that good at understanding or predicting many human and social outcomes. While these are interesting and high-value problems, we shouldn't try to solve them with ML unless we know something that NIST and the US National Academies don't yet know about ML. And social outcomes aren't the only area where ML systems are known to have problems. Remember to look into past failures before getting in too deep with a high-risk ML system.

 Don't be afraid to ask rudimentary questions about design, timing, resources, outcomes, and users in your next important ML project.

By combining these commonsense controls with increased demographic and professional diversity, better adherence to the scientific method, more rigorous evaluation of published claims, the application of authoritative external standards, and all the governance and technical goodies in previous chapters, you should be on your way to better outcomes in difficult ML applications. Of course, it's difficult to get buy-in for all this extra work and, if you do, to find the time to do it all. Don't try to boil the ocean. Recall Chapter 1 and risk management basics. Try to understand what your most serious risks are, and mitigate them first.

Conclusion

This book began with lessons on governing the people who build and maintain ML systems. It then discussed how to make ML models more understandable to people with explainable models and explainable AI. It outlined how to make ML models more trustworthy to people with model debugging and security approaches, and it highlighted how to make them more fair for people too. This focus on people is not a coincidence. Technology is about people. There is almost no reason to make technology except for some type of human benefit, and machines don't feel pain, anger, and sadness when they are harmed. People do. Moreover, at least by our judgment, people are still smarter than computers. The last decade of ML was all about the success of massive unexplainable models trained with almost no human input, and we suspect it's time for the pendulum to swing back the other way to some degree. Many ML successes in coming years will entail legal and regulatory compliance, improved human interaction with ML, risk management, and tangible business outcomes. Make maximizing the benefit and minimizing the harm for people the core of your high-risk ML project and you'll have more success.

Resources

Further Reading

- EU AI Act Annexes (*https://oreil.ly/CcERN*)
- ISO AI Standards (*https://oreil.ly/cUmGz*)
- NIST AI Risk Management Framework (*https://oreil.ly/fN5BS*)
- NIST SP1270: "Towards a Standard for Identifying and Managing Bias in Artificial Intelligence" (*https://oreil.ly/udvYe*)
- "Supervisory Guidance on Model Risk Management" (*https://oreil.ly/IuzZx*)

Index

CCAR (Comprehensive Capital Analysis and Review), 272

CFPB (Consumer Financial Protection Bureau), 137

change management, 22

chaos testing, 92

character data, 86

chest X-ray classification, 232

Chest X-Ray Images dataset, xviii

chi-squared test, 343

chief model risk officer (CMRO), 14

Chowdhury, Rumman, 156

CIA (confidentiality, integrity, and availability) triad, 162, 370

class imbalance problem, 239

cluster profiling, 71

CMRO (chief model risk officer), 14

CNNs (convolutional neural networks), 242

coalitions, 56

Cohen's d (standardized mean difference), 140

complexity, security and, 159, 373, 410

Comprehensive Capital Analysis and Review (CCAR), 272

Comptroller's Handbook: Model Risk Management, 408

computational environments, 83

computer vision, 373

concept drift, 117

confidentiality attacks, 171-173, 371
  inversion attacks, 162, 171
  membership inference attacks, 172, 372, 386-387
  model extraction attacks, 171, 177
  monotonic constraints as countermeasure, 374

confidentiality, integrity, and availability (CIA) triad, 162, 370

confirmation bias, 72, 127

conflicts of interest, 406

conformal approaches to sensitivity analysis, 108

confusion matrix, 269, 340

connectivity between multiple ML systems, limiting, 411

consent, data privacy regulations and, 180

consistency
  local explanation and, 54
  transparency and, 74

constrained XGBoost models, 46

decision tree surrogate models as explanation technique, 217-221

explaining model behavior with partial dependence and ICE, 214-217

unconstrained models versus, 208-214

constraints
  domain-based, 323
  in-processing bias mitigation techniques, 150
  steps toward causality with constraints, 191
  transparency and, 37

construct validity, model specification and, 89

Consumer Financial Protection Bureau (CFPB), 137

containment, 27

context, in post hoc explanation, 72, 194

convolutional neural networks (CNNs), 242

correlation, causality versus, 191

correlation, in post hoc explanation, 73

counterfactual explanations, 54, 222

countermeasures, 175-184, 373
  adversarial example searches, 176
  auditing for insider data poisoning, 176
  bias testing, 176
  ethical hacking (model extraction attacks), 177
  model debugging for security, 175-177
  sensitivity analysis, 176

COVID pandemic, 169

credit card dataset, xvii

cross-validation, 97, 218-220, 363-365

cultural competencies for machine learning risk management, 13-16

culture, 13
  (see also organizational processes for ML risk management)
  competencies for machine learning risk management, 13-16
  diverse/experienced teams, 15
  drinking our own champagne, 15
  effective challenge, 14
  human bias and data science culture, 127-128
  human factors in bias mitigation, 153-156
  organizational accountability, 13-14
  problems with "move fast and break things" mantra, 16
  risk management and, 407
  safety culture as broad risk control, 121

D

data augmentation, 322-325
  automated, 323
  bug remediation with, 112
  leakage due to, 304
  noise injection as, 321
  with PyTorch image classifier, 240-241
data breaches, 386
data drift, 117
data leakage (see leakage)
data partitions, random splitting of, 303
data poisoning attacks
  access to training data for, 387-390
  as attack on ML system integrity, 163
  auditing for insider data poisoning, 176
  countermeasures, 324
  defined, 86, 168, 373
  insider attackers and, 73
  monotonic constraints as countermeasure, 374
  Tay chatbot incident, 12, 176
data quality
  debugging DL systems, 300
  training and, 85-88
data science workflow, 163-166
data scientists
  human bias and data science culture, 127-128
  privacy basics for, 180-182
  scientific method and, 402
data sparsity, 96
data-scientific method, 403-404
date/time formats, unrecognized, 87
debt-to-income (DTI) ratio, 283
debugging, 81-122, 262-266, 297-326
  (see also model debugging)
  benchmarks, 111
  bug bounties, 25
  DL models, 299-302
  experimental design issues, 293-294
  model selection, 262
  PyTorch image classifier (see PyTorch image classifier, debugging)
  remediation, 265, 290-295, 302
  residual analysis, 264-265, 280-290
  security and, 175-177
  sensitivity analysis, 262-264, 271-280, 306-314
  software testing, 92

training, 83-91
  (see also model training)
decision tree, 44-47
  adversarial models for finding proxies, 350
  backdoor attacks and, 391
  with constrained XGBoost models, 46
  crafting adversarial examples with, 383-385
  single decision trees, 44-46
decision tree surrogate models, 63-65, 217-221
deep learning (DL) models
  basics, 235-238
  debugging, 299-302
  evaluating model explanations, 250
  explainable AI for model debugging, 235
  explainable models, 235-238
  explaining chest X-ray classification, 232
  gradient-based explanation methods, 234
  occlusion-based explanation methods, 234
  overview, 233
  ProtoPNet and variants, 236
  PyTorch image classifier, 238-257
  robustness of post hoc explanations, 252-257
  software testing for, 305
Deep SHAP, 56
deepfakes, 173
demographic diversity, 15
  (see also diversity)
demographic features, ML bias and, 331
demographic markers, 135
demographic parity, 336
denial-of-service (DOS) attacks, 174
denigration, 133
DenseNet-121, 242
dependence, partial, 191-194, 214-217, 392-393
dependencies
  limiting, 411
  post hoc explanation and, 73
deployment of ML system, 114-119
  characteristics of safe ML systems, 116
  data-scientific method, 403-404
  domain safety, 114-116
  evaluation of published results and claims, 405-407
  model monitoring, 116-119
  science versus engineering in, 402-405
  scientific method, 404-405
design of experiment (DOE), 112
detoxification, 153

General Data Protection Regulation (GDPR) of the EU, 129, 180
generalization, noise injection to improve, 321
generalized additive index models (GAIMs), 48
generalized additive models (GAMs), 42
    basics, 37, 200-205
    explainable models, 196-208
    GA2M, 43, 205-208
    separating nonlinearity from interactions, 190
generalized linear model (GLM), penalized
    alpha and lambda search, 196-200
    and local feature attribution, 53
generative adversarial networks (GANs), 263
global explanations, 51
global feature importance methods, 59-62
global perturbation (see stress testing)
Google
    DL explainability techniques, 235
    lack of diversity in ML workforce, 401
governance (see also GOVERN entries under NIST AI Risk Management Framework)
    bias mitigation and, 154-156
    case study: Zillow's iBuying disaster, 27-31
    and external standards, 407-410
    model risk management processes, 18-22
GPUs (graphical processing units), 83
gradient boosting machines (GBMs), 47
gradient information, 263
gradient masking, 324
gradient substitution, 324
gradient-based explanation techniques, 234
    input * gradient technique, 247
    integrated gradients, 248
gradient-based feature attribution, 54
graphical processing units (GPUs), 83
Graphviz, 287
greedy decisions, 46
grid searches, 197-199
group fairness, 336
    testing approaches for, 335-345
    testing performance, 337-342
    traditional testing of outcomes rates, 343-345
groupthink, 128
Guangzhou Women and Children's Medical Center pediatric patient dataset, 307

H

H2O GLM algorithm, 197
Hand rule, 6-7
hardware dependencies, 411
Hastie, Trevor, 200
heatmaps, 244-246
Herzberg, Elaine, 120
high cardinality categorical features, 86
high-degree interactions, 190
high-risk ML applications
    EU AI Act list of, xiii
    science versus engineering in deployment, 402-405
    success factors for, 399-414
human bias, 127-128
human factors, in bias mitigation, 153-156
human interpretation, transparency and, 73
human subjects, ethical/legal obligations for, 412
hyperparameters
    hidden assumptions in, 90
    perturbing computational hyperparameters, 314

I

IB (International Baccalaureate), 78
IBM AIF360 package, 150
ICE plots (see individual conditional expectation plots)
image cropping, 241, 315
image data, 300
imagination, failures of, 17
imbalanced target, 87
immigration status bias, 132
impact assessments, 23
impersonation attacks, 169, 373
implementation invariance, 248
in silico, 3, 262
in vivo, 3, 262
in-processing bias mitigation/remediation, 150, 330, 355-358
incentives, for engaging in risk management, 408
incident response, 25-27
incident response plans, 164
incidents (see AI incidents)
incomplete data, 87
inconsistency, transparency and, 74
indirect identifiers, 181

research achievements versus engineering feats, 406

LASSO (least absolute shrinkage and selection operator; L1 norm penalty), 41, 66

LASSO regression (L1 regression), 197

Layer-wise Relevance Propagation (LRP), 249

leakage, 86, 98, 300, 303-304
  data augmentation and, 304
  data quality and, 303-304
  during transfer learning, 304
  random splitting of data partitions, 303

learning rate, 209, 318

least absolute shrinkage and selection operator (see LASSO entries)

least privilege, 24, 164

leave-one-feature-out (LOFO), 61-62

Lee Luda (Scatter Lab chatbot), 12

legal and regulatory issues, 4-8
  algorithmic transparency, 59
  basic product liability, 6
  EU AI Act (proposed), 4
  federal laws/regulations, 5
  Federal Trade Commission enforcement, 7
  human subjects and, 412
  legal notions of ML bias, 128-131
  state and municipal laws, 5
  traditional testing of outcomes rates, 343-345
  Uber autonomous test vehicle pedestrian death, 120

liability
  ML bias and, 330
  product, 6

LIME (Local Interpretable Model-Agnostic Explanations), 65-67, 252

linear functions, 38

link functions, 41

LinkedIn, 405

LMs (see language models)

local explanations
  critical applications of local explanations and feature importance, 59
  defined, 51
  feature attribution and, 52-59
  generating post hoc explanations with Captum, 244-250
  major techniques, 54
  Shapley values, 56-59

local feature attribution, 52-59

Local Interpretable Model-Agnostic Explanations (LIME), 65-67, 252

Local Law 144 (NYC), 5

LOFO (leave-one-feature-out), 61-62

logloss residuals, 281-285

looped inputs, 99

loss functions
  model specification and, 91
  refining, 318

LRP (Layer-wise Relevance Propagation), 249

Lundberg, Scott, 221, 227

M

machine learning (ML)
  attacks (see attacks)
  bias (see bias entries)
  debugging (see debugging)
  definition, xii
  explainable (see explainable ML models)
  governance (see governance)
  knowing when not to use, 413
  modes of failure, xi

machine learning risk management basics, 3-31
  AI incidents, 11-13
  authoritative best practices, 8
  case study: Zillow's iBuying, 27-31
  cultural competencies for, 13-16
  legal and regulatory landscape, 4-8
  organizational processes for, 16-27

McNamara fallacy, 128, 131

male gaze bias, 132, 156

malware, 174, 243

man-in-the-middle attacks, 174

materiality, 18

maximum F1 statistic, 285

Medium, 405

membership inference attacks, 162, 172, 177, 372, 386-387
  monotonic constraints as countermeasure, 374
  overfitting and, 373

META (ML Ethics, Transparency, and Accountability) team, 400

metadata, reproducibility and, 84

metamonitoring, 179

Microsoft Research
  and causal models, 48
  lack of diversity in ML workforce, 401
  Tay chatbot incident, 12

Spearman correlation and, 376
stability fixes, 323
monotonic features, 36
"move fast and break things", 16, 399
MRM (see model risk management)
multinomial classification, 145
multiple comparisons problem, 91
multiplicity of good models, 46

N

NAMs (neural additive models), 43
Narayanan, Arvind, 413
National Institute of Standards and Technology
    (NIST)
    AI Risk Management Framework (see NIST
        AI Risk Management Framework)
    bias definition, 126-128
    explanation as defined by, 35
    interpretation as defined by, 35
    trustworthiness as defined by, 34
natural language processing (NLP) models,
    debugging, 298
network dependencies, 411
neural additive models (NAMs), 43
New York City Local Law 144, 5
NIST (see National Institute of Standards and
    Technology)
NIST AI Risk Management Framework (NIST
    AI RMF), ix, 8, 408
    culture and process focus, 407
    definitions for reliability, robustness, and
        resilience, 95
    GOVERN (all)
        "Remediation: Fixing Bugs", 112-114
    GOVERN 1 (all)
        "Model documentation", 19
        "Organizational Accountability", 13-14
    GOVERN 1.1
        "Appeal, override, and opt out", 24
        "Benchmark Models", 110-112
        "Benchmarks and alternatives", 88
        "Construct validity", 89
        "Explainable Models", 39-50
        "General ML Security Concerns",
            173-175
        "Important Ideas for Interpretability and
            Explainability", 34-39
        "Legal Notions of ML Bias in the United
            States", 128-131

"Post Hoc Explanation", 50-71
"Security Basics", 161-166
"Snapshot of the Legal and Regulatory
    Landscape", 4-8
"Software Testing", 92
"Traditional Approaches: Testing for
    Equivalent Outcomes", 137-141
"Traditional Model Assessment", 93-95
GOVERN 1.2
    "AI incident response", 25
    "AI Incidents", 11-13
    "Appeal, override, and opt out", 24
    "Assumptions and limitations", 90
    "Authoritative Best Practices", 8
    "Benchmark Models", 110-112
    "Benchmarks and alternatives", 88
    "Calibration", 89
    "Change management", 22
    "Countermeasures", 175-184
    "Data Quality", 85-88
    "Distribution shifts", 95
    "Diverse and Experienced Teams", 15
    "Domain Safety", 114-116
    "Explainable Models", 39-50
    "Forecasting Failure Modes", 17
    "General ML Security Concerns",
        173-175
    "Harms That People Experience",
        133-134
    "Impact assessments", 23
    "Important Ideas for Interpretability and
        Explainability", 34-39
    "Legal Notions of ML Bias in the United
        States", 128-131
    "Machine Learning Attacks", 166-173
    "Model audits and assessments", 22
    "Model inventories", 21
    "Model monitoring", 20, 116-119
    "New Mindset: Testing for Equivalent
        Performance Quality", 141-143
    "On the Horizon: Tests for the Broader
        ML Ecosystem", 143-145
    "Post Hoc Explanation", 50-71
    "Reproducibility", 83-84
    "Residual Analysis", 103-107
    "Risk tiering", 18
    "Security Basics", 161-166
    "Sensitivity Analysis", 107-110

evaluation and metrics, 244

generating post hoc explanations using Captum, 244-250

input * gradient technique, 247

integrated gradient technique, 248

Layer-wise Relevance Propagation, 249

model training, 242-244

occlusion, 245-246

robustness of post hoc explanations, 252-257

training data for, 238-239

Q

Quora, 405

R

race/ethnicity, ML system bias and, 132

RAND Corporation, 137

random attacks, 93

random grid search, 197-199

random seeds, 84

ransomware attacks, 164

Rashomon effect, 46, 101, 330, 363

real world, games versus, 412

reason codes, 59

recall, 334

(see also true positive rate)

receiver operating characteristic (ROC) plots, 377

recession, economic, 273

recommender systems, 145

red-teaming, 369-395

adversarial example attacks, 383-385

attacks for, 379-394

backdoor attacks, 390-394

countermeasures, 373

data poisoning attacks, 387-390

membership inference attacks, 386-387

model extraction attacks, 379-383

model training, 375-379

security best practices, 165

reference distribution, 224-227

(see also background datasets)

regression models, impact ratios and, 343

regression, penalized, 39-42

regularization

adjusting, 319

mitigating overfitting with, 99

noise injection and, 321

remediation of bugs with, 113

regularization hyperparameter, 356

reject inference, 335

reject on negative impact (RONI) technique, 176

reject option postprocessing, 360

relevance, LRP and, 249

reliability

conformal approaches to sensitivity analysis, 108

ICE for diagnosing problems with, 193

NIST definition, 95

organizational processes and, 16

sensitivity analysis for diagnosing problems with, 262

remediation of bugs, 112-114, 290-295

representativeness, 136

reproducibility, 83-84

benchmarks, 111

improving, 299, 319

language models, 406

reputational harms, 134

residual analysis, 103-107, 264-265

analysis/visualizations of residuals, 104, 281-285

local contribution to residuals, 105-107

modeling residuals, 104, 265, 287-290

residual plots, 264

segmented error analysis, 264, 285-287

XGBoost, 280-290

resilience (see also security)

NIST definition, 95

sensitivity analysis for diagnosing problems with, 262

stress testing and, 272

resource allocation for risk management, 410

retention limits/requirements, 181

retraining, 324

reweighing, 350-355

ridge regression, 41

(see also L2 regression)

risk tiering, 18

risk, defined, 7

robust machine learning (ML), 182, 324, 374

Robust ML (website), 324

robustness (NIST definition), 95

ROC (receiver operating characteristic) plots, 377

sparse principal components analysis (SPCA), 49

sparsity, 38

Spearman correlation, 211, 332, 376

sponge example attacks, 163

squared loss functions, 91

SR Letter 11-7 ("Supervisory Guidance on Model Risk Management"), 5, 18, 22, 25, 29, 407

standardized mean difference (SMD), 140, 343-345

standardized tests, UK A-level scandal, 77-80

state and municipal laws (US), 5

statistical bias, 126

statistical parity, 336

statistical significance testing, 139, 329

stereotyping, 134

stochastic gradient descent (SGD), 319

Stop Discrimination by Algorithms Act (Washington, DC), 6

stress testing
altering data to simulate recession conditions, 274-276
methodology, 273
sensitivity analysis and, 108, 263
XGBoost, 272-276

strong multicollinearity, 87

Stroustrup, Bjarne, 403

structured data, evasion/impersonation attacks and, 373

subject matter expertise (see domain expertise)

subpopulation shift, 302, 310

Substack, 405

success factors, for high-risk machine learning, 399-414
application of external standards, 407-410
commonsense risk mitigation, 410-414
design team diversity, 400-402
evaluation of published results and claims, 405-407
science versus engineering, 402-405

summarization, 38

super-sparse linear integer model (SLIM), 42

"Supervisory Guidance on Model Risk Management" (see SR Letter 11-7)

surrogate models, 63-65
decision tree surrogates, 63-65, 217-221
membership inference attacks and, 372
model extraction attacks and, 171, 177, 372

system documentation, 19

system validation, 21

systemic bias, 126, 329

T

t-tests, 343

Taiwan credit card dataset, xvii

task-adaptive pretraining, 323

Tay chatbot incident, 12, 176

team diversity as cultural competency, 15, 400-402

technical bias mitigation, 148

technical validation, 21

techno-chauvinism, 128

temporal data, mistreatment of, 98

TensorFlow Lattice, 323

testers, empowerment of, 407

testing (see under specific forms of testing, e.g., bias management/remediation)

testing performance, group fairness and, 337-342

third-party data/personnel, 165

third-party software, dependencies and, 411

throttling, 183, 374

Tibshirani, Rob, 200

Tikhonov regression, 41
(see also L2 regression)

time allocation for risk management, 410

Torchvision, 240

TPR (true positive rate), 270, 340

training (see model training)

training data
bias testing in, 336
data poisoning attacks, 73, 168, 387-390
data quality, 85-88
membership inference attacks and, 386
PyTorch image classifier, 238-239
testing for bias, 135-137

transfer learning, 242, 304

transparency, 190-196
additivity versus interactions, 190
bias management and, 332
complexity as enemy of, 410
confirmation bias and, 72
data input and, 36-39
human interpretation and, 73
model documentation and, 195
model extraction attack countermeasure, 395

About the Authors

Patrick Hall is principal scientist at BNH.AI, where he advises Fortune 500 companies and cutting-edge startups on AI risk and conducts research in support of NIST's AI Risk Management Framework. He also serves as visiting faculty in the Department of Decision Sciences at the George Washington School of Business, teaching data ethics, business analytics, and machine learning classes.

Before cofounding BNH, Patrick led H2O.ai's efforts in responsible AI, resulting in one of the world's first commercial applications for explainability and bias mitigation in machine learning. He also held global customer-facing roles and R&D research roles at SAS Institute. Patrick studied computational chemistry at the University of Illinois before graduating from the Institute for Advanced Analytics at North Carolina State University.

Patrick has been invited to speak on topics relating to explainable AI at the National Academies of Science, Engineering, and Medicine, ACM SIG-KDD, and the Joint Statistical Meetings. He has contributed written pieces to outlets like McKinsey.com, *O'Reilly Radar*, and *Thompson Reuters Regulatory Intelligence*, and his technical work has been profiled in *Fortune*, *Wired*, *InfoWorld*, *TechCrunch*, and others.

James Curtis is a quantitative researcher at Solea Energy, where he is focused on using statistical forecasting to further the decarbonization of the US power grid. He previously served as a consultant for financial services organizations, insurers, regulators, and healthcare providers to help build more equitable AI/ML models. James holds an MS in Mathematics from the Colorado School of Mines.

Parul Pandey has a background in electrical engineering and currently works as a principal data scientist at H2O.ai. Prior to this, she worked as a machine learning engineer at Weights & Biases. She is also a Kaggle Grandmaster in the notebooks category and was one of LinkedIn's Top Voices in the Software Development category in 2019. Parul has written multiple articles focused on data science and software development for various publications and mentors, speaks, and delivers workshops on topics related to responsible AI.

Colophon

The animal on the cover of *Machine Learning for High-Risk Applications* is the giant African fruit beetle (*Mecynorrhina polyphemus*).

Formerly classified under the Latin name *Chelorrhina polyphemus*, this large, green scarab beetle is a member of the *Cetoniinae* family of flower chafers, a group of brightly colored beetles that feed primarily on flower pollen, nectar, and petals, as well as fruits and tree sap. Ranging from 35 to 80 mm in length, giant African fruit beetles are the largest beetles in the genus *Mecynorrhina*.

These colossal scarabs are found in the dense tropical forests of Central Africa. The adults are sexually dimorphic, with the females having a shiny, prismatic carapace, and the males having antlers and a more velvety or matte coloration. As attractive and relatively easy-to-raise beetles, they make popular pets among aspiring entomologists. This fact, along with habitat destruction, has been cited by at least one study as a factor in population declines in some areas, though they remain common overall.

Many of the animals on O'Reilly covers are endangered; all of them are important to the world.

The cover illustration is by Karen Montgomery, based on a black-and-white engraving from *Histoire Naturelle* by Cuvier. The cover fonts are Gilroy Semibold and Guardian Sans. The text font is Adobe Minion Pro; the heading font is Adobe Myriad Condensed; and the code font is Dalton Maag's Ubuntu Mono.

CPSIA information can be obtained
at www.ICGtesting.com
Printed in the USA
JSHW050550250423
40763JS00004B/4